Women, Gender, and Crime

For Jeff, Taylor, and Keegan

Sara Miller McCune founded SAGE Publishing in 1965 to support the dissemination of usable knowledge and educate a global community. SAGE publishes more than 1000 journals and over 800 new books each year, spanning a wide range of subject areas. Our growing selection of library products includes archives, data, case studies and video. SAGE remains majority owned by our founder and after her lifetime will become owned by a charitable trust that secures the company's continued independence.

Los Angeles | London | New Delhi | Singapore | Washington DC | Melbourne

Women, Gender, and Crime
Core Concepts

Stacy L. Mallicoat

California State University, Fullerton

Los Angeles | London | New Delhi
Singapore | Washington DC | Melbourne

FOR INFORMATION:

SAGE Publications, Inc.
2455 Teller Road
Thousand Oaks, California 91320
E-mail: order@sagepub.com

SAGE Publications Ltd.
1 Oliver's Yard
55 City Road
London EC1Y 1SP
United Kingdom

SAGE Publications India Pvt. Ltd.
B 1/I 1 Mohan Cooperative Industrial Area
Mathura Road, New Delhi 110 044
India

SAGE Publications Asia-Pacific Pte. Ltd.
3 Church Street
#10-04 Samsung Hub
Singapore 049483

Acquisitions Editor: Jessica Miller
Editorial Assistant: Rebecca Lee
Content Development Editor: Laura Kirkhuff
Production Editor: Karen Wiley
Copy Editor: Kimberly Cody
Typesetter: C&M Digitals (P) Ltd.
Proofreader: Jen Grubba
Indexer: Jeanne Busemeyer
Cover Designer: Janet Kiesel
Marketing Manager: Jillian Oelsen

Printed in the United States of America

ISBN: 978-1-5063-9927-0 (pbk)

This book is printed on acid-free paper.

SUSTAINABLE FORESTRY INITIATIVE
Certified Chain of Custody
At Least 10% Certified Forest Content
www.sfiprogram.org
SFI-01028

21 22 10 9 8 7 6 5 4

Brief Contents

Preface   xiii

Acknowledgments   xvii

CHAPTER 1.   Women, Gender, and Crime: Introduction   1

CHAPTER 2.   Theories of Victimization   21

CHAPTER 3.   Women, Gender, and Victimization: Rape and Sexual Assault   35

CHAPTER 4.   Women, Gender, and Victimization: Intimate Partner Abuse and Stalking   59

CHAPTER 5.   International Issues in Gender-Based Violence   83

CHAPTER 6.   Women, Gender, and Offending   99

CHAPTER 7.   Girls, Gender, and Juvenile Delinquency   113

CHAPTER 8.   Female Offenders and Their Crimes   131

CHAPTER 9.   Processing and Sentencing of Female Offenders   151

CHAPTER 10.   The Supervision of Women: Community Corrections, Rehabilitation, and Reentry   165

CHAPTER 11.   Women, Gender, and Incarceration   181

CHAPTER 12.   Women Professionals and the Criminal Justice System:
              Police, Corrections, and Offender Services   197

CHAPTER 13.   Women Professionals and the Criminal Justice System:
              Courts and Victim Services   211

Glossary   225

References   231

Index   261

About the Author   271

Detailed Contents

Preface   xiii

Acknowledgments   xvii

CHAPTER 1. Women, Gender, and Crime: Introduction   1

    The Influence of Feminism on Studies of Women, Gender, and Crime   2

    Spotlight on Women and the Academy   3

    Women, Gender, and Crime   5

        Women as Victims of Violence   5

        Women Who Offend   5

        The Intersection of Victimization and Offending   6

        Women and Work in the Criminal Justice System   6

    Data Sources on Women as Victims and Offenders   6

    The Contributions of Feminist Methodology to Research on Women, Gender, and Crime   17

    Conclusion   18

    SUMMARY   18

    KEY TERMS   19

    DISCUSSION QUESTIONS   19

    WEB RESOURCES   19

CHAPTER 2. Theories of Victimization   21

    Victims and the Criminal Justice System   21

    Spotlight on Victim Rights in Mexico   23

        Victim Blaming   24

    Fear of Victimization   26

    Theories on Victimization   28

    Spotlight on Gender and Kidnapping   30

        Routine Activities Theory   31

        Feminist Pathways Perspective   32

    SUMMARY   33

    KEY TERMS   33

    DISCUSSION QUESTIONS   33

    WEB RESOURCES   34

CHAPTER 3. Women, Gender, and Victimization: Rape and Sexual Assault   35

Historical Perspectives on Rape and Sexual Assault   35
Defining Sexual Victimization   37
Prevalence of Rape and Sexual Assault   38
Rape Myths   38
Acquaintance Versus Stranger Assault   40
Spotlight on Rape Culture   40
Drug-Facilitated Sexual Assault   42
Spotlight on the Invisible War: Rape in the Military   43
Spousal Rape   46
Campus Sexual Assault   47
Spotlight on Statutory Rape   48
LGBQT Sexual Violence   49
Racial Differences in Sexual Assault   51
The Role of Victims in Sexual Assault Cases   53
Conclusion   55
SUMMARY   56
KEY TERMS   56
DISCUSSION QUESTIONS   56
WEB RESOURCES   57

CHAPTER 4. Women, Gender, and Victimization: Intimate Partner Abuse and Stalking   59

Defining and Identifying Intimate Partner Abuse   60
Spotlight on IPA and the NFL   63
The Cycle of Violence   64
Victims of Intimate Partner Abuse   65
    Dating Violence   65
    Children of Intimate Partner Abuse   65
    LGBTQ and Intimate Partner Abuse   66
    Effects of Race and Ethnicity on Intimate Partner Abuse   68
    Unique Issues for Immigrant Victims of Intimate Partner Abuse   69
Spotlight on Intimate Partner Abuse in India   70
Barriers to Leaving an Abusive Relationship   71
Victim Experiences With Police and Corrections   72
    Programming Concerns for Victims of Intimate Partner Abuse   74
Stalking and Intimate Partner Violence   75
Spotlight on Stalking and College Campuses   77
Victims and Offenders of Stalking   77
Cyberstalking   78
Laws on Stalking   80
Conclusion   80
SUMMARY   81
KEY TERMS   81

DISCUSSION QUESTIONS   82
WEB RESOURCES   82

CHAPTER 5. International Issues in Gender-Based Violence   83
Human Trafficking   84
   Labor Trafficking   86
   Responses to Human Trafficking   87
   Promising Solutions to End Human Trafficking   88
Spotlight on Witch Burnings in Papua New Guinea   90
Rape as a War Crime   91
Female Genital Mutilation   91
Honor-Based Violence   92
Spotlight on Malala Yousafzai   95
Conclusion   96
SUMMARY   96
KEY TERMS   97
DISCUSSION QUESTIONS   97
WEB RESOURCES   97

CHAPTER 6. Women, Gender, and Offending   99
Theoretical Perspectives on Female Criminality   99
   Historical Theories on Female Criminality   100
Spotlight on the Manson Women   102
   Traditional Theories of Crime and Gender   103
   Modern Theories of Female Offending Behaviors   106
Spotlight on Men and Masculinity   108
   Feminist Criminology   109
SUMMARY   111
KEY TERMS   112
DISCUSSION QUESTIONS   112
WEB RESOURCES   112

CHAPTER 7. Girls, Gender, and Juvenile Delinquency   113
The Rise of the Juvenile Court and the Sexual Double Standard   113
The Nature and Extent of Female Delinquency   115
Spotlight on the Sexual Abuse of Girls in Confinement   119
The "Violent" Girl   120
Technical Violations: The New Status Offense   121
Risk Factors for Female Delinquency   122
   Family   122
   Abuse   123
   Peers   123
   School   124

    Substance Abuse   124

    Mental Health   125

  Meeting the Unique Needs of Delinquent Girls   125

  Spotlight on Arts Programming and At-Risk Youth   126

  Spotlight on Girls' Voices   127

  SUMMARY   129

  KEY TERMS   130

  DISCUSSION QUESTIONS   130

  WEB RESOURCES   130

CHAPTER 8. Female Offenders and Their Crimes   **131**

  Women and Drugs   134

  Property Crime   137

  Spotlight on Women and Bank Robbery   138

  Prostitution   138

    The Legalization Debate   141

  Women and Violence   142

    Girls and Gangs   142

    Gender and Violent Crime   144

  Spotlight on Women and Self-Defense   145

  Spotlight on the Case of Michelle Carter   147

  Mothers Who Kill Their Children   148

  SUMMARY   149

  KEY TERMS   150

  DISCUSSION QUESTIONS   150

  WEB RESOURCES   150

CHAPTER 9. Processing and Sentencing of Female Offenders   **151**

  Stage of the Criminal Justice System   152

  Race Effects and the Processing of Female Offenders   154

  The War on Drugs and Its Effects for Women   156

  The Effects of Extralegal Factors on Sentencing Women   158

  The Effects of Sentencing Guidelines on Judicial Decision Making   159

  International Perspectives on the Processing of Female Offenders   161

  Conclusion   162

  SUMMARY   163

  KEY TERMS   163

  DISCUSSION QUESTIONS   163

CHAPTER 10. The Supervision of Women: Community Corrections, Rehabilitation, and Reentry   **165**

  Gender-Responsive Programming for Women   165

  The Supervision of Women in the Community   169

  Women on Parole   171

  Reentry Issues for Incarcerated Women   171

Spotlight on Life After Parole 177

Recidivism and Female Offenders 177

    Building Resiliency for Women 178

SUMMARY 178

KEY TERMS 179

DISCUSSION QUESTIONS 179

WEB RESOURCES 179

CHAPTER 11. Women, Gender, and Incarceration   181

Historical Context of Female Prisons 181

Contemporary Issues for Incarcerated Women 185

Spotlight on California Prison Realignment and Its Effect on Female Inmates 187

Physical and Mental Health Needs of Incarcerated Women 189

Spotlight on the Financial Challenges Behind Bars 191

Children of Incarcerated Mothers: The Unintended Victims 192

Spotlight on the Girl Scouts Beyond Bars Program 195

SUMMARY 195

KEY TERMS 196

DISCUSSION QUESTIONS 196

WEB RESOURCES 196

CHAPTER 12. Women Professionals and the Criminal Justice System: Police, Corrections, and Offender Services   197

Women in Policing 198

Spotlight on Pregnancy and Policing 203

Women in Corrections 205

Community Corrections: Female Probation and Parole Officers 208

Conclusion 209

SUMMARY 210

KEY TERMS 210

DISCUSSION QUESTIONS 210

WEB RESOURCES 210

CHAPTER 13. Women Professionals and the Criminal Justice System: Courts and Victim Services   211

Women and the Law 211

Spotlight on Women in Politics 214

Women and the Judiciary 215

Spotlight on Women and the Supreme Court 216

Women and Work in Victim Services 218

    Advocates for Intimate Partner Abuse 219

Spotlight on Self-Care for Victim Advocates 220

    Rape-Crisis Workers 220

Conclusion 223
SUMMARY 223
KEY TERMS 223
DISCUSSION QUESTIONS 224
WEB RESOURCES 224

Glossary 225

References 231

Index 261

About the Author 271

Preface

The purpose of this book is to introduce readers to the issues that face women as they navigate the criminal justice system. Regardless of the participation, women have unique experiences that have significant effects on their perspectives of the criminal justice system. To effectively understand the criminal justice system, the voices of women must be heard. This book seeks to inform readers on the realities of women's lives as they interact with the criminal justice system. These topics are presented in this book through summary essays highlighting the key terms and research findings and incorporating cutting-edge research from scholars whose works have been published in top journals in criminal justice, criminology, and related fields.

Organization and Contents of the Book

This book is divided into thirteen chapters, with each chapter dealing with a different subject related to women, gender, and crime. Each chapter begins with an introduction to the issues raised within each topic and summarizes some of the basic themes related to the subject area. Each chapter also includes case studies on critical issues or current events related to the topic. Each introductory essay concludes with a discussion of the policy implications related to each topic. These thirteen chapters include

- Women, Gender, and Crime: Introduction

- Theories of Victimization

- Women, Gender, and Victimization: Rape and Sexual Assault

- Women, Gender, and Victimization: Intimate Partner Abuse and Stalking

- International Issues in Gender-Based Violence

- Women, Gender, and Offending

- Girls, Gender, and Juvenile Delinquency

- Female Offenders and Their Crimes

- Processing and Sentencing of Female Offenders

- The Supervision of Women: Community Corrections, Rehabilitation, and Reentry

- Women, Gender and Incarceration

- Women Professionals and the Criminal Justice System: Police, Corrections, and Offender Services

- Women Professionals and the Criminal Justice System: Courts and Victim Services

The first chapter provides an introduction and foundation for the book. In setting the context for the book, this chapter begins with a review of the influence of feminism on the study of crime. The chapter looks at the different types of data sources that are used to assess female offending and victimization. The chapter concludes with a discussion on feminist methodology and how it can contribute to the discussions of Women, gender, and crime. The Spotlight in this chapter highlights the role of gender within the study of criminology.

The second chapter begins with a review of the victim experience in the criminal justice system. This chapter highlights the experience of help seeking by victims and the practice of victim blaming. The chapter then turns to a discussion of victimization and focuses on how fear about victimization is a gendered experience. The chapter then turns to the discussion of victimization and how theories seek to understand the victim experience and place it within the larger context of the criminal justice system and society in general. The Spotlights in this chapter look at the issue of victim rights in Mexico and the femicides of women along the border cities, and cases of kidnapping involving women and girls.

The third chapter focuses on the victimization of women by crimes of rape and sexual assault. From historical issues to contemporary standards in the definition of sexual victimization, this chapter highlights the various forms of sexual assault and the role of the criminal justice system in the reporting and prosecution of these crimes, and the role of victims in the criminal justice system. This chapter also looks at critical issues such as campus sexual assault, sexual violence in the LGBTQ communities, and racial and ethnic issues in sexual assault. The Spotlights in this chapter look at issues of rape culture and sexual assault within the military.

The fourth chapter presents the discussion of victimization of women in cases of intimate partner abuse and stalking. A review of the legal and social research on intimate partner violence addresses a multitude of issues for victims, including the barriers to leaving a battering relationship. This chapter also highlights how demographics such as race, sexuality, and immigration status impact the abusive experience.

The fifth chapter focuses on international issues for women and includes discussions on crimes such as human trafficking, honor-based violence, witch burnings, genital mutilation, and rape as a war crime. The Spotlights in this chapter look at the issue of witch burnings in Papua New Guinea and the case of Malala Yousafzai.

The sixth chapter focuses on the theoretical explanations of female offending. The chapter begins with a review of the classical and modern theories of female criminality. While the classical theories often described women in sexist and stereotypical ways, modern theories of crime often ignored women completely. Recent research has reviewed many of these theories to assess whether they might help explain female offending. The chapter concludes with a discussion of gender-neutral theories and feminist criminology. The Spotlights in this chapter look at the Manson Women as a classical example of strain theory.

Chapter 7 focuses on girls and the juvenile justice system. Beginning with a discussion on the patterns of female delinquency, this chapter investigates the historical and contemporary standards for young women in society and how the changing definitions of delinquency have disproportionately and negatively impacted young girls. The Spotlights in this chapter look at the issue of sexual abuse in confinement, arts programming for at-risk youth, and listening girls' voices to assess what girls need from the juvenile justice system.

Chapter 8 deals with women and their crimes. While female crimes of violence are highly sensationalized by the media, these crimes are rare occurrences. Instead, the majority of female offending is made up of crimes that are nonviolent in nature or are considered victimless crimes, such as property-based offenses, drug abuse, and sexually based offenses. The Spotlights in this chapter look at how a typically masculine crime of bank robbery can be gendered, a discussion of gender and self-defense, and an examination of the case of Michelle Carter, who was convicted for using text messages to encourage her boyfriend to commit suicide.

The ninth chapter details the historical and contemporary patterns in the processing and sentencing of female offenders. This chapter highlights research on how factors such as patriarchy, chivalry, and paternalism within the criminal justice system impact women. The Spotlight in this chapter looks at international perspectives in the processing of female offenders.

The tenth chapter looks at the experience of women in the community corrections setting. The chapter begins with a discussion of gender-specific programming and how correctional agents and programs need to address unique issues for women. The chapter then looks at the role of risk assessment instruments and how they need to reflect gender differences between male and female offenders. The chapter concludes with a discussion on the reentry challenges of women exiting from prison. The Spotlight in this chapter looks at life after parole.

Chapter 11 examines the incarceration of women. Here, the text and readings focus on the patterns and practices of the incarceration of women. Ranging from historical examples of incarceration to modern-day policies, this chapter looks at how the treatment of women in prison varies from that of their male counterparts and how incarcerated women have unique needs based on their differential pathways to prison. The Spotlights in this chapter look at how California's experience with realignment has impacted the incarceration of women, the financial challenges for women while they are in prison, and the Girl Scouts Beyond Bars program.

Chapter 12 focuses on women who work within criminal justice occupations within traditionally male-dominated environments: policing and corrections. The Spotlight in this chapter looks at issues of pregnancy on policing.

Chapter 13 concludes this text with a discussion of women in the legal and victim services fields. The chapter looks at both women who work as attorneys as well as women in the judiciary. While women are a minority in this realm of the criminal justice system, women are generally overrepresented within victim services agencies. Here, gender also plays a significant role both in terms of the individual's work experiences as well as in the structural organization of the agency. The Spotlights in this chapter highlight the impact of gender on the U.S. Supreme Court, women in politics, and the value of self-care for victim services' workers.

As you can see, this book provides an in-depth look at the issues facing women in the criminal justice system. Each chapter of this book presents a critical component of the criminal justice system and the role of women in it. As you will soon learn, gender is a pervasive theme that runs deeply throughout our system, and how we respond to it has a dramatic effect on the lives of women in society.

There is coverage of critical topics, such as

- Representation of women in criminal justice academia

- Victim blaming

- Multiple marginalities and LGBT populations, including LGBTQ sexual violence

- Marital rape and rape as a war crime

- Campus sexual assault

- Economic abuse

- Cyberstalking

- Labor trafficking

- Women and pretrial release

- Challenges faced by female police officers

- The increasing number of women in the legal field

Spotlights cover key issues, such as

- Victims' Rights in Mexico

- Sexual Victimization at Military Academies

- Stalking and College Campuses
- The Manson Women
- Life After Parole
- Financial Challenges for Incarcerated Women
- Pregnancy and Policing
- Women in Politics
- Self-Care for Victim Advocates

Statistics, graphs, and tables have all been updated to demonstrate the most recent trends in criminology.

Digital Resources

http://study.sagepub.com/mallicoat3e

The open-access **Student Study Site** includes the following:

- Mobile-friendly **eFlashcards** reinforce understanding of key terms and concepts that have been outlined in the chapters.
- Mobile-friendly **web quizzes** allow for independent assessment of progress made in learning course material.
- EXCLUSIVE! Access to certain full-text **SAGE journal articles** that have been carefully selected for each chapter.
- **Web resources** are included for further research and insights.
- Carefully selected **video links** feature relevant interviews, lectures, personal stories, inquiries, and other content for use in independent or classroom-based explorations of key topics.

The password-protected **Instructor Resource Site** includes the following:

- A **Microsoft® Word® test bank** is available containing multiple choice, true/false, short answer, and essay questions for each chapter. The test bank provides you with a diverse range of prewritten options as well as the opportunity for editing any question and/or inserting your own personalized questions to effectively assess students' progress and understanding.
- Editable, chapter-specific **Microsoft® PowerPoint® slides** offer you complete flexibility in easily creating a multimedia presentation for your course. Highlight essential content, features, and artwork from the book.
- **Lecture notes** summarize key concepts on a chapter-by-chapter basis to help with preparation for lectures and class discussions.
- **Sample course syllabi** for semester and quarter courses provide suggested models for use when creating the syllabus for your courses.
- EXCLUSIVE! Access to certain full-text **SAGE journal articles** that have been carefully selected for each chapter. Each article supports and expands on the concepts presented in the chapter.
- **Web resources** are included for further research and insights.

Acknowledgments

I have to give tremendous thanks to Jessica Miller, acquisitions editor for the Criminology and Criminal Justice Division at SAGE Publications. I am also deeply thankful to Jerry Westby and Craig Hemmens, who created the opportunity for me to become involved in this project many years ago. Special thanks as well to the staff at SAGE Publications who have also helped breathe life into this book.

Throughout my career, I have been blessed with amazing colleagues and mentors. I am so appreciative of your love and support. Your wisdom and friendship inspires me every day to be a better scholar, teacher, and human being. I also have to give thanks to my amazing network of friends from the Division on Women and Crime and the Division on People of Color and Crime. I am honored to get to work in an environment that is caring and supportive of my adventures in research and scholarship.

Finally, I am deeply indebted to my family for their love, support, and care and their endless encouragement for my adventures in academia and beyond.

SAGE Publications gratefully acknowledges the contributions of the following reviewers for this third edition:

Dr. Dorinda L. Dowis, Professor, Columbus State University

Leah Grubb, Georgia Southern University

Susan L. Wortmann, Nebraska Wesleyan University

Sandra Pavelka, PhD, Florida Gulf Coast University

Katherine J. Ely, Lock Haven University

Reviewers for the second edition:

Kathleen A. Cameron, Pittsburgh State University

Dorinda L. Dowis, Columbus State University

Katherine J. Ely, Lock Haven University

Allison J. Foley, Georgia Regents University

Bob Lilly, Northern Kentucky University

Johnnie Dumas Myers, Savannah State University

Sue Uttley-Evans, University of Central Lancashire

CHAPTER 1

Women, Gender, and Crime
Introduction

Chapter Highlights

- Introduction to women as victims, offenders, and workers in the criminal justice system
- The emergence of feminism in criminology
- Data sources that estimate female offending and victimization rates
- The contributions of feminist methodologies in understanding issues about women and crime

Since the creation of the American criminal justice system, the experiences of women either have been reduced to a cursory glance or have been completely absent. **Gendered justice**, or rather injustice, has prevailed in every aspect of the system. The unique experiences of women have historically been ignored at every turn—for victims, for offenders, and even for women who have worked within its walls. Indeed, the criminal justice system is a gendered experience.

Yet the participation of women in the system is growing in every realm. Women make up a majority of the victims for certain types of crimes, particularly when men are the primary offender. These gendered experiences of victimization appear in crimes such as rape, sexual assault, intimate partner abuse, and stalking, to name a few. While women suffer in disproportionate ways in these cases, their cries for help have traditionally been ignored by a system that many in society perceive is designed to help victims. Women's needs as offenders are also ignored because they face a variety of unique circumstances and experiences that are absent from the male offending population. Traditional approaches in criminological theory and practice have been criticized by feminist scholars for their failure to understand the lives and experiences of women (Belknap, 2007). Likewise, the employment of women in the criminal justice system has been limited, because women were traditionally shut out of many of these male-dominated occupations. As women began to enter these occupations, they were faced with a hyper-masculine culture that challenged the introduction of women at every turn. While the participation of women in these traditionally male-dominated fields has grown significantly in modern-day times, women continue to struggle for equality in a world where the effects of the "glass ceiling" continue to pervade a system that presents itself as one interested in the notion of justice (Martin, 1991).

In setting the context for the book, this chapter begins with a review of the influence of feminism on the study of crime. Following an introduction of how gender impacts victimization, offending, and employment experiences in the criminal justice system, the chapter presents a review of the different data sources and statistics within these topics. The chapter concludes with a discussion on the research methods used to investigate issues of female victimization, offending, and work in criminal justice-related fields.

The Influence of Feminism on Studies of Women, Gender, and Crime

As a student, you may wonder what **feminism** has to do with the topic of women and crime. Feminism plays a key role in understanding how the criminal justice system responds to women and women's issues. In doing so, it is first important that we identify what is meant by the term *woman*. Is "woman" a category of *sex* or *gender*? Sometimes, these two words are used interchangeably. However, *sex* and *gender* are two different terms. *Sex* refers to the biological or physiological characteristics of what makes someone male or female. Therefore, we might use the term *sex* to talk about the segregation of men and women in jails or prison. In comparison, the term *gender* refers to the identification of masculine and feminine traits, which are socially constructed terms. For example, in early theories of criminology, female offenders were often characterized as *masculine*, and many of these scholars believed that female offenders were more like men than women. While sex and gender are two separate terms, the notions of sex and gender are interrelated within the study of women and crime. Throughout this book, you will see examples of how sex and gender both play an important role in the lives of women in the criminal justice system.

The study of women and crime has seen incredible advances throughout the 20th and 21st century. Many of these changes are a result of the social and political efforts of feminism. The 1960s and 1970s shed light on several significant issues that impacted many different groups in society, including women. The momentum of social change as represented by the civil rights and women's movements had significant impacts for society, and the criminal justice system was no stranger in these discussions. Here, the second wave of feminism expanded beyond the focus of the original activists (who were concerned exclusively about women's suffrage and the right to vote) to topics such as sexuality, legal inequalities, and reproductive rights. It was during this time frame that criminology scholars began to think differently about women and offending. Prior to this time, women were largely forgotten in research about crime and criminal behavior. When they were mentioned, they were relegated to a brief footnote or discussed in stereotypical and sexist ways. Given that there were few female criminologists (as well as proportionally few female offenders compared to the number of male offenders), it is not surprising that women were omitted in this early research about criminal behavior.

Some of the first feminist criminologists gained attention during the 1960s and 1970s. The majority of these scholars were focused primarily on looking at issues of equality and difference between men and women in terms of offending and responses by the criminal justice system. Unfortunately, these liberal feminists focused only on gender and did not include discussions that reflected a multicultural identity. Such a focus resulted in a narrow view of the women that were involved in crime and how the system responded to their offending. As Burgess-Proctor (2006) notes,

> By asserting that women universally suffer the effects of patriarchy, the dominance approach rests on the dubious assumption that all women, by virtue of their shared gender, have a common "experience" in the first place. . . . It assumes that all women are oppressed by all men in exactly the same ways or that there is one unified experience of dominance experienced by women. (p. 34)

While second-wave feminism focused on the works by these White liberal feminists, third-wave feminism addresses the multiple, diverse perspectives of women, such as race, ethnicity, nationality, and sexuality. With these new perspectives in hand, feminist criminologists began to talk in earnest about the nature of the female offender and began to ask questions about the lives of women involved in the criminal justice system. Who is she? Why does she engage in crime? And, perhaps most important, how is she different from the male offender, and how should the criminal justice system respond to her?

As feminist criminologists began to encourage the criminal justice system to think differently about female offenders, feminism also encouraged new conversations about female victimization. The efforts of second- and third-wave feminism brought increased attention to women who were victims of crime. How do women experience victimization? How does the system respond to women who have been victims of a crime? How have criminal justice systems and policies responded to the victimization of women? Indeed, there are many crimes that are inherently gendered that have historically been ignored by the criminal justice system.

▲ **Photo 1.1** The icon of Lady Justice represents many of the ideal goals of the justice system, including fairness, justice, and equality.

Feminism also brought a greater participation in the workforce in general, and the field of criminal justice was no exception. Scholars were faced with questions regarding how gender impacts the way in which women work within the police department, correctional agencies, and the legal system. What issues do women face within the context of these occupations? How has the participation of women in these fields affected the experiences of women who are victims and offenders?

Today, scholars in criminology, criminal justice, and related fields explore these issues in depth in an attempt to shed light on the population of women in the criminal justice system. While significant gains have been made in the field of **feminist criminology**, scholars within this realm have suggested that "without the rise of feminisms, scholarly concerns with issues such as rape, domestic assault, and sex work—let alone recent emphases on intersectionality and overlapping biases of race, class, sexualities, and gender—would arguably never have happened" (Chancer, 2016, p. 308). Consider the rise of black feminist criminology, which looks at how the relationship between race, gender, and other issues of oppression create multiple marginalities for women of color (Potter, 2015).

Spotlight on Women and the Academy

Like many other fields, the academy has historically been a male-dominated profession. Yet the number of women faculty has grown significantly over the past four decades. This is also true in the academic study of crime and the criminal justice system. While the number of men in senior faculty positions outnumbers women, the presence of women entering the academy is growing. In 2007, 57% of doctoral students were female (Frost & Clear, 2007). This marks a significant trend for a field (practitioners and the academy) that has been historically, and continues to be, dominated by men.

(Continued)

(Continued)

As a national organization, the roots of the American Society of Criminology date back to 1941. The founding members of the organization were all male (ASC, n.d.). It was not until 1975 that the annual conference showcased a panel on women and crime. Even with the growing interest in female crime and victimization, not to mention an increase in the number of female scholars, the majority of the association members questioned whether gender was a valuable variable to study. In response to these challenges, a small group of female scholars combined their efforts to lobby for more panels on the study of women and crime. In 1984, the Division on Women and Crime was instituted as an official branch of the American Society of Criminology. Today, the Division is the largest division of the ASC, with 384 members in 2012.

As a result of the work of these early female criminologists, the number of panels and papers presented annually on issues related to gender and crime research has grown substantially and includes discussions related to offending, victimization, and employment issues within the criminal justice system. Between 1999 and 2008, there were 3,050 (16.13%) presentations on themes related to the study of women and crime. The top five topic areas of these presentations include (1) domestic violence/intimate partner violence, (2) gender-specific programming and policies, (3) gender differences in criminal behavior, (4) victimization of women, and (5) international perspectives on women and crime (Kim & Merlo, 2012).

While much of the work of feminist criminology involves female scholars, there are also men who investigate issues of gender and crime. At the same time, there are female scholars whose work does not look at issues of gender. Over the past decade, a body of work has looked at the productivity of criminologists and in particular how female scholars compare to male scholars. While men publish more than women, the gender gap on publishing is reduced when we take into account the length of time in the academy, because the men generally report a longer career history (Snell, Sorenson, Rodriguez, & Kuanliang, 2009). However, achieving gender equity is a long road. A review of three of the top publications in criminology and criminal justice from 2013 notes that while women are well represented as first authors in *Justice Quarterly* (45.2%) and *Theoretical Criminology* (40.7%), they are underrepresented in *Criminology* (28.6%) (Chesney-Lind & Chagnon, 2016). Research by female authors is also less likely to be cited. A review of research publications in the field for the past 2 years notes that white men are most likely to have their work cited in subsequent research (77.1%) compared to white women (12.4%), while both men and women of color are rarely likely to find their research referenced by others (men of color = 1.3%; women of color = 0.7%) (Kim & Hawkins, 2013). Indeed the rise of female scholars led some researchers to note that the future of the "most productive and influential scholars will have a more markedly feminine quality" (Rice, Terry, Miller, & Ackerman, 2007, p. 379).

Women are also becoming more active in the leadership roles within these academic organizations. What was once a "boys club" now reflects an increase in the participation of women on the executive boards as well as officer positions within the organization. Between 2014 and 2018, four of the five presidents of the American Society of Criminology were women—Joanne Belknap, Candace Kruttschnitt, Ruth Peterson, and Karen Heimer. Women are also being elected to the highest position within the Academy of Criminal Justice Sciences, where four women have served as president since 2000, and Nicole Piquero has been elected for 2018. Female criminologists have also chipped away at the glass ceiling at the national level with the appointment of Nancy Rodriguez as Director of the National Institute of Justice in 2014.

While feminist scholars have made a significant impact on the study of crime over the past 40 years, there are still several areas where additional research is needed.

Women, Gender, and Crime

How does the criminal justice system respond to issues of gender? While there have been significant gains and improvements in the treatment of women as victims, offenders, and workers within the criminal justice system and related fields, there is still work to be done in each of these areas.

Women as Victims of Violence

The experience of victimization is something that many women are intimately familiar with. While men are more likely to be a victim of a crime, women compose the majority of victims of certain forms of violent crime. In addition, women are most likely to be victimized by someone they know. In many cases when they do seek help from the criminal justice system, charges are not always filed or are often reduced through plea bargains, resulting in offenders receiving limited (if any) sanctions for their criminal behavior. Because of the sensitive nature of these offenses, victims can find their own lives put on trial to be criticized by the criminal justice system and society as a whole. Based on these circumstances, it is no surprise that many women have had little faith in the criminal justice system. You'll learn more about the experience of victimization in Chapter 2.

Women who experience victimization have a number of needs, particularly in cases of violent and personal victimization experiences. While these cases can involve significant physical damage, it is often the emotional violence that can be equally, if not more, traumatic for victims to deal with. While significant gains have been made by the criminal justice system, the high needs of many victims, coupled with an increased demand for services, means that the availability of resources by agencies such as domestic violence shelters and rape crisis centers are often limited. You'll learn more about the experience of women in crimes such as rape, sexual assault, intimate partner violence, and stalking in Chapters 3 and 4, while Chapter 5 highlights issues of victimization of women around the globe.

Women Who Offend

How do female offenders compare to male offenders? When scholars look at the similarities and differences between the patterns of male and female offending, they are investigating the *gender* gap. What does this research tell us? We know that men are the majority of offenders represented for most of the crime categories, minus a few exceptions. **Gender gap** research tells us that the gender gap, or difference between male and female offending, is larger in cases of serious or violent crimes, while the gap is narrower for crimes such as property and drug related offenses (Steffensmeier & Allan, 1996).

While men are more likely to engage in criminal acts, women offenders dominate certain categories of criminal behavior. One example of this phenomenon is the crime of prostitution. Often called a victimless crime, prostitution is an offense where the majority of arrests involve women. Status offenses are another category where girls are overrepresented. Status offenses are acts that are considered criminal only because of the offender's age. For example, the consumption of alcohol is considered illegal only if you are under a designated age (generally 21 in the United States). Chapter 8 highlights different offense types and how gender is viewed within these offenses. A review of these behaviors and offenders indicates that most female offenders share a common foundation—one of economic need, addiction, and abuse.

Gender also impacts the way that the criminal justice system responds to offenders of crime. Much of this attention comes from social expectations about how women "should" behave. When women engage in crime (particularly violent crimes), this also violates the socially proscribed gender roles for female behavior. As a result, women in these cases may be punished not only for violating the law but also for violating the socially proscribed gender roles. In Chapter 9, you'll learn more about how women can be treated differently by the criminal justice system as a result of their gender. As more women have come to the attention of criminal justice officials, and as policies and practices for handling these cases have shifted, more women are being sent to prison rather than being supervised in the community. This means that there is a greater demand on reentry programming and services for women. These collateral consequences in the incarceration of women are far reaching, because the identity as an *ex-offender* can threaten a woman's chances for success long after she has served her sentence.

The Intersection of Victimization and Offending

One of the greatest contributions of feminist criminology is the acknowledgment of the relationship between victimization and offending. Research has consistently illustrated that a history of victimization of women is a common factor for many women offenders. Indeed, a review of the literature finds that an overwhelming majority of women in prison have experienced some form of abuse—physical, psychological, or sexual—and in many cases, are victims of long-term multiple acts of violence. Moreover, not only is there a strong relationship that leads from victimization to offending but the relationship between these two variables continues also as a vicious cycle. For example, a young girl who is sexually abused by a family member runs away from home. Rather than return to her abusive environment, she ends up selling her body as a way to provide food, clothing, and shelter because she has few skills to legitimately support herself. As a result of her interactions with potentially dangerous clients and pimps, she continues to endure physical and sexual violence and may turn to substances such as alcohol and drugs to numb the pain of the abuse. When confronted by the criminal justice system, she receives little if any assistance to address the multiple issues that she faces as a result of her life experiences. In addition, her *criminal* identity now makes it increasingly difficult to find valid employment, receive housing and food benefits, or have access to educational opportunities that could improve her situation. Ultimately, she ends up in a world where finding a healthy and sustainable life on her own is a difficult goal to attain. You will learn more about these challenges in Chapters 10 and 11 and how the criminal justice system punishes women for these crimes.

Women and Work in the Criminal Justice System

While much of the study of women and crime focuses on issues of victimization and offending, it is important to consider how issues of sex and gender impact the work environment, particularly for those who work within the justice system. Here, the experiences of women as police and correctional officers, victim advocates, probation and parole case managers, and lawyers and judges provide valuable insight on how sex and gender differences affect women. Just as the social movements of the 1960s and 1970s increased the attention on female offenders and victims of crime, the access to opportunities for work within the walls of criminal justice expanded for women. Prior to this era of social change, few women were granted access to work within these occupations. Even when women were present, their duties were significantly limited compared to those of their male counterparts, and their opportunities for advancement were essentially nonexistent. In addition, these primarily male workforces resented the presence of women in "their" world. Gender also has a significant effect for fields that are connected to criminal justice. One example of this is found within the field of victim services, which has typically been viewed as women's work.

Women continue to face a number of sex- and gender-based challenges directly related to their status as women, such as on-the-job sexual harassment, work-family balance, maternity, and motherhood. In addition, research reflects on how women manage the roles, duties, and responsibilities of their positions within a historically masculine environment. The experience of womanhood can impact the work environment, both personally and culturally. You'll learn more about these issues in Chapters 12 and 13 of this book.

Data Sources on Women as Victims and Offenders

To develop an understanding of how often women engage in offending behaviors or the frequency of victimizations of women, it is important to look at how information about crime is gathered. While there is no one dataset that tells us everything that we want to know about crime, we can learn something from each source because they each represent different points of view. Datasets vary based on the type of information collected (quantitative and/or qualitative), who manages the dataset (such as government agencies, professional scholar, community organization), and the purpose for the data collection. Finally, each dataset represents a picture of crime for a specific population, region, and time frame, or stage, of the criminal justice system.

The **Uniform Crime Reports (UCR)** represents one of the largest datasets on crime in the United States. The Federal Bureau of Investigations (FBI) is charged with collecting and publishing the arrest data from over 17,000 police agencies in the United States. These statistics are published annually and present the rates and volume of crime by offense type, based on arrests made by police. The dataset

▲ **Photo 1.2** Most official crime statistics, such as the Uniform Crime Reports, are based on arrest data.

includes a number of demographic variables to evaluate these crime statistics, including age, gender, race/ethnicity, location (state), and region (metropolitan, suburban, or rural).[1]

UCR data give us a general understanding of the extent of crime in the United States and are often viewed as the most accurate assessment of crime. In addition, the UCR data allow us to compare how crime changes over time, because it allows for the comparison of arrest data for a variety of crimes over a specific time frame (e.g., 1990–2000) or from one year to the next. Generally speaking, it is data from the UCR findings that are typically reported to the greater society through news media outlets and that form the basis for headline stories that proclaim the rising and falling rates of crime.

A review of arrest data from the UCR indicates that the overall levels of crime for women decreased 11.8% between 2006 and 2015. For the same time period, the number of arrests for men declined 25.6%. Such results might lead us to question why the percentage of men involved in crime decreased at more than twice the percentage of female arrests. To understand this issue, we need to take a deeper look. Figure 1.1 and Table 1.1 illustrate the UCR data on arrest trends for men and women for 2006 and 2015. In 2006, the UCR shows that women made up 23.8% of all arrests (8,676,456 total number of arrests, with women accounting for 2,070,999 arrests). In contrast, 2015 UCR data indicate that 8,739,363 arrests were made, and women accounted for 27.0% of these arrests (2,140,934) (Crime in the United States 2012 [CIUS], 2012). Note that while the number of arrests involving women decreased by approximately almost a quarter of a million arrests (244,835), the total number of arrests over the decade decreased by almost 800,000. This change notes that while both the proportion of men and women decreased, the rate of male arrests decreased at a greater rate than that of women between these two time periods.

When assessing trends in crime data, it is important to consider the time period of evaluation, because this can alter your results. While both the 10-year and 1-year overall arrest trends demonstrate a decrease for both women and men, the data for 2015 demonstrates areas where arrests increased for women compared to men (and vice versa) compared to 2014. Figure 1.2 and Table 1.2 demonstrate the arrest trends for these 2 years. The proportion of crime involving men fell 3.7%, while the proportion for women decreased 2.9%, indicating that the proportion of men arrested is similar to that of women between these 2 years. While this gives us a picture of overall crime trends, we see the picture differently when we look at the trends for specific crime categories. Here, a deeper look at the

[1]Up-to-date statistical reports on crime data from the Uniform Crime Reports can be accessed at http://www.fbi.gov/ucr/ucr.htm

Figure 1.1 ● 10-Year UCR Arrest Trends

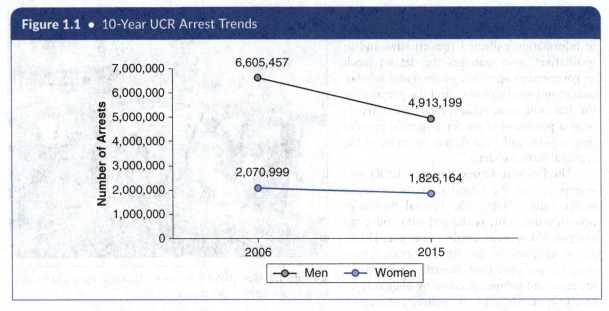

SOURCE: Crime in the United States 2015 (CIUS), 2015.

Table 1.1 ● 10-Year UCR Arrest Trends

	Men			Women		
	2006	2015	% Change	2006	2015	% Change
All arrests	6,605,457	4,913,199	−25.6	2,070,999	1,826,164	−11.8
Violent crime	297,166	244,197	−17.8	64,235	61,780	−3.8
Homicide	6,292	5,463	−13.2	812	738	−9.1
Rape*	13,932	13,546	—	188	409	—
Robbery	60,460	46,060	−23.8	7,977	7,943	−0.4
Aggravated assault	216,482	179,138	−17.3	55,258	52,690	−4.6
Property crime	645,926	576,178	−10.8	304,581	366,152	+20.2
Burglary	159,767	110,416	−30.9	28,355	26,049	−8.1
Larceny-theft	418,187	424,956	+1.6	261,103	328,713	+25.9
Motor vehicle theft	59,234	36,177	−38.9	13,416	10,286	−23.3
Arson	8,738	4,633	−47.0	1,707	1,104	−35.3

SOURCE: Crime in the United States 2015 (CIUS), 2015.

NOTE: 9,581 agencies reporting; 2015 estimated population 199,921,204; 2006 estimated population 186,371,331.

*The 2006 rape figures are based on the legacy definition, and the 2015 rape figures are aggregate totals based on both the legacy and revised UCR reporting definition.

Figure 1.2 ● 1-Year UCR Arrest Trends

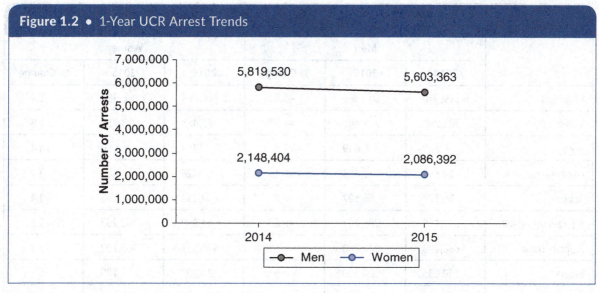

SOURCE: Crime in the United States 2012 (CIUS), 2015.

data shows that violent crime increased for both men and women while property crime declined for both groups. However, these changes were minor. In addition, there were no gender differences for specific crime categories. When the percentage of men involved in burglary decreased, it also decreased for women. When the percentage of men involved in aggravated assault increased for men, it also increased for women.

While the UCR data can illustrate important trends in crime, the reporting of UCR data as the true extent of crime is flawed for the majority of the crime categories (with the exception of homicide), even though these data represent arrest statistics from approximately 95% of the population. Here, it is important to take several issues into consideration. First, the UCR data represent statistics on only those crimes that are reported to the police. As a result, the data are dependent on both what police know about criminal activity and how they use their discretion in these cases. If the police are not a witness to a crime or are not called to deal with an offender, they cannot make an arrest. Arrests are the key variable for UCR data. This means that unreported crimes are not recognized in these statistics. Sadly, many of the victimization experiences of women, such as intimate partner abuse and sexual assault, are significantly underreported and therefore do not appear within the UCR data.

Second, the UCR collects data only on certain types of crime (versus all forms of crime). The classification of crime is organized into two different types of crime: Part 1 offenses and Part 2 offenses. Part 1 offenses, known as *index crimes*, include eight different offenses: aggravated assault, forcible rape, murder, robbery, arson, burglary, larceny-theft, and motor vehicle theft. However, these categories may have limited definitions that fail to capture the true extent of arrests made for these crimes. Consider the category of rape. Historically, the UCR defined forcible rape as "the carnal knowledge of a female forcibly and against her will" (CIUS, 2012, para. 1). While the UCR also collects data on attempted rape by force or threat of force within this category, the definition failed to capture the magnitude of sexual assaults, which may not involve female victims or may involve other sexual acts beyond vaginal penetration. In January 2012, the FBI announced a revised definition for the crime of rape to include "the penetration, no matter how slight, of the vagina or anus with any body part or object, or oral penetration by a sex organ of another person, without the consent of the victim" (FBI, 2012a, para. 1). This new definition went into effect in January 2013. Not only does the new law allow for both males and females to be identified as victims or offenders

Table 1.2 • 1-Year UCR Arrest Trends

	Men			Women		
	2014	2015	% Change	2014	2015	% Change
All arrests	5,819,530	5,603,363	−3.7	2,148,404	2,086,392	−2.9
Violent crime	283,298	287,487	+1.5%	72,463	73,754	−1.8
Homicide	6,201	6,639	+7.1	843	880	+4.4
Forcible rape	14,563	15,453	+6.1	428	481	+12.4
Robbery	55,379	56,502	+2.0	9,233	9,636	+4.4
Aggravated assault	207,155	208,893	+0.8	61,959	62,757	+1.3
Property crime	686,290	648,880	−5.5	430,517	405,792	−5.7
Burglary	140,035	126,630	−9.6	31,402	29,789	−5.1
Larceny-theft	503,460	475,551	−5.5	388,081	363,323	−6.4
Motor vehicle theft	37,311	41,807	+12.1	9,716	11,508	+18.4
Arson	5,484	4,892	−10.8	1,318	1,172	−11.1

SOURCE: Crime in the United States 2012 (CIUS), 2015.

NOTE: 11,437 agencies reporting; 2015 estimated population 229,446,072; 2014 estimated population 228,153,502.

but it also allows the UCR to include cases where the victim either was unable or unwilling to consent to sexual activity (for example, in cases involving intoxication). In addition, the new definition removes the requirement of force. As a result of these changes, the category of rape will now capture a greater diversity of sexual assaults. This new definition is more in line with the variety of laws related to rape and sexual assault that exist for each state. With this change in how these sexually based offenses are counted, it is not currently possible to compare data on the number of these cases prior to 2012. Over time, these changes will help present a more accurate picture of the prevalence of rape and sexual assault in society.

Third, the reporting of the crimes to the UCR is incomplete, because only the most serious crime is reported in cases where multiple crimes are committed during a single criminal event. These findings skew the understanding of the prevalence of crime, because several different offenses may occur within the context of a single crime incident. For example, a crime involving physical battery, rape, and murder is reported to the UCR by the most serious crime, murder. As a result, the understanding of the prevalence of physical battery and rape is incomplete.

Fourth, the reporting of these data is organized annually, which can alter our understanding of crime as police agencies respond to cases. For example, a homicide that is committed in one calendar year may not be solved with an arrest and conviction until the following calendar year. This might initially be read as an "unsolved crime" in the first year but as an arrest in the subsequent year.

Finally, the participation by agencies in reporting to the UCR has fluctuated over time. While there are no federal laws requiring agencies to report their crime data, many states today have laws that direct law enforcement agencies to comply with UCR data collection. For example, notice how there were 11,437 agencies that reported data in 2014 and 2015, but only 9,581 agencies that reported their arrest data in both 2006 and 2015. However, this means that the analyzers of crime trends over time need to take into consideration the number of agencies involved in the reporting of crime data. Failure to do so could result in a flawed analysis of crime patterns over time.

These flaws of UCR data can have significant implications for members of society about the understanding of crime data. Most of us get our information about crime from news headlines or other media reports about crime. These 30-second clips about crime rates do little to explain the intricate nature of UCR data definitions and collection practices. Indeed, when the UCR was first assigned to the FBI, early scholars commented, "In light of the somewhat questionable source of the data, the Department of Justice might do more harm than good by issuing the Reports" (Robison, 1966, p. 1033).

In an effort to develop a better understanding of the extent of offending, the **National Incident-Based Reporting System (NIBRS)** was implemented in 1988. Rather than compile monthly summary reports on crime data in their jurisdictions, agencies now forward data to the FBI for every crime incident. The NIBRS catalog involves data on 22 offenses categories and includes 46 specific crimes known as Group A offenses. Data on 11 lesser offenses (Group B offenses) are also collected. In addition to an increased diversity in the types of crimes that data are collected on, the NIBRS abolished the hierarchy rule that was part of the UCR. This means that cases that involve more than one specific offense will now count all the different offenses that are reported and not just the most serious event. In addition, NIBRS data are collected on both completed as well as attempted crimes.

Overall, NIBRS allows for a more comprehensive understanding of crime in terms of the types of crimes that we collect information about and the data that is collected on these offenses. In 2015, NIBRS data noted that 63.3% of offenders were male, 25.7% were female (while gender was unknown in 11.0% of cases). NIBRS also tells us that half of victims in these crimes were women (50.9%). The majority of victims knew the perpetrator(s) (52.3%), and an additional 24.8% of victims were related to the offender (NIBRS, 2016a). Figure 1.3 and Table 1.3 shows the NIBRS arrest data

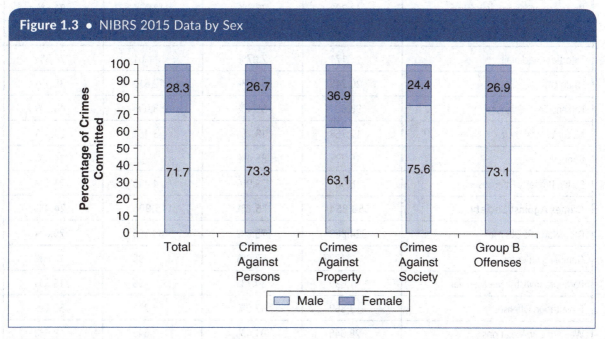

Figure 1.3 • NIBRS 2015 Data by Sex

SOURCE: NIBRS (2016b).

Table 1.3 ● NIBRS 2015 Data by Sex

	Male	%	Female	%
Total	**2,208,567**	**71.7%**	**873,042**	**28.3%**
Crimes Against Persons	**323,371**	**73.3%**	**117,955**	**26.7%**
Assault Offenses	302,144	72.2%	116,390	27.8%
Homicide Offenses	2,380	87.1%	353	12.9%
Human Trafficking Offenses	6	75.0%	2	25.0%
Kidnapping/Abduction	5,469	89.2%	663	10.8%
Sex Offenses	11,877	96.5%	427	3.5%
Sex Offenses, Nonforcible	1,495	92.6%	120	7.4%
Crimes Against Property	**359,557**	**63.1%**	**210,006**	**36.9%**
Arson	1,719	80.1%	426	19.9%
Bribery	124	70.1%	53	29.9%
Burglary/Breaking & Entering	39,801	84.2%	7,459	15.8%
Counterfeiting/Forgery	9,107	63.0%	5,354	37.0%
Destruction/Damage/Vandalism	43,708	78.4%	12,024	21.6%
Embezzlement	2,797	45.3%	3,380	54.7%
Extortion/Blackmail	171	73.7%	61	26.3%
Fraud Offenses	20,248	61.6%	12,615	38.4%
Larceny/Theft Offenses	196,601	55.4%	158,008	44.6%
Motor Vehicle Theft	12,768	78.7%	3,461	21.3%
Robbery	15,933	85.4%	2,720	14.6%
Stolen Property Offenses	16,580	78.9%	4,445	21.1%
Crimes Against Society	**358,854**	**75.6%**	**115,805**	**24.4%**
Drug/Narcotic Offenses	324,869	75.0%	108,555	25.0%
Gambling Offenses	432	82.0%	95	18.0%
Pornography/Obscene Material	1,639	84.7%	295	15.3%
Prostitution Offenses	3,869	47.9%	4,211	52.1%
Weapon Law Violations	28,045	91.4%	2,649	8.6%

	Male	%	Female	%
Total	**2,208,567**	**71.7%**	**873,042**	**28.3%**
Group B Offenses	**1,166,785**	**73.1%**	**429,276**	**26.9%**
Bad Checks	3,717	48.4%	3,969	51.6%
Curfew/Loitering/Vagrancy Violations	9,567	71.3%	3,851	28.7%
Disorderly Conduct	82,781	71.7%	32,656	28.3%
Driving Under the Influence	228,773	74.5%	78,204	25.5%
Drunkenness	80,625	79.5%	20,851	20.5%
Family Offenses, Nonviolent	20,212	71.3%	8,134	28.7%
Liquor Law Violations	66,333	70.8%	27,358	29.2%
Peeping Tom	289	92.9%	22	7.1%
Trespass of Real Property	58,830	77.9%	16,689	22.1%
All Other Offenses	615,658	72.2%	237,542	27.8%

SOURCE: NIBRS (2016b).

for men and women in 2015. Comparing these two sources of data, we find similar results in the number of arrests for women and men. While UCR data shows that women made up 27.1% of all arrests in 2015, NIBRS data notes that 28.3% of all arrests involved women. Similarities are also noted when we can compare like-defined categories. For example., women make up 11.7% of all homicide arrests in the UCR. In NIBRS, they make up 12.9% of arrests. In cases of larceny-theft, UCR data notes that women are 43.3% of all arrests. In NIBRS, women are 44.6% of arrests.

However, the transition of agencies to the NIBRS has been slow. Currently, the data obtained represents 36.1% of the reported crime and 58.1% of all police agencies in the United States. While the NIBRS is an improvement over the UCR, this system still carries over a fatal flaw from the UCR in that both are limited to reported crimes. In spite of this, it is hoped that the improvements in official crime data collection will allow an increased understanding of the extent of female offending patterns. NIBRS is slated to be fully implemented with all agencies reporting to it by January 1, 2021.

In contrast to the limitations of the UCR and NIBRS datasets, the **National Crime Victimization Survey (NCVS)** represents the largest victimization study conducted in the United States. National-level victimization data were first collected in 1971 to 1972 as part of the Quarterly Household Survey conducted by the Census Bureau. In 1972, these efforts evolved into the National Crime Survey (NCS), which was designed to supplement the data from UCR and provide data on crime from the victims' perspective. The NCS was transferred to the Bureau of Justice Statistics in 1979, where the bureau began to evaluate the survey instrument and the data collection process. Following an extensive redesign process, the NCS was renamed the National Crime Victimization Survey in 1991.

The greatest achievement of the NCVS lies in its attempt to fill the gap between reported and unreported crime, often described as the **dark figure of crime**. The NCVS gathers additional data about crimes committed and gives criminologists a greater understanding of the types of crimes committed and characteristics of the victims. In 2015, the NCVS interviewed 163,880 individuals aged 12 and older in 95,760 households. Based on these survey findings,

Table 1.4 • NCVS Crime Rates by Sex: 2002, 2010, and 2015

	Violent Crime					Serious Violent Crime*				
	Rates			Percent Change		Rates			Percent Change	
	2002	2010	2015	2002–2015	2010–2015	2002	2010	2015	2002–2015	2010–2015
Total	32.1	19.3	18.6	−42.2	−3.6	10.1	6.6	6.8	−32.7	+3.0
Sex:										
Male	33.5	20.1	15.9	−52.5	−20.9	10.4	6.4	5.4	−48.1	−15.6
Female	30.7	18.5	21.1	−31.3	+14.1	9.5	6.8	8.1	−14.7	+19.1

SOURCE: Truman & Morgan (2016).

*Includes rape or sexual assault, robbery, and aggravated assault.

the Bureau of Justice Statistics make generalizations to the population regarding the prevalence of victimization in the United States (Truman & Morgan, 2016).

In addition to reporting the numbers of criminal victimizations, the NCVS presents data on the rates of crime. You may ask yourself, "What is a crime rate?" A crime rate compares the number of occurrences of a particular crime to the size of the total population. The NCVS presents its findings in relation to how many instances of the crime per 1,000 people. Crime rates make it easy to understand trends in criminal activity and victimization over time, regardless of changes to the population.

According to the National Crime Victimization Survey, the rate of violent victimization of women in 2002 was 30.7 per 1,000 people. By 2015, the crime rate had fallen to 21.1. Serious violent victimization also saw a significant decrease from 9.5 (2002) to 6.7 (2011), though in 2015 the rate had rebounded to 8.1 per 1,000 people.[2] Table 1.3 highlights the rates of crime for 2015 for violent and serious violent victimization. While NCVS data highlight these decreases, these patterns are not necessarily reflected in the UCR/NIBRS data, because many victims do not report these crimes to the police. With only 46.5% of victims reporting violent crime and 34.6% of victims reporting property crime, the NCVS provides valuable insight about the dark figure of crime that is missing in official crime statistics. This dark figure of crime varies by offense. For example, while 61.9% of cases of aggravated assault were reported, victims reported only 41.7% of simple assault cases. Similar patterns are observed in cases involving property crimes. While 69% of cases of motor vehicle theft were reported, other thefts were only reported 28.6% of the time (Truman & Morgan, 2016).

Just as the UCR/NIBRS is not the only data source on offending, the NCVS is not the only national-level data source on victimization. A number of different studies investigate victims of crime and how the justice system responds to their victimization. One example of this type of survey is the **National Violence Against Women Survey (NVAWS)**. The NVAWS consisted of a random sample of 8,000 women over the age of 18. The NVAWS was first administered between November 1995 and May 1996 and represented one of the first comprehensive data assessments of violence against women for the crimes of intimate partner abuse, stalking, and sexual assault. Another example is the **National Intimate Partner and Sexual Violence Survey (NISVS)**, which is conducted by the Centers for Disease Control and Prevention and the National Center for Injury Prevention and Control. In 2010,

[2]Includes rape, sexual assault, robbery, and aggravated assault.

the NISVS included data from 16,507 interviews. The NISVS reports victimization from a variety of crimes, including sexual assault, intimate partner abuse, and stalking. These findings are then used to create estimates about the extent of crime throughout the United States. Figure 1.4 highlights the lifetime prevalence of rape by race and ethnicity based on data from the NISVS. These results demonstrate that 1 in 5 White (18.8%) and Black (22%) women and 1 in 7 (14.6%) Hispanic women in the United States have been raped at some point in their lifetime. By breaking up these data based on race and ethnicity, we can highlight how the issue of rape is even more dramatic within the American Indian/Alaska Native population, where 1 in 4 (26.9%) women experience rape in their lifetime. Unfortunately, we do not know much about how race and ethnicity impact rates of male rape from these data, only to say that less than 1 in 50 (2%) White men are impacted by the crime of rape in their lifetime (Black et al., 2011). Figure 1.5 presents the findings from this study for the crime of sexual assault. Here, we can see that not only are these crimes much more prevalent in general but also that we are able to see differences for both men and women by race/ethnicity. Studies such as these provide valuable data in understanding the experiences of victims (both men and women) that may not be reflected by the NCVS or UCR data.

While the UCR, NIBRS, and NCVS are examples of official data sources in the United States, several examples of international crime surveys can shed light on the nature of crime and victimization in other countries. The Australian Bureau of Statistics (ABS) collects data on arrested individuals throughout Australia. Unlike the UCR, which collects data on a calendar year basis, the ABS data cycle runs from July 1 to June 30. In its 2015–16 cycle, there were 422,067 individuals aged 10 and older processed by the police for eight different offenses (homicide, assault, sexual assault, robbery, kidnapping, unlawful entry with intent, motor vehicle theft, and other theft; Australian Bureau of Statistics, 2017). Another example of an official source of crime statistics is the annual report produced by the Bundeskriminalamt (Federal Criminal Police Office of Germany). The Bundeskriminalamt (BKA) statistics include data for all crimes handled by the police. In 2015, of the 6,330,649 crimes reported to the police, 5,927,908 were considered "cleared" or solved. Violent crime represents only 2.9% of crime in Germany. The largest crime category is theft and represents 39.2% of all criminal offenses. Men are much more likely to be considered a

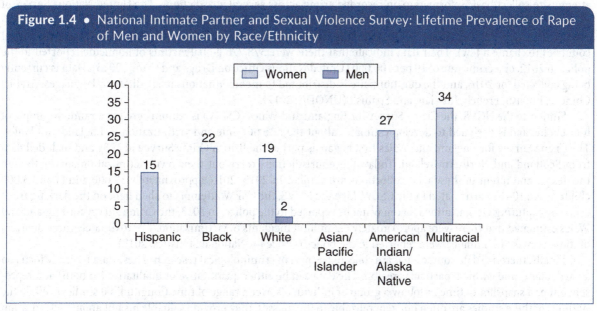

Figure 1.4 • National Intimate Partner and Sexual Violence Survey: Lifetime Prevalence of Rape of Men and Women by Race/Ethnicity

SOURCE: Black et al. (2011).

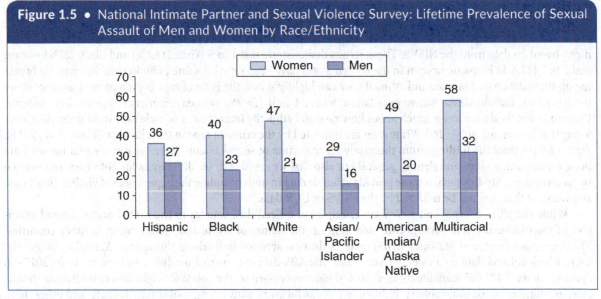

Figure 1.5 • National Intimate Partner and Sexual Violence Survey: Lifetime Prevalence of Sexual Assault of Men and Women by Race/Ethnicity

SOURCE: Black et al. (2011).

suspect by the police in these criminal activities—out of 2,369,036 suspects, only 24.8% are women. Men are also more likely to be victims (59.6%) (BKA, 2015). Australia's and Germany's crime statistical agencies are just two examples of official international data sources on criminal offending at the country level. Because of the differences in laws and reporting practices, it is difficult to compare such statistics at a global level. However, there have been attempts to collect basic information on recorded crime across several jurisdictions. The United Nations Survey of Crime Trends and Operations of Criminal Justice Systems (UN-CTS) compiles crime data from a variety of different sources, including the World Health Organization, Eurostat, and national police organizations from individual countries (to name a few). Their data indicate that there were 378,776 global victims of homicide reported to the police in 2012, or a crime rate of 10 per 100,000 (United Nations Office on Drugs and Crime, 2013). Data is currently being collected for 2016, and the questionnaire is distributed to member nations in six different languages: Arabic, Chinese, English, French, Russian, and Spanish (UNODC, 2017).

Similar to the NCVS, the Crime Survey for England and Wales (CSEW) is administered to a random sample of households and is designed to develop estimates about the rate of crime and victimization in England and Wales. The Crime Survey for England and Wales first began as part of the British Crime Survey in 1984 and included data from Scotland and Northern Ireland. Today, these jurisdictions carry out their own victimization survey though the design and intent of these data collections are similar. In 2015–2016, approximately 35,000 adults and 3,000 children age 10–15 participated in the CSEW. Like the NCVS, the CSEW attempts to shed light on the dark figure of crime by capturing victimizations that may not be reported to the police. In 2013, the Crime Survey for England and Wales estimated that there were approximately 6.2 million incidents of victimization. Approximately three quarters of these crimes (4.7 million) were reported to the police (Office for National Statistics, 2017).

Finally, there are data sources that are collected as part of criminological research. These data typically focus on a particular crime within a particular region. The data can be either quantitative or qualitative (or both) and represent either a snapshot in time or follow a group of individuals over a range of time (longitudinal studies). While the findings of these studies are often not generalizable to the masses, they provide valuable insight about victimization and offending. Throughout this text, you'll be exposed to a number of these studies, within both the chapters and the highlighted readings.

In summary, official crime statistics offer only one perspective on the extent of crime in society. While the UCR and NCVS data and other international data sources provide a wealth of statistics about crime, their results are limited. Through the use of these official data programs, combined with self-report studies and victimization surveys, scholars can investigate issues of gender and crime in a variety of different ways. While each source of data has its strengths and weaknesses in terms of the types of data that are collected and the methods that are utilized, together, they provide a wealth of information that is invaluable in understanding the complex nature of gender and crime.

The Contributions of Feminist Methodology to Research on Women, Gender, and Crime

One of the criticisms of traditional mainstream criminology (and a central theme of feminist criminology) is that traditional perspectives on crime fail to recognize the intricate details of what it means to be a woman in society. The feminist movement has had a significant effect on how we understand women and their relationships with crime. As a result, the methods by which we conduct research on gender have also evolved. While many scholars who do research on gender engage in quantitative methods of research and analysis, this is not the only approach, particularly when dealing with sensitive issues. Here, the influence of feminism can alter the ways in which we conduct research, evaluate data, and make conclusions based on the findings yielded from the research experience. By incorporating a feminist perspective to the research environment, scholars are able to present a deeper understanding of the realities of women's lives by placing women and women's issues at the center of the research process.

The concept of giving women a voice, particularly in situations where they have been historically silenced, is a strong influence on **feminist research methods**. Many of the research studies in this book draw on feminist research methods. From the conceptualization of the research question to a discussion of which methods of data collection will be utilized and how the data will be analyzed, feminist methods engage in practices that are contrary to the traditional research paradigms. While the scientific method focuses on objectivity and the collection of data is detached from the human condition, the use of feminist methods requires a paradigm shift from what is traditionally known as research. While many of the researchers who first engaged in research through a feminist lens were women, feminist methodology does not dictate that the gender of the research participant or researcher be a woman. Rather, the philosophy of this method refers to the types of data a researcher is seeking and the process by which data are obtained (Westervelt & Cook, 2007). Feminist methods are largely qualitative in nature and allow for emotions and values to be present as part of the research process. While some feminist methodologists have criticized the process by which data are often quantified, because it does not allow for the intricate nature and quality of women's lives to be easily documented, others argue that quantitative data have a role to play within a feminist context. Regardless of the approach, the influence of feminism allows for researchers to collect data from a subject that is theoretically important for their research versus data that are easily categorized (Hessy-Biber, 2004; Reinharz, 1992).

There is no single method of research that is identified as the *feminist method*. Rather, the concept of feminist methodology refers to *the process by which data are gathered* and *the relationship between the researcher and the subject*. This process involves five basic principles: (1) acknowledging the influence of gender in society as a whole (and inclusive of the research process); (2) challenging the traditional relationship between the researcher and the subject and its link to scientific research and the validity of findings; (3) engaging in consciousness raising about the realities of women's lives as part of the methodological process; (4) empowering women within a patriarchal society through their participation in research; and (5) an awareness by the researcher of the ethical costs of the research process and a need to protect their subjects (Cook & Fonow, 1986).

For many researchers who study women in the criminal justice system, the use of feminist methodologies is particularly beneficial. Not only does it allow for researchers to explore in depth the issues that women face as victims and offenders but it also provides the opportunity for the researchers to delve into their topics in a way that traditional methods fail to explore, such as the context of women's lives and their experiences in offending and victimization. For example, a simple survey question might inquire about whether an incarcerated woman has ever been victimized. We know that scholarship on incarcerated women has consistently documented the relationship between early life victimizations and participation in crime in their adolescent and adult lives. Yet traditional methods may underestimate the extent and nature of the victimization because the women may not understand the question or identify their experiences in this way. Feminist methodologies allow not only for the exploration of these issues at a deeper level but also they allow for scholars to develop an understanding of the multifaceted effects of these experiences.

While many feminist researchers largely employ qualitative tactics, it is important to note that the use of feminist methods does not exclude the use of quantitative methods. In fact, quantitative methods can yield valuable data on the experiences of women (Westmarland, 2001). For example, survey data can yield information on the presence of gender discrimination, such as the sexual harassment among women in policing. In addition, the use of quantitative data and statistics is often useful for legislators when developing policies. Reinharz (1992) provides the example of the use of statistics in the development of sexual harassment policies whereby quantitative data "encouraged the establishment of sexual harassment committees in universities and . . . eventually provided legal redress for individuals" (p. 80). Indeed, researchers who study issues of women and crime can benefit from the lessons of feminist methodologies in their use of both quantitative and qualitative methods.

While feminist methods can provide valuable resources for the study of women and crime, feminist methods are not limited to issues of gender. Rather, feminist methodologies employ tools that are applicable across criminological topics.

By recognizing from the outset the class, racial, and gendered structures of oppression that may be at work in women's lives, this method gives voice to the larger structural processes that shape the experiences that often go unseen and unheard by others. Thus, this method provides a framework for building trust with those participants who may be unsure about the research process and creates opportunities for understanding individuals and groups who may very well be inaccessible when approached in any other way (Westervelt & Cook, 2007, p. 35).

Conclusion

The feminist movement has had a significant effect on the experience of women in the criminal justice system—from victims to offenders to workers. Today, the efforts of the pioneers of feminist criminology have led to an increased understanding of what leads a woman to engage in crime and the effects of her life experiences on her offending patterns, as well as the challenges in her return to the community. In addition, the victim experience has changed for many women in that their voices are beginning to be heard by a system that either blamed them for their victimization or ignored them entirely in years past. The feminist movement has also shed light on what it means to be a woman working within the criminal justice system and the challenges that she faces every day as a woman in this field. While women have experienced significant progress over the last century, there are still many challenges that they continue to face as offenders, victims, and workers within the world of criminal justice.

/// **SUMMARY**

- The terms *sex* and *gender* are often used interchangeably, but they have different implications for research on women and crime.

- Women are significantly more likely to be victimized by someone they know and are overrepresented in crimes such as sexual assault and intimate partner violence.

- Feminist criminologists have identified a significant link between victimization and offending.

- Many criminal justice occupations are male dominated and reflect gendered assumptions about women and work within these realms.

- Data from the Uniform Crime Reports (UCR) and National Incident-Based Reporting System (NIBRS) often fail to identify much of female victimization, because crimes of rape, sexual assault, and intimate partner abuse go largely underreported.

- Victimization studies, such as the National Crime Victimization Survey (NCVS), help illuminate the dark figure of crime by collecting data on crimes that are not reported to police.

- Self-report studies, such as the National Intimate Partner and Sexual Violence Survey (NISVS), provide estimates of the prevalence of rape, sexual assault, intimate partner abuse, and stalking in the United States.

- Feminist research methods give women a voice in the research process and influence how data on gender are collected.

/// KEY TERMS

Dark figure of crime 13

Feminism 2

Feminist criminology 3

Feminist research methods 17

Gender gap 5

Gendered justice 1

National Crime Victimization Survey (NCVS) 13

National Incident-Based Reporting System (NIBRS) 11

National Intimate Partner and Sexual Violence Survey (NISVS) 14

National Violence Against Women Survey (NVAWS) 14

Uniform Crime Reports (UCR) 7

/// DISCUSSION QUESTIONS

1. What impact has feminism had in the study of women and crime?

2. Discuss how the Uniform Crime Reports (UCR) and the National Incident-Based Reporting System (NIBRS) represent the measure of female offending and victimization in society.

3. How do datasets, such as the National Crime Victimization Survey (NCVS), the National Violence Against Women Survey (NVAWS), and National Intimate Partner and Sexual Violence Survey (NISVS), investigate issues of violence against women?

4. How do feminist research methods inform studies on women and crime?

/// WEB RESOURCES

Centers for Disease Control and Prevention: http://www.cdc.gov

Crime in the United States 2015: https://ucr.fbi.gov/crime-in-the-u.s/2015/crime-in-the-u.s.-2015

National Crime Victimization Survey: http://www.icpsr.umich.edu/icpsrweb/NACJD/NCVS/

National Incident-Based Reporting System: http://www.icpsr.umich.edu/icpsrweb/NACJD/NIBRS/

Uniform Crime Reports: http://www.fbi.gov/about-us/cjis/ucr/ucr

United Nations Survey of Crime Trends and Operations of Criminal Justice Systems: https://www.unodc.org/unodc/en/data-and-analysis/statistics/data.html

 Visit **www.sagepub.com/mallicoat3e** to access additional study tools, including eFlashcards, web quizzes, web resources, video resources, and SAGE journal articles.

CHAPTER 2

Theories of Victimization

Chapter Highlights

- Victims and the criminal justice system
- Gender and fear of victimization
- Theories on victimization

This chapter is divided into three topics. The chapter begins with a review of the victim experience in the criminal justice system. This chapter highlights the experience of help seeking by victims and the practice of victim blaming. The chapter then turns to a discussion of victimization and focuses on how fear about victimization is a gendered experience. The chapter concludes with a discussion of victimization and how theories seek to understand the victim experience and place it within the larger context of the criminal justice system and society in general.

Victims and the Criminal Justice System

Why do victims seek out the criminal justice system? Do they desire justice? What does *justice* mean for victims of crime? Is it retribution? Reparation? Something else? Victims play an important role in the criminal justice process—indeed, without a victim, many cases would fail to progress through the system at all. However, many victims who seek out the criminal justice system for support following their victimization are often sadly disappointed in their experiences. In many cases, human victims of crime are reduced to a tool of the justice system or a piece of evidence in a criminal case. As a result, many of these victims express frustration over a system that seems to do little to represent their needs and concerns; victims can even be further traumatized based on their experiences in dealing with the criminal justice system.

As a result of increased pressures to support the needs of victims throughout the criminal justice process, many prosecutors' offices began to establish victim-assistance programs during the mid-1970s to provide support to victims as their cases moved through the criminal justice process. In some jurisdictions, nonprofit agencies for particular crimes, such as domestic violence and rape crisis, also began to provide support for victims during this time

(Perona, Bottoms, & Sorenson, 2006; U.S. Department of Justice, 1998). Community agencies such as rape crisis centers developed in response to the perceived need for sexual assault prevention efforts, a desire for increased community awareness, and a wish to ameliorate the pain that the victims of crime often experience (Parsons & Bergin, 2010). In response to a backlash against the rights of criminal defendants as guaranteed by the U.S. Constitution, citizens and legislatures increased their efforts toward establishing rights for victims in the criminal justice process.

In an effort to increase the rights of victims in the criminal justice system, several pieces of federal legislation have passed. These policies increase the voice of victims throughout the process, training for officials who deal with victims, and funding programs that provide therapeutic resources for victims. Some of these focus on victims of a specific crime. For example, the Violence Against Women Act provides support for criminal justice researchers studying issues related to intimate partner violence. You'll learn more about this important piece of legislation in Chapter 3. Other examples of federal legislation provide protections for all crime victims, such as the Crime Victims' Rights Act of 2004. While attempts to pass an amendment to the U.S. Constitution on victims' rights have been unsuccessful, each of the 50 states includes references to the rights of victims in criminal cases. Table 2.1 illustrates some of the **core rights of victims** that are included in many state laws and constitutions.

Much of what we know about victims comes from official crime datasets or research studies on samples of victimized populations. A comparison between official crime data (arrest rates) and victimization data indicates that many victims do not report their crime to law enforcement, which affects society's understanding regarding the realities of crime. According to the Bureau of Justice's National Crime Victimization Survey, only about half of all victims surveyed report their victimization to law enforcement (Hart & Rennison, 2003). Victims of serious violent crime are generally more likely to report these crimes compared to property offenses. Robbery was the most likely crime reported (66%), followed by aggravated assault (57%). While women are generally more likely to report crimes to law enforcement than men, cases of personal violence are significantly underreported among female victims (Patterson & Campbell, 2010). For example, the NCVS indicates that only 42% of rapes and sexual assaults are reported, and the Chicago Women's Health Risk Study showed that only 43% of women who experience violent acts from a current or former intimate partner contacted the police (Davies, Block, & Campbell, 2007). Certainly, the relationship between the victim and offender is a strong predictor in reporting rates, because women who are victimized by someone known to them are less likely to report than women who are victimized by a stranger (Resnick, Acierno, Holmes, Dammeyer, & Kilpatrick, 2000).

Table 2.1 ● Core Rights of Victims

The core rights for victims of crime include

- the right to attend criminal justice proceedings;
- the right to apply for compensation;
- the right to be heard and participate in criminal justice proceedings;
- the right to be informed of proceedings and events in the criminal justice process, of legal rights and remedies, and of available services;
- the right to protection from intimidation and harassment;
- the right to restitution from the offender;
- the right to prompt return of personal property seized as evidence;
- the right to a speedy trial; and
- the right to enforcement of these rights.

SOURCE: From VictimLaw (n.d.).

There are many reasons why victims might choose not to report their victimization to the police. Some victims feel embarrassed by the crime. Still others may decide not to report a crime to the police out of the belief that nothing could be done. In many cases, people do not report their crime because they believe that the crime was not serious enough to make a big deal over it, while others believe it is a personal matter.

However, a failure to report does not mean that victims do not seek out assistance for issues related to their victimization experience. Several studies on sexual assault and intimate partner violence indicate that victims often seek help from personal resources outside of law enforcement, such as family and friends, and many seek assistance through formal mental health services following a victimization experience

▲ **Photo 2.1** Much of the victimization that women experience involves offenders known to them. In many cases, their relationship with an offender leads many victims to not report the crime to the police.

(Kaukinen, 2004). While many victims may be reluctant to engage in formal help seeking, research suggests that victims who receive positive support from informal social networks, such as friends and family, are subsequently more likely to seek out formal services, such as law enforcement and therapeutic resources. In these cases, informal networks act as a support system for seeking professional help and for making an official crime report (Davies et al., 2007; Starzynski, Ullman, Townsend, Long, & Long, 2007).

The literature on barriers to help seeking indicates that fears of retaliation can affect a victim's decision to make a report to the police. This is particularly true for victims of intimate partner violence where research indicates that violence can indeed increase following police intervention in intimate partner violence (Dugan, Nagin, & Rosenfeld, 2003). The presence of children in domestic violence situations also affects reporting rates as many victims may incorrectly believe that they will lose their children as a result of intervention from social service agents.

Spotlight on Victim Rights in Mexico

While there are laws protecting crime victims for each state and U.S federal level, such is not the case in many other regions of the world. Victimization is often a stigmatizing experience, leading many crime victims to suffer in silence. This is further compounded by the fact that in many countries, crime victims do not have any legal rights and agencies to support the needs of victims are limited.

Consider the case involving hundreds, if not thousands of victims of femicide along the Ciudad-Juarez and Chihuahua borders. Since the mid-1990s, young women have been murdered in and around these border towns, which have become synonymous with high levels of violence and narcotics trafficking. Their bodies are discovered days, weeks, and months following their disappearance and are typically abandoned in vacant lots in Juarez and the surrounding areas; some women are never found. Many of these cases involve significant acts of sexual torture, including rape and the slashing of the breasts and genitals of the female victims (Newton, 2003). Many

(Continued)

(Continued)

of these women had traveled to these border towns from their villages in search of work in the maquiladoras—factories that assemble or manufacture products, which are then returned to the United States duty free under the North American Free Trade Agreement.

In describing the murders of these women, several commentaries have pointed toward a clash between the traditional roles for women, a machista (chauvinistic) culture, and the rise of women's independence as an explanation for the violence. According to a 2003 report by the Inter-American Commission on Human Rights (IACHR), the crimes against women in Ciudad Juarez have received international attention because of the extreme levels of violence in the murders and the belief that these killings may have been the result of a serial killer. However, their research indicates that these cases of femicide are not the result of a single serial killer but are part of a larger social issue related to a pattern of gender-based discrimination where the violence against women is not considered to be a serious issue. Given the relationship with gender in these cases, any official response to address these crimes must consider the larger social context of crimes against women and the accessibility of justice for women in these cases.

While the Mexican government created a victims services fund designed to provide monetary compensation to the families of the women and girls who have been murdered in Juarez, the program is poorly organized, and few families have been able to access the funds (Calderon Gamboa, 2007). Meanwhile, non-profit organizations such as *Justicia para Nuestras Hijas* (Justice for our Daughters) work to combat the myths and victim blaming surrounding these cases through public education. They also provide legal assistance and therapeutic support services for victims of crime. The organizing also works to document these cases of femicide and lobby for support and legal change to the government (Villagran, n.d.).

The grassroots movement for victims in Mexico has continued to grow. While groups are united in an effort to end violence in their communities, provide support for victims, and call attention to a failing justice system, there are significant debates within these efforts on how to accomplish these goals. In January 2013, the Mexican government passed the General Law of Victims. However, the law was heavily criticized and many groups did not feel that the law went far enough to meet the needs of victims. The law was revised in May 2013 and incorporated a number of provisions for victims, including a national registry of victims, a governmental victim services agency, and a victim assistance fund (Villagran, n.d.). At the same time, the judicial system is working through several reforms to their process. In the words of Ernesto Canales, the cofounder of RENACE, "what is needed is an integral reform of the system . . . we cannot think that by augmenting the rights of victims and leaving the current system in place we'll be protecting (victims)" (Villagran, n.d., p. 138). While progress has been made in these areas, there is still significant work to be done.

Victim Blaming

Reporting practices and help-seeking behaviors by victims are also influenced by the potential of **victim blaming**. Victim blaming is the practice whereby the responsibility of the crime is diffused from the offender and blame is shifted to the victim.

Why do we blame the victim? The process of victim blaming is linked to a belief in a just world. The concept of a just world posits that society has a need to believe that people deserve whatever comes to them—bad things happen to bad people, and good things happen to good people (Lerner, 1980). Under these assumptions, if a bad thing happens to someone, then that person must be at fault for the victimization because of who he or she is and what he or she does. A just world outlook gives a sense of peace to many individuals. Imagining a world where crime victims must have done something foolish, dangerous, or careless allows members of society to distinguish themselves from this identity of victimhood—"I would never do that, so therefore I must be safe from harm"—and allows individuals to shield themselves from feelings of vulnerability and powerlessness when it comes to potential acts of victimization. There are several negative consequences stemming from this condition: (1) Victim blaming assumes that people are able to change the environment in which they live, (2) victim blaming assumes that only "innocent" victims are true victims, and (3) victim blaming creates a false sense of security about the risks of crime.

Given the nature of victimization patterns in society, few meet the criteria of a culturally ideal victim. This process of victim blaming allows society to diffuse the responsibility of crime between the victim and the offender. For example, the battered woman is asked, "Why do you stay?"; the rape victim is asked, "What were you wearing?"; the assault victim is asked, "Why didn't you fight back?"; the burglary victim is asked, "Why didn't you lock the door?"; and the woman who puts herself in harm's way is asked, "What were you thinking?" Each of these scenarios shifts the blame away from the perpetrator and assigns responsibility to the victim. Victim blaming enables people to make sense of the victimization. In many cases, the process of victim blaming allows people to separate themselves from those who have been victimized—"I would never have put myself in that situation"—and this belief allows people to feel safe in the world.

How does the **just world hypothesis** work, and what are the implications for this application in the criminal justice system? Consider the crime of sexual assault. Under the just world hypothesis, victim blaming occurs in subtle ways in typical cases and may be more obvious in high-profile cases. For example, in the accusations against Kobe Bryant, extensive news reports questioned why the victim entered the hotel room with Mr. Bryant. There was also significant speculation about the victim's sexual activity prior to and following the alleged act with Mr. Bryant. Under the just world hypothesis, the victim begins to assume responsibility for this alleged assault in the eyes of the public. This can impact future reporting trends, because victims may be less likely to report their own victimizations after observing what happened to the victim in the Bryant case. A belief in the just world hypothesis also leads to an increased support of rape myths. For example, college males who view newspaper articles in support of myths about rape were less likely to view nonconsensual sexual acts as criminal compared to females in general or males who read neutral news accounts of sexual assault (Franiuk Seefelt, Cepress, & Vandello, 2008).

Given that women tend to be disproportionately represented in many forms of victimization such as rape, sexual assault, and intimate partner violence, victim blaming can be disproportionately gendered and directed toward women (Eigenberg & Garland, 2008). Research on victim blaming finds that men are more likely to blame female victims in cases of rape and sexual assault (Kohsin Wang & Rowley). Victim blaming is also more prevalent among older individuals and those with lower levels of education or lower socioeconomic status (Gracia & Tomas, 2014). Victim characteristics can also impact how much blame is attributed to the victim. For example, victims who violate traditional gender roles or who are intoxicated are more likely to experience victim blaming (Grubb & Turner, 2012). Attributions of responsibility are often levied against victims who do not physically fight back against their attacker (Spears & Spohn, 1996).

The presence of victim blaming has also been linked to the low reporting rates of crime. Here, victims reach out to law enforcement, community agencies, and family or peer networks in search of support and assistance and are often met with blame and refusals to help. These experiences have a negative effect on the recovery of crime victims. The media can also perpetuate victim blaming, particularly in cases involving celebrities. For example, during the alleged sexual assault by Kobe Bryant in 2003 the media used the term *accuser* in this particular case, whereas most accounts of sexual assault generally use the term *victim* (Franiuk et al., 2008). Another example is the high profile assault of Janay Rice by her husband, Baltimore Ravens running back Ray Rice. In September 2014, a video of Mrs. Rice surfaced where she was beaten unconscious by Mr. Rice. The NFL initially suspended Rice for two games for his behavior and the Ravens later terminated his contract. In addition to articles expressing outrage over the incident, there were also several articles that questioned what Janay did to provoke her then-fiance (now husband). Still others asserted that Ray Rice may also be a victim. At a press conference on the incident, Janay stated that she regretted "the role that she played in that night" (Weymouth, 2014; Giris, 2014; Marcotte, 2014). In addition to the effects of victim blaming for these specific individuals, such high profile cases involving victim blaming can also impact reporting rates. "I talked to specific survivors (of sexual assault) that said, 'I don't want to report this because I saw what happened in the Kobe Bryant case'" (Lopez, 2007, para. 8).

Victim blaming is not limited to high-profile cases that make news headlines. Victims are often blamed by those closest to them, such as friends and family, who suggest that the victim "should have known better." Victim blaming can even be internalized whereby victims engage in self-doubt and feel shame for allowing themselves to become a victim (Kohsuro, Wang, & Rowley, 2007). Victim blaming can also inhibit how victims recover from their trauma (Campbell, Ahrens, Sefl, Wasco, & Barnes, 2001).

Victim blaming can also come from formal sources. The concept of **secondary victimization** refers to the practice whereby victims of crime feel traumatized as a result of not only their victimization experience but also by the official criminal justice system response to their victimization. For those cases that progress beyond the law enforcement investigative process, few have charges filed by prosecutors, and only rarely is a conviction secured. Indeed, the "ideal" case for the criminal justice system is one that represents stereotypical notions of what rape looks like rather than the realities of this crime. The practice of victim blaming through **rape myth acceptance** is an example of secondary victimization. Given the nature of the criminal justice process, the acceptance of rape myths by jurors can ultimately affect the decision-making process. Victim blaming can also occur by police and related justice professionals in cases of intimate partner violence, particularly in cases where a victim returns to her abuser (DeJong, Burgess-Proctor, & Elis, 2008). The experience of secondary victimization can have significant consequences of reporting, because research indicates that victims would not have reported the crime if they had known what was in store for them (Logan, Evans, Stevenson, & Jordan, 2005).

Fear of Victimization

The majority of Americans have limited direct experience with the criminal justice system. Most are left with images of crime that are generated by the portrayal of victims and offenders in mass media outlets (Dowler, 2003). These images present a distorted view of the criminal justice system, with a generalized understanding that "if it bleeds, it leads." This leads to the overexaggeration of violent crime in society (Maguire, 1988; Potter & Kappeler, 2006; Surette, 2003). Research indicates that as individuals increase their consumption of local and national television news, their fears about crime increase, regardless of actual crime rates, gender, or a personal history of victimization (Chiricos, Padgett, & Gertz, 2000). In addition to the portrayal of crime within the news, stories of crime, criminals, and criminal justice have been a major staple of television entertainment programming. These images, too, present a distorted view of the reality of crime, because they generally present crime as graphic, random, and violent incidents (Gerbner & Gross, 1980).

Consider the following scenario:

> Imagine yourself walking across a parking lot toward your car. It's late and the parking lot is poorly lit. You are alone. Standing near your car is a man who is watching you. Are you afraid?

When this scenario is presented to groups, we find that men and women respond to this situation differently. When asked who is afraid, it is primarily women who raise their hands. Rarely do men respond to this situation with emotions of fear. Research also notes that girls are more likely than boys to indicate fears about victimization in situations that involve things such as poorly lit parking lots and sidewalks, overgrown shrubbery, and groups loitering in public spaces (Fisher & May, 2009). This simple illustration demonstrates the **fear of victimization** that women experience in their daily lives. As De Groof (2008) explains, "Fear of crime is, in other words, partly a result of feelings of personal discomfort and uncertainty, which are projected onto the threat of crime and victimization" (p. 281).

Why are girls more fearful in these types of situations? Much of this can be attributed to how girls are socialized differently than their male peers. From a young age, girls are often taught about fear, because parents are more likely to demonstrate concern for the safety of their daughters, compared to their sons (De Groof, 2008). This fear results in a relative lack of freedom for girls, in addition to an increase in the parental supervision of girls. These practices, which are designed to protect young women, can significantly affect their confidence levels in regarding the world around them. The worry that parents fear for their daughters continues as they transition from adolescence to adulthood (De Vaus & Wise, 1996). Additionally, this sense of fear can be transferred from the parent to the young female adult as a result of the gendered socialization that she has experienced throughout her life.

Gender also plays a role in feelings of vulnerability, which can translate to fears about victimization. Research indicates that the fear of crime for women is not necessarily related to the actual levels of crime that they personally experience. Overall, women are less likely to be victimized than men, yet they report overall higher levels of fear of crime than their male counterparts (Fattah & Sacco, 1989). These high levels of overall fear of victimization may be perpetuated by a specific fear of crime for women—rape and sexual assault. Indeed, rape is the crime that generates the highest levels of fear for women. These levels of fear are somewhat validated by crime statistics, because women make up the majority of victims for sexually based crimes (Warr, 1984, 1985). However, research indicates that this fear of sexual victimization extends beyond fear of rape to fear of all crimes, not just crimes of a sexual nature. The "shadow of sexual assault" thesis suggests that women experience a greater fear of crime in general, because they believe that any crime could ultimately become a sexually based victimization (Fisher & Sloan, 2003). Yet even when women engage in measures to keep themselves safe, their fear of sexual assault appears to increase rather than decrease (Lane, Gover, & Dahod, 2009). This sense of vulnerability is portrayed by "movie of the week" outlets that showcase storylines of women being victimized by a strange man who lurks in dark alleys and behind bushes (Jones-Brown, 2007; Skolnick, 1966). Unfortunately, these popular culture references toward criminal victimization generally (and rape and sexual assault specifically) paint a false picture of the realities of crime and victimization. Most women are victimized not by strangers, as these films would indicate, but instead by people known to them (Black et al., 2011). Indeed, research indicates that many women fail to see *acquaintance rape* as something that could impact them personally (Pryor & Hughes, 2013). While the fear of sexual assault is a common theme in the literature, some scholars indicate that fears about crime can involve acts other than sexual assault. Cook and Fox (2012) found that fear of physical harm is a stronger predictor of fear about crime for women over the fear of sexual assault. Snedker (2012) found similar evidence, because the majority of women in her study expressed fears over being robbed, not raped.

While there is a significant body of research on how demographics such as gender can impact fear about crime, research is just beginning to look at how multiple marginalities can influence these fears. In a survey of hate crime victimization among the LGBT community, researchers noted that one-third (33.6%) of the study's participants had been victimized as a result of their sexuality. Indeed, LGBT individuals are likely to experience multiple victimizations over the course of their lifetime (Burks et al., 2015). Unlike research using samples of heterosexual men and women (which tend to find that women experience greater fears about crime than men), research by Otis (2007) found that LGBT men and women tend to have similar fears about crime and victimization. One explanation for this may be that gay men experience similar forms of marginalization and vulnerability to that of heterosexual women, particularly when it comes to fears about physical, emotional, and sexually based violence. Meanwhile, women who identify as lesbian may find these fears enhanced not just by their gender but through their sexual identity as well. Fear about crime among the LGBT population is also linked to prior experiences of victimization. Such fear is likely not only a reflection of their own personal victim experiences but is also related to the awareness of hate crimes against LGBT individuals in their community (Tiby, 2001).

The fear of crime and victimization has several negative consequences. Women who are fearful of crime, particularly violent or sexual crimes, are more likely to isolate themselves from society in general. This fear reflects not only the concern of potential victimization but also a threat regarding the potential loss of control that a victim experiences as a result of being victimized. Fear of crime can also be damaging toward one's feelings of self-worth and self-esteem. Here, potential victims experience feelings of vulnerability and increased anxiety.

The effects of fears of victimization are also reflected in societal actions (Clear & Frost, 2007). For example, public transit agencies may increase security measures, such as the presence of personnel, the use of video cameras in stations, and improving service reliability (Yavuz & Welch, 2010). Fear also impacts policy practices within the criminal justice system. Agents of criminal justice can respond to a community's fear of crime by increasing police patrols, while district attorneys pursue tough-on-crime stances in their prosecution of criminal cases. Politicians respond to community concerns about violent crime by creating and implementing tough-on-crime legislation, such as habitual sentencing laws such as "three strikes," and targeting perceived crimes of danger, such as the war on drugs. While the public's concern about crime may be very real, it can also be inflamed by inaccurate data on crime rates or a misunderstanding about the community supervision of offenders and recidivism rates. Unfortunately, "public policy is influenced more by media misinformation and sensationalized high profile cases than by careful or thoughtful analysis" (Frost & Phillips, 2011, p. 88).

Theories on Victimization

In an effort to understand the victim experience, social science researchers began to investigate the characteristics of crime victims and the response by society to these victims. While criminology focuses predominantly on the study of crime as a social phenomenon and the nature of offenders, the field of victimology places the victim at the center of the discussion. Early perspectives on victimology focused on how victims, either knowingly or unconsciously, can be at fault for their victimization, based on their personal life events and decision-making processes.

One of the early scholars in this field, **Benjamin Mendelsohn** (1956), developed a typology of victimization that distinguished different types of victims based on the relative responsibility of the victims in their own victimization. Embedded in between his typology is the degree to which victims have the power to make decisions that can alter their likelihood of victimization. As a result of his work, the study of victimology began to emerge as its own distinct field of study.

Mendelsohn's theory of victimology is based on six categories of victims. The first category is the innocent victim. This distinction is unique in Mendelsohn's typology, because it is the only classification that does not have any responsibility for the crime attributed to the victim. As the name suggests, an innocent victim is someone who is victimized by a random and unprecipitated crime, such as a school shooting. Unlike the other categories in Mendelsohn's typology, the innocent victim is one with no responsibility in his victimization. In contrast, the other five categories assign a degree of blame or responsibility to the victim. Mendelsohn's second category is the victim with minor guilt. In this case, victimization occurs as a result of one's carelessness or ignorance. The victim with minor guilt is someone who, if she had given better thought or care to her safety, would not have been a victim of a crime. For instance, someone who was in the wrong place at the wrong time or one who places herself in dangerous areas where she is at risk for potential victimization is characterized as a victim with minor guilt. An example of this is a case of a victim who is walking alone down the street in a high-crime area and is robbed. Mendelsohn's third category is a victim who is equally as guilty as the offender. This victim is someone who shares the responsibility of the crime with the offender by deliberately placing himself or herself in harm's way. An example of this classification is the individual who seeks out the services of a sex worker, only to contract a sexually transmitted infection as a result of their interaction. The fourth category represents the case whereby the victim is deemed "more guilty" than the offender. This is a "victim" who is provoked by others to engage in criminal activity. An example of this category is one who kills a current or former intimate partner following a history of abuse. The fifth category is a victim who is solely responsible for the harm that comes to him or her. These individuals are considered to be the "most guilty" of victims as they engaged in an act that was likely to lead to injury on their part. Examples of the most guilty victim

Table 2.2 • Mendelsohn's Categories of Victims		
Category	**Definition**	**Example**
Innocent victim	No responsibility for the crime attributed to victim	Institutionalized victims, the mentally ill, children, or those who are attacked while unconscious
Victim with minor guilt	Victim precipitates crime with carelessness/ignorance	Victim lost in the "wrong part of town"
Voluntary victim	Victim and offender equally responsible for crime	Victim pays prostitute for sex; then prostitute robs victim ("rolling Johns")
Victim who is more guilty than the offender	Victim who provokes or induces another to commit crime	Burning bed syndrome: victim is killed by the domestic partner he abused for years
Victim who alone is guilty	Victim who is solely responsible for his or her own victimization	An attacker who is killed in self-defense; suicide bomber killed by detonation of explosives
Imaginary victim	Victim mistakenly believes he or she has been victimized	Mentally ill person who reports imagined victimization as real event

SOURCE: Adapted from Sengstock (1976).

include a suicide bomber who engages in an act that results in his or her death or when a would-be attacker is killed by another in an act of self-defense. Mendelsohn's final category is the imaginary victim. This is an individual who, as a result of some mental disease or defect, believes that he or she has been victimized by someone or something, when in reality this person has not been victimized.

While Mendelsohn focused on the influence of guilt and responsibility of victims, **Hans von Hentig's** (1948) typology of victims looked at how personal factors, such as biological, psychological, and social factors, influence risk factors for victimization. The categories in von Hentig's typology of victims include the young, the female, the old, the mentally defective and deranged, immigrants, minorities, dull normals, the depressed, the acquisitive, the wanton, the lonesome or heartbroken, the tormentor, and the blocked, exempted, or fighting.

While the application of von Hentig's theory helped develop an understanding of victims in general, his typology includes only a single category for females. However, experiences of female victimization can fit within each of von Hentig's other categories. For instance, young girls who run away from home are easy targets for pimps who "save" girls from the dangers of the streets and "protect" them from harm. The youth of these girls places them at a higher risk for violence and prostitution activities under the guise of protection. While von Hentig's category of mentally defective was designed to capture the vulnerability of the mentally ill victim, he also referenced the intoxicated individual within this context. Under this category, women who engage in either consensual acts of intoxication or who are subjected to substances unknown to them can be at risk for alcohol- or drug-facilitated sexual assault. Likewise, consider von Hentig's category of immigrants and the way in which immigration status can also play a key role for women victims. Many abusers use a woman's illegal immigration status as a threat to ensure compliance. In these cases, women may be forced to endure violence in their lives or are induced into sexual slavery out of fear of deportation. Von Hentig also discusses how race and ethnicity can affect the victim experience, and significant research has demonstrated how these factors affect the criminal justice system at every stage.

Spotlight on Gender and Kidnapping

Over the past decade, several stories of women who were kidnapped and held captive for decades hit the national news. One of these cases involves three women who were held in a dilapidated home in Cleveland, Ohio On May 6, 2013, three women were rescued from a home in Cleveland, Ohio. Amanda Berry, Georgina "Gina" DeJesus, and Michelle Knight had been held captive by Ariel Castro, a 52-year-old man who had emigrated to the United States as a child from Puerto Rico. Each of the women had accepted a ride from Castro, who then abducted them and forced them into his basement where he kept the girls physically restrained. Michelle Knight was his first victim and was 21 years old when she was taken on August 22, 2002. His next victim, Amanda Berry, disappeared on April 21, 2003, just before her 17th birthday. Finally, Gina DeJesus was abducted on April 2, 2004. She was only 14. All three girls endured significant physical and sexual assaults throughout their captivity. Michelle Knight reported that she suffered several miscarriages, and Amanda Berry gave birth to a daughter fathered by Castro, born on Christmas Day 2006 (BBC, 2013). After a decade in hell, the women were rescued after garnering the attention of a neighbor who helped them escape (Steer, 2013).

While the prosecutors originally considered charging Castro with aggravated murder (in the cases of the forced miscarriages of Knight), he ultimately pled guilty to 937 counts of kidnapping, rape, and other crimes such as child endangerment and gross sexual imposition (Krouse, 2013; Mahoney, 2013; Sheeran, 2013). In speaking at his sentencing hearing, Michelle Knight told Castro, "I spent 11 years in hell, where your hell is just beginning" (DeLuca, 2013). However, Castro served very little of his sentence before he hung himself by a bedsheet in his cell. Some might argue that Castro's suicide cheated the justice system—"This man couldn't take, for even a month, a small portion of what he had dished out for more than a decade" (Mungin & Alsup, 2013).

© Aaron Josefczyk/ Reuters/Corbis

▲ **Photo 2.2** Amanda Berry reads her victim impact statement during the sentencing hearing for Ariel Castro. Castro was convicted on several counts of kidnapping and rape against Berry and her two co-victims.

Another story with similar circumstances was that of Jaycee Dugard. Dugard was kidnapped by husband and wife Phillip and Nancy Garrido when she was just 11 years old and was held for 18 years. Dugard was abducted walking home from a school bus stop in South Lake Tahoe. Phillip Garrido was a convicted sex offender who was on parole at the time of Jaycee's abduction. Much of her captivity was spent in makeshift tents or a shed that was located behind Garrido's home. Even though parole agents visited the home sixty times, they never checked the sheds in the yard. Meanwhile, Phillip Garrido sexually assaulted Jaycee on a regular basis and she gave birth to two daughters during this time. The children were homeschooled and ultimately Phillip and Nancy allowed Jaycee and her daughters to have contact with the public, under the guise that Jaycee was their sister, not their mother. Jaycee was even allowed to work for the Garridos' printing business, yet she was forbidden to tell anyone about her true identity. On August 24, 2009, Garrido traveled to U.C. Berkeley with the girls to seek permission to hold a special event on campus related to his ministry. The incident was referred to both the local police as well as Garrido's parole officer. While Dugard initially maintained her false identity, she ultimately told investigators who she was.

Phillip Garrido and his wife ultimately pled guilty to kidnapping and rape. On June 2, 2011, Phillip was sentenced to 431 years to life and Nancy received 36 years to life. While Jaycee Dugard filed a suit against the U.S. Government for failing to effectively monitor Garrido when he was a federal parolee, her suit was dismissed. Meanwhile, the state of California approved a settlement of $20 million dollars. She has since written two books about her experience (Dooley, Scott, Ng, & Effron, 2016; Egelko, 2016; Salonga, 2016).

Routine Activities Theory

While early theories of victimization provided a foundation to understand the victim experience, modern victimization theories expand from these concepts to investigate the role of society on victimization and to address how personal choices affect the victim experience. One of the most influential perspectives in modern victimology is Cohen and Felson's (1979) **routine activities theory**. Routine activities theory suggests that the likelihood of a criminal act (and in turn, the likelihood of victimization) occurs with the convergence of three essential components: (1) someone who is interested in pursuing a criminal action (offender), (2) a potential victim (target) "available" to be victimized, and (3) the absence of someone or something (guardian) that would deter the offender from making contact with the available victim. The name of the theory is derived from a belief that victims and guardians exist within the normal, everyday patterns of life. Cohen and Felson posit that lifestyle changes during the second half of the 20th century created additional opportunities for the victim and offender to come into contact with each other as a result of changes to daily routines and activities. Cohen and Felson's theory was created to discuss the risk of victimization in property crimes. Here, if individuals were at work, or out enjoying events in the community, they were less likely to be at home to guard their property against potential victimization, and burglary was more likely to result.

Routine activities theory has been used to understand a variety of different forms of crime, particularly related to demographic differences in victimization. For example, research on routine activities theory demonstrates that minority women are more likely to experience risk of victimization when riding public transportation, and neighborhood factors can affect the odds of women's victimization (Like-Haislip & Miofsky, 2011). Gender can also mediate the types of victimization risk. While men are more likely to experience increased risks of violent victimization because they go out at night, women have an increased risk of theft based on increased shopping activities (Bunch, Clay-Warner, & Lei, 2012).

Routine activities theory has also been used to look at cybercrimes. Research by Navarro and Jasinski (2013) indicates that girls are at a greater risk for cyber-bullying than boys, even though boys engage in similar risky online behaviors. Among adolescents, the use of digital medias such as social networking and texting can place youth at risk of cyber dating abuse. For example, youth who engage in sexting with their boy/girlfriend are more likely to be involved in an abusive dating relationship. The risk of victimization increases with the amount of time that they spend online (Van Ouytsel, Ponnet, & Walrave, 2016).

Routine activities theory has been criticized by feminist criminologists, who disagree with the theory's original premise that men are more vulnerable to the risks of victimization than women. Indeed, the guardians that Cohen and Felson suggest protect victims from crime may instead be the ones most likely to victimize women, particularly in cases of intimate partner abuse and sexual assault. For example, research by Schwartz, DeKeseredy, Tait, and Alvi (2001) indicates that women who engage in recreational substance use (such as alcohol or drugs) are considered to be a suitable target by men who are motivated to engage in certain offending patterns. Attempts by administrators to increase safety on college campuses by implementing protections, such as escort patrols, lighted paths, and emergency beacons (modern-day guardians), may have little effect on sexual assault rates on campus, given that many of these incidents take place behind closed doors in college dormitories and student apartments. In addition, the concept of self-protective factors (or self-guardians) may not be able to ward off a potential attacker, given that the overwhelming majority of sexual assaults on college campuses are perpetrated by someone known to the victim (Mustaine & Tewksbury, 2002). In addition, perceptions of being a "good" girl can also lead women to believe they are at a reduced risk for victimization. "I'm not running around in tiny little dresses anymore" (Snedker, 2012, p. 86). Another woman expressed a similar sentiment of recognizing potential risks of victimization based on her patterns of behavior: "I'm not going to do anything stupid. If I'm coming home really late drunk and I'm by myself, I might be more of a target" (Snedker, 2012, p. 89). This scenario highlights the perception that a shift in routine activities can reduce the risk of victimization. Unfortunately, this adds to the myth that girls who dress provocatively or consume alcohol somehow deserve to be sexually assaulted, which shifts the blame to the victim and not the perpetrator.

Like routine activities theory, **lifestyle theory** seeks to relate the patterns of one's everyday activities to the potential for victimization. While routine activities theory was initially designed to explain victimization from property crimes, lifestyle theory was developed to explore the risks of victimization from personal crimes. Research by Hindelang, Gottfredson, and Garafalo (1978) suggests that people who engage in risky lifestyle choices place themselves at risk for victimization. Based on one's lifestyle, one may increase the risk for criminal opportunity and victimization through both an increased exposure to criminal activity and an increased exposure to motivated offenders. However, crime is not the only lifestyle that can place people at risk for victimization, because nonviolent deviant behaviors, mental health status, and substance use can place people at potential victimization. Gender also plays a role in how these factors influence victimization risk. For example, males who engage in binge drinking have an increased risk of victimization while females who abuse prescription drugs experience significantly higher odds of victimization (Zaykowski & Gunter, 2013).

Given the similarities between the foundations of lifestyle theory and routine activities theory, many researchers today combine the tenets of these two perspectives to investigate victimization risks in general. These perspectives have been used to explain the risks of sexual assault of women on college campuses. For example, young women in the university setting who engage in risky lifestyle decision-making processes (such as the use of alcohol) and have routine activity patterns (such as living alone or frequenting establishments such as bars and clubs where men are present and alcohol is readily available) are at an increased risk for sexual victimization. In addition, women who are at risk for a single incident remain at risk for recurrent victimizations if their behavior patterns remain the same (Fisher, Daigle, & Cullen, 2010).

Feminist Pathways Perspective

Feminist pathways perspective research draws on the historical context of women's and girls' lives to relate how events (and traumas) affect their likelihood to engage in crime. Researchers have identified a cycle of violence for female offenders that often begins with their own victimization and results with their involvement in offending behavior. While the pathways perspective is discussed at length in Chapter 4, the topic deserves a brief introduction as we conclude our discussion on theories of victimization.

The feminist pathways approach may provide some of the best understanding about female offending. Research on women's and girls' pathways to offending provide substantial evidence for the link between victimization and offending, because incarcerated girls are three to four times more likely to have been abused compared to their male counterparts (Belknap & Holsinger, 2006). A review of case files of delinquent girls in California indicates that 92% of delinquent girls in California reported having been subjected to at least one form of abuse, including emotional (88%), physical (81%), or sexual (56%) abuse (Acoca & Dedel, 1998b). Particularly for young female offenders, a history of abuse leads to a propensity to engage in certain types of delinquency, such as running away and school failures. The effects of sexual assault are also related to drug and alcohol addiction and mental health traumas, such as post-traumatic stress disorder and a negative self-identity (Raphael, 2005). In a **cycle of victimization and offending**, young girls often run away from home in an attempt to escape from an abusive situation. In many cases, girls were forced to return home by public agencies, such as the police, courts, and social services—agencies designed to "help" victims of abuse. Unfortunately, in their attempt to escape from an abusive situation, girls often fall into criminal behaviors as a mechanism of survival.

Indeed, there are several ways to think about the victimization of women and girls. As you move through the next three chapters in this text, consider how each of these theoretical perspectives impact the victim experience for women and how the criminal justice system responds to these cases. How would you improve the experience of women as victims? What police recommendations would you recommend to agents of criminal justice? Finally, what remedies exist to limit the victimization of women, and what can you as a member of society do to affect change in this realm?

/// SUMMARY

- Not all victims report their crimes to the police but may seek out support from other sources.

- Victim-assistance programs have emerged as a key response to the secondary victimization often experienced by victims who come forward to the criminal justice system.

- Victim blaming has been linked to low reporting rates.

- Women experience higher rates of fear of crime than males.

- Gendered socialization and vulnerability to specific crime types such as rape may explain the gendered fear of crime.

- Mendelsohn's typology of victimization distinguishes different categories of victims based on the responsibility of the victim and the degree to which victims have the power to make decisions that can alter their likelihood of victimization.

- Von Hentig's typology of victimization focuses on how personal factors, such as biological, social, and psychological characteristics, influence risk factors for victimization.

- The just world hypothesis, which holds that people get what they deserve, is a form of victim blaming.

- Routine activities theory and lifestyle theory have been used to investigate the risk of sexual assault of women.

- The pathways perspective suggests a cycle of criminal justice involvement for women whereby early victimization is sometimes a precursor to later criminal offending.

/// KEY TERMS

Core rights of victims 22

Cycle of victimization and offending 32

Fear of victimization 26

Feminist pathways perspective 32

Just world hypothesis 25

Lifestyle theory 32

Mendelsohn, Benjamin 28

Rape myth acceptance 26

Routine activities theory 31

Secondary victimization 26

Victim blaming 24

von Hentig, Hans 29

/// DISCUSSION QUESTIONS

1. How do early theories of victimization distinguish between different types of victims? How might the criminal justice system use these typologies in making decisions about which cases to pursue?

2. What types of help-seeking behaviors do female crime victims engage in? How are these practices related to the reporting of crimes to law enforcement?

3. What effects does the practice of victim blaming have for future potential crime victims and the criminal justice system?

4. In what ways do media outlets support or dispel rape myths and victim blaming? How is this related to help-seeking behavior, official reporting, and revictimization?

5. How is fear of crime a gendered experience? What factors contribute to the differences in male versus female fear of crime? Do official crime statistics support or dispel the basis for these fear differences?

6. How might feminist criminologists critique modern-day victimization theories, such as routine activities theory and lifestyle theory?

7. How have historical theories on female offending failed to understand the nature of female offending?

8. What contributions has feminist criminology made in understanding the relationship between gender and offending?

 ## WEB RESOURCES

Bureau of Justice Statistics: http://bjs.ojp.usdoj.gov

Feminist Criminology: http://fcx.sagepub.com

The National Center for Victims of Crime: http://www.ncvc.org

Office for Victims of Crime: https://www.ovc.gov

 Visit **www.sagepub.com/mallicoat3e** to access additional study tools, including eFlashcards, web quizzes, web resources, video resources, and SAGE journal articles.

CHAPTER 3

Women, Gender, and Victimization

Rape and Sexual Assault

Chapter Highlights

- Historical perspectives on the sexual victimization of women
- Contemporary paradigms for sexual victimization
- Rape myths and rape myth acceptance
- Categories of sexual assault
- Criminal justice treatment and processing of female sexual assault victims

Historical Perspectives on Rape and Sexual Assault

Rape is one of the oldest crimes in society and has existed in every historical and contemporary society around the world. Laws prohibiting the act of rape, or intercourse under force, threat, or without the consent of the individual, have existed for almost 4,000 years. One of the first laws prohibiting the crime of rape can be found in the Code of Hammurabi from Babylon. Ancient Greek, Roman, and Judaic societies also criminalized the act of rape under various circumstances. Some laws distinguished between the rape of a married versus an unmarried woman, and the punishments for these crimes varied based on the status of the victim (Ewoldt, Monson, & Langhinrichsen-Rohling, 2000). Others viewed rape not as a violent sexual offense but as a property crime (Burgess-Jackson, 1999). If the victim was an unmarried woman, the rape tainted her status and value for potential marriage. As a result, many fathers negotiated to have their daughters marry their rapists (Dodderidge, 1632). Even cases of forcible **sexual assault** (where the victim is compelled to engage in sexually based acts other than intercourse) brought shame to the victim, because the acknowledgment of a rape was an admission of sexual activity. In many cases of forcible sexual assault, women were blamed for tempting offenders into immoral behaviors. During criminal rape trials, a woman's sexual history was often put on display in an attempt to discredit her in front of a jury. By portraying female victims of sexual assault as complicit in the behavior, the responsibility of an offender's actions was mitigated. Such a practice represented a double standard because the courts did not request similar information about a man's sexual history, because it would be considered prejudicial in the eyes of the jury (Odem, 1995).

Until the 20th century, early American statutes on rape limited the definition to a narrow view of sexual assault. Consider the following definition of rape that was included in the Model Penal Code in 1955:

Section 213.1: Rape and Related Offenses

1. Rape. A male who has sexual intercourse with a female not his wife is guilty of rape if

   a. he compels her to submit by force or by threat of imminent death, serious bodily injury, extreme pain or kidnapping, to be inflicted on anyone; or

   b. he has substantially impaired her power to appraise or control her conduct by administering or employing without her knowledge drugs, intoxicants or other means for the purpose of preventing resistance; or

   c. the female is unconscious; or

   d. the female is less than 10 years old.

© Scott Houston/Corbis

▲ **Photo 3.1** In response to a Toronto police officer's comment that "women should avoid dressing like sluts in order not to be victimized," over 3,000 people gathered at Queen's Park in Toronto in 2012 to protest the rape myth that women ask to be sexually assaulted based on their appearance. Since then, "Slut Walks" have been organized around the world to raise awareness about the danger of rape myths and their effects on victims.

What is wrong with this definition? First, it reduces the definition of rape to the act of intercourse, and it excludes other acts of sexual assault, such as oral sex, sodomy, or penetration by a foreign object. Second, it limits the victim-offender relationship to a male perpetrator and a female victim. While women make up the majority of victims, such a definition excludes cases of **same-sex sexual assault**, such as a female sexually assaulting another female or a male-on-male assault, or cases where the victim is a male (and the offender is female). Third, this definition requires that force, or the threat of force, must be used in order for an act to qualify as rape, and it focuses on violence and brutality as proof of the crime. Fourth, this definition creates a marital status exemption such that men could not be prosecuted for raping their wives. Finally, the definition fails to acknowledge attempted rapes as a crime and the traumatic effects of these "near misses" of victimization. However, we do see some positive influences from the Model Penal Code that has influenced present-day laws on rape and sexual assault. First, the Model Penal Code acknowledges that the absence of consent for sexual intercourse (including in cases involving intoxication or unconsciousness) constitutes rape. Second, the definition (while limited) acknowledges that sexual acts involving children are a crime.

While contemporary definitions of rape vary from state to state, many present-day laws include similar provisions. Today, most laws broadly define sexual victimization as sexual behaviors that are unwanted and harmful to the victim. Most emphasize the use of force or coercion that is displayed by the offender rather than focusing on the response or conduct of the victim. This is not to say that the actions of the victim (such as her attire or behaviors) are not chastised by defense counsel or members of the jury, but the law itself does not require victims to demonstrate physical levels of resistance.

Another development in contemporary rape laws involves the abolishment of the marital-rape exemption clause. Historical acceptance of the marital-rape exception is rooted in biblical passages, which state that "a man should fulfill his duty as a husband and a woman should fulfill her duty as a wife, and each should satisfy the other's needs. A wife is not the master of her own body, but her husband is" (I Corinthians 7, 3–5). Today, every state has laws on the books that generally identify rape within the context of marriage as a criminal act. In an effort to resolve some of the limitations with the word *rape*, the term *sexual assault* is often used to identify forms of sexual victimization that are not included under the traditionally narrow definition of rape. These laws have expanded the definitions of sexual assault beyond penile-vaginal penetration and include sodomy, forced oral copulation, and unwanted fondling and touching of a sexual nature. Cases of child sexual assault are treated differently in many jurisdictions, and age of consent laws have led to the development of statutory rape laws. Finally, sex offender registration laws, such as Megan's Law and Jessica's Law, require the community receive notification of sexual offenders and the placing of residential, community, and supervision restrictions on offenders.

Defining Sexual Victimization

What behaviors are included within the definitions of rape and sexual assault? The answer to this question depends on the source. Historically, the Uniform Crime Reports considered only cases of forcible rape. Such a definition excluded the majority of cases of rape and sexual assault. In addition, this practice by the UCR did not account for cases of attempted rape/sexual assault. Although the Federal Bureau of Investigation (2012a, c) changed their data collection practice in 2012 to include both completed and attempted cases of rape and sexual assault, the National Crime Victimization Survey (NCVS) defines rape as the "forced sexual intercourse. . . (including) vaginal, oral, or anal penetration by offender(s)."[1] The NCVS collects data not only on penile penetration but also includes cases of penetration with a foreign object. At the same time, states vary significantly on their own definitions of these crimes. Some states limit rape to penile-vaginal penetration and use sexual assault as a catch-all category of other crimes, while other states use multiple statutes to distinguish between different forms of sexual assault. While some of these statutes are very specific, others combine multiple forms of assault under a single penal code definition.

The limited clarity on the legal definitions of rape and sexual assault, coupled with the personification of these crimes in popular culture and the media, can have a significant effect on victims. In many cases, people who experience acts that are consistent with a legal definition of rape or sexual assault may not label their experience as such. As a result, they do not see themselves as such and therefore do not report these crimes to the police, nor do they seek out therapeutic resources. In many of these cases, women who experience these acts do not define themselves as victims because their experience differs from their personal definitions of what rape and sexual assault look like. For example, the crime of sexual assault is perpetuated throughout fiction novels and made for television movies as a stranger who attacks a victim in his home or on a dark sidewalk at night. Despite the high degree to which such events are manifested within popular culture, real life cases of this nature are relatively rare. Indeed, findings from the NCVS data demonstrate that cases of **stranger rape** with female victims account for only 22% of all sexual assaults (Planty, Langton, Krebs, Berzofsky, & Smiley-McDonald, 2013). Such findings highlight that the majority of rapes and sexual assault are perpetuated by people who are known to the victim.

The lack of an understanding of a definition of rape and sexual assault affects offenders, as well. Many people who admit to engaging in behaviors that meet the legal criteria for rape or sexual assault generally do not define

---

[1]See definitions at http://www.bjs.gov/index.cfm?ty=tda.

their own actions as criminal. One of the most frequently cited studies on rape and sexual assault surveyed 2,971 college men regarding self-reported conduct that met the legal definitions of rape, attempted rape, sexual coercion, and unwanted sexual contact. Based on these reports, the results indicated that 1,525 acts of sexual assault had occurred, including 187 acts of rape. Of those whose acts met the legal definition of rape, 84% of the "perpetrators" believed that their acts did not constitute rape (Warshaw, 1994).

Prevalence of Rape and Sexual Assault

Despite the acknowledgment that rape and sexual assault are two of the most underreported types of crimes, the known data indicate that these crimes pervade our society. According to the Rape, Abuse and Incest National Network (RAINN), a rape, attempted rape, or sexual assault occurs approximately once every 2 minutes. According to the National Crime Victimization Survey, there were 431,840 victims of rape and sexual assault in 2015. When we think about how common these crimes are, this data translates to 1.6 victims per 1,000 individuals age 12 or older (Truman & Morgan, 2016). While the U.S. Department of Justice (2003) found that 40% of victims report their crime to the police, other research has placed this number significantly lower, at 16% for adult women (Kilpatrick, Resnick, Ruggiero, Conoscenti, & McCauley, 2007). Given the stigmatizing nature of this crime, it is not surprising that rape, attempted rape, and sexual assault are some of the most underreported crimes, making it difficult to determine the extent of this problem. While researchers attempt to estimate the prevalence of sexual assault, they are faced with their own set of challenges, including differences in defining sexual assault, the emphasis on different sample populations (adolescents, college-aged adults, adults, etc.), or different forms of data (arrest data vs. self-report surveys). Regardless of these issues and the data it yields, it appears that sexual assault affects most individuals in some way (either personally or through someone they know) at some point in their lifetime.

Prevalence studies report a wide range of data on the pervasiveness of rape and sexual assault in the United States. A national study on rape published in 2007 indicated that 18% of women in America have experienced rape at some point in their lifetime, with an additional 3% of women experiencing an attempted rape. A comparison of these findings to the Violence Against Women survey in 1996 indicates that little change has occurred in the prevalence of this crime over time (15% of all women). Indeed, these results demonstrate an increase in the number of rape cases, which is contrary to the belief that rape has declined significantly in recent times. Findings from studies such as these have led researchers, rape-crisis organizations, and policy makers to posit that one in four American women will be victimized by rape or sexual assault (or an attempt) within their lifetime.

Rape Myths

Rape myths are defined as "attitudes and beliefs that are generally false but are widely and persistently held, and that serve to deny and justify male sexual aggression against women" (Lonsway & Fitzgerald, 1994, p. 134). Table 3.1 highlights some of the most commonly perpetuated myths about rape.

The acceptance of rape myths by society is a contributing factor in the practice of victim blaming. First, the presence of rape myths allows society to shift the blame of rape from the offender to the victim. By doing so, we can avoid confronting the realities of rape and sexual assault in society. This denial serves as a vicious cycle: As we fail to acknowledge the severity of rape and sexual assault, which leads to victims not reporting their crime to authorities, this results in greater acceptance that the crime is not taken seriously by society as a whole. Second, the presence of rape myths lends support to the notion of a just world hypothesis, which suggests that only good things happen to good people and bad things happen to those who deserve it. Rape myths, such as "she asked for it," serve to perpetuate the notion of the just world in action (Lonsway & Fitzgerald, 1994).

Offenders often use rape myths to excuse or justify their actions. Excuses occur when offenders admit that their behavior was wrong but blame their actions on external circumstances outside of their control. In these instances, offenders deny responsibility for their actions. Statements such as "I was drunk" or "I don't know what came over me" are examples of excuses. In comparison, justifications occur when offenders admit responsibility for their actions but argue that their behavior was acceptable under the circumstances. Examples of justifications include "She asked for it" or "Nothing really happened." Miscommunication appears to play a significant role for men, as well, who ask, "When does no mean no, or when does no mean yes?" By suggesting that men "misunderstand" their victim's refusal for sexual activity, the responsibility of rape is transferred from the offender back to the victim.

Some victims accept these excuses or justifications for their assault that minimize or deny the responsibility of their offender. In cases where the male offender "got carried away," female victims often accept the actions of the offender as a natural consequence of male sexuality. In these cases, victims feel that they deserve their victimization as a result of their own actions. Many victims argue that "they should have known better" or that "they didn't try hard enough to stop it." In these cases, victims believe that they put themselves at risk as a result of their own decision-making process.

The prevalence and acceptance of rape myths in society does a significant disservice for both victims and society in general in terms of understanding the realities of rape. These myths permit us to believe that stranger rape is "real" rape, whereas **acquaintance rape,** by persons known to the victim, is interpreted as less serious, less significant, and less harmful because the offender is known to the victim. Rape myths perpetuate the belief that women should be more fearful of the **symbolic assailant**—the stranger who lurks in the alley or hides in the bushes and surprises the victim. Rape myths suggest that in order for a woman to be raped, she needs to fight back against her attacker and leave the scene with bruises and injuries related to her efforts to thwart the assault. Rape myths also suggest that real rape victims always report their attackers and have evidence collected and that an offender is identified who is then arrested, prosecuted, and sentenced to the fullest extent under the law. Alas, this rarely occurs within our criminal justice system. Instead, the majority of cases involve victims who know their offender, and victims who do not report these cases to the police. Even when such cases are reported, the prosecution of an offender can be a difficult task. Here, the consequence of pervasive rape myths in society serves to limit the public's understanding about the realities of rape, which in turn can limit the victim's opportunity for justice.

Table 3.1 • Rape Myths
• A woman who gets raped usually deserves it, especially if she has agreed to go to a man's house or park with him.
• If a woman agrees to allow a man to pay for dinner, then it means she owes him sex.
• Acquaintance rape is committed by men who are easy to identify as rapists.
• Only women can be raped or sexually assaulted by men.
• Women who do not fight back have not been raped.
• Once a man reaches a certain point of arousal, sex is inevitable, and he cannot help forcing himself on a woman.
• Most women lie about acquaintance rape because they have regrets after consensual sex.
• Women who say "No" really mean "Yes."
• Certain behaviors such as drinking or dressing in a sexually appealing way make rape a woman's responsibility.
• If she had sex with me before, she has consented to have sex with me again.
• A man cannot rape his wife.
• Only bad women get raped.
• Women secretly enjoy being raped.

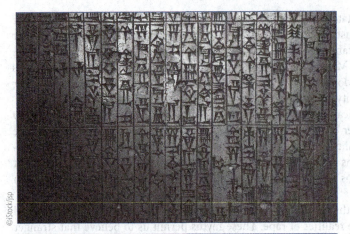

▲ **Photo 3.2** The Code of Hammurabi is one of the oldest legal artifacts in the world and dates back to 1772 BC. It includes punishments for 282 different crimes, including rape. Today it is housed at the Louvre Museum in Paris, France.

Acquaintance Versus Stranger Assault

As illustrated above, cases of stranger rape are not the most common type of sexual assault. Young women are socialized to be wary of walking alone at night, to be afraid that a scary man will jump out of the bushes and attack them. Unfortunately, many prevention efforts that advise women on what they can do to keep themselves safe from sexual assault often focus on these situations of stranger danger. While these tools are certainly valuable in enhancing women's safety, they fail to acknowledge the reality of sexual assault. Acquaintance rape accounts for 90% of all rapes of college women (Sampson, 2003). Additionally, 60% of all rape and sexual assault incidents occur either at the victim's home or at the home of a friend, neighbor, or relative (Greenfeld, 1997).

Cases of acquaintance rape and sexual assault tend to entail lower levels of physical force by the offender and involve less resistance by the victim compared to cases of stranger rape (Littleton, Breitkopf, & Berenson, 2008). Alas, each of these realities is missing from the stereotypical scripts about rape and sexual assault.

It is difficult to assess how many sexual assault victims disclose their victimization to police. Research conducted by Millar, Stermac, and Addison (2002) documented that 61% of acquaintance rapes are not reported to the police. In comparison, Rickert, Wiemann, and Vaughan (2005) found that only one of 86 study participants made a report to law enforcement authorities, and an additional four victims sought services from a mental health professional. While these findings demonstrate a dramatic range of reporting rates, it is safe to conclude that acquaintance rape is significantly underreported. Society tends to discount the validity of acquaintance rape, suggesting that it is a lesser criminal act than to stranger rape (i.e., real rape). Yet research demonstrates that victims of acquaintance rape suffer significant mental health trauma as a result of their victimization. This trauma is often exacerbated by the fact that many victims of acquaintance rape tend to blame themselves for their own victimization. In many cases, these victims are less likely to seek assistance from rape crisis or counseling services.

Spotlight on Rape Culture

In August 2012, Steubenville was thrust into the national spotlight after a 16-year-old girl was sexually assaulted by several of her peers. What made this case particularly noteworthy is that her assault was videotaped and her assailants posted the video on social media sites, such as YouTube and Twitter. In the photos and videos, two Steubenville High football team members, Trent Mays and Ma'lik Richmond (both 16 at the time of the offense), are shown carrying the victim by her hands and feet because she was so intoxicated that she was unable to walk. Video also documents the accused penetrating the victim's vagina with their fingers and flashing her breasts to the camera (Abad-Santos, 2013).

Many blamed the victim (who was so intoxicated that she did not know she had been violated until she saw the photos and videos online) and called her a "train whore." Even one of the football coaches joined in on the blaming, stating, "What else are you going to tell your parents when you come home drunk like that and after a night like that? She had to make up something. Now people are trying to blow up our football program because of it" (Abad-Santos, 2013). During the trial, the defense counsel introduced testimony that tried to paint the victim as culpable in her own attack by calling two former friends who testified that the victim not only had a history of drinking in excess but also told contradic-tory stories about the events of the evening (Welsh-Huggins, 2013a).

The judge found that the victim was so intoxicated that she lacked the cognitive abil-ity to consent to sexual activity (Oppel, 2013). Both Mays and Richmond were found guilty in juvenile court and sentenced to one year in the state juvenile correctional facility. Mays received an additional one-year sentence for the crime of distributing nude images of a minor

▲ **Photo 3.3** Santa Clara County Superior Court Judge Aaron Persky drew significant criticism for his decision to sentence former Stanford University student Brock Turner to only six months in jail for sexually assaulting an unconscious woman. Prosecutors had requested that Turner be sentenced to six years. Turner was released after serving three months of his sentence.

(Ng, 2013). In her report of the verdict, CNN reporter Poppy Harlow critiqued the court's decision, stating that it had been "incredibly difficult [to watch] as these two young men—who had such promising futures, star football players, very good students—literally watched as they believed their life fell apart" (Harlow, 2013). Richmond was released from cus-tody after serving 9 months of his sentence (Fox News, 2014). Mays served 2 years in a youth facility (Jablonski, 2015).

Alas, cases such as Steubenville are more common than we think. In 2015, three high school football players from Dietrich, Idaho, sexually assaulted a mentally disabled teammate by inserting a coat hanger into his rectum in the school locker room following a football practice. The victim's family argued that the attack occurred after months of racist abuse and bullying. The judge in the case was quoted as saying "this is not a rape case . . . this is not a sex case. This started out as penetration with a foreign object. . . . Whatever happened in that locker room was not sexual. It wasn't appropriate. There's nothing in this record that supports anything close to the sexual allegation against this young man" (LaGanga, 2017). School officials waited for several days before reporting the event to the local authorities and instead conducted their own investigation and collected evidence from the locker room. Evidence also suggests that they recorded conversations with the victim in an effort to discredit him. Ultimately, the offenders went unpunished for the crime. One of the offenders was 18 years old at the time of the event, yet was sentenced to just probation for his crime, which was pled down to felony injury to a child (Boone, 2017) and adult felony charges were dropped against at least one of the juveniles involved in the case (KBOI news staff, 2016). The light sentence brought criticism to the judge and drew comparisons to the case of Brock Turner. Turner was sentenced to 6 months for assaulting an unconscious woman at a Stanford University fraternity party. Turner blamed the events of the evening on the culture of drinking that pervades university life. Under state sentencing recommendations, he could have faced 14 years in prison, though prosecutors only asked for 6 years. In handing down his sentence, Judge Persky expressed concern that a harsher sentence could have a "severe impact" on the offender (Koren, 2016). Turner's father also defended his son's actions and advocated that his son should receive probation, stating "that is a steep price to pay for 20 minutes of action out of his 20 plus years of life" (Miller, 2016).

Following his release, Turner will be required to register as a sex offender for life. In December 2017, Turner's attorney filed an appeal for a new trial and requested that the registration requirement be removed.

Cases such as Steubenville, Dietrich, and Brock Turner highlight the role that rape culture continues to play in our society. These forms of violence contribute to a culture of rape whereby offender actions are minimized and blame for these events is often diverted.

Drug-Facilitated/Incapacitated Sexual Assault

A **drug-facilitated rape** is defined as an unwanted sexual act following the deliberate intoxication of a victim. In comparison, an **incapacitated rape** is an unwanted sexual act that occurs after a victim voluntarily consumes drugs or alcohol. In both cases, the victim is too intoxicated by drugs and/or alcohol to be aware of her behavior, and she is therefore unable to consent. Kilpatrick et al. (2007) found that 5% of women experience drug-facilitated or incapacitated rape.

Recent research has discussed a rise in incapacitated rapes through the involuntary drugging of victims. The terms *date rape drug* and *drug-facilitated sexual assault* have been used to identify how the involuntary consumption of substances have been used in sexual assault cases. Table 3.2 provides a description of the different types of substances that are commonly used in cases of drug-facilitated sexual assault. In many cases, these substances are generally colorless, odorless, and/or tasteless when dissolved in a drink and result in a rapid intoxication that renders a potential rape victim unconscious and unable to recall events that occurred while she was intoxicated. One research study identified that less than 2% of sexual assault incidents were directly attributed to the deliberate covert drugging of the victim (Scott-Ham & Burton, 2005). However, these findings document reported cases of sexual assault, and it is reasonable to conclude that many cases of drug-facilitated sexual assault go unreported, because victims may be reluctant to report a crime for which they have little recollection.

With the exception of alcohol, the majority of the substances that are used in cases of drug-facilitated sexual assault (such as GHB, or gamma-hydroxybutyrate, ketamine, and Rohypnol) are labeled as controlled substances, and the possession of these drugs is considered a federal offense under the Controlled Substances Act of 1970. In addition, the Drug-Induced Rape Prevention and Punishment Act of 1996 provides penalties for up to 20 years for the involuntary drugging of an individual in cases of violence (National Drug Intelligence Center, n.d.). Many states have enacted laws that provide specific sanctions in cases of drug-facilitated sexual assault. For example, Colorado Penal Code § 18–3–402(4d) distinguishes cases of drug-facilitated sexual assault as one where "the actor has substantially impaired the victim's power to appraise or control the victim's conduct by employing, without the victim's consent, any drug, intoxicant, or other means for the purpose of causing submissions." Here, state law provides an assessment of a victim's ability to consent to sexual relations and holds that the level of intoxication, combined with the resulting mental impairment of the individual, must affect the victim's ability to exercise reasonable judgment. Here, the law provides for an elevated punishment of these cases. While sexual assault is generally considered a class 4 felony (punishable by 2–6 years in prison), drug-facilitated sexual assault is considered a class 3 felony and calls for a punishment range of 4–12 years. The mandatory parole in these cases also increases from 3 to 5 years.

While there has been increased attention to sexual assault due to involuntary intoxication, this is not the primary form of drug-facilitated sexual assault. Rather, cases where the victim is sexually assaulted following her voluntary intoxication of alcohol make up the majority of drug-facilitated sexual assaults. In a sample of rape cases of college-aged women, alcohol was involved in 79% of cases of nonforcible rape (Kilpatrick et al., 2007). The use of drugs and alcohol places women at a greater risk for sexual assault. Not only may women be less aware of the risk for sexual assault and labeled as a target for potential offenders due to a reduction of their inhibitions but they may also be unable to resist their attackers due to their incapacitated state. Additionally, while voluntarily intoxicated individuals are legally incapable of giving consent for sexual activity (Beynon, McVeigh, McVeigh, Leavey, & Bellis, 2008), these victims are often held as the most responsible of all sexual assault victims, since they chose to use intoxicating substances recreationally. As a result, the actions of perpetrators in these cases are most likely to be excused or diminished (Girard & Senn, 2008).

Table 3.2 • Substances Commonly Used in Drug-Facilitated Sexual Assaults

GHB (Gamma-Hydrozybutyric acid)

- GHB comes in a few forms—a liquid that contains no odor or color, a white powder, and a pill. GHB has not been approved by the FDA since 1990, so it is considered illegal to possess or sell. GHB can take effect in as little as 15 minutes and can last for 3 to 4 hours. GHB is considered a Schedule 1 drug under the Controlled Substances Act. GHB leaves the body within 10 to 12 hours, making it very difficult to detect.

Ketamine

- Ketamine is an anesthetic that is generally used to sedate animals in a veterinarian's office. Ketamine can be particularly dangerous when used in combination with other drugs and alcohol. It is very fast acting and can cause individuals to feel as if they are dissociated from their body and be unaware of their circumstances. It can cause memory loss, affecting the ability of a victim to recall details of the assault.

Rohypnol (Flunitrazepam)

- Rohypnol is a dissolvable pill of various sizes and colors (round, white, oval, green-gray). Rohypnol is not approved for medical use in the United States, and much of the supply comes from Mexico. However, the manufacturer of this drug recently changed the chemistry of the pill such that if it is inserted into a clear liquid, it will change the color of the drink to a bright blue color, allowing for potential victims to increase the chance that they could identify whether their drink has been altered. Rohypnol effects can be noticeable within 30 minutes of being ingested; the individual appears overly intoxicated, and the drug affects their balance, stability, and speech patterns. Like many other substances, Rohypnol leaves the body in a rapid fashion, generally between 36 and 72 hours of ingestion.

Alcohol

- Alcohol is one of the most common "date rape" drugs. Here, victims drink to excess, placing themselves at risk for sexual assault. Not only do victims willingly consume alcohol, it is (generally, based on the age of the individual) legal and easily obtained. The consumption of alcohol impairs judgment, lowers inhibition, and affects a victim's ability to recognize potentially dangerous situations.

Spotlight on the Invisible War: Rape in the Military

As a prestigious military academy, the Air Force Academy in Colorado Springs, Colorado, receives high rankings for its training of pilots (as well as its football team). However, 2003 brought a new level of attention to the Academy, as allegations of sexual abuse among the ranks were made public. Not only did victims suggest that rape and sexual assault occurred within the student body on a regular basis, victims suggested that military officials knew of the abuse but did little to stop the systematic assault of female cadets by their male counterparts. Women who came forward with allegations were often punished by their superiors, leading many victims to remain silent about the abuse they endured. While six cadets came forward as part of the allegations, a survey of female graduates that same year suggested that the issue of rape, sexual assault, and sexual harassment is much more prevalent than these few cases. Over 88% of the female graduates participated in the survey, and 12% of women acknowledged that they experienced completed or attempted rape at some point during their college career. An additional 70% of women referenced cases of sexual harassment, including pressure to engage in sexual behaviors (Schemo, 2003). While the most common form of victimization involved sexual harassment, female cadets were significantly more likely to indicate that they had experienced forms of unwanted sexual

(Continued)

(Continued)

touching, sexual coercion, or rape. In addition, women were almost four times more likely to experience multiple acts of victimization compared to men (Snyder, Fisher, Scherer, & Daigle, 2012). Table 3.3 highlights some of the findings from this study.

Table 3.3 ● Sexual Victimization at Military Academies

Type of Victimization	All Victims (%)	Males (%)	Females (%)
Unwanted sexual attention	22.65	10.79	41.24
Sexual harassment	55.73	38.40	82.89
Unwanted sexual contact	15.85	8.96	26.65
Sexual coercion	7.99	4.39	13.64
Rape	3.45	2.41	5.07
Total victimization	58.90	41.85	85.57
Multiple victimizations	25.00	12.23	45.04

SOURCE: Snyder, Fisher, Scherer, & Daigle (2012).

In response to these events, a Sexual Assault Prevention and Response (SAPR) team was developed in June 2005 and provides two victim advocates as well as a 24/7 hotline. When a sexual assault is reported, victims have the choice of filing a restricted or unrestricted report. While a restricted report allows victims to receive counseling and other services from the sexual assault response team, these reports remain confidential and no charges are filed. In an unrestricted case, the Air Force Office of Special Investigations is able to assess whether criminal charges will be filed against the perpetrator (Branum, 2013). In addition, SAPR delivers approximately 11 hours of training over the cadet's four-year educational experience on rape and sexual assault prevention. Similar programs are in place at all the military academies. In addition, each campus has added a special victims legal counsel to help individuals whose cases are handled through the military justice system.

The most recent data from the 2015–2016 academic year notes that while the overall number of cases has decreased, the number of reports at West Point and the Naval Academy have increased. At West Point, there were 26 reported cases of sexual assault, compared to 17 cases in the previous year. Similarly, there were 28 cases reported at the Naval Academy, compared to 25 in 2014–2015. Meanwhile, the number of reported incidents at the Air Force Academy dropped significantly. In 2014–2015 there were 49 reported cases. This year, there were 32 reported cases. In addition, more victims are choosing to have their cases handled by the military justice system (Cooper, 2017; Department of Defense, 2017).

Unfortunately, cases of rape and sexual assault are not limited to the military academies. In an effort to bring attention to the issue of rape in the military, filmmakers Kirby Dick and Amy Ziering presented their film *The Invisible War* at the Sundance Movie Festival in 2012. Drawing from real stories from military personnel, the film portrays the victimization of these soldiers and the response, or lack thereof, by military officials. Their story paints a grim picture about sexual violence in the military as they suggest that 20% of all active duty women are sexually victimized. Other scholars have indicated that 34% of active duty women (and 6% of men) suffer harassment of a sexual nature (Lipari, Cook, Rock, & Matos, 2008). Official data from 2015[2] notes that 6,083 incidents of sexual assault involving service members as either victims and/or subjects were reported. Most of these reports were unrestricted and allowed for these cases to be reviewed by the military justice system. Since [the documentary's] release, the Invisible No More Campaign has generated new conversations about how to combat this issue. Following his review of the film, Secretary of Defense Leon Panetta ordered that all sexual assault investigations be altered to provide multiple avenues for victims to report cases of assault. Previous military policy dictated that the assault be reported to the victim's immediate supervisor. Panetta also directed each branch to develop a Special Victims Unit to respond to allegations of sexual assault.[3]

▲ **Photo 3.4** Ariana Klay was gang raped in 2009 by a fellow marine and his civilian friend. When she reported the rape to her commanding officer, he replied, "It's your fault for wearing running shorts and makeup." One of her perpetrators was given immunity in the case while the other was convicted to adultery and indecent language and was sentenced to only 45 days in military jail. Klay and others have fought for changes to the way sexual assault cases are handled in the military.

Despite recent changes, rape in the military continues to be a problem. In 2012, Air Force Staff Sergeant Luis Walker was convicted on twenty-eight counts of rape, sexual assault, and aggravated sexual misconduct against ten victims and received 20 years for his crimes (Peterson, 2012). While this one case led to a successful outcome, there are many others where victims fail to secure meaningful justice. Meanwhile the culture of sexual violence continues within our military branches. Recently, a criminal investigation was opened into a secret Facebook group involving over 30,000 active and veteran men from the U.S. Marines where photos of female Marines are posted without their permission. Many of the photos involve either nude images or women in various states of undress and are accompanied by sexist and derogatory commentary (Phillips, 2017).

In an effort to create systemic changes on how sexual assault cases are handled by the military, members of the U.S. Senate have made attempts to change the Uniform Military Code of Justice. Senators Kirsten Gillibrand (D-NY) and Claire McCaskill (D-MO) who are both members of the Senate Armed Services Committee have tackled this issue head on and have challenged military officials to increase their understanding about rape in the military. According to Gillibrand, "Not every single commander necessarily wants women in the force. Not every single commander believes what a sexual assault is. Not every single commander can distinguish between a slap on the ass and a rape because they merge all these crimes together" (*NY Daily News*, 2013, para. 11). In December 2013, Congress passed the Military Justice Improvement Act, which makes a number of significant reforms for how cases of sexual assault are handled within the military ranks. These include an end to the statute of limitations for rape and sexual assault cases, makes retaliation against victims a crime, and bars military commanders from overturning convictions on sexually based crimes. It also mandates a dishonorable discharge for those convicted of such crimes (O'Keefe, 2013).

---

[2]Data are collected for the fiscal year.

[3]See http://www.notinvisible.org/the_movie for information about the film *The Invisible War*.

Spousal Rape

Earlier in this chapter, you learned about how early laws on rape included a marital exception clause, which argues that women automatically consent to sex with their husbands as part of their marriage. Even once the legal rights of women began to increase, the relationship between a man and wife was viewed as a private manner, not one for public scrutiny. This belief system permitted the criminal justice system to maintain a "hands-off" policy when it came to **spousal rape**. As existing rape laws began to change throughout the 1970s and 1980s, increased attention was brought to the marital rape exception. In 1978, only five states defined marital rape as a crime. While all 50 states have either eliminated laws that permitted marital rape or had expressly included laws that prohibited this practice, several states still have exceptions in the law that limit how marital rape is defined. For example, in Oklahoma, the crime of spousal rape requires that there be the use of force (or threats of use of force) (O.S. §, 21 45 1111). In South Carolina, cases of sexual battery must be reported to law enforcement within 30 days of the offense (SC Code §16-3-615).

While U.S laws generally prohibit marital rape, it is still legal in many other countries around the world (Fus, 2006). While Nigerian criminal law has criminalized rape in general (and provides for a life sentence for offenders), the law does not acknowledge rape by a spouse as a crime. In fact, "Section 282 of the Penal Code expressly states that sexual intercourse by a man with his own wife is not rape" (Chika, 2011). India also provides legal immunity in cases of rape when the victim is their wife (Mandal, 2014). Meanwhile, other regions of the world (such as South Africa and Britain) have criminalized marital rape but provide for lenient sentencing structures for offenders (Rumney, 1999; S v Modise, 2007)

The majority of cases of marital rape involve cases of emotional coercion rather than physical force in the assault. Examples of emotional coercion include inferences that it is a *wife's duty* to engage in sex with her husband (referred to as social coercion) or the use of power by a husband to exert sexual favors from his wife (referred to as interpersonal coercion). A third form of emotional coercion involves cases where a wife engages in sex for fear of unknown threats or damages that may occur if she refuses. Many of these occurrences are related to cases of domestic violence, where the possibility of violence exists. Cases of marital rape by the use of physical force are referred to as battering rape. In cases of battering rape, the sexual assault is an extension of the physical and emotional violence that occurs within the context of the relationship (Martin, Taft, & Resick, 2007). The physical effects of marital rape are generally greater compared to cases of stranger and acquaintance rape.

Contrary to popular belief, marital rape is as prevalent as other forms of rape, but this victimization is generally hidden from public view. Results from randomized studies showed that 7% to 14% of women experienced completed or attempted rape within the context of marriage, cohabitating, or intimate relationship (Bennice & Resick, 2003). Community samples tend to yield significantly higher rates of marital rape; however, they tend to draw from shelters or therapeutic settings, which offer skewed results. These studies find that 10% to 34% of women studied experienced rape within the context of marriage (Martin et al., 2007).

One of the challenges in the reporting and punishment of marital rape is that the perception persists that marital rape is not *real* rape. Research notes that acts of sexual assault (such as oral sex without consent) are less likely to be viewed as a form of marital rape. However there is a gender difference in these perceptions, because women are more likely than men to view nonconsensual acts such as vaginal and anal penetration, as well as penetration with an object, as marital rape. Marital rape is also viewed as the least serious form of rape, compared to rape by a stranger or acquaintance (Kirkwood & Cecil, 2001; Ferro, Cermele, & Saltzman, 2008). Martial rape is only viewed as a serious act when there is a history of violence in the relationship, and victims receive greater levels of blame if there is a history of infidelity in the relationship. Such perceptions not only impact how others view these situations but can also lead to self-blaming behaviors by the victim (Langhinrichsen-Rohling & Monson, 1998; Munge, Pomerantz, Pettibone, & Falconer, 2007).

Despite the criminalization of spousal rape, the cultural acceptance of marital rape still fails to identify these women as victims. By leaving these victims with the belief that their experiences are not considered real rape, these women are less likely to seek assistance for their victimization. Thus, marital rape remains a significant issue in the United States and around the world.

Campus Sexual Assault

When defining **campus sexual assault,** many assume that these incidents are limited to crimes that occur on a college campus. However the term is much broader and includes experiences of rape and sexual assault that occur during the collegiate experience. Rates of sexual assault appear to be higher on college campuses, where it is estimated that between 20% and 25% of women will experience a completed or attempted rape at some point during their collegiate career (Fisher, Cullen, & Turner, 2000). University life contains many variables that may increase the risk for sexual assault—campus environments that facilitate a "party" atmosphere, easy access to alcohol and drugs, increases in freedom, and limited supervision by older adults (Sampson, 2003). In this environment, the majority of sexual assaults against university women occurred between the evening and early morning hours during or after a party. Alcohol was involved in most of these cases where the victims knew their attackers. Victims are also more likely to be younger and less knowledgeable about the dangers of sexual assault and its relationship to the school/party experience. In addition, the more that students engage in substance use, the greater the risk for victimization because they are more likely to cross paths with a motivated offender (Hines, Armstrong, Reed, & Cameron, 2012).

Research notes that the risk of sexual assault among college-age individuals is highest during the first year of the university experience. During this year, one in six female students experience either an attempted or completed incapacitated or forcible sexual assault. In addition, women who have previously experienced sexual violence during adolescence are more likely to be revictimized in college (Carey, Durney, Shepardson, & Carey, 2015).

The recent attention on campus sexual assault involves Title IX from the Education Amendments of 1972 and states that "no person in the United States shall, on the basis of sex, be excluded from participation in, be denied the benefits of, or be subjected to discrimination under any education program or activity receiving Federal financial assistance" (20 U.S.C. §1681). At the time of its implementation, it was primarily used to ensure that women have equal access to programs such as law school and medical school (which had historically used quota systems to limit access to women) or to provide support and access for women's programs within college athletics (which had been either missing or lacked adequate funding). Directives such as the 2011 Dear Colleague letter where the Department of Education stated that the provisions in Title IX, which prohibit discrimination and harassment on the basis of sex, were also applicable in cases of sexual violence, initiated many of the changes that we see today on campuses. This call to action, coupled by the creation of the White House Task Force to Protect Students from Sexual Assault, resulted in increased requirements for schools to both respond to current acts of harassment and take steps to prevent similar acts in the future (Office of Civil Rights, 2011). One of the challenges facing colleges has been that these mandates are generally unfunded. This means that campuses must find a way to support these new or enhanced infrastructures. Perhaps the best way to describe these efforts is to expand the focus from a responsive framework (albeit, one that many colleges and universities were doing a poor job at) to one that includes prevention efforts as well as the addition of an accountability factor. For example, campuses have created requirements for training employees, procedures for reporting cases, and processes for responding to complaints. In addition, campuses are required to adopt prevention curriculum for students as well as provide support systems and resources for victims. While faculty are often mandatory reporters of any known incidents (regardless of whether they occurred on or off campus), most campuses have options for both confidential and anonymous reporting. Victims also have the option to pursue their case through campus disciplinary structures and to report the case to local authorities for criminal processing.

©iStock/iofoto

▲ **Photo 3.5** Emma Sulkowicz, a visual arts major from Columbia University, carried a mattress everywhere on campus during her senior year as part of a performance demonstration and protest of the way that her allegations of sexual assault were managed by the university.

What effect have these changes had on campus sexual assault? Research notes that despite a renewed focus on educating students about campus resources in this area, students remain unfamiliar with the resources that are available (Burgess-Proctor, Pickett, Parkhill, Hamill, Kirwan, & Kozak, 2016). Bystander education programs are also showing positive effects in changing attitudes about sexual assault (Banyard, Moynihan, & Plante, 2007) and increasing bystander effectiveness (Katz & Moore, 2013). In addition, there is significant variation between institutions of higher education on how allegations of sexual assault are managed. For example, while some campuses use an adversarial trial-like model where evidence is presented and witnesses provide testimony and are cross-examined, others have implemented a process that is more focused on information gathering (Konradi, 2016). Such processes typically adopt a preponderance of the evidence for their burden of proof standard. While significant progress has been made to address issues of campus sexual assault, there is still significant work to be done.

Spotlight on Statutory Rape

Statutory rape refers to sexual activity that is unlawful because it is prohibited by legal statute. Unlike other forms of violent sexual assault, statutory rape generally involves individuals who are legally unable to consent to sexual activity because of their age.

While statutory rape laws were initially introduced to protect adolescents from adults, particularly in cases where there was a dramatic age difference, these laws have also been used against adolescents and their peers. Some would consider these to be victimless crimes because individuals in these cases often do not define themselves as a victim. Rather, they see themselves as willing participants in sexual activity. It is purely the legal distinction of who can, and who cannot, consent that makes these acts a crime. There are two different types of statutory rape laws. The first category includes states where the age of consent is considered a minimum age and sex with anyone under that age is considered a crime. For example, the age of sexual consent in California is 18, and anyone engages in intercourse with someone under the age of 18 is in violation of the state's statutory rape law. So two 17-year-olds that engage in intercourse would be considered to be breaking the law. In the second category are states that define an age range between the individuals. In these cases, it would be considered a crime if one of the individuals was of a minimum age and the other individual was older by a specified number of years under the statute. For example, in Missouri, someone who is at least 21 years old who has sexual intercourse with someone younger than 17 is considered guilty of second-degree statutory rape. (§ 566.034 (1)). In comparison, Tennessee state law considers statutory rape a criminal act if (1) it involves sexual penetration; (2) the victim is at least 13, but younger than 18; and (3) the offender is at least 4 years older than the victim. In addition, Tennessee requires that offenders under the age of 18 be tried as juveniles (§ 39-13-506).

Several states have increased their prosecution of statutory rape cases in an effort to reduce teen pregnancy and the demand on welfare. During the 1990s, legislators targeted welfare reform as a major cause of action. In passing The Personal Responsibility and Work Opportunity Reconciliation Act (PRWORA), legislators noted a significant increase in the number of unwed teen mothers between 1976 and 1991 and indicated that these young single mothers were more likely to apply for welfare benefits. In responding to this issue, legislators noted that "an effective strategy to combat teenage pregnancy must address the issue of male responsibility, including statutory rape culpability" (H.R. 3734-7). Encouraged by this directive, states began to increase their prosecutions of statutory rape cases. One of the most significant examples of this practice comes from California, where then-Governor Pete Wilson allocated additional funding to form a vertical prosecution unit specifically for statutory rape cases. Vertical prosecution units (where prosecutors stay with a case from the beginning and specialize in a particular offense category) generally yield a higher conviction rate because victims are more likely to participate in the process (Donovan, 1996). However, California is not the only state involved in increasing the prosecutions of these crimes. In an effort to assist prosecutors, Mississippi recently passed a law that requires the collection of DNA from babies born to mothers under the age of 16 in case the evidence is needed in statutory rape criminal cases (Diep, 2013).

The increased prosecution of statutory rape cases leads to collateral consequences for offenders. In many states, the conviction of statutory rape requires that offenders must register as a sex offender, which can significantly limit their academic standing as well as their ability to secure employment. Unfortunately, the minimum age of consent laws and state registry requirements fail to distinguish between "two immature high school kids hooking up at a party [and] a pedophile molesting the toddler next door" (Downey, 2007, B1). One suggestion is for states to adopt age-gap provisions to their statutory rape laws. Meanwhile, other states have adopted Romeo and Juliet laws, which maintain the age-gap provision, but do not include the sexual registry requirement. In Florida, if a victim is at least 14 years old and consented to sexual activity with someone who is no more than 4 years older, the offender can petition to have the registration requirement removed (The Florida Senate, 2011). However, these Romeo and Juliet clauses are not without problems in their own right, because many states do not provide exceptions for cases of same-sex statutory rape. Here, it is important that LGBT youth be protected in the same ways under the law, and states should work to close these gaps (Higdon, 2008). Provisions such as this can help ensure that the focus of statutory rape prosecution returns to situations of coercion of a victim by an offender, not on youthful offenders engaging in consensual sexual activity.

LGBTQ Sexual Violence

Much of the existing research on rape and sexual violence involves a male offender and a female victim. Many of the theories to explain rape involve the use of violence by men to exert power and control over women. This explanation is rooted in a heterosexist ideology. Indeed, our laws, which in many states identify the crime of rape as the unlawful penetration of a penis into a vagina, do not allow for us to legally identify these same-sex cases as rape (though most have additional statutes of sexual assault that would be inclusive of same-sex acts of sexual violation).

Historically, much of the discussion about same-sex rape was limited to male-on-male sexual assault, and many of these studies were conducted within an incarcerated setting. Over the past decade, the focus on same-sex victimization has increased. Research from the National Alcohol survey noted that women who identified as bisexual were almost three times as likely (14.9%) to report sexual abuse as adults compared to heterosexual women. Rates for women who identified as lesbian had lower rates of victimization than those who identified as bisexual (8.1%), but higher rates of violence compared to heterosexual adult women (Drabble, Trocki, Hughes, Korcha, & Lown, 2013). Racial differences in victimization are also prevalent among the LGBT population with Latina and Asian American LGBT women experiencing higher rates of adult sexual violence compared to white women (Balsam, Molina, Blayney, Dilworth, Zimmerman, & Kaysen, 2015). In addition, women who identify as lesbian are more likely to be abused by a family member (Sigurvindottir & Ullman, 2015). Over the course of their lifetime, a significant portion of the LGBTQ population experience some form of sexual victimization. The National Intimate Partner and Sexual Violence Survey estimates that 46% of lesbian women and 75% of bisexual women are sexually assaulted in their lifetime. Similar results are noted for gay men (40%) and men who identify as bisexual (47%) (Walters, Chen, & Breiding, 2013). While the data on the prevalence of victimization vary from study to study, these studies have one key theme in common; LGBTQ individuals experience sexual violence at significantly higher rates compared to heterosexual individuals.

Research on recovery for victims of sexual violence notes that women who identify as bisexual or lesbian report higher levels of psychological and social challenges as a result of their victimization. Dealing with symptoms of post-traumatic stress disorder was the most common psychosocial outcome for all victims, yet women who identified as bisexual or lesbian reported significantly higher levels of PTSD compared to heterosexual women. Bisexual and lesbian women also report higher levels of problem drinking, drug abuse, and depression, compared to heterosexual women. Black bisexual women also reported higher levels of problem drinking compared to white bisexual women (Sigurvindottir & Ullman, 2015).

While the research on sexual violence among lesbian, gay, and bisexual communities is increasing, a significant gap remains in studying violence and trauma within the transgendered community. Transgendered individuals are more than twice as likely to experience rape or sexual assault compared to LGBQ individuals (Langenderfer-Magruder, Wells, Kattari, Whitfield, & Ramos, 2016). The National Center for Transgendered Equality notes that nearly half (47%) of all transgendered individuals are sexually assaulted at some point in their lifetime. For many transgendered individuals, violence begins at a young age with 13% of individuals reporting sexual violence in K–12 as a result of being transgendered. Such rates are particularly high for trans women (21%) and crossdressers (18%). Rates of violence significantly increase for individuals who engage in prostitution and other acts of sex work (72%) with nearly one in five engaging in sex work to obtain money, food, or shelter. Of those who are arrested for sex work and other criminal violations, nearly one quarter (22%) believed that their identity as transgender influenced the officer's decision to make an arrest (James, Herman, Rankin, Keisling, Mottet, & Anafi, 2016). The effects of this violence are significant because transgendered men and women are significantly more likely to attempt suicide, compared to transgendered individuals who do not have a history of sexual violence (Testa, Sciacca, Wang, Hendricks, Bradford, & Bongar, 2012).

Reporting rates for sexual violence among the LGBTQ population are low. Research by Langenderfer-Magruder et al. (2016) notes that 23.2% of cisgender individuals (with cisgender females more likely to report than cisgender males) and 15% of transgendered victims report their victimization to the police. LGBTQ individuals who report same-sex sexual violence are often confronted with a system where agents of the criminal justice system may reflect homophobic views (Wang, 2011). Such perspectives can potentially silence victims and prevent them from seeking legal remedies and social services. In cases where individuals do report these crimes to law enforcement, many victims state that their cases are mishandled by authorities (Stotzer, 2014).

While federal law states that crimes against someone on the basis of their "actual or perceived gender-related characteristics" is illegal, few states have incorporated such language into their statutes (Human Rights Campaign Foundation, 2014). Advocacy services have also been slow in responding to the unique and multiple needs of this population (Turrell & Cornell-Swanson, 2005). Given the unique intersectionality between sexual identity and sexual violence, programs need to consider how programs need to be adapted to deal with these multiple marginalities. While the recent reauthoritization of the Violence Against Women Act includes provisions for the LGBTQ community, some community service providers express a fear that offering services to the lesbian, gay, bisexual, and transgender (LGBT) population could potentially restrict their donations from government or socially conservative individuals and organizations. These conflicts limit the opportunities to identify same-sex sexual assault as a social problem (Girshick, 2002).

Racial Differences in Sexual Assault

Research suggests that women of color have different experiences of sexual assault, compared to Caucasian women. These differences can be seen in prevalence rates, reporting behaviors, disclosure practices, help-seeking behaviors, and responses by the justice system. For example, research indicates that 18% of White women, compared to 19% of Black women, 34% of American Indian/Alaska Native women, and 24% of women who identify as mixed race report a rape or sexual assault during the course of their lifetime (Tjaden & Thoennes, 2006). Two important issues are raised with these statistics: (1) We already know that rape generally is underreported, so it is possible to assume that the true numbers of rape and sexual assault within different races and ethnicities may be significantly higher than these data indicate; and (2) given the unequal distribution of these statistics by race and ethnicity, compared to their representation in the general population, it is reasonable to conclude that women of color are victimized at a disproportionate rate compared to their White sisters. Despite these issues, the experience of rape and sexual assault within minority communities is significantly understudied in the scholarly research. Here, we ask the question: How do race and ethnicity affect the experience of rape and sexual assault and the response to these crimes by the criminal justice system?

While much of the literature on racial differences in rape and sexual assault focuses on the African American female experience, statistics by Tjaden and Thoennes (2006) highlight the extreme rates of rape within the American Indian and Alaska Native population (AIAN). These data are particularly troubling given that the AIAN population is a small minority in the population, making up only 1.5% of the U.S. population (U.S. Bureau of the Census, 2000). Research using the National Crime Victimization data indicates that compared to other racial and ethnic groups, AIAN women are most likely to experience rape within an intimate partner relationship, versus stranger or acquaintance relationships. Within this context, they were more likely to have a weapon used against them and to be physically assaulted as part of the attack. Alcohol and drugs also play a stronger role in the attacks of AIAN women, with more than two-thirds of offenders under the influence of intoxicants, compared to only one third of offenders in cases involving White or Black victims. While AIAN victims are more likely to report these crimes to the police, the majority of these reports come from people on behalf of the victim (family, officials, others) rather than the victim herself (Bachman, Zaykowski, Lanier, Poteyva, & Kallmyer, 2010).

Data is also limited on the Asian American/Pacific Islander experience with sexual violence. While data notes that women from these communities report lower rates of rape and sexual assault, they are also unlikely to believe that rape can occur within a relationship (NAWHO, 2002). Research also notes that Asian American men and women are more likely to engage in victim blaming in cases of rape and sexual assault (Lee, Pomeroy, Yoo, & Rheinboldt (2005). These findings likely influence the low reporting rates for Asian American victims, because they are the less likely to disclose their victimization (Shenoy, Neranartkomol, Ashok, Chaing, Lam, & Trieu, 2010). Many victims also fail to seek support to cope with their victimization, with a majority of victims citing feelings of shame as a barrier in help seeking (Lee & Law, 2001). This is particularly important because it can have long-term consequences, such as increases in alcohol use as a way to cope with their victimization (Nguyen, Kaysen, Dillworth, Brajcich, & Larimer, 2010).

Research by Boykins et al. (2010) investigates the different experiences of sexual assault among Black and White women who sought emergency care following their attack. While no racial and ethnic differences were found between victims in terms of the location of the assault (home, car, outdoors) or whether the offender was known to the victim, Black women were significantly more likely to have a weapon used against them during the attack than to White women (42% vs. 16.7%). The intoxication of the victim (and offender) also varied by race, because White women were more likely to be under the influence of alcohol (47.2% of White women reported being under the influence, compared to 23.8% of Black women), as were their perpetrators (47.2% of offenders against White women were under the influence, compared to 23.8% of offenders against Black women). In contrast, the use of illicit drugs prior to the assault was more common among Black victims compared to White victims (28.7% vs. 12.5%). However, there were no racial or ethnic differences in the reporting of the assault to police or of the offering or acceptance of counseling resources. Despite the importance of these findings, it is important to keep in mind that few victims seek out emergency services following their assault, which may skew the interpretation of these results.

Not only are women of color less likely to disclose sexual assault but there are also a number of factors that vary by race and ethnicity that can affect the disclosure and recovery process. Research by Washington (2001) showed that less than half of the women interviewed had disclosed their victimization; when they did disclose, they did so to friends or family members within 24 hours of the assault. However, most of these women experienced incidents of victim blaming as a result of their disclosure. As a result of historical personal and cultural experiences with law enforcement, the majority of these women did not seek out the police to make an official report of their attack. In addition, many of the Black women talked about not reporting as a cultural expectation of keeping their business to themselves. They also mentioned not wanting to perpetuate additional racist views against members of the African American community, particularly if their assailant was also Black.

> We have this element in our community that it's the White man or the White race that causes most, if not all, of the problems we have in our communities. If we begin to point out the Black male for specific problems, we tend to get heat . . . and even from some women because we as women have been socialized as well. And it's "Don't bring the Black man down. . . . He's already going to jail, dying, rumored to be an endangered species; so why should we as Black women bring our wrath against him?" (Washington, 2001, p. 1269)

Cultural expectations also limited the help seeking for some African American victims. These women assumed the identity of the "strong Black woman," which in turn restricted many women from seeking out therapeutic resources because "only crazy people went to therapy" (Long & Ullman, 2013, p. 310). Rather than share their victimization, which could make them appear weak, victims would not disclose their assaults, even to close friends or family members. Alas, the lack of support often led to psychological challenges for many survivors. For these women, finding someone that they could trust and talk to about their victimization proved to be a healing experience (Long & Ullman, 2013).

Likewise, cultural expectations also can inhibit the official reporting practices of women within the Asian American and Pacific Islander population (AAPI). As in the African American community, there is a high level of distrust of public officials (often because of negative experiences either in the United States or in the cases of immigrant and refugee individuals, in their home country) as well as a cultural expectation to keep personal issues in the private sphere. Research has highlighted that many AAPI women fail to understand the definitions of rape and sexual assault, which limits the likelihood that such incidents will be reported (Bryant-Davis, Chung, & Tillman, 2009). Concerns over immigration status and language barriers also limit victim reporting. These same factors also affect the use of therapeutic resources because AAPIs have the lowest utilization of mental health services of any racial or ethnic minority group (Abe-Kim et al., 2007).

Within the Hispanic community, Latina women have the highest rates of attempted sexual assault of all ethnic groups. Stereotypes of Latina women as passionate and sexual women can lead to victim blaming by the victim herself and therefore limits the likelihood that they will report (or that their reports will be taken seriously). Given these challenges, it is important for agencies in Hispanic/Latino communities to reach out to the population and dismantle some of the stereotypes and attitudes that can inhibit reporting and help-seeking behaviors (Bryant-Davis et al., 2009). Indeed, research indicates that Hispanic/Latina women are more likely to seek out informal resources (68.9%) versus make a report to the police (32.5%). Their utilization of informal resources included seeking medical attention (34.7%) and disclosing their victimization to a parent (26.6%). However, the rates of disclosure (both formally and informally) were significantly reduced if the victim had a history of childhood victimization (Sabina, Cuevas, & Schally, 2012).

Culture shapes the manner in which people represent themselves, make sense of their lives, and relate to others in the social world. Indeed, the experience of trauma is no different, and we find that women of color are less likely to engage in help-seeking behaviors from traditional models of assistance. While many women of color believe that agencies such as rape-crisis centers can provide valuable resources to victims of sexual assault, they may be hesitant to call on these organizations for fear that these organizations would be unable to understand their experiences as women of color. In addition, many victims may be unaware that such services are available, particularly given the potential language barriers (Sabina et al., 2012). Instead, victims may turn to sympathetic leaders and women within their own communities. To increase the accessibility of these services to women of color, victims and scholars argue that services need to be culturally sensitive and address the unique considerations that women of various racial and ethnic identities face as victims of sexual assault (Tillman, Bryant-Davis, Smith, & Marks, 2010).

The Role of Victims in Sexual Assault Cases

Many women do not identify themselves as victims. According to a national survey of college women, 48.8% of women who were victimized did not consider the incident to be rape. In many cases, victims may not understand the legal definition of rape. Others may be embarrassed and not want others to know. Finally, some women may not want to identify their attacker as a rapist (Fisher et al., 2000).

According to the National Crime Victimization Survey, 32.5% of victims of rape and sexual assault reported their victimization to the police (Truman & Morgan, 2016). Several factors increase the likelihood that a victim will report the crime to the police, including injury, concern over contracting HIV, and their identification of the crime as rape. Victims are less likely to report the crime if the offender is a friend or if they were intoxicated (Kilpatrick et al., 2007). For college-age women, less than 5% of completed and attempted rapes were reported to the police. While women do not report these crimes to law enforcement or school officials, they do not necessarily stay silent, because over two-thirds of victims confided in a friend about their attack. The decision by victims to not report their assault to the police stems from a belief that the incident was not harmful or important enough to report. For these women, it may be that they did not believe that they had been victims of a crime or did not want family members or others to know about the attack. Others had little faith in the criminal justice system, because they were concerned that the criminal justice system would not see the event as a serious incident or that there would be insufficient proof that a crime had occurred (Fisher et al., 2000).

Victims who do report their crimes often do so to prevent the crime from happening to others (Kilpatrick et al., 2007). Documented key findings from the National Violence Against Women Survey show that only 43% of reported rapes resulted in an arrest of the offender. Of those reported, only 37% of these cases were prosecuted. Fewer than half (46.2%) of those prosecuted were convicted, and 76% of those convicted were sentenced to jail or prison. Taking unreported rapes into consideration, this means that only 2.2% of all rapists are incarcerated. Of those who reported their rape, less than half of victims indicated that they were satisfied with the way their case was handled by the authorities (Tjaden & Thoennes, 2006).

In addition to the low levels of initial reports to the police, victims may also withdraw their participation as their case moves through the criminal justice system. This is particularly common in cases where the assault experience does not reflect stereotypical notions of what rape and sexual assault look like to the average individual. For example, a case involving an assault by a stranger where a weapon was used against the victim is a mythological view of what sexual violence looks like. These cases are most likely to involve participation by the victim. Cases where there are witnesses to the attack are also more likely to encourage victim participation in the criminal justice process, particularly in cases where the witness can corroborate a victim's story of the assault. At the same time, some victims may be discouraged by the criminal justice process and withdraw their participation, particularly when victims are aware of the low conviction rates (Alderden & Long, 2016).

In other cases, victims decide to report their assaults in an effort to increase community awareness and attention by the criminal justice system to crimes of sexual violence. These victims acknowledge that the small number of successes within the legal system in these types of cases may mean that traditional avenues of justice may not be available to them. In some cases, victims talk of wanting to protect future victims from their assailant, even if nothing came of their report personally. Here, the need to raise awareness in their community trumped their own needs for closure. In the words of one victim,

> I looked back and thought; well I'm not going to let one situation put me off from doing the right thing and going through. I know it would be a harrowing experience sitting there telling them what happened over and over again, but at the end of the day you know people need to be accountable for what they've done. And I thought I've, whether it goes to court or whether it doesn't I've done everything in my power you know to prevent something. (Taylor & Norma, 2012, p. 34)

Many victims make these reports knowing that people and officials may not respond favorably or that family members may reject them, particularly in cases where the offender is a close relative or family friend. These are significant hardships that influence many victims to not disclose their victimization to both officials as well as personal social networks. Despite these challenges, some victims believed that reporting the crime helped in their survival because it validated their victimization experience (Taylor & Norma, 2012).

Victims of rape and sexual assault have both immediate and long-term physical and emotional health needs. Over half of the victims of sexual assault experience symptoms of posttraumatic stress disorder (PTSD) at some point during their lifetime. Symptoms of PTSD can appear months or even years following the assault. The levels of emotional trauma that victims experience lead to significant mental health effects, such as depression, low self-esteem, anxiety, and fear for personal safety. Women with a history of sexual assault are more likely to have seriously considered attempting suicide and are more likely to engage in behaviors that put them at risk, including risky sexual behaviors with multiple partners, extreme weight loss measures, and substance abuse involving alcohol and illegal drugs (Gidycz, Orchowski, King, & Rich, 2008; Kaukinen & DeMaris, 2009). Women who are victimized by strangers may experience anxiety and fear about their surroundings, particularly if the assault occurred in a public setting. For women who were assaulted by a family member, acquaintance, or date, they may experience issues with trusting people.

Given the limits of the criminal justice system, how can we meet the needs of victims in rape and sexual assault cases? The current rape crisis movement developed in response to the perceived need for prevention, community awareness, and amelioration of victims' pain. However, even the best community services are limited and lack adequate resources to effectively combat all needs for victims of sexual assault. While attempts to help survivors of sexual assault involve friends, family members, community agencies, and criminal justice personnel, efforts in help seeking may actually enhance the trauma that victims experience because of lack of support, judgment, and blame by support networks. Additionally, victims may experience further trauma by being forced to relive their trauma as part of the official processing of the assault as a crime (Kaukinen & DeMaris, 2009). Because of these negative experiences in disclosure, many victims choose to keep their assault a secret.

Ultimately, cases of rape and sexual assault can be very difficult to prove in a court of law. Convictions are rare, and many cases are plea-bargained to a lesser charge, many of which carry little to no jail time. Alas, the acceptance of rape myths by police, prosecutors, judges, and juries limits the punishment of offenders in cases of sexual assault.

Figure 3.1 • Punishment and Rape

39% of rapes are reported to the police

⬇

If a rape is reported, there is a 50.8% chance of an arrest

⬇

If an arrest is made, there is an 80% chance of prosecution

⬇

If there is a prosecution, there is a 58% chance of a conviction

⬇

If there is a felony conviction, there is a 69% chance the convict will spend time in jail

⬇

So even in the 39% of attacks that are reported to the police, there is only a 16.3% chance the rapist will end up in prison

⬇

Factoring in unreported rapes, only about 6% of rapists will ever spend a day in jail

⬇

15 of 16 walk free

Figure 3.1 highlights how each stage of the criminal justice system reduces the likelihood that offenders will be arrested, charged, and punished for these cases. The effects of these practices can further discourage victims from reporting these crimes, believing that little can be done by criminal justice officials.

Conclusion

Research on rape and sexual assault indicates a number of areas where the criminal justice system and other social institutions can improve prevention and intervention efforts. Given that adolescents and young adults have higher rates of acquaintance rape and sexual assault, much of these prevention efforts have been targeted toward college campuses. While college campuses have increased their educational activities aimed toward preventing rape on campuses in recent times, these efforts may still be inadequate given the number of assaults that occur on campuses around the nation each year. However, the age of victimization appears to be decreasing, indicating a need for education efforts focused on high school students.

Victims indicate that an increase in public education about acquaintance rape and increased services for counseling would encourage more victims to report their crimes (Kilpatrick et al., 2007). Programs focusing on rape and sexual assault prevention should provide accurate definitions of sexual assault behaviors, the use of realistic examples, discussions about alcohol use and sexual assault, and an understanding of what it means to consent to sexual activity. By tailoring education efforts toward combating myths about rape, these efforts can help reduce the levels of shame that victims may experience as a result of their victimization and encourage them to seek help following a sexual assault. Services need to be made available and known to students, in terms of both services and outreach on campus and information available online.

/// SUMMARY

- Rape is one of the most underreported crimes of victimization.

- The risk of rape and sexual assault appears to be higher on college campuses.

- The acceptance of rape myths by society contributes to the practice of victim blaming.

- Many victims of rape and sexual assault fail to identify their experiences as a criminal act.

- Excuses and justifications allow perpetrators of rape and sexual assault to deny or minimize levels of blame and injury toward their victims.

- The majority of rapes and sexual assaults involve individuals who are known to the victim prior to the assault.

- The term *date rape drugs* has been used to identify a group of drugs, such as GHB, Rohypnol, and ketamine, that have been used to facilitate a sexual assault.

- Victims of rape and sexual assault are at risk for long-term physical and emotional health concerns.

/// KEY TERMS

Acquaintance rape 39	Rape 35	Statutory rape 48
Campus sexual assault 47	Same-sex sexual assault 36	Stranger rape 37
Drug-facilitated rape 42	Sexual assault 35	Symbolic assailant 39
Incapacitated rape 42	Spousal rape 46	

/// DISCUSSION QUESTIONS

1. How has the definition of rape evolved over time?

2. Why do many victims of rape and sexual assault choose not to report their crimes to the police?

3. What impact do rape myths play in victim blaming and the denial of offender culpability?

4. Why do many victims of rape and sexual assault fail to identify themselves as victims of a crime?

5. Why are acquaintance rape cases not viewed as "real" rape?

6. What tactics do perpetrators use to coerce sex from their victims?

7. In what ways can prevention efforts be used to educate women and men about the realities of rape and sexual assault?

8. What are the short- and long-term effects of sexual assault? How might early sexual assault yield a pathway to later victimization or offending?

/// WEB RESOURCES

Bureau of Justice Statistics: http://bjs.ojp.usdoj.gov

The National Center for Victims of Crime: http://www.ncvc.org

National Clearinghouse on Marital and Date Rape: http://ncmdr.org/

NCVC Rape Shield Laws: http://www.ncvc.org/ncvc/main.aspx?dbID=DB_FAQ:RapeShieldLaws927

Office of Victims of Crime: http://www.ojp.usdoj.gov

RAINN—State resources for sexual assault: http://www.rainn.org/get-help/local-counseling-centers/state-sexual-assault-resources

Rape, Incest and Abuse National Network: http://www.rainn.org

 Visit **www.sagepub.com/mallicoat3e** to access additional study tools, including eFlashcards, web quizzes, web resources, video resources, and SAGE journal articles.

CHAPTER 4

Women, Gender, and Victimization
Intimate Partner Abuse and Stalking

Much of history has documented the presence of violence within relationships. Throughout history, women were considered the property of men. Wife beating was a legal and accepted form of discipline of women by their husbands. During ancient Roman times, men were allowed to beat their wives with "a rod or switch as long as its circumference is no greater than the girth of the base of the man's right thumb" (Stevenson & Love, 1999, table 1, 753 B.C.). The "rule of thumb" continued as a guiding principle of legalized wife beating throughout early European history and appeared in English common-law practices, which influenced the legal structures of the early settlers in America. While small movements against wife beating appeared in the United States throughout the 18th and 19th century, it was not until 1871 that Alabama and Massachusetts became the first states to take away the legal right of men to beat their wives. However, significant resistance still existed in many states on the grounds that the government should not interfere in the family environment. In 1882, wife beating became a crime in the state of Maryland. While defining wife beating as a crime meant that the act would receive criminal consequences, the enforcement of the act as a crime was limited, and husbands rarely received any significant penalties for their actions.

The rise of the feminist movement in the late 1960s and early 1970s gave a foundation for the **battered women's movement**. Shelters and counseling programs began to appear throughout the United States during the 1970s; however, these efforts were small in scale, and the need for assistance significantly outweighed the availability of services. While police officers across the nation began to receive training about domestic violence calls for service, most departments had a nonarrest policy toward cases of domestic violence, because many officers saw their role as a peacemaker or interventionist rather than as an agent of criminal justice. In these cases, homicide rates continued to increase because of the murders of women at the hands of their intimate partners, and more officers were dying in the line of duty responding to domestic violence calls.

The grassroots battered women's movement of the 1970s led to systemic changes in how the police and courts handled cases of domestic violence. Many of these changes occurred in response to research findings by the **Minneapolis Domestic Violence Experiment** (MDVE). The MDVE illustrated that when an arrest was made in a misdemeanor domestic violence incident, recidivism rates were significantly lower compared to cases in which police simply "counseled" the aggressor (Sherman & Berk, 1984). Many departments ushered in new policies based on these findings. However, replication studies did not produce similar experiences and instead indicated that arresting the offender led to increases in violence.

Throughout the 1980s, state and nonprofit task forces assembled to discuss the issues of intimate partner abuse. By 1989, the United States had over 1,200 programs for battered women and provided shelter housing to over 300,000 women and children each year (Dobash & Dobash, 1992; Stevenson & Love, 1999). In 1994, Congress passed the **Violence Against Women Act** (VAWA) as part of the Federal Crime Victims Act. The VAWA provided funding for battered women's shelters and outreach education, as well as funding for domestic violence training for police and court personnel. It also provided the opportunity for victims to sue for civil damages as a result of violent acts perpetrated against them. In 1995, the Office on Violence Against Women (OVW) was created within the U.S. Department of Justice and today is charged with administering grant programs aimed at research and community programming toward eradicating intimate domestic and intimate partner abuse in our communities (Office on Violence Against Women [OVW], n.d.). Table 4.1 highlights the allocation of resources and the provision of services through the different reauthorizations of the Violence Against Women Act.

Defining and Identifying Intimate Partner Abuse

A number of different terms have been used to identify acts of violence against women. Many of these descriptions fall short in capturing the multifaceted nature of these abusive acts. The term *wife battering* fails to identify cases of violence outside of marriage, such as violent relationships between cohabiting individuals, dating violence, or even victims who were previously married to their batterer. Excluding these individuals from the official definition of *battered* often denies these victims any legal protections or services. The most common term used in recent history is *domestic violence*. However, this term combines the crime of woman battering with other contexts of abuse found within a home environment, such as the abuse of children or grandparents. Today, many scholars and community activists prefer the term **intimate partner abuse** (IPA) because it captures any form of abuse between individuals who currently have, or have previously had, an intimate relationship (Belknap, 2007). However, the use of these terms can vary significantly between different research studies, which can make it difficult to understand the extent of these victimizations. For example, the Centers for Disease Control and Prevention defines intimate partner abuse as "physical, sexual or psychological harm by a current or former partner or spouse" (Centers for Disease Control and Prevention [CDC], n.d., para. 1). Meanwhile, the National Violence Against Women survey extended the definition of intimate partner abuse to include cases of rape/sexual assault, physical assault, and stalking behaviors. Other agencies such as the Bureau of Justice Statistics (2006) include additional crimes within the discussion of IPA, such as homicides and robberies involving intimate partners (Catalano, 2012).

According to the National Crime Victimization Survey, an estimated 1.3 million women are physically victimized each year by a current or former intimate partner. In the majority of cases, men are the aggressor and women are

Table 4.1 • The Violence Against Women Act

1994	**Violent Crime Control and Law Enforcement Act of 1994** **Title IV—Violence Against Women** • Allocated $1.6 billion in grant funds (1994–2000) for investigation and prosecution of violent crimes against women, community services for victims, and the creation of domestic violence helplines • Created new laws that target violators of civil restraining orders and that make interstate domestic violence a federal crime • Allows offenders to use civil justice in cases that prosecutors decline to prosecute • Established the Office on Violence Against Women within the Department of Justice
2000	**Victims of Trafficking and Violence Protection Act of 2000** **Division B—Violence Against Women Act** • Allocated $3.33 billion in grant funds (2001–2005) • Enhanced federal laws for domestic violence and stalking • Added protections for immigrant victims • Added new programs for elderly and disabled victims • Included victims of dating violence into VAWA protections and services
2005	**Violence Against Women Act and Department of Justice Reauthorization Act of 2005** • Allocated $3.935 billion in grant funds (2007–2011) • Created repeat offender penalties • Added protections for trafficked victims • Provides housing resources for victims • Enhanced resources for American Indian and Alaska Native populations • Provides increased training for health care providers to recognize signs of domestic violence • Enhanced protections for illegal immigrant victims
2013	**Violence Against Women Act Reauthorization of 2013** • Allocated $3.378 billion in grant funds (2013–2018) • Continues funding for grants for research and services • Maintains and expands housing protections • Expands options for tribal courts to address domestic violence • Requires reporting procedures for dating violence on college campuses • Prohibits discrimination for LGBT victims in accessing services • Maintains and increases protections for immigrant victims

SOURCES: Seghetti, L. M., & Bjelopera, J. P. (2012). The Violence Against Women Act: Overview, legislation and federal funding. Congressional Research Service. Retrieved from http://www.fas.org/sgp/crs/misc/R42499.pdf.; National Coalition Against Domestic Violence. (2006). Comparison of VAWA 1994, VAWA 2000 and VAWA 2005 Reauthorization Bill. Retrieved from http://www.ncadv.org/files/VAWA_94_00_05.pdf; Office on Violence Against Women. (n.d.). VAWA 2013 summary: Changes to OVW-administered grant programs. Retrieved from http://www.ncdsv.org/images/OVW_VAWA+2013+summary+changes+to+OVW-administered+Grant+Programs.pdf

▲ **Photo 4.1** Intimate partner violence is composed of a variety of different behaviors used by an offender to have power and control over their victim. These include physical, sexual, emotional, and psychological abuse.

the victim (85%)[1] (CDC, 2003). Alas, most crimes of intimate partner abuse are considered a misdemeanor offense, even for repeat offenders. In these cases, prosecutors charge offenders with the crime of simple assault (77.9% of cases), which carries with it a penalty of no more than one year in jail (Klein, 2004; Smith & Farole, 2009).

Much of the abuse within an intimate relationship occurs behind closed doors and is not visible to the community. This makes it difficult for researchers to measure the extent of these acts or for community agencies to provide outreach and services for victims. Many are reluctant to report cases of abuse to anyone (police, friends, or family members) due to the high levels of shame that they feel as a result of the abuse. Others believe that the police will be unable to help. This belief is not unfounded. Research indicates that in some cases, the police scolded victims for not following through on previous court cases. Other victims were either blamed for causing the violence or were told to fix the relationship with the offender (Fleury-Steiner, Bybee, Sullivan, Belknap, & Melton, 2006).

Most people think of physical battering/abuse as the major component of intimate partner abuse. However, abuse between intimates runs much deeper than physical violence. Perhaps one of the most common (and some would argue the most damaging in terms of long-term abuse and healing) is **emotional abuse**. Those who batter their partner emotionally may call them derogatory names, prevent them from working or attending school, or limit access to family members and friends. An abuser may control the finances and limit access and information regarding money, which in turn makes the victim dependent on the perpetrator. Emotional abuse is a way in which perpetrators seek to control their victims, whether it be in telling them what to wear, where to go, or what to do. They may act jealous or possessive of their partner. In many cases, emotional abuse turns violent toward the victim, child(ren), or pet(s). Following acts of physical or sexual violence, the emotional abuse continues when a batterer blames the victim for the violent behavior by suggesting that "she made him do it" or by telling the victim that "you deserve it." Research indicates that emotional abuse is more common with younger males and females and women are more likely to experience social isolation and property damage within the context of emotional abuse compared to men (Karakurt & Silver, 2013). Emotional abuse is particularly damaging because it robs the victim of her self-esteem and self-confidence. In many cases, victims fail to identify that they are victims of intimate partner abuse if they do not experience physical violence. Yet the scars left by emotional abuse are significant and long lasting. Unfortunately, few laws characterize the acts of emotional abuse as a criminal offense.

Economic abuse is another tool in which perpetrators of intimate partner abuse try and control their partner. Economic abuse involves acts that damage the victim's ability to be self-sufficient. It can also serve as a way to make it difficult for a victim to leave their batterer. Economic abuse includes acts such as restricting access to the family's bank account or prohibiting individuals from having their own bank account. This also extends to both jeopardizing one's employment status or prohibiting them from working, which only makes the individual more dependent on their abuser. While much of the research has looked at economic abuse from a very narrow view (and as such, the available data posits that such

---

[1]Given that the majority of data find men as the perpetrator and women as the victim, this text generally uses the term *he* to refer to the abuser and the term *she* as the victim. The use of these terms is not meant to ignore male victims of violence or abuse within same-sex relationships but only to characterize the majority of cases of intimate partner abuse.

abuse is rare), recent studies have attempted to increase the measurements of this phenomenon. These findings acknowledge that economic abuse is just as common as physical and emotional abuse (Postmus, Plummer, & Stylianou, 2015).

For a small number of women, physical violence in an intimate relationship escalates to murder. For these women, death was the culmination of a relationship that had been violent over time, and in many cases, the violence occurred on a frequent basis. The presence of a weapon significantly increases the risk of homicide, because women who are threatened or assaulted with a gun or other weapon are 20 times more likely to be killed (Campbell et al., 2003). Three-fourths of intimate partner homicide victims had tried to leave their abusers, refuting the common question of "why doesn't she leave?" While many of these women had previously sought help and protection from their batterers' abuse, their efforts failed (Block, 2003).

Spotlight on IPA and the NFL

In Chapter 2, you learned about the case of Ray Rice, who was suspended from the NFL for a domestic incident involving his then fiancée, Janay Rice. However, this is not the only incident of intimate partner abuse involving a football star. In fact, there are several active players that have a history of domestic violence. Between 2000 and 2014, there were 83 domestic violence arrests involving 80 players. Given that there are a maximum of 53 players on each of the 32 teams, this means that approximately 20% of all players in the NFL have a history of domestic violence. Indeed, cases of this nature make up 55.4% of all arrests within the league (McCann, 2014).

Brandon Marshall, who most recently played for the New York Jets, has had nine reported incidents related to intimate partner abuse and has been arrested on three separate occasions. In 2007, he was arrested on suspicion of domestic violence against his then girlfriend (Rasheedah Watley) and was arrested in 2009 for disorderly conduct during a fight with his fiancée (Michi Nogami-Campbell). In 2011, Marshall was stabbed by Nogami-Campbell, who claimed that she was acting in self-defense. During that same year, Marshall was diagnosed with borderline personality disorder. His most recent incident was in 2012, when he was accused of striking a woman at a club in New York City. None of these incidents led to a criminal conviction, though he was suspended for one game by the NFL in 2008. Since then, he has made several public appearances related to domestic violence awareness and prevention to speak out about his actions and history with violence. As a free agent, he is being considered by teams such as the Baltimore Ravens, which has not drafted or signed anyone with a history of domestic violence since the events involving Ray Rice in 2014 (Hensley, 2017). In the first 3 months of 2017, there were two cases involving arrests of active players for intimate partner violence: Ethan Westbrooks and Rodney Astin. Westbrooks, who was most recently a defensive tackle with the LA Rams, was booked on suspicion of domestic violence stemming from an incident with the mother of his child. While the charges were ultimately dropped, Westbrooks remains a free agent (McAtee, 2017). A third incident involved Trent Richardson (last played for the Ravens in 2014). Richardson was arrested and charged with third-degree domestic violence in Alabama (Sports Illustrated, 2017).

In August 2014, NFL Commissioner Roger Goodell sent a letter to all team owners about a new disciplinary policy within the National Football League in cases of intimate partner abuse and sexually based offenses. Any player that is arrested and charged with one of these offenses must undergo a personal evaluation, which could include a requirement for counseling or other services. Players would also be suspended without pay for six games. Subsequent offenses would result in a banishment from the NFL, though a player could apply for reinstatement after one year (Pelissero, 2014). However, the policy appears to be applied unevenly. Since its introduction, the six-game policy has only been applied in two of the eighteen allegations of domestic violence. Former Detroit Lions offensive lineman Rodney Austin was found guilty on domestic violence charges following a fight with his girlfriend. While he was suspended by the league (and was released by the Lions), Exekiel Elliott (Dallas Cowboys) and Ra'Shede Hageman (Atlanta Falcons) were both allowed to continue to play during the 2016–2017 post-season despite pending investigations (Pilon, 2017).

The Cycle of Violence

The greatest tool of perpetrators of intimate partner abuse is their ability to have power and control over their victim. To explain how violence and abuse occurs in an intimate relationship, Lenore Walker (1979) conceptualized the **cycle of violence**. The cycle of violence is made up of three distinct time frames (see Figure 4.1). The first is referred to as tension building, where a batterer increases control over a victim. As anger begins to build for the perpetrator, the victim tries to keep her partner calm. She also minimizes any problems in the relationship. During this time, the victim may feel as though she is walking on eggshells because the tension between her and her partner is high. It is during the second time frame, referred to as the abusive incident, where the major incident of battering occurs. During this period, the batterer is highly abusive, and engages in an act of violence toward the victim. Following the abusive incident, the perpetrator moves to stage three, which is often described as the honeymoon period. During this stage, the offender is apologetic to the victim for causing harm. He often is loving and attentive and promises to change his behavior. In this stage, the perpetrator is viewed as sincere and in many cases is forgiven by the victim. Unfortunately, the honeymoon phase does not last forever, and in many cases of intimate partner abuse, the cycle begins again, tensions increase, and additional acts of violence occur. Over time, the honeymoon stage may disappear entirely.

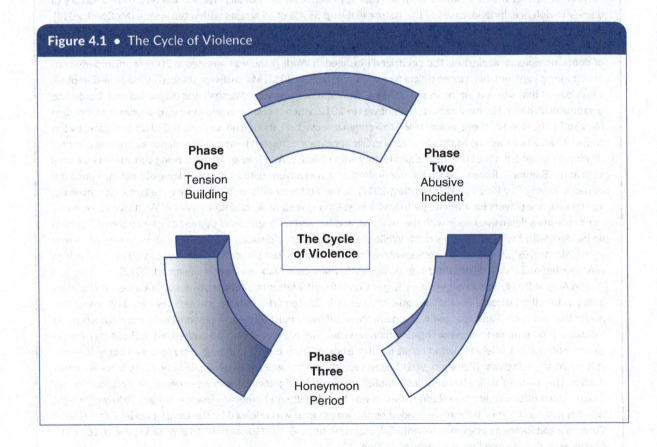

Figure 4.1 • The Cycle of Violence

Phase One
Tension Building

Phase Two
Abusive Incident

The Cycle of Violence

Phase Three
Honeymoon Period

Victims of Intimate Partner Abuse

Intimate partner abuse can impact victims of any sex, age, race, ethnicity, religion, nationality, and sexual orientation. Offenders who perpetuate these acts of violence are spouses, intimates (boyfriend/girlfriend, cohabitating partners), and ex-intimates. This chapter highlights some of the different relationship types and populations where IPA occurs. The chapter also includes a discussion of the challenges that victims face within intimate partner abuse.

Dating Violence

While initial laws on intimate partner abuse recognized only physical violence between married couples, recent laws have been changed to reflect the variety of relationship types where intimate partner abuse can occur. One such example is **dating violence**. Even though two people are unmarried and may or may not be living together, such relationships are not immune from violence. Prevalence rates of dating violence vary. According to the Centers for Disease Control and Prevention High School Youth Risk Behavior Survey, 11.7% of girls and 7.4% of boys have experienced physical violence within a dating relationship. Sexual violence in a dating relationship also impacts 15.6% of girls and 5.4% of boys (CDC, 2015). In contrast, research on dating violence on college campuses indicates that 32% of students report a history of dating violence in a previous relationship, and 21% of students indicate that they currently experience violence in their dating relationship (Sellers & Bromley, 1996). Similar results are noted from Copp, Giordano, Longmore, & Manning (2015) who found that 35% of youth had experienced some form of violence in either their current or most recent dating relationship. Teens, in particular, are at high risk for dating violence as a result of their inexperience in relationships and their heightened views of "romantic love," combined with a desire to be independent from their parents (Alabama Coalition Against Domestic Violence [ACADV], n.d.). Given the severity of this issue, it is concerning that few parents believe that dating violence is a significant issue for their children (Women's Health, 2004). The early onset of violence and abuse in a relationship continues for victims into adulthood, because adolescent victims often find themselves in a pattern of abusive relationships as adults (Silverman, Raj, Mucci, & Hathaway, 2001).

Children of Intimate Partner Abuse

Children are significantly affected by violence within the home environment, even if they are not the direct victims of the abuse. Research indicates that 68% to 87% of incidents involving intimate partner abuse occur while children are present (Raphael, 2000). One battered woman spoke of the effects this victimization has on children: "Our kids have problems dealing with us. When we argue and fight in front of them, when they see our husbands humiliating, beating, and cursing us, they will get affected. They will learn everything they see" (Sullivan, Senturia, Negash, Shiu-Thornton, & Giday, 2005, p. 928).

Children who reside in a home where violence is present tend to suffer from a variety of negative mental health outcomes, such as feelings of low self-worth, depression, and anxiety. Affected children often suffer in academic settings and have higher rates of aggressive behavior (Goddard & Bedi, 2010). Additionally, many children exposed to violence at a young age continue the cycle of violence into adulthood, because they often find themselves in violent relationships of their own. Research indicates that 30% of young boys who are exposed to acts of intimate partner abuse will engage in violence against an intimate partner later in life. In an effort to respond to families in need, many agencies that advocate for victims of intimate partner violence are connecting with child welfare agencies to provide a continuum of care for children and their families. However, it is important for agencies to make sure that they do not overemphasize this risk factor and label these children as potential offenders and victims, because it could lead to a self-fulfilling prophecy (Boyd, 2001).

LGBTQ and Intimate Partner Abuse

While the majority of intimate partner abuse involves a female victim and a male offender, data indicate that battering also occurs in same-sex relationships. The National Crime Victimization survey found that 3% of females who experienced IPA were victimized by another woman, while 16% of male victims were abused by their male counterpart (Catalano, 2007). However, these official statistics may not necessarily reflect the reality of this issue. Research on teen dating violence note that LGBTQ youth have significantly higher rates compared to heterosexual youth. Figure 4.2 highlights data for dating violence for LGBTQ and heterosexual youth. Is same-sex IPA a rare phenomenon (as official data may suggest), or is this issue more common yet hidden within this community? Like heterosexual victims of intimate partner abuse, many same-sex victims are reluctant to report their abuse. The decision to report same-sex IPA involves the same challenges as a heterosexual battering relationship. But these challenges are enhanced for LGBT victims because it exposes their sexual orientation to police, community organizations, peers, and family members (Irwin, 2008).

Research indicates that female victims of **same-sex intimate partner abuse** face many of the same risk factors for violence as heterosexual battering relationships. Figure 4.3 presents the power and control wheel for the LGBTQ community. While heterosexual IPA relationships face many of these same factors such as economic abuse, emotional abuse, and coercion, this figure adds factors such as heterosexism, external homophobia, and internalized homophobia as (further) influences on LGBTQ IPA relationships. For some victims, these additional factors can complicate their efforts to find support within the LGBTQ community. As one victim notes, "I think that people are very afraid to add to (the stigma of being queer) by saying . . . not only are we queer but we also have violence in our relationships and in our community" (Bornstein, Fawcett, Sullivan, Senturia, & Shiu-Thornton, 2006, p. 169). In addition, the connection that an IPA victim has to the LGBTQ community (or lack thereof) can also play a role in disclosure practices. For example, women who experienced abuse within the context of their first lesbian

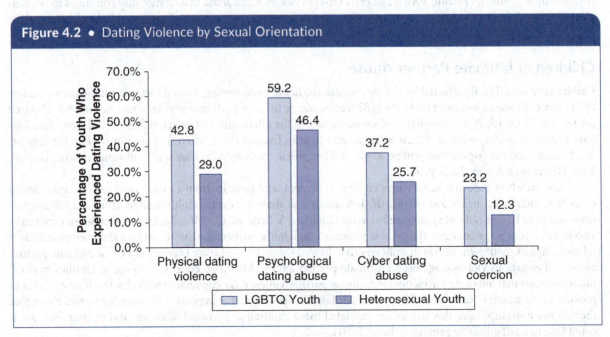

Figure 4.2 • Dating Violence by Sexual Orientation

SOURCE: Dank, M. Lachman, P., Zweig, J. M., & Yahner, J. (2014). Dating violence experiences of lesbian, gay, bisexual, and transgender youth. *Journal of Youth Adolescence*, 43: 846–857.

relationship tended to express fear about discrimination. Since many of these victims lacked a connection to the LGBTQ community, some wondered whether the abuse was a normal component of a lesbian relationship. This fear of being "outed" also led some victims to stay in the relationship for a longer period of time (Irwin, 2008). In comparison, women who had strong networks or attachments with the LGBTQ community were more likely to seek out help when their relationships turned violent (Hardesty, Oswald, Khaw, & Fonseca, 2011).

Given that LGBTQ victims of intimate partner abuse are in the minority, few programs and services exist to meet the unique needs of this population. In addition, resources that are often available to heterosexual victims of

Figure 4.3 ● Lesbian/Gay Power and Control Wheel

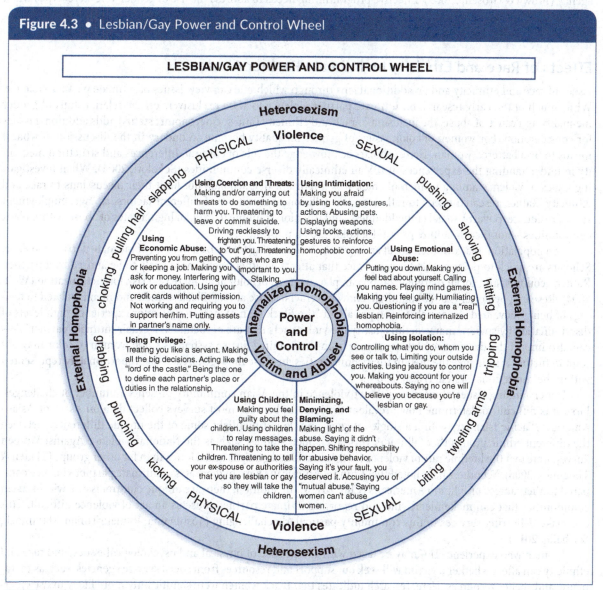

SOURCE: Developed by Roe & Jagodinsky, Texas Council on Family Violence. Adapted from the Power & Control and Equity Wheels developed by the Domestic Abuse Intervention Project.

IPA are expressly denied for the LGBTQ population. Three states have explicitly denied LGBT victims from seeking out a protective order in cases involving IPA (Montana, Louisiana, and South Carolina). Only one state (Hawaii) specifically includes language that allows LGBTQ individuals to seek out a **restraining order** against a current or former intimate. The remaining laws at the state level are silent on the issue because they neither permit nor exclude victims from seeking a restraining order. In these cases, the interpretation of the law is left up to the judiciary (American Bar Association Commission on Domestic Violence, 2008). Even service providers may view same-sex IPA incidents as less serious than cases of heterosexual IPA. This assumption can impact the level and type of services provided by an agency (Brown & Groscup, 2009). Effective programming needs to address the use of gender-role stereotypes when developing education and intervention efforts for the community. Agencies also need to develop "queer-specific" services to meet the needs for the LGBT community (Bornstein et al., 2006).

Effects of Race and Ethnicity on Intimate Partner Abuse

Issues of race and ethnicity add an additional lens through which one can view issues of intimate partner violence. While much of the early research on intimate partner violence focused exclusively on the relationships of gender inequality as a cause of abuse, the inclusion of race and ethnicity (and socioeconomic status) adds additional issues for consideration. For women of color, issues of gender inequality become secondary in the discussion of what it means to be a battered woman. Here, scholars acknowledge the role of cultural differences and structural inequality in understanding the experiences of IPV in ethnically diverse communities (Sokoloff, 2004). When investigating issues of violence among women of color, it is important that scholars not limit their discussions to race and ethnicity. Rather, research needs to reflect on the collision of a number of different factors, as "age, employment status, residence, poverty, social embeddedness, and isolation combine to explain higher rates of abuse within black communities—not race or culture per se" (Sokoloff, 2004, p. 141).

As a population, Black women are at an increased risk of being victimized in cases of intimate partner violence. Scholars are quick to point out that it is not race that affects whether one is more likely to be abused by a partner. Rather, economic and social marginalization can place women of color at an increased risk for victimization (West, 2004). Research by Potter (2007b) highlights how interracial abuse among Black women and men is related to feelings of being "devalued" by social stereotypes about "the Black man." Since men of color experience high levels of discrimination by society, many victims justify the violent acts that are perpetuated by their intimate partner. This can also impact the decision to seek assistance from the criminal justice system as some women of color may not want to further criminalize the men in their communities, because they are already disproportionately represented within the correctional system (Nash, 2006).

Understanding issues of intimate partner violence in the Asian community presents a number of challenges. First, it is difficult to determine how prevalent the issue is, because most surveys collect data on Asian or Asian-American/Pacific Islanders within a single category and do not highlight some of the unique differences between the different ethnic groups that fall under this label. Such studies, such as the National Violence Against Women Survey, note that the lifetime rate of violence for this combined group is much lower than for other groups (Tjaden & Thoennes, 2006). Yet others have noted that Chinese Americans have higher rates of intimate partner violence compared to Vietnamese or Filipino Americans (Cho, 2012a). In addition, there are unique cultural issues within Asian communities that can make identifying and reporting intimate partner abuse as an act of violence difficult. This can make delivering services to this community particularly challenging (Yoshihama, Ramakrishnan, Hammock, & Khaliq, 2012).

Women who experience IPA may be faced with a multitude of physical and psychological issues, and race and ethnicity can affect whether a victim will seek out support and resources from social service agencies, such as therapeutic and shelter resources. Here, research indicates that Black women were significantly more likely to use emergency hospital services, police assistance, and housing assistance, compared to White and Hispanic/Latina women. For example, 65.4% of Black IPA females indicated that they had used housing assistance during the past year, compared to only 26.9% of White IPA women and 7.7% of Hispanic/Latina IPA women (Lipsky, Caetano, Field, & Larkin, 2006). Meanwhile, Asian victims of IPA are also less likely to use mental health services than Latinas (Cho, 2012b). Women of color also express a need for culturally relevant support in their communities. For example, traditional therapeutic communities may be ineffective for some victims of violence: "Black folks don't 'do' group. We 'do' church. . . . I will not sit there and [tell] all these White women my business. [Blacks] don't talk about our stuff [in public]—and especially to White folks" (Nash, 2006, p. 1437).

Unique Issues for Immigrant Victims of Intimate Partner Abuse

While intimate partner abuse is an issue for any community, the effects are particularly significant for immigrant communities. Research indicates that men in these communities often batter their partner as a way to regain control and power in their lives, particularly when their immigrant status has deprived them of this social standing. Battering becomes a way in which these men regain their sense of masculinity. For many, the education and training they may have received in their home countries does not easily transfer on their arrival to the United States. As Bui and Morash (2008) note, "Vietnamese immigrant men have lost power after immigrating to the United States. Many felt bad because they lack[ed] language and occupational skills and could not support their families" (p. 202).

Faced with their husband's inability to find a job to support the family, many immigrant women are faced with the need to work, which many immigrant men find to be in opposition to traditional cultural roles and a threat to their status within the family. This strain against traditional roles leads to violence. Many men blame the American culture for the gender clash occurring in their relationships. However, many women accept the violence as part of the relationship, because such behavior is considered normative for their culture. For example, violence is accepted behavior in Vietnamese traditional cultures, wherein men are seen as aggressive warriors and women are seen as passive and meek. Research on intimate partner violence within this community reveals high levels of verbal (75%), physical (63%), and sexual abuse (46%), with 37% experiencing both physical and sexual abuse (Bui & Morash, 2008). Within immigrant Asian communities, feelings of shame significantly impact the help-seeking behaviors. One woman characterizes these fears: "I do not share with others because if I share with someone, then that someone might tell another person who might happen to know my mother-in-law and so on. And the news will spread and it will bring bad name to my family" (Tonsing & Barn, 2016, p. 5).

For Ethiopian-immigrant women, the violent behavior of men is also accepted within the community, making it difficult for women to develop an understanding that battering is a crime and that they should seek out services. Help seeking is seen as a complaint by women, and in such cases, members of the community turn to support the perpetrator, not the victim (Sullivan et al., 2005). Intimate partner abuse is also discussed as a normal part of relationships for Russian-immigrant women. One woman stated that domestic violence "is part of the destiny, and you have to tolerate it" (Crandall, Senturia, Sullivan, & Shiu-Thornton, 2005, p. 945). These cultural expectations may inhibit women from seeking out assistance, because it would bring shame on the victim and her family, both immediate and extended. Strict gender-role expectations may lead women to believe that they do not have the right to disobey their partner, which legitimizes the abuse.

Many perpetrators use the fear of deportation to prevent victims from leaving an abusive relationship. Many Latina immigrant women are likely to remain in a battering relationship for a longer period of time due to fear surrounding their undocumented immigration status. In these cases, Latina immigrants are less likely to seek out help for intimate partner abuse compared to Latina nonimmigrants (Ingram, 2007). While the 2005 reauthorization of the Violence Against Women Act increased the protection of immigrant women who are victims of a crime (including domestic violence), it is unclear how many immigrant women are aware of these protections.

Perpetrators often build on a negative experience of law enforcement from their home country in an effort to create a sense of distrust of the U.S. legal system. For many Vietnamese women, a call to the police for help was a last resort and often done not to facilitate an arrest but rather to improve the relationship between the perpetrator and the victim by stopping the violence. Most victims did not want to have their partner arrested or prosecuted for domestic violence but rather they wanted to send a message that the abuse was wrong. Unfortunately, many were reluctant to seek police intervention because they fear the civil implications that a criminal record would bring, particularly in jurisdictions with mandatory arrest policies (Bui, 2007).

Language barriers may also affect victims' ability to seek help, because they may not be able to communicate with law enforcement and court personnel, particularly when resources for translators may be significantly limited (National Coalition Against Domestic Violence, n.d.). Lack of language skills, combined with a lack of understanding of the American legal system, also can prevent an immigrant/refugee woman from leaving her violent relationship. Not only may a victim not know what services are available; she may not understand how to navigate social systems, such as welfare and housing, and educational opportunities that are necessary in order to achieve economic independence from her batterer (Sullivan et al., 2005). In an effort to expand access to the courts in domestic violence cases, California amended its domestic violence laws in 2001 to ensure that legal documents in domestic violence cases would be made available in multiple languages. Today, paperwork to request a restraining order and other related documents is available in five different languages: English, Chinese, Spanish, Vietnamese, and Korean.[2]

Spotlight on Intimate Partner Abuse in India

Intimate partner abuse is a worldwide problem. Alas, issues such as patriarchy, power, and control know no geographical boundaries. In many countries, it is these values about women that exacerbate the abuse of women. Consider the case of India. As in many regions of the world, the marital relationship is considered private, and there are few laws against the abuse of women. Indeed, the cultural values reign supreme and essentially promote the power differential between men and women. It is some of these cultural indicators, such as the dowry and arranged marriages, that can encourage violence. For many families, the arranged marriage is an opportunity for the bride's family to increase their social status within the community because they "marry up" their daughters.

The inability to provide an adequate dowry then serves as a trigger for the abuse. For these women, the abuse begins almost as soon as the marriage begins (44% indicate that it began within a month of the marriage), and it is a regular occurrence. Seventy-nine percent of the women reported abuse within their marriage on a daily basis and another 15.6% once every two days. In many cases, the violence comes not only from her husband but also her in-laws. Women were not only physically beaten (100%) but were also threatened by knives and other weapons (47.8%). Psychological violence was also a common tactic because they were prohibited from contacting their families, friends, and even their own children (82.2%; Panchanadeswaran & Koverola, 2005).

Given the cultural context for these abusive relationships, women seek help from a variety of sources. For those women that do leave these abusive relationships, community legal aid and counseling shelters are the most helpful in exiting an abusive situation. The police are essentially useless in dealing with these incidents. Meanwhile, families are only moderately helpful because they are caught up within maintaining their image in the community:

My parents and sister were very supportive and provided shelter from [sic] my daughter and me whenever we went. But after 3–4 days, my parents would always ask me to go back and try to reconcile with my husband. They were worried that if I stayed longer, he would not take me back . . . and the family honor will be affected, and I would be a stigma to the family and no one would marry my younger sister. (Panchanadeswaran & Koverola, 2005, p. 750)

---

[2]Each state has different policies on the availability of legal documents in languages other than English. Forms for the State of California are located at http:www.courtinfo.ca.gov.

Barriers to Leaving an Abusive Relationship

When hearing of cases of domestic violence, many members of the public ask, "Why doesn't she just leave?" Leaving a relationship where intimate partner abuse is present is a difficult and complex process. There are many issues that a victim must face. One of the greatest barriers to leaving a battering relationship is the financial limitations that victims face. Women who lack economic self-sufficiency are less likely to report intimate partner abuse and less likely to leave the relationship. The support from extended family and friends can play a critical role in a victim's ability to successfully depart from an abusive partner. However, these same individuals can increase the potential for victim blaming and a withdrawal of support and empathy if the victim returns to the relationship (Moe, 2007).

Inherent in the question of "why doesn't she just leave?" is the question of "why does she stay?" This question places the responsibility on the victim for staying with a violent partner rather than focusing on why her partner chooses to be violent. The reality is that many women do leave their batterers. The average battered woman leaves seven to eight times before she is successful in leaving for good (ACADV, n.d.). Violence does not always end when women report their crimes or leave their abuser. For some women, the levels of violence increase; women who were separated from their batterers reported higher rates of violence, compared to women who were married or divorced from their batterer (Catalano, 2007). These acts of violence can involve not only the initial victim but also can spread out, placing children, friends, and extended family members of the woman at risk. Concerns regarding these potential increases in violence may influence these women to remain in the relationship out of concern for their loved ones.

For some women, their children are the reason why they leave an abusive situation and seek help. For some women, the desire to provide their children with a happy childhood was their motivation to leave. For others, it was to demonstrate that abusive and violent behaviors are not normal parts of a healthy relationship. One woman states: "I wouldn't have left if it wasn't for her because I saw the damage that I was . . . she was . . . going through and when she told me she was scared, that really explained why I try not to be scared of her father" (Stephens & Melton, 2016, p. 7). At the same time, the desire to maintain the family unit can also delay help-seeking behaviors.

> I think they impact me a lot from the past because they love their dad and he is a good dad for them . . . I have always tried to keep my family together and it is really hard for them to be away from him. Like they cry for him and it hurts, you know, but I think this time, it's just getting too bad. I don't want them to end up seeing the violence. You know . . . I mean they can hear him call me names and stuff like that, you know, but they love their dad and so I think that['s] a lot of the reason why I just stayed. (Stephens & Melton, 2016, p. 8)

Given that a significant portion of intimate partner abuse occurs in young adulthood, how do factors such as age and relationship status impact the decision to leave these relationships? It is interesting to note that the presence of physical violence did not impact the decision to stay in or leave a relationship for these youth. Rather, it was experiences with other negative relationship characteristics, such as emotional abuse or difficulties in communication that led to the ending of the relationship. The acceptance of the significant other by parents and peers also had an impact on this decision; those whose significant other was viewed favorably by their family and friends were more likely to stay, while negative perceptions were more likely to influence the decision to leave the relationship. Youth were also more likely to exit these relationships if they believed there was an opportunity to meet someone new.

In their search for support, some women may turn toward religious institutions for assistance in leaving a relationship characterized by intimate partner abuse. For many women, their faith gives them strength to leave (Wang, Horne, Levitt, & Klesges, 2009). Unfortunately, for some of these women, their spirituality may hinder their abilities to leave. Cultural scripts of some religious doctrines may encourage women to try to resolve the struggles of their relationship, because divorce and separation are not viewed as acceptable under the eyes of the church.

▲ **Photo 4.2** A domestic violence victim wears an alarm necklace that silently signals police in event of danger. Domestic violence agencies distribute the devices, called the A.W.A.R.E. alarm, which stands for Abused Women's Active Response Emergency.

Here, congregations encourage women to forgive the violence that their partners display (Potter, 2007a). Additionally, clergy may be ill equipped to deal with the issue of intimate partner abuse within their congregations because of a lack of understanding of the realities of the problem and limited training on service and support needs (Shannon-Lewy & Dull, 2005).

Many women struggle with their decision to leave an abusive relationship. Some women may still love their partner, despite the violence that exists within the relationship. Others may hope that their partner will change and believe the promises made by their loved one for a different life. In some multicultural communities, there is a greater pressure outside of the family unit to return to one's batterer. Members of these communities often place significant pressures on victims to reunite with their batterer (Sullivan et al., 2005). For many women, they fear what their lives will be like without their partner. These fears may include how they will support themselves (and their children), the possibility that future relationships will have similar results, and even fear of loneliness. A key to successfully leaving an abusive relationship is the victim's belief that she will be better off without her batterer and have the confidence to make a new life free from violence.

Victim Experiences With Police and Corrections

As the criminal justice system becomes more involved in cases of intimate partner abuse, scholars have begun to ask questions about the victim experience with the criminal justice system. The findings of these studies vary. While some suggest that victims are satisfied by their experience with the police and courts in these cases, others highlight areas for significant improvement within the justice process.

The first step in asking for assistance often involves the police. The victim can either request the presence of the police or the police may be summoned on behalf of a victim, usually by a neighbor or other family member. Unlike cases where a third party reports the abuse, victims who initiate contact with the police are more likely to want to press charges against their assailant (Boivin & Leclerc, 2016). Research on this topic provides feedback on how victims feel about these interactions with the police. Women who felt that the officer listened to their concerns and provided information and referrals for help (such as shelters and other protective options) were the most satisfied with their experience with the police (Johnson, 2007). Gender of the responding officer also has an impact on victim satisfaction levels, because victims indicated that female officers were more receptive to their concerns overall and were not just focused on facilitating an arrest (Stalens & Finn, 2000). These positive experiences can encourage victims to seek out police assistance in the future should they need it (Johnson, 2007). There are also factors that can influence whether a case moves forward following a police report. If a perpetrator has a history of violent behavior, both the prosecutor and the victim are more likely to want to see the case move forward, whereas first-time offenders are more likely to have their charges dismissed or to be handled informally (Cerulli et al., 2015).

In contrast, women who do not feel that the justice system effectively responded to their concerns may be less likely to seek out help in the future. If an offender is let off with a "slap on the hand," victims may experience increased risks of violence in the future (Moe, 2007). Here, the criminal justice system did not serve as an effective deterrent for these offenders. This is also true in cases where the intimate partner abuse is limited to verbal abuse. Some women did not feel that the police took the issue of verbal violence seriously. At the same time, victims often minimized the severity of the verbal violence in order to discourage the police from making an arrest (Stewart, Langan, & Hannem, 2013). Negative experiences with the police can also contribute to experiences with posttraumatic stress disorder for victims of IPV (Srinivas & DePrince, 2015). However, failing to achieve a desired outcome with the criminal courts does not necessarily dissuade victims from seeking out other avenues such as emergency departments or the civil court for remedies such as protection orders (Cerulli, et al., 2015).

Drawing from criticisms regarding the **discretionary arrest** policies of many police departments, mandatory arrest or pro-arrest policies began to surface in police departments across the nation during the 1980s and 1990s. **Mandatory arrest** policies refer to the legal duty of a police officer to make an arrest if the officer has reason to believe that domestic violence has occurred. The laws vary from state to state, but most state laws recognize both current and previous spouses or cohabitants as protected categories under the law, though not all states cover dating or prior dating relationships. Currently, 22 states have some form of mandatory arrest policy in place. In addition, the laws vary when a mandatory arrest can be made. For example, laws in Alaska and Missouri require that a report be made within 12 hours of the assault, whereas Mississippi and Nevada extend the time frame to 24 hours. Washington State and South Dakota represent some of the most narrowly defined time frames and require that the police make an arrest within 4 hours of the assault. Washington State law is also unique in that it limits cases to individuals who are 16 or older (Hirschel, 2008).

The movement toward mandatory arrest clarified roles for officers when dealing with domestic violence calls for service. It also removed the responsibility of arrest from the victim's decision and onto the shoulders of police personnel. For many women, they believed that a mandatory arrest policy would make officers understand that domestic violence is a serious issue and that it would legitimize their victimization. At the same time, the threat of arrest would serve as a deterrent for the offender. Here, women believed that an arrest would decrease levels of violence and send a message to the offender that battering is a crime and he would be punished. However, they acknowledged that the decrease in violence was only a temporary measure and that there existed a possibility of increased violence after an offender returned to the family home following an arrest or court proceedings (Barata & Schneider, 2004; Moe, 2007). Victims can feel disempowered by the mandatory arrest process, because it takes away their decision-making abilities. While mandatory arrest policies removed the victim's responsibility for instituting formal charges against an offender, there were some unintentional consequences. In many cases, a victim's call to the police for help resulted in her own arrest, leaving many victims feeling betrayed by the system that they sought help from (Burgess-Proctor, 2012). Other victims may be less likely to call for intervention knowing that their batterer (or themselves) would be arrested (Gormley, 2007; Miller & Peterson, 2007).

Dual arrests are more likely to occur when state laws or policies do not include a primary aggressor designation. As a result, officers are required to make a determination about who the "real" offender is. Even with a primary aggressor designation, officers may lack the training or experience to make a professional judgment about whom to arrest, resulting in both parties being arrested. These dual-arrest practices result in women being arrested for domestic violence with their partner. As a result, many women victims find themselves labeled as offenders of IPA by police and the courts for engaging in acts of self-defense (Miller, 2005). Dual-arrest policies also have negative consequences for the LGBT community. Research by Hirschel et al. (2007) found that in cases of intimate partner violence, same-sex couples were more likely to be involved in dual-arrest situations (female-to-female = 26.1% and male-to-male = 27.3%) compared to heterosexual couples (3.8%).

The increase in arrests has far-reaching implications for women, including the refusal of help by shelter services and challenges in child custody battles as a result of their "criminal" history (Miller & Meloy, 2006). In addition, gender differences in battering impact programming options for women who engage in acts of IPA. Here, scholars have noted that traditional batterer intervention programming (which is designed primarily for male offenders) may not be appropriate for women. Instead, therapeutic options should focus on the rationale and factors behind women who engage in IPA (Kernsmith, 2005).

In response to many mandatory arrest policies, many jurisdictions have instituted **no-drop policies**. Rather than force a victim to participate against her will, these jurisdictions developed evidence-based practices that would allow the prosecutor to present a case based on the evidence collected at the scene of the crime, regardless of any testimony by the victim (Gormley, 2007). Such policies were developed in response to a victim's lack of participation in the prosecution of her batterer. These policies may actually work against victims. When victims feel that their voice is not being heard by the criminal justice system, they may be less likely to report incidents of intimate partner abuse. While no-drop policies were designed to prevent victims from dismissing charges against their batterer, they instead led to disempowering victims.

When victims feel that the criminal justice system does not meet their needs in a case of intimate partner violence, they are less likely to seek assistance for subsequent victimizations. In many cases, victims felt that the event was not serious enough to report or expressed concerns that they would not be believed by the police. In addition, several victims were concerned about how contacting the police could lead to potential negative consequences for themselves or their families. Here, victims expressed concerns over the possibility of mandatory arrests or dual arrests (and the effects on children in the home), custody battles, and fear of how the offender would respond. Finally, even after multiple victimizations, some victims still express love and compassion for their abuser (Gover, Welton-Mitchell, Belknap, & Deprince, 2013).

Over time, many victims and advocates have expressed concern that the traditional criminal justice system may not be an effective tool to address the issues posed by intimate partner abuse. In response to these concerns, many jurisdictions have developed specialized courts that deal exclusively with cases of domestic violence. The professionals in these specialized courts (prosecutor, judges) often have specific training on issues such as the cycle of violence and the role of power and control within an intimate partner relationship. Research demonstrates that the use of specialized court practices can impact the level of satisfaction that victims experience as a result of their interactions with these environments. In their evaluation of a domestic violence court program in South Carolina, researchers Gover, Brank, and MacDonald (2007) found that a collaborative courtroom environment between the prosecutor, victim advocate, and judge had a significant effect on victim satisfaction levels. Unlike traditional criminal justice options that generally focus on punitive measures, this program emphasized the therapeutic options designed to treat the offender. As a result, the majority of victims and defendants believed that the outcome of their case was fair, positive, and respectful.

Programming Concerns for Victims of Intimate Partner Abuse

Not only are programs needed to address the needs of victims but it is also important to consider the value of battering prevention programs for men. Over the past three decades, batterer intervention programming has become one of the most popular options when sentencing offenders in cases of intimate partner abuse. Given the high correlation between substance use and intimate partner abuse, most programs also include substance abuse treatment as a part of their curriculum. The majority of these programs offer group therapy, which is popular not only for its cost-effectiveness but also because scholars suggest that the group environment can serve as an opportunity for program participants to support and mentor one another. One criticism of battering intervention programs is that they generally assume that all batterers are alike. This approach does not offer the opportunity for programs to tailor their curriculum to address the differences among men who abuse (Rosenbaum, 2009). In addition, victims of domestic violence voice their dissatisfaction with many of these types of programs, arguing that they are ineffective in dealing with the issues that the men face in their lives (Gillum, 2008).

Intimate partner abuse attacks every community, age, religion, race, class, and sexual identity. Programs that provide services for victims of battering must acknowledge the need for programming that is culturally diverse and reflect the unique issues within different racial and ethnic communities. The need for culturally relevant programming also extends to shelter programs for victims of domestic violence. In one program, participants noted the absence of women of color (particularly Black women) within the shelter administration and staff, even though the majority of the clientele was Black. Feeling culturally connected to program practitioners (as women of color and IPV survivors themselves) helped survivors understand what they were going through. As one woman notes, "Black womens understand other Black womens. Ain't no way a White woman understands what a Black women going through. . . . Because . . . we're different, we are totally different" (Gillum, 2009, p. 67). In addition, programs to be based within the targeted community ensure participation from the community residents—if programs are difficult to access geographically, women are less likely to seek out services as a result of time, money (loss of work hours and cost of child care), and transportation limitations. Programs also need to be proactive and engage in prevention efforts with young women and men in the community (Bent-Goodley, 2004).

Culturally diverse programs are not enough to combat issues of violence between intimate partners. Rather, intervention efforts need to attack the systems that create social inequalities—racism, sexism, classism, and so on. In addition, the legal system and program providers need to understand how these issues are interrelated and not dominated by a single demographic factor (Sokoloff, 2004). Regardless of their individual effects on a single person, many of these interventions have the potential to fail at the macro level, as long as the social culture of accepting male violence against women remains (Schwartz & DeKeseredy, 2008).

Stalking and Intimate Partner Violence

According to the National Crime Victimization Survey, **stalking** is defined as "a course of conduct directed at a specific person that would cause a reasonable person to feel fear" (Baum, Catalano, Rand, & Rose, 2009, p. 1). Estimates by the Supplemental Victimization Survey (SVS) indicate that more than 5.9 million adults[3] experience behaviors defined as stalking[4] or **harassment**.[5] Table 4.2 illustrates the types and prevalence of stalking behaviors. In most cases, the acts that constitute stalking, such as sending letters or gifts, making phone calls, and showing up to visit, are not inherently criminal. These acts appear harmless to the ordinary citizen but can inspire significant fear and terror in victims of stalking.

Much of what the general public understands about stalking comes from Hollywood, where celebrities have long experienced acts of stalking. Consider the actions of John Hinckley Jr. who became infatuated with Jodie Foster when she first appeared as a child prostitute in the film *Taxi Driver*. Hinckley's obsession with Foster continued while she was a student at Yale, but he failed to gain her attention after numerous letters and phone calls. In 1981, Hinckley attempted to assassinate President Ronald Reagan in an effort to impress Foster. He was found not guilty by reason of insanity for his crimes and was committed to St. Elizabeth's Hospital for treatment. Another example of celebrity stalking is Madonna's stalker Robert Dewey Hoskins. He was convicted in 1996 for making threats against the star—he told the star that he wanted to "slice her throat from ear to ear" ("After Court Order," 1996, para. 6) and attempted to break into her house on two separate occasions. During one event, he successfully scaled the security wall of her home and was shot by one of her bodyguards. Other Hollywood victims of stalking include David Letterman, Sandra Bullock, Tyra Banks, and Lindsay Lohan, to name a few. Indeed, it seems that a number of Hollywood personalities have been stalked by an obsessed fan at some point during their careers. While noteworthy

---

[3]The Supplemental Victimization Survey (SVS) includes only data on respondents aged 18 and older who participated in the National Crime Victimization Survey (NCVS) during January–June 2006. The data assess victimization incidents that occurred during the 12 months prior to the interview.

[4]According to these data, 3.4 million people are victims of stalking each year.

[5]Harassment is defined by the SVS as acts that are indicative of stalking behaviors but do not incite feelings of fear in the victim.

Table 4.3 • Prevalence of Stalking	
Experienced at least one unwanted contact per week	46.0%
Victims were stalked for 5 years or more	11.0%
Experienced forms of cyberstalking	26.1%
Received unwanted phone calls or messages	66.2%
Received unwanted letters and e-mail	30.6%
Had rumors spread about them	35.7%
Were followed or spied on	34.3%
Experienced fear of bodily harm	30.4%
Believed that the behavior would never stop	29.1%

events of Hollywood stalkers brought significant attention to the crime of stalking, the attention was done in ways that reduced the social understanding of this crime to one that was limited to celebrities and the Hollywood circuit. Many of these cases involved perpetrators who suffered from mental disease or defect. This narrow definition had significant effects on the legitimization of this crime for ordinary victims of stalking.

Outside of the Hollywood context, a victim's relationship with her future stalker began in a very ordinary sense. Victims described these men as attentive, charming, and charismatic. But these endearing qualities soon disappeared, and their interactions became controlling, threatening, and violent. Many women blamed themselves for not recognizing the true colors of their stalker earlier. This pattern of self-blaming affected their ability to trust their own judgment and led these women to be hesitant about their decision-making abilities in future relationships as a result of their victimization.

As with many crimes, victims of stalking often do not report their victimization to police. According to SVS data, more than half of the individuals who were victims of stalking did not report their victimization. For many victims, their decision to not report these crimes stemmed from a fear of intensifying or escalating the stalking behaviors. Others dealt with their victimization in their own way, believing that their experience was a private and personal matter. Additionally, many believed that stalking was not a serious enough offense (or did not believe that a crime had occurred) to warrant intervention from the criminal justice system. Finally, some victims felt that nothing could be done to stop the behavior by their stalkers. For those individuals who did report their crimes, SVS data indicate that charges were filed in only 21% of these cases, further solidifying a belief for many victims that the criminal justice system was unable to effectively punish their stalkers in a court of law.

Victims engage in several different strategies in an effort to cope with their stalking victimization. Some victims attempted to solve the trauma through self-reflection and sought out therapeutic resources. Women also made significant changes to their behavior patterns. They might avoid community events out of a fear that their stalker would show up at the same function. Other women moved out of the area yet still expressed fear that their stalker would find them. Some victims tried to renegotiate the definitions of their relationship with their offender through bargaining, deception, or deterrence. Finally, some victims moved against their attackers by issuing warnings or pursuing a legal case against them (Cox & Speziale, 2009; Spitzberg & Cupach, 2003).

Spotlight on Stalking and College Campuses

In Chapter 3, you learned about Title IX and how recent attention on this legislation has led college campuses across the United States to revisit how they respond to cases of sexual assault, as well as implement prevention-based education for all students. Such efforts have also led to increased attention of cases of stalking on college campuses. In addition, the Jeanne Clery Act, which requires universities to annually publish their crime statistics, was recently amended to make stalking a mandatory reporting offense.

What is the prevalence of stalking on college campuses? It is the most common type of victimization among college-age individuals. Research by Myers, Nelson, and Forke (2016) notes that 16.0% of survey respondents from an urban university in Philadelphia reported experiencing stalking during their college experience, compared to 12.0% who reported sexual victimization, and 7.0% who reported physical victimization. Victims were more likely to be female (22.1%), and their perpetrators were more likely to be acquaintances or friends (41.1%). Intimate partners engaged in stalking in only 13.7% of cases. Other studies have noted that 27% of students experienced stalking while at campus (Spitzberg, 2016). While traditional research has identified a relationship between stalking and intimate partner abuse, research on college-age students note that the majority of stalking cases involve acquaintances or friends as offenders (Myers, Nelson, & Forke, 2016).

College students often fail to understand the definition of stalking and are often unlikely to label their experiences as stalking, even though they feel threatened or fearful as a result (Spitzberg, 2016). Research notes that many of the behaviors that constitute stalking are common occurrences within college-age relationships (Shorey, Cornelius, & Strauss, 2015). Similarly, behaviors that can be identified as cyberstalking are often rationalized among college-age students as a form of modern-day courtship and were not considered by the majority of the students to be of any particular significance, particularly in cases where the offender is known to the victim (Lee, 1998).

Recent changes to the Jeanne Clery Act (which requires that universities publish statistics about crime that occurs on or near campus) have included stalking as a reportable offense. In addition, the Dear Colleague letter on sexual violence has led universities to shift the way that they respond to cases of stalking under Title IX legislation. As you learned above, experiences of stalking can have negative mental health consequences. Within a university population, these challenges can present in a variety of ways, including issues with academic attendance and poor academic performance. Given the increasing presence of stalking behaviors on college campuses, colleges and universities are faced with expanding both their educational programming as well as their provision of services for victims (Myers, Nelson, & Forke, 2016).

Victims and Offenders of Stalking

Who are the victims of stalking? They are men and women, young and old, of every race, ethnicity, and socioeconomic status. Data indicate that there are certain groups that make up the majority of victims of stalking. A meta-analysis of 22 studies on stalking found that female victims made up 74.59% of stalking victims, while 82.15% of the perpetrators were male. In the majority of cases, the perpetrator was someone known to the victim, with 30.3% of all cases occurring as a result of a current or former intimate relationship. Only 9.7% of stalking cases involved someone who was a stranger to the victim (Spitzberg & Cupach, 2003).

While stalking is a crime in its own right, it is also a common experience for victims of intimate partner abuse. The degree to which victims are stalked is directly related to the levels of physical, emotional, and sexual abuse that they experienced with their intimate partner: The greater the abuse in the relationship, the higher the levels of

▲ **Photo 4.3** Many victims of stalking experience the constant fear or being followed and observed as they attempt to manage their daily lives. In this situation, the psychological terror that victims experience can be just as violent as any physical confrontation.

stalking can be. Several factors appear to influence whether a victim of domestic violence will be stalked. Women who are no longer in a relationship with their abuser are more likely to experience stalking compared to women currently involved in an IPA relationship. Additionally, domestic violence abusers who are more controlling and physically violent toward their victims are more likely to stalk them. Finally, abusers who use drugs and alcohol are more likely to stalk their partners. For those women who had moved on to new relationships, almost three fourths of them indicated that their new partner was harassed, threatened, or injured by their stalker (Melton, 2007).

Economics also impact the stalking experience for victims. Many victims find that they do not have the economic resources or abilities to move out of their communities to escape their stalker. Many of these women received governmental subsidies for housing—moving would mean giving up this assistance. This lack of mobility made it easier for their perpetrators to continue to stalk and harass their victims. In addition, the close-knit nature of many of these communities led to cases where a batterer's friends and family members were able to help the offender harass and intimidate their victim. Unfortunately, these cases of third-party stalking are not always recognized by the criminal justice system, or are not connected to the behaviors of the individual. As a result, many victims believe that an escape from the violence is impossible (Tamborra, 2012).

The experience of stalking has a significant effect on a woman's mental health. Women who experience significant levels of stalking over time are more likely to be at risk for depression and posttraumatic stress disorder. These rates of depression and posttraumatic stress disorder are significantly higher for women who blame themselves for the behaviors of their perpetrator (Kraaij, Arensman, Garnefski, & Kremers, 2007). Victims indicate feelings of powerlessness, depression, sleep disturbances, and high levels of anxiety (Pathe & Mullen, 1997). They are also likely to develop a chronic disease or other injury in response to the high levels of stress that victims of stalking experience (Davis, Coker, & Sanderson, 2002). It is clear that mental health services need to acknowledge how the experience of stalking affects the mental health status of victims and determine how to better provide services to this community.

Cyberstalking

The use of technology has changed the way in which many victims experience stalking. The use of devices such as e-mail, cell phones, and global-positioning systems (GPS) by offenders to track and monitor the lives of victims has had a significant effect on the experience of stalking. The term **cyberstalking** was created to address the use of technology as a tool in stalking. Of the 3.2 million identified victims of stalking identified by the SVS, one out of four individuals reported experiencing acts that are consistent with the definition of cyberstalking. Table 4.3 highlights examples of stalking aided by technology. As the use of technology continues to expand in our social world, so will its use to stalk, harass, and engage in acts of violence against individuals.

Like traditional methods of stalking, cyberstalking involves incidents that create fear in the lives of its victims. Just because cyberstalking does not involve physical contact does not mean that it is less damaging or harmful than physical stalking. Indeed, some might argue that the anonymity under which cyberstalkers can operate creates significant opportunities for offenders to control, dominate, and manipulate their victims, even from a distance, because there are no geographical limits for stalking within the domain of cyberspace. Indeed, someone can be stalked from just about anywhere in the world. For many victims of "traditional" stalking, cyberstalking presents a new avenue through which victims can be harassed, threatened, and intimidated. In cases of intimate partner abuse, technology and cyberstalking is a way in which abusers can continue to control and harass their victims from afar. "Some perpetrators text and phone repeatedly, creating dread and fear in the victim that the harassment will never end. Some women receive only one text or call daily or weekly, but this can be equally as terrifying in the context of their specific domestic-abuse history" (Woodlock, 2017, p. 586).

While cyberstalking is a relatively new phenomenon, research indicates that the prevalence of these behaviors is expanding at an astronomical rate. Youth and young adults appear to be particularly at risk for these forms of victimization, given their connections to the electronic world through the use of the Internet, blogs, text messaging, and social networking sites, such as Facebook. Consider that the simple act of tagging a friend in a photo on Facebook, Instagram, or other social media platform can provide valuable information to a stalker as it could inadvertently disclose their location (Dimond, Fiesler, & Bruckman, 2011). In addition, participation in activities such as sexting can increase the likelihood that one will be victimized online. Research indicates that 38% of study participants had either sent or received sexually explicit texts or photos. Participation in these activities increases the likelihood of cybervictimization (Reyns, Burek, Henson, & Fisher, 2013). In addition, stalkers can use information to publicly post information that is not only embarrassing but could jeopardize their relationships with friends, family, and employers (Woodlock, 2017). Given the limited understanding of these crimes by victims (and the larger society), it is important that advocates and justice professionals have an understanding about the realities of these crimes in order to provide adequate support for victims.

Table 4.4 ● Experiences of Stalking via Mobile Technologies	
Method	**%**
Used text messages, phone, and so on to call her names, harass her, or "put her down"	78
Used mobile technology to check her location	56
Made her feel afraid to not respond to a phone call or text because of what the caller might do (e.g., threaten suicide)	56
Checked her text messages without her permission	47
Threatened her via text, e-mail, and/or social media	44
Shared private photographs or videos of her without her permission	39
Posted negative information about her on social media	33
Tracked her via GPS (e.g., using applications such as Find My Friends)	17
Demanded her electronic password/s	17
Impersonated her in e-mails, text messages, and or/social media	14
Purchased a phone for her for the purpose of keeping track of her	8

SOURCE: Woodlock (2017).

Laws on Stalking

For the majority of the 20th century, stalking was not considered to be a crime. The first law criminalizing the act of stalking was created in 1990 by the state of California following the murder of actress Rebecca Schaeffer in 1989 by an obsessed fan. Schaeffer had risen to fame as an actress in the popular television show *My Sister Sam*. Robert Bardo had become obsessed with "Patti," the character played by Schaeffer on the show, and made several attempts to contact her on the set. He sent Schaeffer several letters and had built a shrine to her in his bedroom. Undeterred, he traveled cross-country, and he paid a private investigator $250 to obtain her home address. On making contact with Schaeffer at her residence, he shot her in the chest, killing her. Bardo was convicted of murder and sentenced to life in prison. Since the death of Rebecca Schaeffer and the creation of the first antistalking law in California, all 50 states, the District of Columbia, and the federal government have created criminal laws against stalking. In addition, the majority of state laws on stalking include details on stalking via electronic methods.

To prosecute someone for stalking, many state laws require victims to indicate that they experienced *fear* as a result of the offender's actions. Research indicates that women are more likely to experience fear as a result of being stalked compared to men (Davis et al., 2002). Using data from the National Violence Against Women Survey, Dietz and Martin (2007) found that nearly three fourths of women who were identified as victims of stalking behaviors indicated that they experienced fear as a result of the pursuit by their stalker. The levels of fear depended on the identity of the stalker (women indicated higher levels of fear when they were stalked by a current or former intimate or acquaintance) and how they stalked their victims (physical and communication stalking experiences generated higher levels of fear). Fear levels are also predicted by the severity and frequency of the contact (Reyns & Englebrecht, 2012). But what about women who experienced behaviors consistent with the definition of stalking but who did not feel fearful as a result of these interactions? Are these women not victims of stalking? In many states, they would not be considered victims, and the behaviors perpetrated against them would not be considered a crime.

The challenge with stalking is that many do not perceive stalking to be a significant event. Much of the research in this area is based on hypothetical scenarios, investigating what victims might do in these sorts of situations. From this research, we learn that the perceptions about stalking vary based on the gender of the victim and the offender and the type of relationship as well as the gender of the study participant. In addition, men are more likely to view stalking as a minor event and to engage in victim blaming toward stalking victims (Lambert, Smith, & Geistman, 2013). Victim blaming can be predicated by the type of relationship between the victim and the offender. Victims are the least blameworthy if the offender is a stranger but are considered culpable if the stalking results from a casual sexual relationship, such as a one-night stand. This can in turn impact perceptions of victim reporting—"When the victim reports this to the police, she will have to tell them everything, including how she had sex with him on the first night. This makes her look bad and she might be blamed for leading him on" (Cass & Mallicoat, 2014). If people do not perceive that victims will report these crimes to the police in hypothetical scenarios, we can assume that it is unlikely that they will reach out to the police should they face a similar victimization in their own lives.

Conclusion

Many victims of intimate partner violence and stalking did not report their victimization because they did not believe that what was happening to them was a criminal act, particularly in cases where there was no experience of physical violence. One victim noted that in assessing whether a relationship is healthy, women should look at themselves and any changes in their personal behaviors rather than obsessing on the actions of their stalker. "Think about how you were before this happened and how happy you were, and I think once ladies reminisce on that, I think that's where strength comes from" (Cox & Speziale, 2009, p. 12). Others advised that women should not stay silent on the issues of intimate partner abuse and stalking in order to protect their own safety, whether that meant filing a police report and obtaining a restraining order or letting friends, family, and coworkers know of their victimization. Here, victims acknowledge an increased need for community awareness about the nature of these victimizations and the resources available to them.

/// SUMMARY

- Intimate partner abuse is difficult to identify, because much of the abuse occurs behind closed doors and victims are reluctant to report cases of abuse.

- The Violence Against Women Act of 1994 provided funding for battered women shelters, outreach education, and training on domestic violence for police and court personnel.

- Children who are exposed to violence in the home are at risk for negative mental health outcomes and may continue the cycle of violence as adults.

- Gender-role stereotypes and homophobic views have a significant effect on identifying victims of same-sex IPA and giving them the assistance they need.

- Immigrant victims of domestic violence face a variety of unique issues such as cultural norms regarding violence, gender-role expectations, and a fear of deportation that affect their experience with battering.

- Walker's cycle of violence (1979) helps explain how perpetrators maintain control within a battering relationship.

- Women are confronted with a variety of barriers in their attempts to leave a relationship where intimate partner abuse is present.

- For many women, mandatory arrest policies have resulted in only a temporary decrease in the violence in their lives, with the potential of increased violence in the future.

- Stalking is defined as a "course of conduct directed at a specific person that would cause a reasonable person to feel fear."

- Cyberstalking involves the use of technology to track and monitor the lives of victims of stalking.

- Many victims do not report their experiences of being stalked to law enforcement, because they fear that a report will escalate the behavior, or they do not believe that stalking is a serious matter or that anything can be done to stop the stalking behavior.

- Stalking is often related to incidents of intimate partner abuse.

/// KEY TERMS

Battered women's movement 59

Cyberstalking 78

Cycle of violence 64

Dating violence 65

Discretionary arrest 73

Economic abuse 62

Emotional abuse 62

Harassment 75

Intimate partner abuse 60

Mandatory arrest 73

Minneapolis Domestic
   Violence Experiment 60

No-drop policies 74

Restraining order 68

Same-sex intimate partner abuse 66

Stalking 75

Violence Against Women Act 60

DISCUSSION QUESTIONS

1. How have mandatory arrest and no-drop policies improved the lives of women involved in cases of intimate partner abuse? How have these policies negatively affected victims?

2. What unique issues do immigrant victims of intimate partner abuse face?

3. Describe the different forms of violence that can occur within an intimate partner abusive relationship.

4. Explain how the cycle of violence attempts to explain incidents of intimate partner battering.

5. What barriers exist for women in their attempts to leave a battering relationship?

6. How has the use of technology changed the way in which victims experience stalking? What challenges do these changes present for law enforcement and the criminal justice system in pursuing cases of cyberstalking?

7. How do victims cope with the experience of being stalked?

WEB RESOURCES

Bureau of Justice Statistics: http://bjs.ojp.usdoj.gov

The National Center for Victims of Crime: http://www.ncvc.org

National Coalition Against Domestic Violence: http://www.ncadv.org/

The National Domestic Violence Hotline: http://www.ndvh.org/

Office of Victims of Crime: http://www.ojp.usdoj.gov/

Office on Violence Against Women: http://www.ovw.usdoj.gov/

Stalking Resource Center: http://www.ncvc.org/src/Main.aspx

Stalking Victims Sanctuary: http://www.stalkingvictims.com

 Visit **www.sagepub.com/mallicoat3e** to access additional study tools, including eFlashcards, web quizzes, web resources, video resources, and SAGE journal articles.

CHAPTER 5

International Issues in Gender-Based Violence

Chapter Highlights

- Honor-based violence
- Rape as a war crime
- Human trafficking of women
- Genital mutilation

Within a global environment, millions of women personally experience violence or live representations of savagery and brutality that can last for decades. You've already learned about the issues of intimate partner abuse and rape/sexual assault in Chapters 3 and 4. However, these are not the only acts of violence that women around the world endure. Some of the most common forms of violence against women include human trafficking, femicide, genital mutilation, and murder in the name of honor. Each of these crimes are related to the status of women within their communities, and suggestions for change are rooted within a shift of gendered normative values and the treatment of women in these societies. Within this chapter, you will learn about the nature of these crimes, the implications for women in these regions, and how criminal justice policies address these issues within an international context.

As you read through the experiences of the women and their victimizations, it is important to consider how the cultural context of their lives affects their victimization experience. The effects of culture are significant, because it can alter not only how these crimes are viewed by agents of social control (police, legal systems) but also how the community interprets these experiences. These definitions play a significant role in determining how these crimes are reported (or if reports are made), as well as any response that may arise from these offenses. It can be dangerous to apply a White, middle-class lens or an "Americanized identity" to these issues; what we might do as individuals may not necessarily reflect the social norms and values of other cultures.

Human Trafficking

Rathana was born to a very poor family in Cambodia. When Rathana was 11 years old, her mother sold her to a woman in a neighboring province who sold ice in a small shop. Rathana worked for this woman and her husband for several months. She was beaten almost every day, and the shop owner never gave her much to eat. One day, a man came to the shop and bought Rathana from the ice seller. He then took her to a faraway province. When they arrived at his home, he showed Rathana a pornographic movie and then forced her to act out the movie by raping her. The man kept Rathana for more than 8 months, raping her sometimes two or three times a day. One day, the man got sick and went to a hospital. He brought Rathana with him and raped her in the hospital bathroom. Another patient reported what was happening to the police. Rathana was rescued from this man and sent to live in a shelter for trafficking survivors.

Salima was recruited in Kenya to work as a maid in Saudi Arabia. She was promised enough money to support herself and her two children. But when she arrived in Jeddah, she was forced to work 22 hours a day, cleaning 16 rooms daily for several months. She was never let out of the house and was given food only when her employers had leftovers. When there were no leftovers, Salima turned to dog food for sustenance. She suffered verbal and sexual abuse from her employers and their children. One day while Salima was hanging clothes on the line, her employer pushed her out the window, telling her, "You are better off dead." Salina plunged into a swimming pool three floors down and was rescued by police. After a week in the hospital, she returned to Kenya with broken legs and hands.

Katya, a student athlete in an Eastern European capital city, dreamed of learning English and visiting the United States. Her opportunity came in the form of a student visa program, through which international students can work temporarily in the United States. But when she got to America, rather than being taken to a job at a beach resort, the people who met her put her on a bus to Detroit, Michigan. They took her passport away and forced her and her friends to dance in strip clubs for the traffickers' profit. They controlled the girls' movement and travel, kept keys to the girls' apartment, and listened in on phone calls the girls made to their parents. After a year of enslavement, Katya and her friend were able to reach federal authorities with the help of a patron of the strip club in whom they had confided. Due to their bravery, six other victims were identified and rescued. Katya now has immigration status under the U.S. trafficking law. (U.S. Department of State, 2011)

Each of these scenarios represents a common story for many victims of human trafficking. These examples reflect a life experience where women victims of trafficking have been manipulated, abused, and exploited. These are but a few examples of the crimes that make up the category of human trafficking.

Human trafficking is the second largest criminal activity and the fastest growing criminal enterprise in the world. Estimates by the United Nations (2008) suggest that approximately 2.5 million people from 127 countries are victims of trafficking. Due to the nature of these crimes, it is difficult to determine a precise number of human trafficking victims worldwide. According to data provided by the U.S. State Department, between 600,000 and 820,000 men, women, and children are trafficked across international borders every year. These numbers do not include the thousands, and potentially millions, of individuals who are trafficked within the boundaries of their homelands (U.S. Department of State, 2013).

Trafficking can involve cases within the borders of one's country as well as transport across international boundaries. Thailand is a well-known location for the sexual trafficking of women and girls who migrate from other Southeast Asian countries, such as Cambodia, Laos, Myanmar (Burma), and Vietnam, as well as other Asian countries, such as China and Hong Kong. Others find their way to Thailand from the United Kingdom, South Africa,

Czech Republic, Australia, and the United States (Rafferty, 2007). However, examples of trafficking are not limited to countries from the Southeast Asian region. The trafficking of women and children is an international phenomenon and can be found in many regions around the world, even in the United States.

Within the discussion of human trafficking, it is sex trafficking that receives the greatest amount of attention. Between January 2007 and September 2008, there were 1,229 documented incidents[1] of human trafficking in the United States. An astounding 83% of these cases were defined as alleged incidents of sex trafficking (such as forced prostitution and other sex crimes), of which 32% of these cases involved child sex trafficking and 62% involved adults (Kyckelhahn, Beck, & Cohen, 2009). According to the U.S. Trafficking Victims Protection Act (TVPA), which was passed by Congress in 2000, sex trafficking occurs when

> a commercial act is induced by force, fraud or coercion, or in which the person induced to perform such an act has not attained 18 years of age; or the recruitment, harboring, transportation provision, or obtaining a person for labor or services through the use of force, fraud or coercion [is] for the purpose of subjection to involuntary servitude, peonage, debt bondage, or slavery. (U.S. Department of State, 2011, p. 8)

Trafficked victims may find themselves working in a variety of settings, including brothels, strip clubs, and sex clubs. They also appear in pornographic films, live Internet sex chats, and on the streets where they solicit money in exchange for sexual services. Traffickers use several methods to manipulate women and girls into the sex trade and prey on their poor economic standing and desires for improving their financial status. These enticements include offers of employment, marriage, and travel. Each of these opportunities is a shield to trap women into sexual slavery. In some cases, women may be kidnapped or abducted, although these tactics are rare compared to the majority of cases, which involve lies, deceit, and trickery to collect its victims (Simkhada, 2008). In some cases, young children are recruited by "family friends" or community members or may even be intentionally sold into servitude by their own parents. According to Rafferty (2007)

> Traffickers use a number of coercive methods and psychological manipulations to maintain control over their victims and deprive them of their free will, to render them subservient and dependent by destroying their sense of self and connection to others, and to make their escape virtually impossible by destroying their physical and psychological defenses. The emotional and physical trauma, as well as the degradation associated with being subjected to humiliation and violence, treatment as a commodity, and unrelenting abuse and fear, presents a grave risk to the physical, psychological and social-emotional development of trafficking victims. (p. 410)

Victims are dependent on their traffickers for food, shelter, clothing, and safety. They may be trafficked to a region where they do not speak the language, which limits opportunities to seek assistance. They may be concerned for the safety of their family members, because many traffickers use threats against loved ones to ensure cooperation (Rafferty, 2007). Girls who are imprisoned in a brothel are often beaten and threatened in order to obtain compliance. They are reminded of their "debts" that they are forced to work off through the sale of their bodies. Most girls have little contact with the world outside the brothel and are unable to see or communicate with the family members that are left behind.

While some girls are able to escape the brothel life on their own, most require the intervention of police or social workers. Girls receive services from "rehabilitation centers," which provide health and social welfare assistance to victims of trafficking. The intent of these agencies is to return girls to their homes; however, many of these girls

---

[1]The Human Trafficking Reporting System (HTRS) is part of the Department of Justice and tracks incidents of suspected human trafficking for which an investigation, arrest, prosecution, or incarceration occurred as a result of a charge related to human trafficking.

indicate they experience significant challenges on return to their communities. Many of these girls are not looked on as victims but rather as damaged goods when they return home. As such, they are shunned and stigmatized not only by society at large but also by their family members (Simkhada, 2008). As a result, many victims keep their trafficking experiences a secret, which can complicate outreach and recovery efforts. Particularly in cases where women leave home for a job, they may be chastised for not sending money back to the family or feel anguish over having left their children. Even when victims did disclose their experiences to family members, they were not believed. In some cases, the husbands accused their wives of marital infidelity and do not understand that the women were victimized. In others, the stigma of trafficking and the fear of others knowing of their experience led many victims to stay silent about their victimization (Brunovskis & Surtees, 2012).

Despite being aware of trafficking as a social issue, many jurisdictions have failed to effectively address the problem in their communities. Much of the intervention efforts against trafficking involve nongovernmental organizations (NGOs), national and international antitrafficking agencies, and local grassroots organizations. While several countries have adopted legislation that criminalizes the sale and exploitation of human beings, many have yet to enact antitrafficking laws. In some cases, countries may have laws on the books but have limited resources or priorities for enforcing such laws. Still other countries punish the victims of these crimes, often charging them with crimes such as prostitution when they seek out assistance from the police. While grassroots and antitrafficking organizations have developed policies and practices designed to punish traffickers and provide assistance to the victims, few of these recommendations have been implemented effectively or on a worldwide scale.

Labor Trafficking

While sex trafficking is the most common discussed form of trafficking, there are other acts of trafficking. **Labor trafficking** is defined as "the recruitment, harboring, transportation, provision, or obtaining of a person for labor or services, through the use of force, fraud, or coercion for the purpose of subjection to involuntary servitude, peonage, debt bondage, or slavery" (Victims of Trafficking and Violence Protection Act of 2000). While men are more likely to be the victims of labor trafficking, women make up approximately one-third of the victims in these cases. Certain types of labor trafficking, such as domestic servitude, are more likely to have female victims (UNODC, 2016). Forced labor can also involve immigrants and migrant workers that are in need of employment. Research on a migrant community in Southern California found that 30% of the undocumented workers were victims of labor trafficking. More than half of these individuals had experienced exploitation and abuse by their employers. In contrast, studies on forced labor in international settings note that temporary migration programs, such as guest worker programs, often place individuals at risk for exploitation (Belanger, 2014). While victims of labor trafficking are subjected to threats to their physical safety and restrictions on their access to friends and family, female victims of labor trafficking are also at risk for sexual harassment and assault (Abdul, Joarder, & Miller, 2014; Zhang, Spiller, Finch, & Qin, 2014). Estimates indicate that forced labor generates more than $30 billion dollars annually (International Labour Organization, 2005).

Often embedded in cases of forced labor trafficking is debt bondage. **Debt bondage** requires victims to pay off a debt through labor. Debt may be inherited as a result of the actions of other family members or may be acquired in response for employment, transportation, and housing or board (U.S Department of Health & Human Services, 2011). In some cases, the costs of these debts are so high that it is impossible for the victim to ever depart the situation. While men, women, and children are all at risk for being victimized, women are disproportionately presented in these cases (U.S. Department of State, 2012).

Cases of labor trafficking are far less likely to be identified by local law enforcement. In many instances, cases of forced labor trafficking are hidden within legal forms of employment (Barrick, Lattimore, Pitts, & Zhang, 2014). In addition, agencies have limited training on how to identify cases of labor trafficking and lack the adequate resources to be able to pursue cases of labor trafficking. These jurisdictions also tend to lack services that are targeted for victims of trafficking (Farrell, Owens, & McDevitt, 2014).

Responses to Human Trafficking

There are a number of items of national legislation and international policies that outline efforts to address human trafficking worldwide. While there is no uniform standard across jurisdictions, these generally include three basic themes involving the prosecution of traffickers, protection of victims, and prevention of human trafficking.

In the United States, legislation known as the **Trafficking Victims Protection Act of 2000** (TVPA)[2] is designed to punish traffickers, protect victims, and facilitate prevention efforts in the community to fight against human trafficking. Enacted by Congress in 2000, the law provides that traffickers can be sent to prison for up to 20 years for each victim. In 2008, the Department of Justice obtained 77 convictions in 40 cases of human trafficking, with an average sentence of 112 months (9.3 years). Over two-thirds of these cases involved acts of sex trafficking. At the state level, 42 states currently have antitrafficking legislation in their jurisdictions and are active in identifying offenders and victims of these crimes (U.S. Department of State, 2008).

While the TVPA includes protection and assistance for victims, these provisions are limited. For example, victims of trafficking are eligible for a **T-visa**, which provides a temporary visa. However, there are only 5,000 T-visas available (regardless of the numbers of demand for these visas), and issuance of this type of visa is limited to "severe forms of trafficking (such as) involving force, fraud or coercion or any trafficking involving a minor" (Haynes, 2004, p. 241). In addition, applications for permanent residency are conditional on a victim's participation as a potential witness in a trafficking prosecution. In the 2 years following the implementation of the T-visa program, only 23 visas had been granted, a far cry from the demand given that over 50,000 people are trafficked into the United States alone each year (Oxman-Martinez & Hanley, 2003).

In an effort to track antitrafficking campaigns on a global level, the U.S. Department of State assesses the efficacy of policies and practices. Each country is organized into one of three tiers, and the United States uses these rankings in making funding decisions for countries in need. Countries need to demonstrate that they are working to prosecute the offenders of trafficking and protect the victims. "If governments fail to meet this minimum standard, or do not make strides to do so, they will be classified as a Tier 3 country. Under those circumstances, the United States will only provide humanitarian and trade-related assistance" (Wooditch, 2011, pp. 475–476). Table 5.1 illustrates data on the global enforcement of trafficking under the Trafficking Victims Protection Reauthorization Act of 2003. While well intentioned, the *Trafficking in Persons (TIP) Report* has been criticized and there have been few policy recommendations that have been implemented as a result of its findings. Research indicates that over the past decade, antitrafficking efforts have remained stable despite the introduction of the tier ranking system. While countries may have made efforts in combating human trafficking, it may not be enough to impact their tier ranking. In addition, the tier system has not always led to decision making in terms of the grant allocation process as it was initially intended to do (Wooditch, 2011).

In 2000, the United Nations proposed the *Protocol to Prevent, Suppress and Punish Trafficking in Persons, especially Women and Children*. While the intent of this multinational legal agreement was to join together international entities to identify and respond to victims and offenders of human trafficking, efforts have been slow to action. For example, the protocol applies to only those countries that have agreed to comply. While 147 countries have joined, several have raised concerns or objections to the process by which conflicts would be resolved (for example, via a third-party arbitration). So while many applaud the United Nations for attempting to tackle the issue of human trafficking, these efforts have been largely unsuccessful.

Similar to the TVPA in the United States, and as suggested by Cho, Dreher, and Neumayer (2011), the European Union policies on trafficking prioritizes the prosecution of offenders over the needs of victims, and visas are granted only for the purposes of pursuing charges against the traffickers. In addition, there is no encouragement or pressure by the EU for states to develop programs to address the needs of trafficked victims (Haynes, 2004). While the push

---

[2]Reauthorized by Congress in December 2008.

Table 5.1 • Global Law Enforcement on Trafficking			
Year	Prosecutions	Convictions	Victims Identified
2008	5,212	2,983	30,961
2009	5,606	4,166	49,105
2010	6,017	3,619	33,113
2011	7,206	4,239	41,210
2012	7,705	4,746	46,570
2013	9,460	5,446	44,758
2014	10,051	4,443	44,462
2015	18,930	6,609	77,823

SOURCE: U.S. Department of State (2017).

to *jail the offender* of these crimes appears positive, the reality is that few prosecutions have succeeded in achieving this task. Even in cases where prosecutions are "successful" and traffickers are held accountable for their crimes, their convictions result in short sentences and small fines, the effect of which does little to deter individuals from participating in these offenses in the future.

Despite the laws that have increased the punishments for traffickers, research notes that most cases within the United States are reactive and focus on the prosecution of offenders rather than proactive strategies that could help identify traffickers and their victims (Farrell, Owens, & McDevitt, 2014). While local law enforcement could serve a valuable role, most officers lack the training in order to identify both offenders and victims in these cases (Farrell, McDevitt, & Fahy, 2010).

In contrast to the prosecution-oriented approach, several international organizations have developed models to fight trafficking that focus on the needs of the victim. These approaches focus on the security and safety of the victims, allow them to regain control over their lives, and empower them to make positive choices for their future while receiving housing and employment assistance. While this approach provides valuable resources for victims, it does little to control and stop the practice of trafficking from continuing.

Promising Solutions to End Human Trafficking

Given the limitations of the **jail the offender and protect the victim models**, research by Haynes (2004) provides several policy recommendations that would combine the best aspects of these two approaches. These recommendations include the following:

1. *Protect, do not prosecute the victim:* As indicated earlier, many victims find themselves charged with prostitution and other crimes in their attempts to seek help. Not only does this process punish the victim but it serves also to inhibit additional victims from coming forward out of fear that they too might be subjected to criminal punishments. Antitrafficking legislation needs to ensure that victims will not be prosecuted for the actions in which they engaged as a part of their trafficked status. In addition, victims need to be provided with shelter and care to meet their immediate needs following an escape from their trafficker.

2. *Develop community awareness and educational public service campaigns:* Many victims of trafficking do not know where to turn for help. An effective media campaign could provide victims with information on how to recognize if they are in an exploitative situation, avenues for assistance such as shelters and safety options, and long-term planning support, such as information on immigration. Media campaigns can also help educate the general public on the ways in which traffickers entice their victims and provide information on reporting potential victims to local agencies. Recent examples of prevention efforts in fighting trafficking have included raising public awareness through billboard campaigns, the development of a national hotline to report possible human trafficking cases, and public service announcements in several languages, including English, Spanish, Russian, Korean, and Arabic, to name a few (U.S. Department of State, 2009). These efforts help increase public knowledge about the realities of human trafficking within the community.

3. *Address the social and economic reasons for vulnerability to trafficking:* The road to trafficking begins with poverty. Economic instability creates vulnerability for women as they migrate from their communities in search of a better life. For many, the migration from their homes to the city places them at risk for traffickers, who seek out these women and promise them employment opportunities only to hold them against their will for the purposes of forced labor and slavery. Certainly, the road to eradicating poverty around the world is an insurmountable task, but an increased understanding of how and why women leave could inform educational campaigns, which could relay information about the risks and dangers of trafficking and provide viable options for legitimate employment and immigration.

4. *Prosecute traffickers and those who aid and abet traffickers:* Unfortunately, in many of these jurisdictions, law enforcement and legal agents are subjected to bribery and corruption, which limits the assistance that victims of trafficking may receive. "Police are known to tip off club workers suspected of harboring trafficked women in order to give owners time to hide women or supply false working papers (and) are also known to accept bribes, supply false papers or to turn a blind eye to the presence of undocumented foreigners" (Haynes, 2004, p. 257). To effectively address this issue, police and courts need to eliminate corruption from their ranks. In addition, agents of justice need to pursue cases in earnest and address the flaws that exist within the system in order to effectively identify, pursue, and punish the offenders of these crimes.

5. *Create immigration solutions for trafficked persons:* An effective immigration policy for victims of trafficking serves two purposes: Not only does it provide victims with legal residency rights and protections but it also helps pursue criminal prosecutions against traffickers, especially since the few effective prosecutions have relied heavily on victim cooperation and testimony. At its most fundamental position, victims who are unable to obtain even temporary visas will be unable to legally remain in the country and assist the courts in bringing perpetrators to justice. In addition, victims who are offered immigration visas contingent on their participation in a prosecution run the risk of jeopardizing potential convictions, because defense attorneys may argue that the promise of residency could encourage an "alleged" victim to perjure his or her testimony. Finally, the limited opportunities to obtain permanent visa status amount to winning the immigration lottery in many cases, because these opportunities are few and far between and often involve complex applications and long waiting periods.

6. *Implement the laws:* At the end of the day, policy recommendations and legislation do little good if such laws are not vigorously pursued and enforced against individuals and groups participating in the trafficking of humans. In addition, such convictions need to carry stern and significant financial and incarceration punishments if they hope to be an effective tool in solving the problem of trafficking.

While efforts to prioritize the implementation of antitrafficking laws may slow the progress of eliminating these crimes against humanity, the best efforts toward prevention focus on eliminating the need for people to migrate in search of opportunities to improve their economic condition. An ecological perspective suggests that the cause of trafficking lies within issues such as poverty, economic inequality, dysfunction within the family, gender inequality, discrimination, and the demand for victims for prostitution and cheap labor. At its heart, human trafficking "is a crime that deprives people of their human rights and freedoms, increases global health risks, fuels growing networks of organized crime and can sustain levels of poverty and impede development in certain areas" (U.S. Department of State, 2009, p. 5). Until these large-scale systemic issues are addressed, the presence of trafficking will endure within our global society.

Spotlight on Witch Burnings in Papua New Guinea

Between 1692 and 1693, 200 people were accused and 19 were executed in Salem, Massachusetts, for practicing witchcraft. The paranoia of this region stemmed from a similar craze between the 12th and 15th century in Europe where people believed that the devil could empower individuals to bring harm on his behalf. While the people of Salem ultimately admitted that these trials were conducted in error and provided compensation to the families of the wrongfully convicted, these witch trials mark a unique point of history for colonial America (Blumberg, 2007).

While the Salem witch trials are a part of history, the beliefs of witchcraft remain alive in a number of global regions. One area that has recently been drawing attention is Papua New Guinea, which is located in the South Pacific north of Australia. As a country of over 800 different cultures and language, one of the unifying factors between them is a belief in black magic (Mintz, 2013).

Consider the following case: Kepari Leniata was burned alive in February 2013 after she was accused of being a witch. She was tortured, bound, and soaked with gasoline and set afire among the community trash (Pollak, 2013). She was blamed for engaging in sorcery and causing the death of a young boy in the village. Rather than accept that the child may have died from illness or natural causes, it is not uncommon for villagers to look to the supernatural to explain death (Bennett-Smith, 2013). "Black magic is often suspected when misfortune strikes, especially after the unexplained death of a young man, because it is said that they have a long life ahead of time and it has been cut short" (Alpert, 2013, para. 4). Leniata's death is not the only case of witch burning in recent times because two women narrowly escaped a similar fate, and in June 2013, a local schoolteacher was beheaded for being a witch (Chasmar, 2013). The punishment for sorcery is generally a public display in an effort to deter others from using magic (OXFAM, 2010). Women are most often the victims of accusations of sorcery, and it is often men who make such accusations. While the most egregious punishment for sorcery is death, people who have been accused of these crimes can also lose their land, homes, and be banished from the community (OXFAM, n.d.). The legal system in Papua New Guinea provides little help in preventing acts of witch burning and other tortures of those accused of sorcery. While there are laws that prohibit sorcery, they do little to deter the practice. The 1971 Sorcery Act punishes those who engage in sorcery with a two-year incarceration sentence, a rather insignificant punishment. In addition, people who commit murder can use sorcery as a mitigating factor. Here, murder is justified in the eyes of the offender as an act of greater good of the community. The United Nations has called for an end to witch burning, because "these reports raise grave concern that accusations of sorcery are used to justify arbitrary and inhumane acts of violence" ("UN: 'Sorcery' murders must end," 2013, para. 8). The Papua New Guinea government recently overturned the Sorcery Act and has called for the expansion of the death penalty for offenders of these crimes. Despite this strong stance by governmental officials, it is unknown what effect, if any, this change will have on the practice of witch burning (UN News Centre, 2013).

Rape as a War Crime

In Chapter 3, you learned about the research on rape and sexual assault. Rape as a crime is an act of power and control. From World War II and the Holocaust to the acts of violence in Uganda, Bosnia-Herzegovnia, and the Democratic Republic of Congo, acts of sexual violence have been perpetuated against civilian women and children. In times of war, acts of sexual assault become a weapon by those who are either in power or seek to be in power. In 2008, the United Nations officially declared rape as a weapon of war. In cases of rape as a war crime, it is not about an individual being targeted and attacked but rather a systematic perpetuation of sexual assault against entire communities.

The case of the Democratic Republic of Congo is one of the most significant events of rape in the context of war in recent history, Located in Central Africa, the country has been involved in civil and continental wars since the mid-90's. These conflicts have led to the rise of armed groups, as well as agents of the government, engaging in violence against each other and citizens of the country (Human Rights Watch, 2017a). Recent conflicts have involved the murders of men, women, and children of the Kamuina Nsapu militia by members of the Congolese army, as well as the murder of two UN experts (Human Rights Watch, 2017b, 2017c).

The extent of sexual violence in this region has led to a characterization of the DRC as the rape capital of the world. Reports indicate that sexual violence is often a public event and is used to incite fear in communities and their residents. Women and children are disproportionately victimized in these cases. While data on these events are difficult to obtain, research suggests that approximately 1.8 million Congolese women experienced rape during the two decades of conflict in the Democratic Republic of Congo (Peterman, Palermo, & Bredenkamp, 2011). Other estimates report that almost 40% of all women are survivors of sexual assault (Johnson et al., 2010). Victims are often unlikely to report their victimization and suffer in silence. Their suffering includes both physical and psychological trauma from these violent events. Ten to twelve percent of victims contract HIV as a result of being raped (Nanivazo, 2012).

In response to these crimes, the United Nations Security Council has officially noted "sexual violence as a tactic of war, which exacerbates situations of armed conflicts and impedes the restoration of peace and security" (Nanivazo, 2012). Due to pervasive corruption throughout the Congolese government, the judicial system of the DRC has historically been unable to effectively respond and punish offenders. However, recent progress has led to several military tribunals and restitution for victims (United Nations, 2015).

Female Genital Mutilation

Female **genital mutilation** (FGM; also known as female cutting or circumcision) includes a number of practices whereby young girls are subjected to the vandalism or removal of their genitalia. The purpose of this process is to both protect the purity of girls' virginity while at the same time eliminating the potential for sexual pleasure. These procedures are far from safe because the tools are rarely sanitized and anesthesia is not used. In addition, the people performing these procedures do not have any sort of medical training. Yirga, Kassa, Gebremichael, and Aro (2012) list the four types of female genital mutilation:

> [T]ype 1, partial or total removal of the clitoris and/or the prepuce (clitoridectomy); type 2, partial or total removal of the clitoris and labia minora, with or without excision of the labia majora (excision); type 3, narrowing of the vaginal orifice with creation of a covering seal by cutting and appositioning the labia minora and/or the labia majora, with or without excision of the clitoris (infibulation); and type 4, all other harmful procedures to the female genitalia for nonmedical purposes, such as pricking, piercing, incising, scraping, and cauterization. (p. 46)

While there has been significant outrage at an international level, genital mutilation remains a significant issue. Estimates indicate that 100–140 million women across Africa are genitally mutilated every year. This means that the majority of women in these countries have endured this experience. For example, 94% of women in Sierra Leone and 79% in Gambia have been circumcised. Many women who undergo this process experience significant infection and are at risk for sterilization, complications during pregnancy, and sexual and menstrual difficulties. In addition to these physical challenges, victims experience high levels of psychological trauma (Foundation for Women's Health Research and Development, 2012).

Genital mutilation is a cultural normative practice, and it is viewed as an expression of womanhood. Females who have not undergone a circumcision process are often viewed as lower status and less desirable, which impacts their value in marriage. In addition, the failure to be circumcised carries significant examples of urban legend and fear: "A girl that is not circumcised cannot have children because the clitoris is still there. When the baby's head touches the clitoris at birth, the baby will die" (Anuforo, Oyedele, & Pacquiao 2004, p. 108). Other myths suggest that uncircumcised women are unclean, that circumcision aids in childbirth, and the vagina is more visually appealing without it (Akintunde, 2010). It is also believed that circumcision helps maintain sexual purity and prevents promiscuity. For many of these tribal communities, they express hope that the practice of female circumcision will continue and resent the belief by Westerners that the practice is abusive. However, migration and modernization may help encourage these communities to abandon the practice. For example, women who immigrate to the United States are more likely to believe that female cutting practices should end. However, change is not just an American ideal, because some research indicates that women's attitudes about FGM are changing, which could lead to shifts in the practice. Here, experiences such as education and employment influence such changes. For example, women who attend college or who are employed outside of the home are significantly less likely to circumcise their daughters. (Boyle, McMorris, & Gomez, 2002). For those that believe that the practice should continue, they suggest some practical changes that would allow the cultural values of FGM to remain. Here, some suggest that the procedure be performed in a medical environment with trained practitioners who could respond to any complications that might arise (Anuforo et al., 2004).

While social change may be possible within the communities that practice female genital mutilation, few laws have been passed to outlaw the practice. However, several groups have engaged in advocacy work within these communities. The World Health Organization conducts extensive research and public awareness campaigns in hopes of educating African women about the detrimental effects of genital mutilation (World Health Organization, 2012). However, these practices are not limited to the African countries and other regions of the world where the practice is commonly accepted. For example, the United Kingdom has been a major source for immigrants and refugees from these regions. Even though people are physically removed from their countries of origin, their cultures and practices follow with them. As a result, nations such as Great Britain need to engage in outreach with these communities that reside within their borders (Learner, 2012).

Honor-Based Violence

The category of **honor-based violence** (HBV) includes practices such as honor killings, bride burnings, customary killings, and dowry deaths. Each of these crimes involves the murder of a woman by a male family member, usually a father, brother, or male cousin. These women are killed in response to a belief that the women have offended a family's honor and have brought shame to the family unit. The notion of honor is one of the most important cultural values for members of these communities. "Honor is the reason for our living now . . . without honor life has no meaning. . . . It is okay if you don't have money, but you must have dignity" (Kardam, 2005, p. 16).

At the heart of the practice of honor-based violence is a double standard rooted in patriarchy, which dictates that women should be modest, meek, pure, and innocent. Women are expected to follow the rules of their fathers and, later, their husbands. In some cases, honor killings have been carried out in cases of adultery, or even perceived infidelity. Consider the recent case of a 15-year-old girl who died after an acid attack in her home in Kashmir, Pakistan. Her crime was that she was talking to a boy outside of her family home. Unfortunately, this case, and the response by her family members, is not uncommon. On their arrest, her parents justified their actions because their daughter had brought shame to their family's honor (Burke, 2012). Hina Jilani, a lawyer and human rights activist, suggests that, in some cultures, the "right to life of women . . . is conditional on their obeying social norms and traditions" (Amnesty International, 1999, para. 2). Women are viewed as a piece of property that holds value. Her value is based on her purity, which can be tainted by acts that many Western cultures would consider to be normal, everyday occurrences, such as requesting a love song on the radio or strolling through the park (Arin, 2001). For many women, their crime is that they wanted to become "Westernized" or participate in modern-day activities, such as wearing jeans, listening to music, and developing friendships. For other women, their shame is rooted in a sexual double standard where a woman is expected to maintain her purity for her husband. To taint the purity of a woman is to taint her honor and, thereby, the honor of her family. The concept of honor controls every part of a woman's identity. As Kardam (2005) explains, "When honor is constructed through a woman's body, it entails her daily life activities, education, work, marriage, the importance of virginity (and) faithfulness" (p. 61).

Women who are accused of bringing negative attention and dishonor are rarely afforded the opportunity to defend their actions (Mayell, 2002). Even women who have been victimized through rape and sexual assault are at risk of death via an honor killing, because their victimization is considered shameful for the family. In many cases, the simple perception of impropriety is enough to warrant an honor killing. Amnesty International (1999) explains the central role of *perception* in honor in Pakistan:

> The distinction between a woman being guilty and a woman being alleged to be guilty of illicit sex is irrelevant. What impacts the man's honour is the public perception, the belief of her infidelity. It is this which blackens honour and for which she is killed. To talk of "alleged kari" or "alleged siahkari" makes no sense in this system nor does your demand that a woman should be heard. It is not the truth that honour is about but public perception of honour. (p. 12)

The practice of honor and customary killings are typically carried out with a high degree of violence. Women are subjected to acts of torture, and their deaths are often slow and violent. They may be shot, stabbed, strangled, electrocuted, set on fire, or run over by a vehicle. In fact, doing so is expected in certain cases, because "a man's ability to protect his honour is judged by his family and neighbors. He must publicly demonstrate his power to safeguard his honour by killing those who damaged it and thereby restore it" (Amnesty International, 1999, p. 12). One would assume that the women in these countries would silently shame these acts of violence. Contrary to this belief, however, research indicates that the women in the family support these acts of violence against their daughters and sisters as part of the shared community understanding about honor (Mayell, 2002).

▲ **Photo 5.1** Supporters of Tehrik-e-Minhaj ul Quran, an Islamic organization, protest against "honor killings" of women in Lahore, Pakistan. Hundreds of women die each year in these honor attacks, which are generally committed by their male relatives (husband, father, brother, etc.) for bringing shame on the family.

© epa/Corbis

While the United Nations (2000, 2010) estimates more than 5,000 honor killings each year around the world, researchers and activists indicate that the true numbers of these crimes are significantly greater. Estimates indicate that tens of thousands of women are killed each year in the practice of honor-based violence. Yet many of these crimes go unreported, making it difficult to develop an understanding of the true extent of the issue. According to research by Chesler (2010), the majority (95%) of the victims of honor killings are young women (mean age = 23). In 42% of cases, there were multiple perpetrators involved in the killing, a characteristic that distinguishes these types of crimes from the types of single-perpetrator femicide that are most commonly reported in Western countries. Over half of these women were tortured to death and were killed by methods such as stoning, burning, beheading, strangulation, or stabbing/bludgeoning. Nearly half (42%) of these cases involved acts of infidelity or alleged "sexual impropriety," while the remaining 58% of women were murdered for being "too Western" and defying the expectations that are set through cultural and religious normative values. Yet men are never criticized for their acceptance of Western culture. Women in such cultures "are expected to bear the burden of upholding these ancient and allegedly religious customs of gender apartheid" (Chesler, 2010, pp. 3–11).

While much of the practice of honor killings occurs outside of the United States (and other Westernized jurisdictions), we do see occasional incidents of honor killings in these regions. These cases are exclusively linked to an immigrant culture or community where honor killings are a more accepted practice. Despite laws that prohibit murder, the perpetrators in these crimes generally maintain that their actions were culturally justified. Perhaps one of the most recent cases of honor violence within the Western world involves the January 2012 conviction of the Shafia family in Ontario, Canada. Mohammad Shafia, his wife Tooba Yahya, and their son Hamen were found guilty of first-degree murder in the deaths of their children/sisters Zainab (age 19), Sahar (age 17), and Geeti (age 13) as well as Rona, Mohammad's first wife from his polygamous marriage. The four women were found in a submerged car staged to look like an accident. Prosecutors argued that the daughters were killed for dishonoring the family. While the Shafia family members all maintained their innocence and have publicly stated their intent to appeal their conviction, evidence in the case included wiretapped conversations, which included Mohammad stating, "There can be no betrayal, no treachery, no violation more than this . . . even if they hoist me up onto the gallows . . . nothing is more dear to me than my honor" ("Canada Honor Killing Trial," 2012, para. 25).

Even if justice officials do become involved in these cases, perpetrators are rarely identified and even more rarely punished to any extent. When human rights organizations and activists identify these incidents as honor-based violence, family members of the victim are quick to dismiss the deaths of their sisters and daughters as "accidents." In Turkish communities, if a woman has fractured the honor of her family, the male members of her family meet to decide her fate. In the case of "customary killings," the task of carrying out the murder is often given to the youngest male member of the family. Typically, these boys are under the age of criminal responsibility, which further reduces the likelihood that any punishments will be handed down in the name of the victim (Arin, 2001).

In their quest to improve the lives of women who may be victims of the practice of honor killings, Amnesty International (1999) outlines three general areas for reform:

1. *Legal Measures.* The current legal system in many of these countries does little to protect victims from potential violence under the normative structures that condone the practice of honor killings. Women have few, if any, legal rights that protect them from these harms. Legal reforms must address the status of women and provide them with opportunities for equal protection under the law. In cases where women survive an attempted honor killing, they need access to remedies that address the damages they experience. In addition, the perpetrators of these crimes are rarely subjected to punishment for their actions. Indeed, the first step toward reform includes recognizing that violence against women is a crime, and such abuses need to be enforced by the legal communities. International law also needs to recognize these crimes and enforce sanctions against governments that fail to act against these offenders. However, it is unclear how effective these legal measures will be for individual communities. In their discussions of what can be done to stop the practice of honor killings, Turkish activists did not feel that

increasing the punishments for honor-based violence would serve as an effective deterrent, particularly in regions where the practice is more common and accepted within the community, because "punishments would not change the social necessity to kill and that to spend long years in jail can be seen as less important than lifelong loss of honor" (Kardam, 2005, p. 51).

2. *Preventive Measures.* Education and public awareness is the first step toward reducing honor-based violence toward women. These practices are rooted in culture and history. Attempts to change these deeply held attitudes will require time and resources aimed at opening communication on these beliefs. This is no easy task given the normative cultural values that perpetuate these crimes. One of the first tasks may be to adopt sensitivity-training programming for judicial and legal personnel so that they may be able to respond to these acts of violence in an impartial manner. In addition, it is important to develop a sense of the extent of the problem in order to provide effective remedies. Here, an enhanced understanding of data on these crimes will help shed light on the pervasiveness of honor-based violence as a first step toward addressing this problem.

3. *Protective Measures.* Given the limited options for women seeking to escape honor-based violence, additional resources for victim services need to be made available. These include shelters, resources for women fleeing violence, legal aid to represent victims of crime, provisions for the protection of children, and training to increase the economic self-sustainability for women. In addition, the agencies that offer refuge for these women need to be protected from instances of backlash and harassment.

While these suggestions offer opportunities for change, many agents working in the regions most affected by honor-based killings indicate feelings of hopelessness that such changes are even possible. Certainly, the road toward reform is a long one, because it is rooted in cultural traditions that present significant challenges for change. "When an honor killing . . . starts to disturb everybody . . . and when nobody wants to carry this shame anymore, then finding solutions will become easier" (Kardam, 2005, p. 66). Indeed, the first step in reform involves creating the belief that success is possible.

Spotlight on Malala Yousafzai

Pakistan has one of the largest populations of children that do not attend school, two-thirds of whom are girls. Spending on education represents only 2.3% of the gross national product (GNP) and over 49 million adults are illiterate (Torre, 2013). Girls were prohibited from attending school under Taliban rule and over 170 schools were destroyed between 2007 and 2009 (Brumfield & Simpson, 2013).

Malala Yousafzai was born on July 12, 1997, in Pakistan. As a young girl, Malala became interested in politics and education and became an outspoken advocate for girls' education in her country. At 11 years old, she gave her first speech titled "How dare the Taliban take away my basic right to education" and at 12 she began blogging for the BBC about life under Taliban rule (Kuriakose, 2013). Her public profile began to rise through her speeches and writings and her efforts were applauded by several international organizations. In 2012, she began to develop a foundation to help young girls receive an education. However, she was considered a threat to the Taliban, and on October 9, 2012, she was shot while riding on a bus home from school (Walsh, 2012). The Taliban argued that she was targeted not for promoting education but for using propaganda against the Taliban. "Taliban are not opposed to girls education, but they could not support anti-Islamic agendas and Westernized education systems"

(Continued)

(Continued)

▲ **Photo 5.2** Malala Yousafzai was shot by the Taliban when she was only 15 years old for speaking out about girls' rights to education. She is a worldwide advocate on the issue and won a Nobel Peace Prize in 2014.

(Brumfield & Simpson, 2013, para. 11). For this crime, they have stated that she will continue to remain a target. While a *fatwa* was issued against the Taliban gunman, he remains at large.

Yousafzai was seriously wounded in the attack as the gunman's bullet fired through her head, neck, and shoulder. She was transported to the United Kingdom for treatment where she went through several surgeries, one of which replaced a piece of her skull with a titanium plate. Amazingly, she did not suffer any neurological damage (Brumfield & Simpson, 2013). Since then, she has resided in Birmingham, England, because it is too dangerous for her to return to Pakistan. However, the violence has not silenced Malala. She continues to speak out about the importance of education for girls and created the Malala fund to raise support for educational projects for girls worldwide. She has received a number of international awards and was nominated for the Nobel Peace Prize. Six months after the shooting, Malala returned to school in the United Kingdom, a day she described as the most important day of her life (Quinn, 2013). One year following her attack, Malala released her biography *I am Malala* (Farid, 2014).

Conclusion

While this chapter covers some of the victimizations that women face around the world, it is by no means an exhaustive discussion. Many of these crimes occur due to the status of women in society and gender-role expectations of women. Alas, the needs for victims in these cases are high, and the nature of these crimes can challenge the accessibility and delivery of services. Ultimately, reform for these victims is linked to changing the gendered cultures of our global society.

/// SUMMARY

- Human trafficking involves the exploitation of individuals for the purposes of forced labor or involuntary servitude, debt bondage, and sexual exploitation. The majority of these cases involve sexual exploitation and abuse, and human trafficking disproportionately affects women.

- Traffickers prey on women from poor communities and appeal to their interests in improving their economic standing as a method of enticing them into exploitative and manipulative work environments.

© Walter McBride/Corbis

- International efforts to combat human trafficking have focused on "3Ps": prosecution (of traffickers), protection (of victims), and prevention (of trafficking cases), but there has been little international progress in reducing the prevalence of human trafficking worldwide.

- Recommendations for best practices against trafficking involve improved victim services, increased public awareness about trafficking, and implementation and enforcement of stricter laws against the practice.

- Honor-based violence involves the murder of women for violating gendered cultural norms. Most incidents of honor-based violence are committed by a male family member, such as a father, husband, brother, or cousin.

- Offenders of honor-based violence are rarely punished, because the killings are an accepted practice within the communities.

- Efforts toward reducing or eliminating honor-based violence include legal reform, education and public awareness, and additional resources for victim services.

- Female genital mutilation is a cultural practice throughout much of Africa. Much of the Western world views these practices as acts of violence toward women.

- Rape has been used as a crime of torture against civilians during times of war.

KEY TERMS

Debt bondage 86

Femicide 83

Genital mutilation 91

Honor-based violence 92

Human trafficking 84

Jail the offender and protect the victim models 88

Labor trafficking 86

Trafficking Victims Protection Act of 2000 87

T-visa 87

DISCUSSION QUESTIONS

1. How is the concept of shame created in cultures where honor-based violence is prevalent?

2. To what extent are offenders in honor-based violence cases punished? What measures need to be implemented to protect women from these crimes?

3. How do women enter and exit the experience of sexual trafficking?

4. Compare and contrast the jail the offender and the protect the victim models of trafficking enforcement. What are the best practices that can be implemented from these two models to address the needs of trafficking victims?

5. What suggestions have been made to work within the communities that support genital mutilation?

6. What challenges exist in responding to cases of rape during times of war?

WEB RESOURCES

Desert Flower Foundation: http://www.desertflowerfoundation.org/en/

Forward UK: http://www.forwarduk.org.uk/key-issues

HumanTrafficking.org: http://www.humantrafficking.org

Not for Sale: http://www.notforsalecampaign.org/about/slavery/

Polaris Project: http://www.polarisproject.org/

Stop Honour Killings: http://www.stophonourkillings.com/

Trafficking in Persons Report: https://www.state.gov/j/tip/rls/tiprpt/2016/

United Nations, Sexual Violence in Conflict: http://www.un.org/sexualviolenceinconflict/

 Visit **www.sagepub.com/mallicoat3e** to access additional study tools, including eFlashcards, web quizzes, web resources, video resources, and SAGE journal articles.

CHAPTER 6

Women, Gender, and Offending

Chapter Highlights

- Critiques of traditional explanations of crime
- Feminist criminology
- The intersections of criminal victimization and offending

This chapter is devoted to the theoretical explanations of female offending. The chapter begins with a review of the failures of mainstream criminology to provide adequate explanations for women who offend. This section first examines how traditional theories of crime failed to understand how female offenders differed from male offenders. While these original authors did little to acknowledge gender, scholars have since looked to whether modern-day applications of these perspectives can help explain female offending. The chapter then turns to a discussion on how feminist scholars have sought out new theories to represent the female offender and her social world. The chapter concludes with a discussion on feminist criminology and how the offending patterns of women are often intertwined with their experiences of victimization.

Theoretical Perspectives on Female Criminality

Theories on criminal behavior try to explain why offenders engage in crime. These theories of crime may focus on causes of crime from either macro or micro explanations for criminal behavior. Macro theories of crime explore the large-scale social explanations for crime, such as poverty and community disorganization. In contrast, micro theories of crime focus on individual differences between law-abiding and law-violating behaviors. Since the late 19th century, researchers have investigated the relationship between gender, crime, and punishment from macro as well as micro perspectives. As Belknap reflects, "Female lawbreakers historically (and to some degree today) have been viewed as abnormal and as worse than male lawbreakers—not only for breaking the law but also for stepping outside of prescribed gender roles of femininity and passivity" (2007, p. 34). Theories on the nature of female criminality have ranged from describing these offenders as aggressive and violent to women who are passive, helpless, and in need of protection. Consequently, theories on the etiology of female offending have reflected both of these

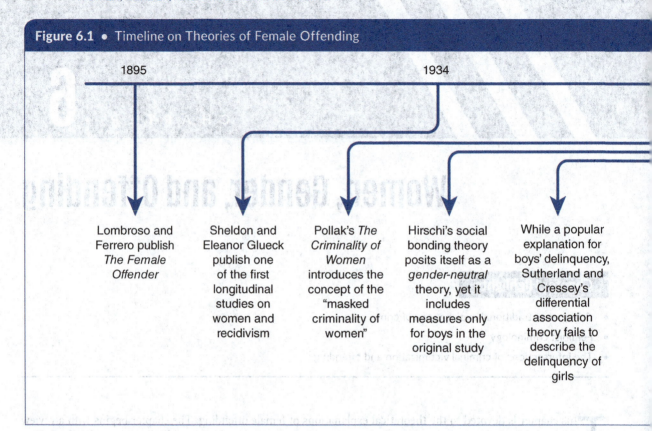

Figure 6.1 • Timeline on Theories of Female Offending

1895

1934

Lombroso and Ferrero publish *The Female Offender*

Sheldon and Eleanor Glueck publish one of the first longitudinal studies on women and recidivism

Pollak's *The Criminality of Women* introduces the concept of the "masked criminality of women"

Hirschi's social bonding theory posits itself as a *gender-neutral* theory, yet it includes measures only for boys in the original study

While a popular explanation for boys' delinquency, Sutherland and Cressey's differential association theory fails to describe the delinquency of girls

perspectives. While theories on female crime have grown significantly from the early perspectives, it is important to debate the tenets of these historical viewpoints, because they provide a foundation for a greater understanding of female offending (see Figure 6.1).

Historical Theories on Female Criminality

Cesare Lombroso and William Ferrero represent the first criminologists to attempt to investigate the nature of the female offender. Expanding on his earlier work, *The Criminal Man,* Lombroso joined with Ferrero in 1895 to publish *The Female Offender.* Lombroso's basic idea was that criminals are biological throwbacks to a primitive breed of man and can be recognized by various "atavistic" degenerative physical characteristics. To test this theory for female offenders, Lombroso and Ferrero went to women's prisons, where they measured body parts and noted physical differences of the incarcerated women. They attributed a number of unique features to the female criminal, including occipital irregularities, narrow foreheads, prominent cheekbones, and a "virile" type of face. Although they found that female offenders had fewer degenerative characteristics compared to male offenders, they explained these differences by suggesting that women, in general, are biologically more primitive and less evolved than men. They also suggested that the "evil tendencies" of female offenders "are more numerous and more varied than men's" (Lombroso & Ferrero, 1895, p. 151). Female criminals were believed to be more like men than women, both in terms of their mental and physical qualities, suggesting that female offenders were more likely to experience suppressed

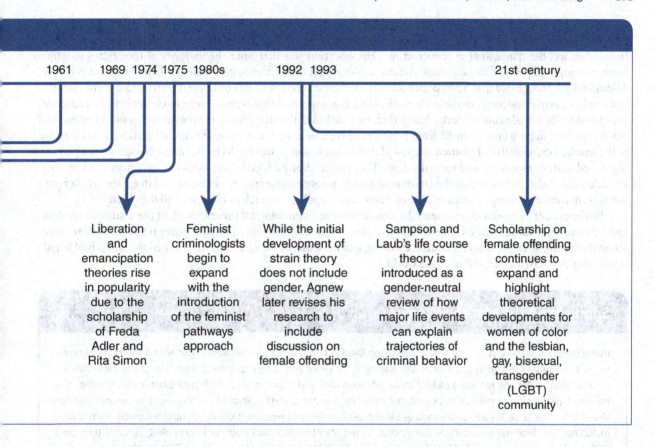

1961	1969	1974	1975	1980s	1992	1993	21st century

Liberation and emancipation theories rise in popularity due to the scholarship of Freda Adler and Rita Simon

Feminist criminologists begin to expand with the introduction of the feminist pathways approach

While the initial development of strain theory does not include gender, Agnew later revises his research to include discussion on female offending

Sampson and Laub's life course theory is introduced as a gender-neutral review of how major life events can explain trajectories of criminal behavior

Scholarship on female offending continues to expand and highlight theoretical developments for women of color and the lesbian, gay, bisexual, transgender (LGBT) community

"maternal instincts" and "ladylike" qualities. They were convinced that women who engaged in crime would be less sensitive to pain, less compassionate, generally jealous, and full of revenge—in short, criminal women possessed all the worst characteristics of the female gender while embodying the criminal tendencies of the male.

The methods and findings of Lombroso and Ferrero have been harshly criticized, mostly due to their small sample size and the lack of heterogeneity of their sample demographics. They also failed to control for additional environmental and structural variables that might explain criminal behavior regardless of gender. Finally, their key assumptions about women had no scientific basis. Their claim that the female offender was more ruthless and less merciful had more to do with the fact that she had violated sex-role and gender-role expectations than the nature of her actual offending behaviors.

The works of Sheldon and Eleanor Glueck represent some of the earliest longitudinal studies on crime and delinquency. In 1934, the Gluecks followed up their study of 500 incarcerated men with a similar study on the female offender, titled *Five Hundred Delinquent Women*. These researchers sought only to distinguish female offenders from male offenders, but this work was also one of the first studies on recidivism among this population. Although *Five Hundred Delinquent Women* was not as well known as their other works, it was similar in philosophy and methodology to their other publications. Most notably, the Gluecks looked at a variety of different factors to explain criminality, which was a dramatically different approach compared to other studies during this time period. For example, they were among some of the first researchers to investigate the role of the family on delinquency. In addition, the Gluecks drew from a multidisciplinary perspective, and they were influenced by a variety of disciplines such as biology, sociology, psychology, and anthropology.

More than a half century passed between the publication of Lombroso and Ferrero's *The Female Offender* and the publication of *The Criminality of Women* by **Otto Pollak** (1961). Pollak believed that criminal data sources failed to reflect the true extent of female crime. His assertion was that since the majority of the crimes in which women engage are petty in nature, many victims do not report these crimes, particularly when the victim is a male. Additionally, he suggested that many police officers exercise discretion when confronted with female crime and may issue only informal warnings in these cases. His data also indicated that women were more likely to be acquitted, compared to their male counterparts. Altogether, he concluded that the crimes of women are underreported, and when reported, these women benefit from preferential treatment by the systems of criminal justice. His discussion of the **masked criminality of women** suggested that women gain power by deceiving men through sexual playacting, faked sexual responses, and menstruation. This power allowed female criminality to go undetected by society. Likewise, Pollak believed that the traditional female roles of homemaker, caretaker, and domestic worker gave women an avenue to engage in crimes against vulnerable populations, such as children and the elderly.

While each of these works represented a new frontier in criminological theory, much of the assumptions about gender were significantly flawed. These early theories of female criminality placed a heavy reliance on stereotypes about the female offender as manipulative, cunning, and masculine—all identities that limited the analysis of female criminality to a narrow perception of the world.

Spotlight on the Manson Women

In the late 1960s, the charismatic Charles Manson lived with a few dozen followers on an abandoned ranch/movie lot near Topanga Canyon in L.A. County, engaging in free love and drug experimentation. He called these followers his "family." Among his more radical ideas, Manson believed a race war called Helter Skelter was coming, and he developed a plan to initiate this inevitable race war. He persuaded several of his followers to commit murder, thereby testing their loyalty and sparking Helter Skelter. Several members of his "family" followed his request, including the "Manson women": Susan Atkins, Leslie Van Houten, and Patricia Krenwinkel. Susan Atkins and Patricia Krenwinkel participated in the infamous murder of the pregnant actress Sharon Tate and her houseguests on August 8, 1969. Two days later, Van Houten joined as Atkins, Krenwinkel, and Watson stabbed a wealthy grocer, Leno LaBianca, and his wife, Rosemary. Leslie Van Houten, Susan Atkins, and Patricia Krenwinkel were convicted and sentenced to death for committing murder. Their death sentences were commuted in 1972 to life sentences with the possibility of parole when state and federal courts declared capital punishment unconstitutional.

To date, there have been many theories that have attempted to explain why Van Houten, Atkins, and Krenwinkel were led to engage in murder. Each of these women were users of LSD, a powerful hallucinogenic drug during their time with Manson, which altered their mental functioning. Van Houten had experimented with LSD during her adolescence and rebelled against her conservative upbringing. To date they have each served over 40 years for crimes that they committed during their 20s and while under the influence of drugs.

In addition, all three women also experienced strain in their family relationships, which led them to seek out new relationships for love and acceptance. For each of the women, Manson and his family fulfilled this need. Van Houten became pregnant at 16 and had an abortion, which increased the tensions between her and her mother. Strain theory can be applied to explain her substance abuse and early delinquency, because she experienced strain from the breakdown of the relationship to her mother (Atchison & Heide, 2011). Susan Atkins grew up in a supportive nuclear family, but her mother died of cancer when she was just 15. While she was a good student throughout childhood, her academic performance suffered following her mother's death. Her home environment also suffered and she ultimately moved out on her own. Patricia Krenwinkle's parents divorced when she was 17 and she had a history of being bullied significantly as a teen (Biography.com).

Following their conviction, the three were finally free of the influence of Manson. They have been model prisoners and have been involved in efforts to rehabiliate themselves. However, each of the women have been denied parole multiple times, despite their good behavior in prison and their efforts to rehabilitate themselves. Leslie Van Houten is very active in the Prison Pups program, which allows inmates to train service dogs for the disabled. In September 2017, Van Houten was recommended by the parole board for release for the 2nd time. It will be up to Governor Brown whether the board's recomendation will be affirmed. After being denied parole thirteen times, Patricia Krenwinkle's recent hearing focused on whether the board should consider her history of abuse by Manson. Under California law, parole commissioners can give greater weight to

▲ **Photo 6.1** Susan Atkins, Patricia Krenwinkel, and Leslie Van Houten walk to their hearing in the murder case of Sharon Tate in 1970. The three women, known as the Manson Women, were sentenced to death, but their sentences were commuted to life in prison. While each of the women has faced numerous parole hearings, Krenwinkel and Van Houten remain incarcerated in California Institute for Women, Chino. Atkins died of cancer in 2009.

experiences of physical or emotional abuse if it impacted their offense. While Krenwinkle testified that Manson was abusive toward her, the board rejected her defense and denied her request for parole (Thompson, 2017). Today, Krenwinkle has served longer than any other female inmate in the state of California. Meanwhile, Susan Atkins was diagnosed with brain cancer in 2008. Her requests for compassionate medical release were denied and the board stated that she remained a danger to society. She passed away on September 24, 2009, as an inmate in the California prison system. Charles Manson passed away in November 2017.

Traditional Theories of Crime and Gender

A number of criminological theories rose to fame during the mid- and late 20th century. The majority of these explanations focused exclusively on male criminality, with little consideration for women's lives. Many of these theorists excluded women from their research on the grounds that they represented such a small proportion of the offending population. Instead, some theorists simply made gross gendered stereotypes about women and girls.

Travis Hirschi's social bond theory (1969) is one example of an alleged gender-neutral theory of crime that failed to consider the lives of girls and women. While most theories up to this point focused on why offenders engage in crime, Hirschi's work was unique in that it looked for explanations as to why people might desist from criminal behavior. His theory focused on four criteria, or *bonds,* that prevent people from acting on potential criminological impulses or desires. He identified these bonds as (1) **attachment**, (2) **commitment**, (3) **involvement**, and (4) **belief**. *Attachment* refers to the bond that people have with family, friends, and social institutions (such as government, education, and religion) that may serve as an informal control against criminality. Hirschi posited that people refrain from criminal behavior as a result of these attachments because they do not want to disappoint people in their lives. For example, youth who have positive attachments to parents or peers may limit their delinquent behavior because they do not want to disappoint these important relationships. The second concept, *commitment,* refers to the investment that an individual has to the normative values of society. In many ways, the concept

▲ **Photo 6.2** Throughout the 20th century, the number of arrests involving females has increased dramatically. Feminist criminologists highlight that many of the traditional theories of crime fail to address the unique needs of offending women. In addition, much of these data reflect changes in policies regarding societal perspectives of female offending versus a direct increase in the rates of offending by women.

of commitment embodies the spirit of rational choice perspectives. For example, if one is committed to obtaining a college degree, then a violation of the law might limit one's ability to achieve that goal. As a result, one might decide not to engage in the illegal behavior out of fear of jeopardizing one's future. *Involvement* refers to the level at which one might participate in conventional activities such as studying or playing sports. The idea behind involvement is that youth who are more involved in these sorts of activities are less likely to engage in delinquent activities. Finally, *belief* refers to a general acceptance of the rules of society—"the less a person believes he should obey the rules, the more likely he is to violate them" (Hirschi, 1969, p. 26).

For Hirschi, families serve as one of the strongest inhibitors of delinquency. Research shows that the attachment to the family unit varies by gender, because girls are more emotionally attached to their parents. It is this bond that serves to protect girls from delinquency (Heimer, 1996). Likewise, research by Huebner and Betts (2002) showed that a strong attachment bond to parents and other adults serves as a protective factor for girls. However, this attachment to the family may also be related to the increased focus of parents on their daughters. As a result, when girls engage in delinquent behavior, they can experience higher levels of shaming by their parents (Svensson, 2004).

While much has been said about the influence of social bond theory on delinquency, the majority of this scholarship has been restricted to the American criminal justice system. Research by Ozbay and Ozcan (2008) investigates whether **social bond theory** can be used to explain the context of male and female delinquency among Turkish youth. Like findings on American youth, their results indicate that social bonds have a stronger effect on the lives of female students. Within Turkish cultures, the family is an important institution, and girls are highly attached to the family unit. Much of this has to do with differential socialization between the sexes. In contrast, the attachment to school and teachers is a stronger influence in preventing delinquency for boys. While studies on American students indicate that an attachment to school can serve as a protective factor against delinquency for both boys and girls (Lowe, May, & Elrod, 2008), girls who are less attached to school are more likely to engage in nonviolent acts of delinquency (Daigle, Cullen, & Wright, 2007). Educational bonds can also help explain why girls are less likely to engage in alcohol and marijuana use compared to boys (Whaley, Hayes-Smith, & Hayes-Smith, 2010).

While Hirschi's social bond theory is considered a macro-level perspective on criminal behavior, his general theory of crime (with Michael Gottfredson) is considered more of a micro-level theory. Gottfredson and Hirschi focus on self-control as the single explanative factor for delinquent and criminal behavior. According to the general theory of crime, those individuals with high levels of social control will remain law abiding, while those with low social control will be more likely to engage in deviant and criminal activities. But the question remains: What influences an individual's self-control, and for the purposes of this discussion, what role does gender play in this process? Gottfredson and Hirschi posit that the development of self-control is rooted in the family. The more involved parents are in their children's lives, the more likely they are to be aware of challenges to the development of their children's self-control. This awareness then leads to action, and parents are more likely to correct these issues at a young age. As a result, Gottfredson and Hirschi's general theory of crime suggests that early intervention efforts are the only effective tool to deter individuals from crime. From their perspective, variables such as gender, race, and class are irrelevant, because everything comes down to self-control (Gottfredson & Hirschi, 1990).

Since the development of Gottfredson and Hirschi's general theory of crime, many researchers have looked at the role of gender in this process using constructs such as impulsivity, risk taking, and aggression as indicators of self-control. However, these findings demonstrate that the general theory of crime can explain the delinquency of boys but fails in its explanation for girls. For example, research by DeLisi et al. (2010) on delinquent youth housed in the California Youth Authority facility indicate that while self-control measures are effective in predicting behavioral violations for incarcerated males, the misconduct in girls is more likely to be explained by other variables such as age (younger girls are more likely to act out) and the presence of a psychiatric disorder. Similarly, research by Shekarkhar and Gibson (2011) noted that while low self-control did predict offending behaviors for Latino boys and girls in terms of violent offenses, it did not predict the behaviors of girls who engage in property offenses (which generally comprise much of female offending patterns). Even in those studies where self-control might explain the offending characteristics for girls, these effects are often eliminated when other variables such as opportunity or social learning theory are introduced (Burton, Cullen, Evans, Alarid, & Dunaway, 1998; LaGrange & Silverman, 1999). In addition, any gender differences in self-control tend to disappear over time (Jo & Bouffard, 2014).

Edwin Sutherland's (Sutherland & Cressey, 1974) **differential association theory** focuses on the influence of how relationships lead to crime, in particular, the influence of peer relationships on delinquent behavior. Differential association theory is influenced by social learning theory, which suggests that criminality is a learned behavior. Differential association theory posits that these learned behaviors are a result of peer associations. As youth spend time with people, these people then influence their knowledge, practices, and judgments on delinquent behavior. The more that people are exposed to these delinquent attitudes and behaviors, the more they are able to influence this person. Like many social theories of the 20th century, discussions of gender were absent in differential association theory.

Recent research has provided mixed results in the application of differential association theory for female offenders. In addition, race and ethnicity also impact the effects of the peer relationship for girls' delinquency. Silverman and Caldwell (2008) find that peer attitudes have the greatest effect on youth behavior for Hispanic girls. Here, the *strength of the peer relationship* plays a key factor—if the peer group deems that delinquency is an acceptable behavior, the rates of violent delinquent behavior increase. In contrast, *time* plays the biggest role for White girls. As the proportion of time that is spent with the peer group increases, the greater the influence these peers have on violent delinquent behavior (Silverman & Caldwell, 2008). However, not all research demonstrates support for the applications of differential association theory to girls. Research by Daigle et al. (2007) and Lowe, May, and Elrod (2008) indicates that influences from delinquent peers do lead to an increase in delinquency for boys but that negative peer influence does not have an effect for girls. Here, it may be that while peer associations can impact delinquency, the effect is stronger for the delinquency of boys than girls (Piquero, Gover, MacDonald, & Piquero, 2005).

Another theory that has frequently been used to explain offending behaviors is *strain theory.* While several theorists have made contributions to the understanding of how an individual's aspirations collide with the goals of society, the works of Robert Agnew represent perhaps the most modern of these applications in terms of criminal behavior. While traditional theories of strain by scholars such as Merton (1938) and Cohen (1955) focused on the structural limitations of success, Agnew's (1992) general strain theory looks into individualized psychological sources as correlates of criminal behavior. Agnew highlights three potential sources of strain: (1) failure in achieving positive goals, (2) the loss of positive influences, and (3) the arrival of negative influences.

Agnew has continued to develop his general strain theory to consider how strain might impact the delinquency and at-risk behaviors for girls as well as boys. Research by Broidy and Agnew (1997) argues that general strain theory can be used to explain gender differences in crime. However, it is important to keep some key distinctions in mind when using a gendered approach to general strain theory. First, males and females have different sources of strain. For example, girls are more likely to experience strain as a result of violence in the home (physical, emotional, and sexual), which in turn leads to delinquent acts, such as running away and substance abuse. Second, boys and girls respond to strain differently. Here, Broidy and Agnew highlight that while strain can manifest as anger for both boys and girls, they exhibit this anger in different ways. For example, girls are more likely to internalize their feelings of anger, which can lead to issues of self-destructive behaviors and depression. In contrast, boys tend to exhibit anger in physical and emotional outbursts (Broidy & Agnew, 1997).

In addition to the work by Broidy & Agnew, other scholars have looked at how gender can impact how youth experience strain. Research notes that males and females tend to experience different types of strain, which in turn can impact the types of offending behaviors (Moon & Morash, 2017). While boys experience higher levels of traditional strain than girls (defined here as aspirations for higher educational success), girls are more likely to have negative life events and report higher levels of conflict with their parents. Yet it is these negative life events and higher levels of conflict that increase the involvement in delinquency. Some research indicates that educational success becomes the vehicle for bringing out these issues (Daigle et al., 2007) while others identify specific experiences with strain (such as a history of physical abuse or living with someone who uses drugs and alcohol) as an indirect cause of daily substance abuse (Sharp, Peck, & Hartsfield, 2012). Meanwhile, research by Garcia and Lane (2012) identifies that a major source of strain among female delinquents is relationship strain. Strain within the family (such as with parents) can manifest in behaviors such as running away, substance abuse, or poor relationships choices. These poor relationship choices can also be their own source of strain, particularly when girls become involved with system-involved or older males. Peer relationships can also perpetuate strain, particularly in the cases of *frenemies*. Unlike other theories that discuss how deviant peers might encourage delinquency, Garcia and Lane find that girls may engage in delinquent acts (such as fights) out of anger toward other female peers or status offenses (such as truancy) in an effort to avoid being bullied. In cases of drug use, research notes that gender does impact the strain that youth experience, particularly in their likelihood to recidivate. For example, youth who live in single parent homes are more likely to relapse in their drug use compared to youth who reside in a two-parent household, and that this behavior is more common for boys than girls (Grothoff, Kempf-Leonard, & Mullins, 2014).

While these classical theories of crime generally offered little evidence or explanation about female criminal activity at their inception, later research has investigated if and how these traditional theories of crime can understand the role of gender in offending. To date, these conclusions are mixed—while some provide evidence that these theories can make contributions to understanding female crime, others are more suited to explaining male criminality, as they were originally conceived. It is also important to consider how issues of intersectionality can impact these findings and future research should consider how issues such as race, ethnicity, and sexuality can also influence gender issues within these classical theories of offending.

Modern Theories of Female Offending Behaviors

The emergence of works by **Freda Adler** and **Rita Simon** in the 1970s marked a significant shift in the study of female criminality. The works of Adler and Simon were inspired by the emancipation of women that was occurring during the 1960s and 1970s in the United States and the effects of the second wave of the feminist movement. Both authors highlighted how the liberation of women would lead to an increased participation of women in criminal activities. While Adler (1975) suggested that women's rates of violent crime would increase, Simon (1975) hypothesized that women would commit a greater proportion of property crimes as a result of their liberation from traditional gender roles and restrictions. While both authors broke new ground in the discussion of female crime, their research has also been heavily criticized. Analysis on crime statistics between 1960 and 1975 indicates that while female crime rates for violent crimes skyrocketed during this time period, so did the rates of male violent crime. In addition, one must consider the reference point of these statistics. True, more women engaged in crime. However, given the low number of female offenders in general, small increases in the number of crimes can create a large percentage increase, which can be misinterpreted and overexaggerated. For example, if women are involved in 100 burglaries in one year and this number increases to 150 burglaries in the next year, this reflects a 50% increase from one year to the next. If, however, men participated in 1,000 burglaries in one year and in 1,250 during the next, this is only a 25% increase, even though the actual numerical increase is greater for men than women.

Another criticism of Adler and Simon's works focuses on their overreliance on the effects of the women's liberation movement. While it is true that the emancipation of women created increased opportunities and freedoms to engage in crime, this does not necessarily mean that women were more compelled to engage in crime. Changing policies in policing and the processing of female offenders may reflect an increase of women in the system as a result of changes in the response by the criminal justice system to crimes involving women.

In addition to Adler and Simon's focus on the emancipation of women as an explanation for increasing crime rates, theories shifted from a focus on individual pathology to one that referenced social processes and the greater social environment. One of the few theories during this time frame that incorporated gender as a major theme was **power control theory,** which assesses how patriarchy can influence gender-role socialization and, in turn, how this process impacts rates of delinquency. Developed by **John Hagan** (1989), power control theory starts with the premise that women and girls are socialized in different ways from men and boys. For example, under a patriarchal family structure, boys will be encouraged to be more aggressive, ambitious, and outgoing and benefit from increased freedom compared to girls. Power control theory suggests that these differences in power lead girls to have lower rates of crime because of reduced opportunities. In contrast, families that are structured in a more egalitarian or balanced manner will socialize their children in a similar fashion regardless of their sex. This in turn leads to fewer gender differences in delinquency. For example, women in South Korea that were raised within a more patriarchal family structure were likely to be law-abiding (regardless if they were high or low risk takers) while families with less patriarchal families were more likely to engage in criminal behaviors (Kim, Gerber, Henderson, & Kim, 2012).

One of the major weaknesses of Hagan's theory is that it focuses on the two-parent family structure; under a patriarchal structure one could assume that the father or male figurehead exerts the primary source of control in the family. As the number of children residing in divorced, separated, and noncohabitating homes continues to increase, it is important to consider how power control theory might apply in these settings. Research by Bates, Bader, and Mencken (2003) finds that single fathers tend to exert similar levels of parental control over their children compared to two-parent patriarchal families, while single mothers exert lower levels of parental control over children. In families with higher levels of parental control, girls are more likely to refrain from deviant behaviors because they view them as risky. Yet the single parent may be less likely to exert parental control over his child due to reduced opportunities to supervise the youth. As a result, this family structure may present an indirect, though important, effect on youth delinquency.

Another modern theory that has been used to investigate the causes of female offending is **Robert Sampson** and **John Laub's** (1993) **life course theory**. Life course theory suggests that the events of one's life (from birth to death) can provide insight as to why one might engage in crime and highlights the importance of adolescence as a crucial time in the development of youthful (and ultimately adult) offending behaviors. Here, ties to conventional adult activities such as family and work can serve as a protective factor in adulthood, even if the individual has engaged in delinquent acts during adolescence. While not specifically a feminist theory of crime, life course theory does allow for a gender-neutral review of how the different developmental milestones in one's life can explain criminal behavior.

Recent applications of life course theory have included discussions of gender in their analyses. Research by Thompson and Petrovic (2009) investigated how variables such as marriage, education, employment, and children can have gendered effects on an individual's illegal substance use. Their research indicates that these social bonds impact men and women differently. While Sampson and Laub suggested that marriage serves to inhibit criminal behavior in men, Thompson and Petrovic (2009) did not find a similar effect for women in terms of illicit drug use. Their findings indicate that marriage alone is not enough to reduce illicit drug use for women. Instead, it is the strength of the marriage that has an effect in reducing substance abuse for women. Adding to the discussion on life course theory and women, research by Estrada and Nilsson (2012) demonstrates that female offenders are more likely to come from childhoods that are traumatized by poverty. In addition, women who engage in chronic offending into adulthood are less likely to have consistent employment histories and be involved in healthy romantic relationships. Indeed, these instabilities may in fact lead women toward lifestyles that can encourage criminal behavior.

While life course theory can have value for understanding offending behaviors of girls and women, scholars suggest that life course theory needs to expand its understanding of what is considered a "significant life event." In particular, Belknap and Holsinger (2006) point to the effects of early childhood abuse traumas, mental health concerns, and sexual identity as a significant life event that can be used to understand criminality.

These modern theories made significant improvements in understanding the relationship between gender and crime. Unlike traditional theorists, these modern theories placed gender as a significant focus in their theoretical development. However, critiques of these theories demonstrate that there is increased need for greater discussions about women and crime, particularly given the relationship between the context of their lives and their offending behaviors.

Spotlight on Men and Masculinity

The concept of masculinity refers to qualities that are typically associated with the male gender. These include characteristics such as dominance, control, aggression, and strength (or the opposite of weakness). Like feminist theory, theories of masculinity also focus on the role of patriarchy and hegemonic ideals. But in this case, masculinity plays upon these constructs to assess how men and boys "should" behave. These definitions are socially constructed, meaning that they are created by the cultural structures of society rather than the biological characteristics of an individual.

While many of the traditional theories of crime focused primarily on male crime, few of these theories looked at the role of gender and the construction of masculinity as it pertained to male-offending behaviors. And while many of the historical theories about female offending suggested that female criminality was best described by women who were less feminine and more masculine (and therefore, more like male offenders), early theories about male criminals were viewed as an abnormal subset of the population. Contemporary theories of crime began to allude to issues of masculinity through discussions of dominance and the physicality of offending behaviors.

The work of James Messerschmidt has been influential in understanding the relationship between masculinity and crime, particularly on issues of violence. His work builds upon the concept of hegemonic masculinity, which was first developed by Raewyn Connell (1987). Hegemonic masculinity explains how a culture of dominance creates social structures whereby men are placed in roles of power and dominance compared to the social culture of women. For Messerschmidt, hegemonic masculinity is measured by "work in the paid labor market, the subordination of women, heterosexism, and the uncontrollable sexuality of men...practices towards authority, competitive individualism, independence, aggressiveness, and the capacity for violence" (1993, p. 82). This notion of maleness was something for men to aspire to and idealize and crime was a normal expression of masculinity. "Crime, therefore, may be invoked as a practice through which masculinities (and men and women) are differentiated from one another. Moreover, crime is a resource that may be summoned when men lack other resources to accomplish gender." (Messerschmidt 1993 , p. 85). From here, it is not a far jump to understand how crimes, such as sexual assault and intimate partner violence, can be illustrations of hegemonic masculinity whereby men exhibit their power over women. As you learned in Sections III and IV of this text, crimes of sexual and intimate violence are most likely perpetuated against women by men and that such acts are best explained as an illustration of power and control. Theories of masculinity can also be used to understand acts of violence by men, in general, in their search for maleness. For example, most of the high-profile school shooting events throughout the 1990s and 2000s involved boys who used their acts of violence to retaliate against individuals who were viewed as popular or who had bullied them throughout their youth. The mass shooting at Columbine High School in 1999 is an example of this type of masculine violence whereby Eric Harris and Dylan Klebold carried out a planned attack against their high school, killing 12 students and a teacher before turning their guns on themselves. The case of masculinity and violence has also been used to describe acts of gang violence (Heber , 2017) and prison violence (Michalski, 2017).

Feminist Criminology

The emergence of feminist criminology builds on the themes of gender roles and socialization to explain patterns of female offending. Here, scholars begin with a discussion on the backgrounds of female offenders in an effort to assess who she is, where she comes from, and why she engages in crime. Feminist criminology reflects several key themes in its development. Frances Heidensohn (1985, p. 61) suggested that "feminist criminology began with the awareness that women were invisible in conventional studies in the discipline. . . . Feminist criminology began as a reaction . . . against an old established male chauvinism in the academic discipline." While some criminologists suggested that traditional theories of crime could account for explanations in female offending, others argued that in order to accurately theorize about the criminal actions of women, a new approach to the study of crime needed to be developed.

> Theoretical criminology was constructed by men, about men. It is simply not up to the analytical task of explaining female patterns of crime. . . . Thus, something quite different will be needed to explain women and crime. . . . Existing theories are frequently so inconsistent with female realities that specific explanations of female patterns of crime will probably have to precede the development of an all-inclusive theory. (Leonard, 1982, pp. xi–xii)

How can feminist thought influence the field of criminology? Daly and Chesney-Lind (1988) point out that feminist discussions about crime are not limited to "women's issues." They argue that it is important that any discussion of women's lives and criminality incorporates conversations on masculinity and patriarchy. Given the historical distortions and the casual assumptions that have been made about women's lives in relationship to their criminal behaviors, incorporating feminist perspectives can provide a richer understanding about not only the nature of female offending but also the role of how experiences with victimization of women shape this process. In addition, feminist perspectives highlight that feminist criminology is not a single identity but an opportunity to consider multiple influences when understanding issues of gender and crime.

The use of feminist theory, methodologies, and activism in discussions of criminology has led to a variety of new understandings about gender and crime. Perhaps one of the most influential perspectives to date on female offending is the feminist pathways approach. Feminist pathways research seeks to show how life events (and traumas) affect the likelihood to engage in crime. While the pathways approach has many similarities with other theories such as life course or cycle of violence perspectives, these theories do not explain women's criminality from a feminist perspective. In comparison, the feminist pathways approach begins with a feminist foundation (Belknap, 2007). Within the feminist pathways approach, researchers have identified a cycle of violence for female offenders that begins with their own victimization and results with their involvement in offending behavior. Belknap and Holsinger (1998) posit that one of the most significant contributions of feminist criminology is understanding the role of victimization in the histories of incarcerated women, because female offenders report substantially high occurrences of physical, emotional, and sexual abuse throughout their lifetimes. "While such an explanation does not fit all female offenders (and also fits some male offenders), the recognition of these risks appears to be essential for understanding the etiology of offending for many girls and women. Yet this link between victimization and offending has largely been invisible or deemed inconsequential by the powers that be in criminology theory building and by those responsible for responding to women's and girls' victimizations and offenses" (Belknap & Holsinger, 1998, p. 32).

Another example of research incorporating a feminist pathways perspective is Wesely's (2006) research on homeless women and exotic dancers. The levels of childhood abuse and victimization that the women in her study experienced were "located within a nexus of powerlessness, gender-specific sexualization and exploitation, economic vulnerability and destitution, and social alienation and exclusion" (Wesely, p. 309). These women grew up to believe that violence was an ordinary and normal experience, which in turn influenced their decision-making practices throughout their lives. For example, these women learned that sexuality is a tool to manipulate and gain control over others. As a result, many of the women chose to engage in sex work at a young age in an effort to escape the physical and sexual abuse they experienced by their parents and family members. Unfortunately, the decision to live and work on the streets placed them at risk for further violence. These "lived experiences contributed to a downward spiral in which the women were preoccupied with daily survival, beaten down, depressed, and unsuccessful at making choices or having opportunities that improved their life conditions" (Wesely, pp. 314–315).

A third approach by Brennan, Breitenbach, Dieterich, Salisbury, and von Voorhis (2012) on feminist pathways identifies multiple pathways to crime. While abuse still plays a theme in some of these pathways, their work identifies eight different pathways within four unique themes. The first theme describes women who have lower experiences with victimization and abuse but whose major criminality revolves around their addiction. The first pathway in this theme contains women who are younger and are the parents of minor children, while the second pathway involves women who are older and do not have children. The second theme highlights the classic role of victimization and abuse within offending. Many of these women also experience emotional and physical abuse by a significant other. The first pathway within this theme involves younger single mothers who may suffer from depression. Many of their offenses involve drugs and dual arrests from intimate partner violence. The second pathway involves women who engage in higher rates of crime and who have greater issues with drugs and mental health. They are older and not involved in parenting. The third and fourth themes have a common foundation in that these women have been highly marginalized throughout their lives. They typically lived in high-crime areas with high rates of poverty. They suffered in school and often lack adequate vocational skills to provide sustenance for their lives. Within these similarities, there are also differences. The first theme involves lower rates of victimization and fewer mental health issues. Many of these women were involved in acts of drug trafficking. Within this theme, the first pathway highlights women who tend to be younger and single parents, while the second pathway describes cases where the women have higher rates of crime and noncompliance with the criminal justice system and are less dependent on a significant other. As in the case with other pathways, these women tend to be older and nonparenting. The final theme involves women who are antisocial and aggressive. They have limited abilities to develop a stable environment for their lives and are often homeless. These women are distinguished primarily by their mental health status. In contrast, the second pathway within this theme involves women who are considered actively psychotic and are at risk for suicide. These women have a significant history with violence and aggression.

Indeed, the feminist pathways approach may provide some of the best information on how women find themselves stuck in a cycle that begins with victimization and leads to offending. Research on women's and girls' pathways to offending provides substantial evidence for the link between victimization and offending, because incarcerated girls are three to four times more likely to be abused than their male counterparts. A review of case files of delinquent girls in California indicates that 92% of delinquent girls in California reported having been subjected to at least one form of abuse (emotional = 88%; physical = 81%; sexual = 56%) (Acoca & Dedel, 1997).

For female offenders, research overwhelmingly indicates that a history of abuse leads to a propensity to engage in certain types of delinquency. However, the majority of research points to women committing such offenses as running away and school failure rather than acts of violence. The effects of sexual assault are also related to drug and alcohol addiction and mental health traumas, such as posttraumatic stress disorder and a negative self-identity (Raphael, 2004). In a cycle of victimization and offending, young girls often ran away from home in an attempt to escape from an abusive situation. In many cases, girls were forced to return home by public agencies, such as the police, courts, and social services—agencies designed to help victims of abuse. Girls who refused to remain in these abusive situations were often incarcerated and labeled as "out of parental control."

A review of case files of girls who had been committed to the California Youth Authority facilities during the 1960s showed that most girls were incarcerated for status offenses (a legal charge during that time frame). Many of these girls were committed to the Youth Authority for running away from home, where significant levels of alcoholism, mental illness, sexual abuse, violence, and other acts of crime were present. Unfortunately, in their attempt to escape from an abusive situation, girls often fell into criminal behaviors as a mechanism of survival. Running away from home placed girls at risk for crimes of survival, such as prostitution, where the level of violence they experienced was significant and included behaviors such as robbery, assault, and rape. These early offenses led these girls to spend significant portions of their adolescence behind bars. As adults, these same girls who had committed no crimes in the traditional sense later were convicted for a wide variety of criminal offenses, including serious felonies (Rosenbaum, 1989). Gilfus's (1992) work characterizes the pathway to delinquency as one of "blurred boundaries," because the categories of victim and offender are not separate and distinct. Rather, girls move between the categories throughout their lives, because their victimization does not stop once they become offenders. In addition to the victimization they experienced as a result of their survival strategies, many continued to be victimized by the system through its failure to provide adequate services for girls and women (Gaarder & Belknap, 2002).

Feminist criminologists have also worked at identifying how issues such as race, class, and sexuality impact criminality (and the system's response to these offending behaviors). From this inquiry, we learn that women of color experience multiple marginalized identities, which in turn impacts their trajectories of offending. Research by Potter (2006) suggests that combining Black feminist theory and critical race feminist theory with feminist criminology allows for an enhanced understanding of how Black women experience crime. This perspective of a *Black feminist criminology* identifies four themes that alter the experiences for Black women in the criminal justice system. First, many Black women experience structural oppression in society. Second, the Black community and culture features unique characteristics as a result of their racialized experiences. Third, Black families differ in their intimate and familial relations. Finally, this perspective looks at the Black woman as an individual, unique in her own right (Potter, 2006). Together, these unique dimensions lead to a different experience for Black women within the criminal justice system that needs to be recognized within theoretical conversations on women and crime.

Developments in feminist research have addressed the significant relationship between victimization and offending. A history of abuse is not only highly correlated with the propensity to engage in criminal behaviors but also it often dictates the types of behaviors in which young girls engage. Often, these behaviors are methods of surviving their abuse, yet the criminal nature of these behaviors brings these girls to the attention of the criminal justice system. The success of a feminist perspective is dependent on a theoretical structure that not only has to answer questions about crime and delinquency but also has to address issues such as sex-role expectations and patriarchal structures within society (Chesney-Lind, 2006). The inclusion of feminist criminology has important policy implications for the justice system in the 21st century. As Belknap and Holsinger (2006, pp. 48–49) note,

> The ramifications of the traditionally male-centered approaches to understanding delinquency not only involve ignorance about what causes girls' delinquency but also threaten the appropriateness of systemic intervention with and treatment responses for girls.

As feminist criminology continues to provide both an understanding of the causes of female offending and explanations for the changes in the gender gap of offending, it will also face its share of challenges. Both Chesney-Lind (2006) and Burgess-Proctor (2006) have suggested that the future of feminist criminology centers on expanding the discussions on the intersections between gender, race, and class. For example, recent research has posited that increases in the number of women that are incarcerated as a result of the war on drugs represent not only a war on women in general (Bloom, Owen, & Covington, 2004) but also has had specific and detrimental effects for women of color (Bush-Baskette, 1998, 1999). Feminist scholars also need to continue to pursue opportunities to link their research and activism, particularly given some of the recent trends in crime control policies that have both intentional and unintentional consequences for the lives of women, their families, and their communities.

/// SUMMARY

- Early biological studies of female criminality were based on gross assumptions of femininity and had limited scientific validity.

- Historical theories of crime saw women as doubly deviant—not only did women break the law but they also violated traditional gender-role assumptions.

- Applications of social bond theory illustrate that family bonds can reduce female delinquency, while educational bonds have a stronger effect for boys.

- Recent tests of differential association theory indicate that peer associations may have a stronger effect on male delinquency than female delinquency.

- Research on general strain theory illustrates that not only do girls experience different types of strain from boys but they also respond to experiences of strain differently.

- Life course theory examines how adverse life events impact criminality over time and can provide insight on both female and male offending patterns.

- Theories of female criminality during the 1960s and 1970s focused on the effects of the emancipation of women, gendered assumptions about female offending, and the differential socialization of girls and boys.

- The feminist pathways approach has identified a cycle for women and girls that begins with their own victimization and leads to their offending.

/// KEY TERMS

Adler, Freda 106

Attachment 103

Belief 103

Commitment 103

Differential association theory 105

Hagan, John 107

Hirschi, Travis 103

Involvement 103

Laub, John 107

Life course theory 107

Lombroso, Cesare, and William Ferrero 100

Masked criminality of women 102

Pollak, Otto 102

Power control theory 107

Sampson, Robert 107

Simon, Rita 106

Social bond theory 104

Sutherland, Edwin 105

/// DISCUSSION QUESTIONS

1. How have historical theories on female offending failed to understand the nature of female offending?

2. What has recent research on gender and traditional theories of crime illustrated about the nature of female offending?

3. What contributions has feminist criminology made in understanding the relationship between gender and offending?

/// WEB RESOURCES

Bureau of Justice Statistics: http://bjs.ojp.usdoj.gov

Feminist Criminology: http://fcx.sagepub.com

 Visit **www.sagepub.com/mallicoat3e** to access additional study tools, including eFlashcards, web quizzes, web resources, video resources, and SAGE journal articles.

Girls, Gender, and Juvenile Delinquency

- The rise of the juvenile court
- The "double standard" for girls in the juvenile justice system
- The new *violent* girl
- Contemporary risk factors associated with girls and delinquency
- Gender-specific needs of young female offenders

While the majority of this book focuses on the needs of women and girls generally, this chapter highlights some of the specific issues facing girls within the juvenile justice system. Beginning with a discussion on the rise of the juvenile courts, this chapter highlights the historical and contemporary standards for young women in society and how the changing definitions of delinquency have disproportionately and negatively affected young girls. These practices have manifested into today's standards of addressing cases of female delinquents. This chapter concludes with a discussion of reforms designed to respond to the unique needs of girls within the juvenile justice system.

The Rise of the Juvenile Court and the Sexual Double Standard

The understanding of adolescence within the justice system is a relatively new phenomenon. Originally, the development of the term *juvenile delinquent* reflected the idea that youth were "malleable" and could be shaped into law-abiding citizens (Bernard, 1992). A key factor in this process was the doctrine of *parens patriae*. **Parens patriae** began in the English Chancery Courts during the 15th century and evolved into the practice whereby the state could assume custody of children for cases where the child had no parents or the parents were deemed unfit care providers. As time passed, *parens patriae* became the government's justification for regulating adolescents and their behaviors under the mantra in the best interests of the child (Sutton, 1988).

Prior to the development of the juvenile court, the majority of cases of youth offending were handled on an informal basis. However, the dramatic population growth, combined with the rise of industrialization, made it increasingly difficult for families and communities to control wayward youth. The doctrine of *parens patriae* led to the development of a separate system within the justice system designed to oversee the rehabilitation of youth who were deemed out of control.

Developed in 1825, the New York House of Refuge was one of the first reformatories for juvenile delinquents and was designed to keep youth offenders separate from the adult population. Unlike adults, youths were not sentenced to terms proportionate to their offenses in these early juvenile institutions. Instead, juveniles were committed to institutions for long periods of time, often until their 21st birthday. The doctrine of *parens patriae* was often used to discriminate against children of the poor, because these youth had not necessarily committed a criminal offense. Rather, youth were more likely to be described as "coming from an unfit home" or displaying "incorrigible behaviors" (Bernard, 1992). The practices at the House of Refuge during the 19th century were based less on controlling criminal behaviors and more on preventing future pauperism, which the reformers believed led to delinquency and crime (Sutton, 1988). Rather than address the conditions facing poor parents and children, reformers chose to respond to what they viewed as the "peculiar weaknesses of the children's moral natures" and "weak and criminal parents" (Bernard, 1992, p. 76).

The Progressive Era of the late 19th and early 20th century in the United States led to the child-saving movement, which comprised middle- and upper-class White citizens who "regarded their cause as a matter of conscience and morality (and) viewed themselves as altruists and humanitarians dedicated to rescuing those who were less fortunately placed in the social order" (Platt, 1969, p. 3). The efforts of the child-savers movement led to the creation of the first juvenile court in Chicago in 1899. The jurisdiction of the juvenile court presided over three youth populations: (1) children who committed adult criminal offenses, (2) children who committed status offenses, and (3) children who were abused or neglected by their parents (Chesney-Lind & Shelden, 2004).

Parens patriae significantly affected the treatment of girls who were identified as delinquent. During the late 19th and early 20th centuries, moral reformers embarked on an **age-of-consent campaign**, which was designed to protect young women from *vicious men* who preyed on the innocence of girls. Prior to the age-of-consent campaign, the legal age of sexual consent in 1885 ranged between 10 and 12 for most states. As a result of the efforts by moral reformers, all states raised the age of consent to 16 or 18 by 1920. While their attempt to guard the chastity of young women from exploitation was rooted in a desire to protect girls, these practices also denied young women an avenue for healthy sexual expression and identity. The laws that resulted from this movement were often used to punish young women's displays of sexuality by placing them in detention centers or reformatories for moral violations with the intent to incarcerate them throughout their adolescence. These actions held women to a high standard of sexual purity, while the sexual nature of men was dismissed by society as normal and pardonable behavior. In addition, the reformers developed their policies based on a White, middle-class ideal of purity and modesty; anyone who did not conform to these ideals was viewed as out of control and in need of intervention by the juvenile court (Chesney-Lind & Shelden, 2004). This exclusive focus by moral reformers on the sexual exploitation of White, working-class women led to the racist implication that only the virtues of White women needed to be saved. While reformers in the Black community were equally interested in the moral education of young women and men, they were unsupportive of the campaign to impose criminal sanctions on offenders for sexual crimes, because they were concerned that such laws would unfairly target men of color (Odem, 1995).

Age-of-consent campaigners viewed the delinquent acts of young women as inherently more dangerous than the acts of their male counterparts. Because of the emphasis on sexual purity as the pathway toward healthy adulthood and stability for the future, the juvenile reformatory became a place to shift the focus away from their sexual desire and train young girls for marriage. Unfortunately, this increased focus on the use of the reformatory for moral offenses allowed for the practice of net widening to occur, and more offenders were placed under the supervision of the juvenile courts. **Net widening** refers to the practice whereby programs such as diversion were developed to inhibit the introduction of youth into the juvenile justice system. However, these practices often expanded the reach to offenses and populations that previously were outside the reach of the juvenile justice system. The effects of this practice actually increased the number of offenders under the general reach of the system, whether informally or formally.

Beyond the age-of-consent campaign, the control of girls' sexuality extended to all girls involved in the juvenile court, regardless of offense. A review of juvenile court cases between 1929 and 1964 found that girls who were arrested for status offenses were forced to have gynecological exams to determine whether or not they had engaged in sexual intercourse and if they had contracted any sexually transmitted diseases. Not only were these girls more likely to be sent to juvenile detention than their male counterparts, but they also spent three times as long in detention for their "crimes" (Chesney-Lind, 1973). Indeed, throughout the early 20th century, the focus on female sexuality and sexually transmitted infections (STI) reached epic proportions, and any woman who was suspected to be infected with a STI was arrested, examined, and quarantined (Odem, 1995).

In addition to being placed in detention centers for engaging in consensual sex, young women were often blamed for "tempting defendants into immoral behavior" (Odem, 1995, p. 68) in cases where they were victims of forcible sexual assault. Other historical accounts confirm how sexual victimization cases were often treated by the juvenile court in the same manner as consensual sex cases—in both situations the girl was labeled as delinquent for having sex (Shelden, 1981). These girls were doubly victimized, first by the assault and second by the system. During these court hearings, a woman's sexual history was put on display in an attempt to discredit her in front of a jury, yet the courts did not request similar information about a man's sexual history because it would "unfairly prejudice the jury against him" (Odem, 1995, p. 70). These historical accounts emphasized that any nonmarital sexual experience, even forcible rape, typically resulted in girls being treated as offenders.

The trend of using sexuality as a form of delinquent behavior for female offenders continued throughout the 20th and into the 21st century. The court system has become a mechanism through which control of female sexuality is enforced. Males enjoy a sense of sexual freedom that is denied to girls. In regard to male sexuality, the only concern generally raised by the court is centered on abusive and predatory behaviors toward others, particularly younger children. Here, probation officer narratives indicate that court officials think about sexuality in different ways for male and female juvenile offenders. For boys, no reference is made regarding noncriminalized sexual behaviors. Yet for girls, the risk of victimization becomes a way to deny female sexual agency. Here, probation officers would comment in official court reports about violations of moral rules regarding sexuality and displays of sexual behavior. In many cases, these officers expressed concern for the levels of sexual activity in which the girls were engaging. In many cases, such professional concerns are used as grounds for identifying these girls as "out of control" and therefore in need of services by the juvenile court (Mallicoat, 2007).

The Nature and Extent of Female Delinquency

Girls are the fastest growing population within the juvenile justice system. Not only have the number of arrests involving girls increased but the volume of cases in the juvenile court involving girls has also expanded at a dramatic rate. Despite the increased attention on females by the agents of the juvenile justice system and the public in general, it is important to remember that girls continue to represent a small proportion of all delinquency cases, because boys' offending continues to dominate the juvenile justice system.

As discussed in Chapter 1, the Uniform Crime Reports (UCR) reflects the arrest data from across the nation. This resource also includes information on juvenile offenders. Given that law enforcement officials represent the most common method through which juvenile offenders enter the system, arrest data provide a first look at the official processing of juvenile cases. Here, we can assess the number of crimes reported to law enforcement involving youth offenders, the most serious charge within these arrests, and the disposition by police in these cases. You have also learned that the UCR data is not without its flaws. Given that juveniles are often involved in acts that are not serious and nonviolent in nature, these practices of crime reporting and how the data are compiled can have a significant effect on the understanding of **juvenile delinquency** by society. Despite these flaws, the UCR remains the best resource for investigating arrest rates for crime (Snyder & Sickmund, 2006).

UCR data on juvenile offenders indicate that in 1980, girls represented 20% of juvenile arrests. By 2003, girls' participation in crimes increased to 27%. Today, juvenile girls make up 29% of the arrests of individuals under the age of 18. Data from 1980 to 2003 show the female proportion of violent crime index offenses increased from 10% to 18%, while property offenses increased from 19% to 32%. These shifts in girls' arrests have certainly increased the attention of parents, juvenile court officials, and scholars (Knoll & Sickmund, 2010; Snyder & Sickmund, 2006). However, it appears that the majority of this increase occurred during the late 1980s to early 1990s when the rise of "tough on crime" philosophies spilled over into the juvenile arena. Figure 7.1 illustrates data on the juvenile arrests and the percentages of males and females involved in crimes for 2003 and 2012. Even though the percentage of female arrests within the juvenile population has increased over the past decade, the actual number of arrests has fallen in every crime category.

Despite the fact that females continue to represent a smaller proportion of the offending population compared to males and that the overall number of arrests has decreased significantly, the hype of the female delinquent continues to dominate discussions about juvenile delinquency. The increased attention on female delinquency by law enforcement has, in turn, affected the handling of these cases by the juvenile courts. In 2007, the U.S. juvenile

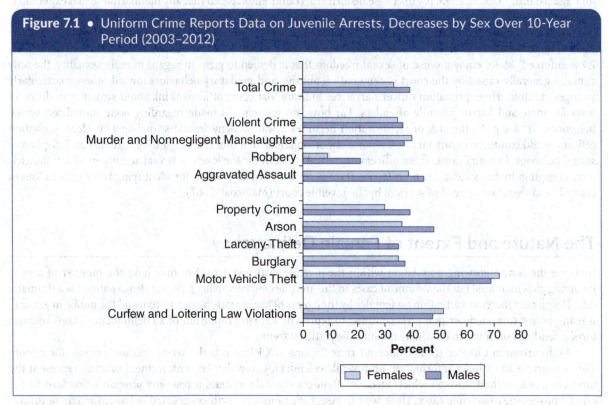

Figure 7.1 • Uniform Crime Reports Data on Juvenile Arrests, Decreases by Sex Over 10-Year Period (2003–2012)

SOURCE: Crime in the United States 2012 (2012).

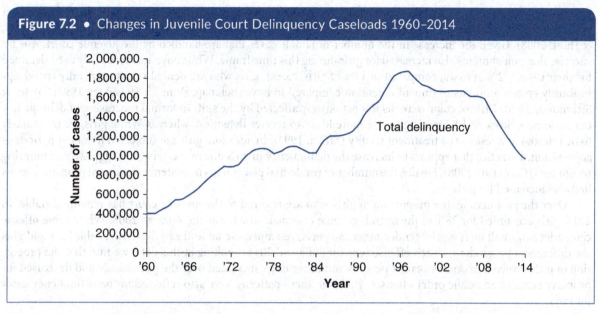

Figure 7.2 • Changes in Juvenile Court Delinquency Caseloads 1960–2014

SOURCE: Hockenberry & Puzzanchera (2017).

courts were dealing with an estimated 1.7 million cases each year. Since the early 1990s, girls have represented a growing proportion of cases in the juvenile courts. In 1991, girls made up 19% of delinquency cases, 26% in 2002, 27% in 2007, and 28% in 2009. Youth of color also continue to represent a disproportionate number of youth in the juvenile court. This is particularly noteworthy given that the percentage of arrests has decreased significantly in recent years (Knoll & Sickmund, 2010, 2012; Snyder & Sickmund, 2006, Hockenberry & Puzzanchera, 2017) (Figure 7.2). However, these trends may be stabilizing as the proportion of girls in the juvenile court has stabilized since 2005.

The dramatic increase of girls in delinquency caseloads during the 1990s and 2000s led many scholars to investigate the causes of these changes. Were girls engaging in higher levels of delinquent behavior or were there changes to the way in which we responded to these cases? Research by Steffensmeier, Schwartz, Zhong, and Ackerman (2005) showed the increase in arrests and **formal processing** of juvenile cases has disproportionately

Table 7.1 • Juvenile Court Cases Involving Girls, 2005 and 2014

Most Serious Offense	2005	2014
Person	30%	28%
Property	34%	37%
Drugs	10%	8%
Public Order	26%	27%

SOURCE: Hockenberry & Puzzanchera (2017).

impacted girls through the practice of up charging by prosecutors and a decrease in tolerance for girls who "act out." Meanwhile, boys benefit from a greater acceptance of these "unacceptable" behaviors (Carr, Hudson, Hanks, & Hunt, 2008). Given the increase in the number of female cases that are handled by the juvenile court, it is no surprise that punishments also increased for girls during this time frame. While boys are more likely to be detained for their cases (22% of cases, compared to 17% of girls' cases), girls who are denied release generally spend significantly greater amounts of time in detention compared to boys (Belknap, Dunn, & Holsinger, 1997; Snyder & Sickmund, 2006). Girls of color were disproportionately affected by the shift to formal processing of delinquency cases, because Black and Hispanic girls are more likely to receive detention, whereas White girls are more likely to be referred to a residential treatment facility (Miller, 1994). In addition, girls are subjected to longer periods of supervision, a practice that appears to increase the delinquency in girls due to excessive and aggressive monitoring techniques (Carr et al., 2008). Finally, the number of residential placements or sentences to formal probation terms had also increased for girls.

Over the past decade, the proportion of girls who are referred to the juvenile court has remained stable. In 2014, girls accounted for 28% of the overall juvenile caseload, which was the same as 2005. While some offense categories saw small increases by gender, other categories remained the same or saw decreases. Table 7.2 highlights the differences by gender for each offense type for 2005 and 2014. Looking at this data, we find that the proportion of girls involved in crimes against persons and drugs cases increased over the past decade and decreased for property crimes and public order offenses. However, these patterns were also reflected in the delinquency cases for boys.

Table 7.2 • Changes in Juvenile Court Cases by Gender, 2005 and 2014

Most Serious Offense	Boys 2005	Boys 2014	% Changes	Girls 2005	Girls 2014	% Changes
Person	25%	25%	+1%	28%	30%	+2%
Property	37%	34%	−3%	37%	34%	−3%
Drugs	8%	10%	+2%	12%	15%	+3%
Public Order	26%	26%	0%	27%	26%	−1%

SOURCE: Hockenberry & Puzzanchera (2017).

While there were efforts to reduce the use of detention in the juvenile court during the early 21st century, recent trends note that the percentage of cases for both boys and girls has increased slightly over the past 5 years. In 2009, 22% of boys were detained compared to 24% in 2014. Similarly, 15% of girls were detained in 2009 compared to 17% in 2014. The likelihood of having cases processed formally also increased slightly for both boys and girls. However, these gains did not translate into an increase in the proportion of cases that were adjudicated delinquent because both boys and girls saw a decrease over the past 5 years. In 2009, 61% of cases involving males and 56% of cases involving females were adjudicated delinquent. Within 5 years, these proportions fell to 55% of boys' cases and 49% of girls' cases (Hockenberry & Puzzanchera, 2017).

Spotlight on the Sexual Abuse of Girls in Confinement

While the historical discussions on facilities for delinquent girls and offending women have indicated that females experienced high levels of physical and sexual abuse by both guards and other inmates, it is assumed that such experiences are ancient history and are not relevant to modern-day discussions about girls in custody. Unfortunately, these abuses still continue at many juvenile institutions.

The Survey of Youth in Residential Placement was administered to over 7,000 youth in custody during Spring 2003. The results from this survey indicate that 4% of youth in custody experienced sexual victimization. Half of these youth identified staff members as the offenders in these cases (Sedlak, McPherson, & Basena, 2013). Fast-forward to several years later, and it appears that the abuse of youth in custody has increased. The National Survey of Youth in Custody surveyed 9,198 adjudicated youth housed in juvenile facilities across the United States between June 2008 and April 2009 (Beck, Harrison, & Guerino, 2010). Like previous studies, the NSYC finds that the majority of these assaults are perpetuated by staff (10.3%); 41.7% of these involved use of force by the staff member and the remaining 58.3% were "consensual" (even though state law would disagree with this definition of consensual given the context of the relationship). Juvenile males were more likely to be victims of staff sexual abuse, and their offenders were typically female staff members. In comparison, juvenile females were more likely to experience acts of abuse from other inmates (9.1% of girls compared to 2.0% of boys). LGBT youth experienced some of the highest levels of victimization (12.1%). In particular, transgendered girls are at extreme risk for victimization (Just Detention International [JDI], 2009). In many cases, staff members not only fail to protect transgendered youth in custody but often join in on the abuse (Fellner, 2010). While surveys such as these yield valuable information about the nature of abuse within juvenile facilities, the data are collected anonymously. This makes it difficult for facility and state officials to follow up on these cases of abuse. In addition, few of these assaults are ever reported to officials. In many cases, victims fear that reporting these crimes will increase the likelihood for future victimization (Human Rights Watch, 2006). While these research findings demonstrate that sexual assault within juvenile confinement facilities is a significant issue, failure to report these cases on even anonymous surveys such as the[se] may skew the findings, and the actual extent of this problem may be even higher.

While the National Prison Rape Elimination Commissions have made a number of recommendations to reduce the extent of abuse within confinement facilities, many of these reforms are costly and out of reach. Public officials have also argued that conducting annual reviews of abuse within juvenile facilities would be too costly. However, allowing such abuse to continue is also an expensive burden, because the emotional experience of victimization impacts youth long after they have departed the facility. In addition, the failure to respond to systemic abuse within the prisons places facilities at risk for lawsuits by youth and their families. In 2007, Alabama paid a $12.7 million settlement in response to a class action lawsuit by 48 girls that served time at a state youth correctional facility. The core of their complaint centered on allegations of significant abuse involving over 15 staff members.[1] While international standards prohibit the supervision of female offenders by male staff (a policy that could reduce the cases of abuse of female youth by male guards), many facilities continue to allow cross-gender supervision, continuing to place these girls at potential risk (Human Rights Watch, 2006).

---

[1]For a state-by-state review of systematic maltreatment within juvenile facilities, go to http://www.aecf.org/OurWork/ JuvenileJustice/~/media/Pubs/Topics/Juvenile%20Justice/Detention%20Reform/NoPlaceForKids/SystemicorRecurring MaltreatmentinJuvenileCorrectionsFacilities.pdf

▲ **Photo 7.1** Recent years have seen an increase in the reporting of cases involving "violent girls." Are girls really becoming more violent or have parents, schools, and police changed the way in which they respond to incidents of girls who are deemed to be "out of control."

The "Violent" Girl

Over the past two decades, media reports have alluded to the rise of the violent juvenile offender. This portrayal of "bad girls" by the media has been linked to data that reflected a significant increase in the number of arrests for crimes of violence involving girls. Based on these findings, researchers ask, Are girls really becoming more violent? Or is there something else to blame for these increases? Have parents, schools, and police changed the way in which they respond to incidents of girls who are deemed to be out of control?

While official crime rates appear to demonstrate that the rate of violent offenses by juvenile girls is increasing, these data reflect only increases in the number of arrests, which is a reflection of the response by the police. Meanwhile, self-report studies do not support this claim and indicate that the levels of violence have actually decreased for both boys and girls. For example, results from the Youth Risk Behavior Survey indicate that between 1991 and 2001, acts of violence by girls decreased 30.5% while boys' violence decreased by 14.1% (Centers for Disease Control and Prevention, 1992–2002).

A review of recent trends in female juvenile cases indicates an overrepresentation of incidents of family-based violence (Brown, Chesney-Lind, & Stein, 2007). The rise in these cases reflects a shift in the way in which families and officials respond to these cases. Consider that adolescence often corresponds with a new discovery for freedom, which often collides with parents' desire to maintain some control and authority over their children. In some cases, parents may turn to the police and the juvenile court for help. Juvenile authorities may talk to or threaten the youth or use fear as a tool to gain compliance from the youth (Davis, 2007). Once upon a time, the police treated these interventions as a social service rather than a criminal matter. But this practice is shifting, and cases of domestic dispute and minor assault against family members are now handled as formal acts of delinquency by the police and court system (Brown et al., 2007; Feld, 2009).

Many parents seek out the police because they do not know what else to do and believe that once their kids are involved in the juvenile justice system, they will have greater opportunities for resources such as individual and family therapy (Sharpe, 2009). Once the formal processing of these cases places these girls under the supervision of probation, any subsequent power struggles between the parent and child may then become the grounds for a technical violation of probation. As a result, the court becomes a new and powerful method for enforcing parental authority. Parents in turn can hold a high level of power in the eyes of the court when it comes to the disposition of their child's case. Indeed, it is not uncommon during juvenile court proceedings for a judge to consult with a parent in judicial decisions. If a parent agrees that a child can come home (under the order of obeying house rules), the court may be more likely to return the youth home. If, however, a parent does not want physical custody of the child, a judge may decide to institutionalize the youth (Davis, 2007).

Family-based cases are not the only type of offense that has increased in recent years. Juvenile courts have also seen a marked increase in the number of cases of school-based violence. Once upon a time, outbursts and minor assaults were handled within the school's administration using punishments such as detention and suspension. As a result of zero-tolerance policies, these cases are now dealt with by local police agencies. Given that girls are more likely to engage in acts of violence against family members or peers (whereas boys are more likely to commit acts of violence against distant acquaintances or strangers), such policies may unfairly target girls (Feld, 2009).

Girls that engage in violence often have a history of violence in their own lives. This is an important characteristic to consider because many girls who act out may simply be reacting to the social and personal conditions of their lives. Research by Tasca, Zatz, and Rodriguez (2012) indicates that girls who engage in violence come from home environments that are significantly impoverished. In some cases, there is a history of parental drug abuse. Many of the girls experience sexual abuse and are exposed to violent acts, such as intimate partner abuse, within the home environment. For these girls, home is not a safe place but is one where violence reigns.

Technical Violations: The New Status Offense

Like the historical and contemporary control of female sexuality, status offenses are another realm where doctrines such as *parens patriae* allow for the juvenile court to intervene in the lives of adolescents. **Status offenses** are acts that are illegal only if committed by juveniles. Examples of status offenses include the underage consumption of alcohol, running away from home, truancy, and curfew violations. While the juvenile court was founded with the idea of dealing with both delinquency and status offenses, today's courts have attempted to differentiate between the two offense categories because of constitutional challenges on status offenses (Bernard, 1992). One of the elements of the **Juvenile Justice and Delinquency Prevention (JJDP) Act of 1974** called for the decriminalization of status offenders in any state that received federal funds. Prior to its enactment, young women were much more likely to be incarcerated for status offenses compared to their male counterparts (Chesney-Lind & Shelden, 2004). While the institutionalization of sexually wayward girls officially ended with the JJDP Act of 1974, funds were not made available to provide resources to address the needs of girls. "Status offenders are not a unique or discrete category of juveniles, and they share many of the same characteristics and behavioral versatility as other delinquent offenders" (Feld, 2009, p. 245). Given that status offense charges were frequently used as the basis to incarcerate girls, many assumed that the presence of girls in the juvenile justice system would decrease following the decriminalization of status offenses. However, this decline did not last long. While youth can no longer be incarcerated specifically for status offenses, we still see cases where youth appear before the juvenile court for these cases. Data from an urban county in Arizona indicate that race and gender have an effect on whether youth will be adjudicated for status offenses, such as curfew violations, running away from home, using alcohol and/or tobacco, and truancy. While White girls were the least likely to be adjudicated delinquent for a status offense, Native American boys were the most likely to be adjudicated, followed by girls of color (African American and Hispanic; Freiburger & Burke, 2011).

In addition, researchers contend that the practice of institutionalizing girls who are deemed out of control continues today (Acoca & Dedel, 1998a; Chesney-Lind & Shelden, 2004). The modern-day practice of institutionalizing girls for status offenses is known as **bootstrapping.** The process of bootstrapping involves cases where a girl is currently on probation or parole for a criminal offense and then is prosecuted formally for a probation violation as a result of committing a status offense, such as running away from home or truancy (Owen & Bloom, 1998). While provisions of the **Reauthorization of the Juvenile Justice and Delinquency Prevention (JJDP) Act (1992)** attempted to make the practice of bootstrapping more difficult for courts, evidence indicates that the practice continues in an inequitable fashion against girls. Research by Feld (2009) suggests that acts that were once treated as status offenses are now processed as minor acts of delinquency due to the expansion of the discretionary powers available to schools, police, and juvenile justice officials. The replacement of status offenses by probation violations has allowed justice officials to recommit girls to these residential facilities. While a commitment to a state institution or detention center for these types of status offenses is prohibited by the original authorization of the JJDP Act in 1974, it appears that the juvenile justice system has found a new method to "incarcerate" young girls deemed out of control by the courts (Carr et al., 2008).

Risk Factors for Female Delinquency

Earlier chapters of this text have highlighted the historical failures of criminology to address the unique causes of women and girls' offending. The theoretical inattention to these issues has significantly affected the identification and delivery of services for women and girls. It is a failure for policy makers and practitioners to assume that, just because girls typically engage in nonviolent or nonserious acts of crime and delinquency, their needs are insignificant (Chesney-Lind & Shelden, 2004). Indeed, a historical review of the juvenile justice system finds that programs and facilities are ill equipped to deal with the needs of girls. While boys and girls can exhibit many of the same risk factors for delinquency, such as family dysfunction, school failures, peer relationships, and substance abuse, the effects of these risk factors may resonate stronger for girls than they do for boys (Moffitt, Caspi, Rutter, & Silva, 2001). In addition, research indicates that girls possess significantly higher risk factors toward delinquency than boys. For example, boys are more likely to increase their underage alcohol consumption due to peer pressure, while this doesn't have an effect for girls, who are more likely to binge drink as a result of personal victimization experiences and feelings of peer approval (Whaley, Hayes, & Smith, 2014). It is interesting to note that while White girls tend to exhibit significantly higher levels of risk for certain categories (such as substance abuse), youth of color, particularly African American youth, are significantly overrepresented in the juvenile court (Gavazzi, Yarcheck, & Lim, 2005). Given these failures of the juvenile courts, it is important to understand the **risk factors for female delinquency** in an effort to develop recommendations for best practices for adolescent delinquent and at-risk girls. For juvenile girls, the most significant risk factors for delinquency include a poor family relationship, a history of abuse, poor school performance, negative peer relationships, and issues with substance abuse. In addition, these risk factors are significantly interrelated.

Family

The influence of the family unit is one of the most commonly cited references in the study of delinquency. The family represents the primary mechanism for the internalization and socialization of social norms and values (Hirschi, 1969), and social control theorists have illustrated that a positive attachment to the family acts as a key tool in the prevention of delinquency. Yet research indicates that girls may have stronger attachments to the family compared to boys, which can serve as a protective factor against delinquency. However, families can serve as a protective factor only when they exist in a positive, prosocial environment. Research indicates that girls benefit from positive communication, structure, and support in the family environment (Bloom, Owen, Deschenes, & Rosenbaum, 2002b). Just as the family unit can protect girls from delinquency, it can also lead girls into delinquency at a young age. Youth may turn to delinquency to enhance their self-esteem or to overcome feelings of rejection by their families (Matsueda, 1992). Research has indicated that delinquent girls have lower bonds with their family compared to nondelinquent girls (Bourduin & Ronis, 2012). In addition, these negative family issues constitute a greater problem for girls than boys (Shepherd, Luebbers, & Dolan, 2013). Family fragmentation because of divorce, family criminality, and foster care placements, in addition to family violence and negative family attachment, has been identified as family risk factors for female delinquents. Girls with blended families (stepparent) are more likely to engage in high rates of delinquency and alcohol use, compared to girls that reside with both birth parents. Girls who live with just one parent are also more likely to engage in frequent alcohol use (Vanassche, Sodermans, Matthijs, & Swicegood, 2014). Families with high levels of conflict and poor communication skills, combined with parents who struggle with their own personal issues, place girls at risk for delinquency (Bloom et al., 2002b). Family factors can also serve to encourage relapse and recidivism because girls are more likely to be at risk for continuing behaviors in families where either the parent is involved in the justice system or uses drugs or alcohol (van der Put et al., 2014). In addition, once a girl becomes immersed in the juvenile justice system, her delinquency can serve to increase the detachment between her and her family (Girls Incorporated, 1996). Indeed, incarcerated girls are less likely to receive support from their parents compared to boys. This has significant implications in two ways. First, girls are more likely to experience depression, and the lack of family support can contribute to their mental health status. Second, many intervention programs within the juvenile court rely on parental involvement. Measures of success in these programs could be compromised if girls feel less supported by their parents (Johnson et al., 2011).

Abuse

Sexual, physical, and emotional abuse has long been documented as significant risk factors for female offenders. The impact of abuse is intensified when it occurs within the family. Such abuse can be detrimental to the positive development of the adolescent female and can result in behaviors such as running away, trust issues, emotional maladjustment, and future sexual risk behaviors. This is not meant to suggest that violence and victimization are not present in the lives of male delinquents, only that it is more common for girls. Research by Belknap and Holsinger (2006) shows that 58.9% of girls (versus 18.5% of boys) indicated they had been sexually abused by either a family member or other individual in their life. While sexual abuse is the most studied form of abuse for girls, other forms of maltreatment can have a significant effect on the development of girls. Girls experience higher rates of physical abuse than their male counterparts (62.9% of girls compared to 42.8% of boys). Research suggests that girls who are abused may have lower (strength) bonds to protective factors, such as parents and school, that could serve to inhibit their involvement in delinquency (Bourduin & Ronis, 2012).

Experiences of childhood abuse are often the tip of the iceberg for the issues that affect preteen and adolescent females. In many cases, acts such as running away from home reflect an attempt to escape from a violent or abusive home environment. Unfortunately, in their attempt to escape from an abusive situation, girls often fall into criminal behaviors as a mechanism of survival. Widom (1989) found that childhood victimization increases the risk that a youth will run away from home and that childhood victimization and running away increase the likelihood of engaging in delinquent behaviors. A history of sexual abuse also affects the future risk for victimization, because girls who are sexually abused during their childhood are significantly more likely to find themselves in a domestically violent relationship in the future (McCartan & Gunnison, 2010).

Peers

The presence of delinquent peers presents the greatest risk for youth to engage in their own acts of delinquency. While much of the research suggests that girls are more likely to associate with other girls (and girls are less likely to be delinquent than boys), research by Miller, Loeber, and Hipwell (2009) indicates that girls generally have at least one friend involved in delinquent behaviors. While girls in this study indicated that they associated with peers of both genders, it is not the gender of the peers that can predict delinquency. Rather, it is the number of delinquent peers that determines whether a youth engages in problem behaviors. Here, the effects of peer pressure and the desire for acceptance often lead youth into delinquency, particularly if the majority of the group is involved in law-violating behaviors.

Several factors can affect one's association with delinquent peers. First, scholars indicate the shift toward unsupervised *free time* among youth as a potential gateway to delinquency, because youth who are involved in after-school structured activities are less likely to engage in delinquency (Mahoney, Cairns, & Farmer, 2003). However, girls tend to spend less time with their delinquent peers compared to boys and experience less peer pressure as a result (Weerman & Hoeve, 2012). Research indicates that negative peer relationships have a stronger effect for African American girls than boys, while boys' delinquency is more likely to be limited by parental monitoring (O'Donnell, Richards, Pearce, & Romero, 2012). Given the slashing of school-based and community programs because of budgetary funds, there are fewer opportunities to provide a safe and positive outlet for youth in the hours between the end of the school day for youth and the end of the work day for parents. Second, age can also affect the delinquent peer relationship. For girls, peer associations with older adolescents of the opposite sex have an impact on their likelihood to engage in delinquent acts if the older male is involved in crime-related behaviors (Stattin & Magnusson,

©iStock/grummana5

▲ **Photo 7.2** Many girls with experiences of childhood sexual abuse engage in a variety of self-injurious behaviors including addiction and cutting.

1990). Finally, negative family attachment also affects the presence of delinquent peers, because girls whose parents are less involved in their daily lives and activities are more likely to engage in problem behaviors (such as substance abuse) with delinquent peers (Svensson, 2003).

School

School failures have also been identified as an indicator of concern for youth at risk. Truancy can be an indication of school failures, such as suspension, expulsion, or being held back. In research by Acoca and Dedel (1998a), 85% of incarcerated girls in their study compared their experience in school to a war zone, where issues such as racism, sexual harassment, peer violence, and disinterested school personnel increased the likelihood of dropping out. For girls, success at school is tied to feelings of self-worth: The more students feel attached to the school environment and the learning process and develop a connection to their teachers, the less likely they are to be at risk for delinquency (Crosnoe, Erickson, & Dornbusch, 2002). Additionally, the slashing of prosocial extracurricular activities has also negatively affected girls. Here, activities that involve creativity, build relationships, and enhance personal safety help build **resiliency** in young women and guard against delinquent behaviors (Acoca & Dedel, 1998a). Finally, the involvement of a parent in the daughter's school progress can help build resiliency for girls (Bloom et al., 2002b).

Substance Abuse

Several risks have been identified for adolescent females' involvement in alcohol and drug use: early experimentation and use, parental use of drugs and alcohol, histories of victimization, poor school and family attachments, numerous social opportunities for use, poor self-concept, difficulties in coping with life events, and involvement with other problem behaviors (Bloom et al., 2002b). Substance abuse affects female delinquency in two ways. First, girls who experience substance abuse in their families may turn to behaviors such as running away to escape the violence that occurs in the home as a result of parental drug and alcohol use. Engagement in substance abuse can also be facilitated by their parents.

> Jenna did OxyContin with her mom the first time. That's how Jenna's mom found out that Jenna was doing it and snorting it because they sniffed it when they did it together, It was weird because her mom patted her on the back for snorting it. Like most kids get patted on the back by their moms for playing sports or something, and Jenna's mom patted her on the back for snorting pills. It made Jenna feel like a badass, kinda cool. (Dehart & Moran, 2015, p. 303)

Second, girls themselves may engage in substance abuse as a mechanism of self-medication to escape from abuse histories (Chesney-Lind & Shelden 2004). In addition, research indicates that the use of substances can be a gendered experience. While boys tend to limit their drug use to marijuana, girls experiment with and abuse a variety of substances, including methamphetamines, cocaine, acid, crack, and huffing chemicals. Not only did their poly-drug use indicate significant addiction issues but their substance abuse also altered their decision-making abilities, influenced their criminal behaviors, and placed them at risk for danger (Mallicoat, 2007). While substance abuse increases the risk for delinquency for girls, the absence of substance abuse serves as a protective factor against delinquency (McKnight & Loper, 2002).

Finally, girls may use illicit substances as an escape from the violence that they have observed in their communities. Often this trauma is a precursor for offending, because it is present long before girls begin to engage in at-risk or delinquent behavior. From viewing murders in their neighborhood to, such events have a damaging impact on the development of youth. In a study of 100 girls involved in the juvenile justice system, 90% had witnessed violence, ranging from witnessing a violent attack with a weapon (55%) to having a close friend or family member who was murdered (46%). Over a third of girls (35%) had witnessed a murder. One girl described an event where she observed a man and woman arguing. "He took a gun out of his back pocket. . . . There was brain everywhere. That image . . . it was terrifying" (DeHart & Moran, 2015, p. 303). Here, violence prevention programs in school and community-based programs could assist in healing these wounds rather than waiting for aggressive and self-harming behaviors to escalate to the point of requiring attention from the juvenile justice system.

Mental Health

Youth in custody experience high rates of trauma throughout the course of their lives. Girls experience higher rates of emotional trauma than boys. (See Hennessey, Ford, Mahoney, Ko, & Siegfried, 2004, for a review of the literature.) For many youth, these traumas place them at risk for post-traumatic stress disorder (Shufelt & Cocozza, 2006) and suicidal ideation. Girls are also more likely to engage in self-injurious behaviors (Shepherd, Luebbers, & Dolan, 2013). This is particularly important for girls under custody because 45% of girls in detention indicated that they had attempted suicide at some point in their lives (Belknap & Holsinger, 2006). Girls are also more likely to suffer from anxiety-related disorders, which typically stem from early childhood experiences with abuse and victimization. In many instances, these anxiety-related disorders are co-occurring with substance abuse and addiction, which can create unique challenges for programming and treatment (Shufelt & Cocozza, 2006). It is important for the juvenile justice system to note and respond to these issues. Unfortunately, many detention facilities are ill equipped to deal with the mental health needs of youth in custody, and these girls end up falling through the cracks. A failure by the system to effectively recognize the mental health needs of delinquent girls not only places these youth at risk for future harm but also places them at risk for increased involvement with the system (Hennessey et al., 2004).

Meeting the Unique Needs of Delinquent Girls

While girls may make up a minority of offenders in the juvenile justice system, their needs should not be absent from juvenile justice policies. As indicated earlier, girls have a number of different and interrelated issues that historically have been ignored by the system. The 1992 Reauthorization of the Juvenile Justice and Delinquency Prevention Act acknowledged the need to provide gender-specific services to address the unique needs of female offenders. Over the past two decades, research has highlighted the factors that may affect a young woman's road to delinquency, and the reauthorization of the JJDP mandates that states incorporate this understanding into the assessment tools and programming options for girls.

What should **gender-specific programming** for girls look like? Programs must be able to address the wide variety of needs of the delinquent girl; given that many of the risk factors for delinquency involve a web of interrelated issues, programs need to be able to address this tangled web of needs rather than attempt to deal with issues on an individual and isolated basis. Research identifies that a history of victimization is the most significant issue facing at-risk and delinquent girls. According to Belknap & Holsinger (2006), 55.8% of girls believe that their experiences with abuse throughout their childhood had an effect on their offending behaviors. The prevalent nature of a victimization history in adolescent females raises this issue to one of central importance in gender-specific programming. Not only do programs need to provide counseling services for both boys and girls that focus on the trauma in their lives but placement services for youth need to be expanded as well. Given that many girls run away from home to escape an abusive environment, punishment in detention is not an appropriate place for girls. Because early childhood victimization often leads to risky sexual behaviors with the conclusion of teenage pregnancy and parenthood, education should be offered to these girls as a preventive measure for pregnancy and sexually transmitted diseases. However, it is important to remember that not even gender responsive programming is a one-size-fits-all-girls model. For girls that have gender-sensitive risk factors such as a history of trauma or physical/mental health needs, gender responsive programming is helpful in preventing recidivism. However, for girls that do not have a abuse history, such programs can actually lead to higher risks for recidivism (Day, Zahn, & Tichavsky, 2015).

Spotlight on Arts Programming and At-Risk Youth

Once upon a time, schools offered arts programming as part of a child's education. Courses in the visual arts and music were as much a part of the curriculum as math and science. However, budget cuts and an emphasis on standardized testing has led to the minimization or cancelation of arts-related programming. The loss of the arts has had a significant effect on the academic successes of our youth population. Research from the National Education Longitudinal Study of 1988 tells us that children who have a rich experience with the arts demonstrate greater achievements in science and writing and a higher GPA compared to those with a lower engagement in the arts. In addition, these youth were more likely to attend college (71% compared to 48%) and receive an associate's (24% compared to 10%) or bachelor's degree (18% compared to 6%). In addition, the effect of art-related education is stronger for those kids with a lower socioeconomic status background (Catterall, Dumais, & Hampden-Thompson, 2012).

Arts education programming has been shown to have a positive impact on the lives of at-risk youth. In their evaluation of three arts education programs, the YouthARTS development project has identified that participation in these programs not only provided youth with a positive outlet to express their emotions and to develop their communication skills but these experiences have also had an impact on recidivism rates for juvenile participants. Not only did the youth in the program receive fewer juvenile court referrals but their offenses were [also] less serious for those that did engage in delinquency (Americans for the Arts, 2000). Arts-related programming has also had a significant impact on youth in custody. Youth that participated in a visual arts program while in juvenile detention demonstrated significantly lower rates of misbehavior (63%), which increased the time that staff could use for positive interactions, versus disciplinary actions (Ezell & Levy, 2003).

But what about girls? Few of the arts education programs in practice utilize gender-responsive practices. The Share Art Program in Flint, Michigan, began as a coed program with youth incarcerated at the Genesee Valley Regional Center. The program focuses on visual art and spoken-word poetry as ways that the youth can express themselves and make sense of their lives, which are often very chaotic. As a short-term detention facility, youth serve an average of 21 days, which gives program providers a limited time with most of the youth. In an effort to meet the unique needs of the girls in the facility, the Share Art Program adapted their program design to reflect gender-responsive practices. The female-only environment provided the opportunity for the girls to have a safe space to share their emotions through their art, and as they developed their writing, the girls began to feel more confident about their abilities. Through their poetry, the girls began to explore their histories, life experiences, and their visions for the future. Many of the girls commented that the program not only increased their self-confidence but also provided them with a skill set to work through their emotions and decision-making processes. In addition, the girls learned how to work with others and build a support network. Finally, the staff of the program also served as important role models for the girls. By creating a space where the girls could focus on the risk and resiliency factors in their lives, the program was able to effectively serve the needs for this female population and provided a valuable resource for the community (Rosenbaum & Spivack, 2013).

As in the case of the needs of high-risk pregnancies, juvenile justice facilities are often ill equipped to deal with the physical and mental health needs of incarcerated females (Tille & Rose, 2007). The emotional needs of developing teenagers, combined with the increase in the prevalence of mental health disorders of incarcerated females, makes this an important component for gender-specific programming for female populations. Physical and mental health complaints by youth need to be interpreted by staff and facilities as a need, not as a complaining or manipulating behavior. Additionally, such interventions must be established on an ongoing basis for continual care, versus limited to an episodic basis (Acoca & Dedel, 1998a).

When designing programs for youth, it is important to consider the variety of different backgrounds and cultures that delinquent girls come from, because this impacts not only their pathways to offending but also affects how they will respond to interventions. Research has indicated that race and ethnicity impact the pathways of girls to the juvenile justice system. While White females experience higher levels of physical and sexual abuse and substance abuse compared to African American girls, the abuse of girls of color remains high. Seventy percent of Black girls indicate a history of physical abuse, and 46% have been sexually abused in their lifetime (compared to 90% of White girls who are physically abused and 62% who are sexually abused; Holsinger & Holsinger, 2005). Other research shows that factors such as lack of parental monitoring, antisocial attitudes, school commitment, and peer pressure can be used to explain delinquency among girls in the Hmong community (Ciong & Huang, 2011).

These factors can alter the way in which girls respond to these experiences. White girls are more likely to engage in self-injurious behaviors compared to girls of color. Here, it appears that White girls are more likely to respond to the abuse experience through internally harming behaviors, whereas girls of color are more likely to engage in outward displays of violence (Holsinger & Holsinger, 2005). The greatest long-term successes come from programs that provide support, not just for the individual girl but for her extended family as well. Unfortunately, many family members resist being involved in programming, because they fail to accept responsibility for the role that they may have played in the development of their daughter's delinquency (Bloom, Owen, Deschenes, & Rosenbaum, 2002a). This lack of involvement raises significant concerns for the family environment of these girls. Although more than one half of girls reported that they do not get along with their parents (51%) and the view that their relationship with their parents contributed to their delinquency (59%), 66% of the girls stated that they would return to live with their parents following their release from custody. This is particularly concerning given that 58% of the girls surveyed reported experiencing some form of violence in the home. It is impossible to develop programs for incarcerated females without reevaluating policies that contribute to the destruction of the family. Gender-specific programming for adolescent females needs to focus on rebuilding the family unit and developing positive role modeling. Here, programs such as family counseling and family substance abuse treatment models can positively affect troubled families.

Spotlight on Girls' Voices

As you learned in earlier chapters of this text, listening to the stories of women and girls is one of the key strengths of feminist research methods. From this type of research, we learn that girls have a lot to share about their lives [and] their experiences with the juvenile justice and criminal justice systems and have ideas about what they need to improve their lives. Research tells us that girls benefit from a structured environment and that tools such as effective discipline, expectations for behavior, and guidance can provide valuable support for girls (Garcia & Lane 2010). Many of the girls in these research studies discuss the power that a positive role model has for their lives. Strong female staff within the juvenile justice system (and related

(Continued)

(Continued)

ancillary organizations) can serve as mentors for girls and provide valuable mentorship support and guidance for girls (Bright, Ward, & Negi 2011). As one female who had spent time in a juvenile facility indicated about the power of a positive mentor, "we depend on that support and that bond with somebody that we can talk to and trust and confide in" (Bright, Ward, & Negi, p. 2011, p. 38). While girls echo the need for therapeutic resources to address drug addiction and victimization histories, they also believe that developing independent life skills and reentry programming is essential in preventing recidivism as a girl transitions into adulthood (Garcia & Lane, 2010). Beyond discussions about the types of programming and the role of mentors in their lives, this research provides a vivid picture of the environments that these girls come from—and ultimately will return to.

The economic marginality that surrounds the lives of girls impacts their future outlooks for success. For many of the girls, what they see within their own families and communities is all they know. To hope and aspire for a better life simply seems like a dream that is out of reach. As a result, many young girls submit themselves to a life filled with violence:

> I came from the ghetto. And people didn't go to college. They barely made it out of high school, if they made it out of high school. So it's not normal for us to think, you know it's just not something that crosses our minds. (Garcia & Lane, 2010, p. 237)

Regardless of the successes that girls may experience within the juvenile justice system, the reality is that these girls will most likely return to the chaotic environments of their families and communities. While some girls fight to maintain the positive changes in their lives by working toward goals for their future, others reference that these will be an uphill battle based on the environments in which they reside:

> It was just harsh, hard. You had to be a rough kid. . . . It was a place that should have been condemned a long time ago. Every day people getting shot. You stand on the sidewalk, you know, somebody running by with a gun, kids getting ran over, people sneaking in people's windows, raping people. (Bright, Ward, & Negi, 2011, p. 40)

For other girls, returning to the juvenile system represents perhaps the safest place for them. Given the economic marginality, violence, and chaos that encompass their lives, it is no surprise that a structured orderly environment that provides food, clothing, and shelter is viewed as a favorable option, even if it means being incarcerated. For families that are involved in abusive and criminal behaviors, a return home for the youth can also mean a return to the behaviors that led them to the juvenile court in the first place.

> Here I am back on the streets and if I do this again and get into trouble then I'm just gonna go back to a place where they are gonna feed me and I don't have to worry about somebody beatin' me there; I don't have to worry about somebody molestin' me there, you know? (Garcia & Lane, 2010, p. 235)

> I think if they would have kept me in longer, I think I probably would have been better off than what I am now. When I first got out . . . I was doing good here. . . . Then I got out of the little program and stuff, came back over here [living at home], and everybody was still doing the same thing they was doing, and I fell right back into the habit. (Morash, Stevens, & Yingling, 2014)

Although traditional research on female offenders has focused on the risk factors that lead to negative behaviors, recent research has shifted to include resiliency or protective factors to fight against the risks of delinquent behavior. These factors include intelligence; brilliance; courage; creativity; tenacity; compassion; humor; insightfulness; social competence; problem-solving abilities; autonomy; potential with leadership; engagement in family, community, and religious activities; and a sense of purpose and belief in the future. While these resiliency factors typically develop within the context of the family, the support for such a curriculum needs to come from somewhere else, since many delinquent girls often come from families in crisis (Acoca & Dedel, 1998a). Research notes that participating in programs that are gender responsive and focus on building resiliency are not only effective in increasing coping skills for life challenges and improving participants' abilities to develop long range goals but engagement in at-risk behaviors and psychological distress also decrease (Javdani & Allen, 2016).

While the intent to provide gender-specific services indicated a potential to address the unique needs of girls, not all scholars are convinced that girls will be able to receive the treatment and programs that are so desperately needed. While many states embarked on data-heavy assessments reflecting the needs of girls, few of these adventures have translated into effective programmatic changes (Chesney-Lind & Shelden, 2004). Funding remains the most significant barrier in providing effective services for girls. Even when gender-specific programming options exist, the need for these services can outweigh the available options. The limited number of placements, combined with long waiting lists for such services, often makes treatment options unavailable for most girls (Bloom et al., 2002a). However, several individual and community factors also affect program delivery, including lack of information or difficulties in accessing services, resistance toward programming by girls and their families, and distrust of service providers. In addition, racial, economic, and cultural issues can affect whether communities will seek out assistance and the degree to which these services will reflect culturally relevant issues (Bloom et al., 2002b). To develop effective and available programming, the system needs to place the allocation of resources as a priority in identifying and addressing the needs of girls in the juvenile justice system.

/// SUMMARY

- Arrest data and self-report data present contradictory images on the nature and prevalence of female violence.

- While arrests for violent offenses involving girls have increased, self-report data among girls indicate a decrease in the levels of violence.

- Police and the courts have altered the way in which they respond to cases of female delinquency, particularly in cases of family or school violence.

- Many incidents of family violence stem from symbolic struggles for adolescent freedom between girls and their parents.

- For juvenile girls, the most significant risk factors for delinquency include a poor family relationship, a history of abuse, poor school performance, negative peer relationships, and issues with substance abuse.

- Issues of emotional and mental health are a high area of need for delinquent girls.

- Effective gender-specific programming needs to provide long-term programming for girls and their social support network that addresses the causes of delinquency in girls' lives.

- Programming that includes resiliency or protective factors plays a significant role in gender-specific programming.

- Programs face significant barriers in implementing services for girls.

/// KEY TERMS

Age-of-consent
    campaign 114

Bootstrapping 121

Formal processing 117

Gender-specific
    programming 125

Juvenile delinquency 116

Juvenile Justice and
    Delinquency Prevention (JJDP)
    Act of 1974 121

Net widening 114

Parens patriae 113

Reauthorization of the Juvenile
    Justice and Delinquency

Prevention (JJDP) Act
    (1992) 121

Resiliency 124

Risk factors for female
    delinquency 122

Status offenses 121

/// DISCUSSION QUESTIONS

1. How did the age-of-consent campaign punish girls and deny healthy expressions of sexuality? What effects of this movement remain today?

2. How have girls continued to be punished for status offenses, despite the enactment of the JJDP Act of 1974?

3. What risk factors for delinquency exist for girls?

4. How has the treatment of girls by the juvenile justice system altered society's understanding of violence among girls?

5. What should gender-specific programming look like? What challenges do states face in implementing these programs?

/// WEB RESOURCES

Girls Study Group: http://girlsstudygroup.rti.org/

National Center for Juvenile Justice: http://www.ncjj.org

Office of Juvenile Justice and Delinquency Prevention: http://www.ojjdp.gov

 Visit **www.sagepub.com/mallicoat3e** to access additional study tools, including eFlashcards, web quizzes, web resources, video resources, and SAGE journal articles.

Female Offenders and Their Crimes

Women engage in every type of criminal activity. Much like their male counterparts, females are involved in a variety of different types of crime. While female crimes of violence are highly sensationalized by the media, these crimes are rare occurrences. Instead, the majority of female offending is made up of crimes that are nonviolent in nature or are considered victimless crimes, such as drug abuse and sexually based offenses.

Males have always engaged in greater numbers of criminal acts. However, women are becoming more involved in crime and the criminal justice system. Research over the past several decades has focused on the narrowing of the gender gap, which refers to the differences in male and female offending for different types of offenses. But what does this really mean? Are women becoming more violent than they were in the past, as media reports have suggested? Is the rise in women's incarceration a result of more women engaging in serious criminal acts? What contributes to these changes? How do we investigate these questions?

In Chapter 1, you learned about the changes in male and female crime participation over a 1-year and 10-year period, using arrest data from the Uniform Crime Reports. Using these same data, we can investigate the gender gap in offending. Figure 8.1 and Table 8.1 compares the percentage of males and females in different offense types. These data illustrate that the proportion of violent crime cases is far greater for males than females. In contrast, the proportion of property crimes is greater for females than males, because property crimes make up 84.6% of all female arrests, compared to 69.3% of male arrests. While these data illustrate that the gender gap may be narrowing in terms of gender proportions of crime, it is important to note that the number of male arrests

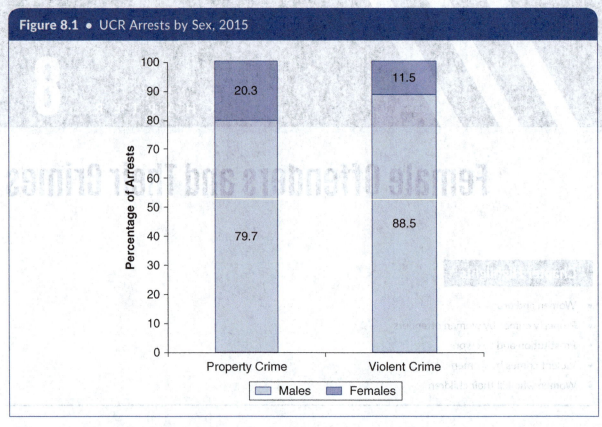

Figure 8.1 • UCR Arrests by Sex, 2015

SOURCE: Crime in the United States 2015. https://ucr.fbi.gov/crime-in-the-u.s/2015/crime-in-the-u.s.-2015/tables/table-42.

is twice that of the number of arrests of women for index crimes and almost three times greater than the number of arrests for all crimes.

Arrest trends over time also demonstrate an overall decrease in violent crimes for both men and women, but they show an increase in property crimes for women. Table 8.2 demonstrates the 5- and 10-year trends in male and female arrests from 2006 to 2015. For example, between 2011 and 2015, women's arrests in property-related crimes decreased 6.5%, yet between 2006 and 2015, arrests for women in this category increased 25.9%. This leads us to conclude that arrests of women for property crimes dramatically increased between 2006 and 2011, and then marked a significant downturn between 2011 and 2015. In addition, much of this variability comes from changes in the number of arrests for larceny-theft crimes. Despite these fluctuations, it is important to remember that women remain a small proportion of the total number of arrests.

While data from the Uniform Crime Reports provide valuable insight into the current state of female offending, research by Steffensmeier and Allan (1996) examines the proportion of male and female arrests for three separate snapshots of time during the 20th century: 1960, 1975, and 1990. Their findings indicate that females make up 15% (or less) of arrestees for most types of major crimes (such as crimes against persons and major property crimes) across all time periods. For minor property offenses, the greatest increases are noted between 1960 and 1975 arrest data. Here, the female percentage of arrests increased from 17% in 1960 to 30% in both 1975 and 1990. The only

Table 8.1 • 2015 UCR Arrest Data: Males Versus Females

	Number of Offenders		Percentage of Offense Type Within Gender (%)	
	Males	**Females**	**Males**	**Females**
Violent crime	309,253	78,829	79.7%	20.3%
Homicide	7,549	984	88.5%	11.5%
Rape	16,990	514	97.1%	2.9%
Robbery	62,721	10,509	85.6%	14.4%
Aggravated assault	221,993	66,822	76.9%	23.1%
Property crime	699,250	434,069	61.7%	38.3%
Burglary	135,064	31,545	81.1%	18.9%
Larceny-theft	511,557	388,520	56.8%	43.2%
Motor vehicle theft	47,169	12,662	78.8%	21.2%
Arson	5,460	1,342	80.3%	19.7%

SOURCE: Crime in the United States 2015. https://ucr.fbi.gov/crime-in-the-u.s/2015/crime-in-the-u.s.-2015/tables/table-42.

NOTE: Total male arrests for index crimes = 1,008,503; total female arrests for index crimes = 512,898. Arrests for index crimes make up 16.6% of male arrests and 22.9% of female arrests.

exception where women make up the majority of arrests is for the crime of prostitution (where women make up between two-thirds and three-fourths of all arrests across all three time periods).

In contrast to Steffensmeier and Allan's research, which relied on UCR data, Rennison (2009) compared offending data from the National Crime Victimization Survey (NCVS) for the 9 years between 1992 and 2001. Her work indicates that there have been negligible differences in the gender gap between male and female offending behaviors during this time frame. By using the data from the NCVS, we see a different view of men's and women's offending behaviors because it includes the dark figure of crime—that is, those crimes that were not reported to the police, as well as the crimes where the police were notified of the crime. These findings note that any differences in the gender gap result not from the increases of female offending but rather from the decreases in male offending rates for particular offenses, which fell at a greater rate than the decrease in female offending rates.

While women participate in many different types of crimes, this chapter highlights five general categories of crime, all which involve gendered assumptions about crime and offending. The first category focuses on a topic that is at the heart of the dramatic rise of female participation in the criminal justice system: drug addiction. The second category investigates the role of women in property crime. The third category focuses on prostitution and sex work. While this is a crime that is often identified as a victimless crime, a review of women who engage in sexually based offenses often face high levels of victimization in their lives. The fourth category looks at the role of women within gang organizations. The chapter concludes with a look at women who engage in acts of murder.

Table 8.2 • 5- and 10-Year Arrest Trends 2006–2015: UCR Arrest Data: Males Versus Females

	Percent Change Within Gender Between 2011 and 2015		Percent Change Within Gender Between 2006 and 2015	
	Males	Females	Males	Females
Violent crime	−6.1	−1.8	−17.8	−3.8
Homicide	+0.8	−1.8	−13.2	−9.1
Rape	−	−	−	−
Robbery	−13.1	+2.7	−23.8	−0.4
Aggravated assault	−5.5	−3.0	−17.3	−4.6
Property crime	−11.1	−6.5	−10.8	+20.2
Burglary	−29.2	−13.4	−30.9	−8.1
Larceny-theft	−6.3	−6.7	+1.6	+25.9
Motor vehicle theft	+9.2	+34.9	−38.9	−23.3
Arson	−24.2	−12.3	−47.0	−35.3

SOURCES: https://ucr.fbi.gov/crime-in-the-u.s/2015/crime-in-the-u.s.-2015/tables/table-33 Crime in the United States 2015. https://ucr.fbi.gov/crime-in-the-u.s/2015/crime-in-the-u.s.-2015/tables/table-35.

Women and Drugs

Throughout the majority of the 20th century, women were not identified as the typical addict or drug abuser. In many cases, the use of prescription and illegal substances by women (particularly White women) was normalized, often as a response to the pressures of gender-role expectations. For example, cocaine and opiates were legally sold in pharmacies and were frequently prescribed by doctors for a variety of ailments. Historically speaking, "women's addiction [was] constructed as the product of individual women's inability to cope with changing versions of normative femininity" (Campbell, 2000, p. 30). Examples of this can be found in advertisements depicting women and antianxiety medications in an effort to calm the frenzied housewife who is overwhelmed with her duties as a wife and mother. In the modern era, drug use was once again promoted as desirable (for White women) with the image of the heroin chic fashionista of the 1990s, personified by supermodel Kate Moss.

Without question, the war on drugs has had a significant impact on women with illicit drug addictions. In the last few decades, female incarceration rates grew 108%, but raw numbers grew eightfold (Harrison & Beck, 2006). These increases can be attributed almost exclusively to the female drug offender (or attributed to the rise in other offenses because of her drug use). This disproportionality continues to increase. In 2012, female drug offenders account for 25% of the state prison population, whereas in male prisons, these crimes make up only 16% of all offenders (Carson & Golinelli, 2013). This is a significant increase compared to 2008 data, where only 9% of drug offenders were women (Guerino, Harrison, & Sabol, 2011).

An endless number of pathways lead to the onset of drug addiction and offending. However, research consistently identifies similar pathways of drug use for women, regardless of race, ethnicity, or drug of choice. Whether the discussion focuses on women addicted to crack cocaine in lower income communities or middle-class women who abuse alcohol or prescription drugs, substance use becomes a method of coping with their lives (Inciardi, Lockwood, & Pottiger, 1993). These primary pathways include exposure to alcohol and drugs at a young age, early childhood victimization and trauma, mental health challenges, and economic challenges (Bloom, Owen, & Covington, 2003).

For some women, their experiences with addiction begin at an early age. These girls are often exposed to drug use within their home environment. A family environment can influence the pathway to addiction in terms of an increased availability of these illicit drugs as well as an environment that is accepting of substance use. In some cases, substance abuse becomes a part of the family culture and a way in which children could spend time with their parents and siblings (Carbone-Lopez, Gatewood Owens, & Miller, 2012). On the other hand, lack of parental supervision may also lead to substance use for girls (Bowles, DeHart, & Webb, 2012). Early experimentation with substance abuse can also lead to a longer term of addiction (Dennis, Scott, Funk, & Foss, 2005).

▲ **Photo 8.1** Research highlights that women and men vary in their drug use, in terms of both their drug of choice and their motivations for use. Here, a woman is shown using drugs intravenously.

Another pathway to addiction is represented through the issues that result from victimization and trauma, particularly during early childhood. Women who experience violence and abuse during their formative years are more likely to abuse alcohol and other drugs compared to women without a history of abuse. Here, research estimates that 48% to 90% of addicted women have endured physical or sexual victimization during their childhood (SAMHSA, 2009). Left untreated, drugs become a way to escape from the pain of childhood abuse and trauma (Carbone-Lopez et al., 2012). The presence of mental health issues can also serve as a pathway to addiction. Mental illness and substance use go hand in hand because 72% of men and women with severe mental disorders have a co-occurring substance abuse problem (Baillargeon, Binswanger, Penn, Williams, & Murray, 2009). Additionally, research indicates that women have higher rates of mental illness compared to men (James & Glaze, 2006). If effective mental health treatment (including psychotropic medication) is unavailable, many may choose to self-medicate with illicit substances, which can lead to issues with addiction (Harris & Edlund, 2005). Finally, women may engage in substance abuse as part of their romantic relationship with a significant other. In many cases, their experimentation quickly translates into addiction and continues even once the relationship ends (Ryder & Brisgone, 2013).

Addiction limits the abilities for many women to develop a self-sustaining life. In addition to placing them at risk for homelessness, violence, and incarceration in an effort to fund their drug use, addiction has collateral consequences, particularly for her minor children. Indeed, the images of the pregnant addicted mother and crack babies of the 80s and 90s represented the greatest form of evil found in the drug-abusing woman. Many women with addiction issues often fail to recognize that they are pregnant until late in their pregnancy where their substance use and lack of prenatal care can place their child at significant risk for health and developmental issues. However, for some women, the realization that they are expecting may encourage them to seek out treatment and give them a reason to change their lives (Silva, Pires, Guerreiro. & Cardoso, 2012). However, relapse issues can threaten this newfound journey toward stability and have lasting effects both for her life as well as for her children. Relapse, incarceration, and time in a treatment facility mean that mothers are separated from their children. Even in cases where these mothers were physically present, their addiction meant that they were often emotionally unavailable for their children. Over time, an intergenerational pattern emerges, and these daughters turn to the same addictions that their mothers endure.

Regardless of their pathway to addiction, increases in number of women using drugs and the marginalization of addicts fed the war on drugs. As the behaviors of addicted women shifted toward criminal activity in an effort to support their drug habit, the perception that drug addiction is *dangerous* spread among the general public. Drug use became something to fear by members of society. The shift of addiction from a public health issue to a criminal justice issue fueled the fear about the link of drug use and crime.

The heightened frenzy over the dangerousness of drugs has fueled the war on drugs into an epidemic. The war on drugs and its effects on the criminal justice system have been documented extensively, and the introduction of mandatory minimum sentencing represented a major change in the processing of drug offenders. While these sentencing structures were applied equally to male and female defendants, the role of women's participation in drug offenses often differs substantially from male involvement in drug-related crimes. With the elimination of judicial discretion, judges were unable to assess the role that women played in these offenses (Merolla, 2008). As a result, women now received long sentences of incarceration where they had once been granted probation and other forms of community supervision. The effect of this shift was dramatic. Between 1986 and 1991, the incarceration rates of women for drug-related offenses increased 433%, compared to a 283% increase for males (Bush-Baskette, 2000). Drug-convicted women make up 72% of the incarcerated population at the federal level (Greenfeld & Snell, 2000). Most of these cases involve women as users of illegal substances. Even in the small proportion of cases where women are involved in the sale of drugs, they rarely participate in mid- or high-level management in the illegal drug market, often because of sexism within the drug economy (Maher, 2004b). For those women who are able to break through the glass ceiling of the drug trade, they are often characterized by justice officials as either more like their male counterparts (much as early criminologists did in describing female criminality) or worse than their male counterparts for violating gender norms about drug dealing. However, for most of the women who enter the drug trade, it is their relationship with an intimate partner that explains their criminality both in terms of drug use and manufacturing. Not only were women introduced to new, serious substances (such as heroin and opioids) through their relationships (Ventura-Miller, Miller, & Barnes, 2016) but courts viewed these women as less culpable in their offending as they were "under the influence" of these criminal men (Mann, Menih, & Smith, 2014).

While recent changes in federal drug sentencing laws have reduced the disparities in sentencing, the damage has already been done. The effects of these laws created a new system of criminal justice where the courts are overloaded with drug possession and distribution cases, and the growth of the prison economy has reached epic proportions. Yet these efforts appear to have done little to stem the use and sale of such controlled substances. At the same time, there is recent chatter by government leaders, such as Attorney General Jefferson Sessions that there should be a return to the war on drugs. Under his leadership, he has instructed federal prosecutors to pursue harsh punishments for drug-related crimes, even low-level offenses. In justifying this change in policy, Sessions has cited a perceived increase in crime rates over the past year, arguing that such increases may be a sign of a new trend (Ford, 2017). This marks a dramatic shift from policy changes that were enacted under President Obama. Indeed, the overall rates of crimes other than drug-related cases have changed little during the last 40 years. The effects of these policies have produced significant consequences for families and communities, particularly given the increase in the incarceration rates of women. Chapters 10 and 11 explore in depth the consequences in the incarceration of women, for both themselves and their families, as well as their communities. It is these consequences that have led some scholars to suggest that the war on drugs has in effect become a war on women (Chesney-Lind, 1997).

Property Crime

The category of property crime is relatively broad and encompasses a number of different offenses. Generally speaking, property crime refers to the illegal acquisition of money, goods, or valuables, but without the use of force or fear to obtain the property. While the Uniform Crime Report includes arson, burglary, larceny-theft, and motor vehicle theft as Part 1 offenses under the category of property crime, the National Crime Victimization Survey (NCVS) includes only burglary, motor vehicle theft, and theft (larceny) in its definition. As a more inclusive representation of crime, the National Incident Based Reporting System incorporates many more types of property offenses into its definition, such as arson, bribery, burglary, vandalism, embezzlement, blackmail, fraud, larceny-theft, motor vehicle theft, stolen property offenses, and bad checks.

According to the Bureau of Justice Statistics, the rate of property crime victimization within U.S. households (property crime per 1,000 households) has steadily declined since 1993. Today's rate is roughly one-third of the 1993 victimization rate (110.7 victimizations per 1,000 households in 2015, compared to 320 in 1993) (Truman & Morgan 2016). While females are more likely to be involved in property offenses compared to other types of crimes, males still commit the overwhelming majority of these crimes. Men committed 62% of property crimes in 2010, while women were responsible for about 38% of these offenses.

Earlier in this chapter, you learned about how women's lives are shaped by addiction. Addiction can also shape women's participation in crimes, particularly for property offenses because women may engage in these crimes to either support their drug habit or commit crime while under the influence. Indeed, drugs are the most common factor among females who engage in property crimes. Research by Johnson (2004) finds that 52% of property offenders engage in crime to get money so that they can buy drugs. In comparison, only 15% of violent offenders stated that their crime was directly related to obtaining drugs for personal use.

Another factor in female property offending is economic survival. Given that only 40% of incarcerated women were employed prior to their arrest, it appears that many women engage in these crimes in order to provide for themselves and their families. Research does note that welfare reform during the 1990s did lead to a small reduction of female involvement in serious property crimes (Corman, Dave, & Reichman, 2014). However, to suggest that poverty and unemployment leads people to engage in property-based offending is a narrow view of the issue. Certainly, addiction can play a role for some offenders. Here, the decision to engage in crime helps not only to fund their substance abuse but it also provides support to maintain a household. This is particularly poignant given that many individuals who suffer from addiction are unable to hold down functional employment.

The image of women in property crimes varies dramatically. On one hand, shoplifting is typically described as a "pink-collar" crime. While shoplifting may be an act that some undertake to support other areas of criminality, such as drug use, others use shoplifting as their primary occupation and sell their goods to buying customers. These women view themselves as professionals, and their ability to shoplift is a skill. Much like the drug dealer, the shoplifter develops a list of clients who will purchase their goods from her. Her attire is based on what types of stores she will steal from so that she blends in with the rest

▲ **Photo 8.2** The majority of crimes involving women are property offenses and include crimes such as burglary and theft. Here, a woman engages in shoplifting from a store.

of the legitimate shoppers and goes undetected by security personnel (Caputo & King, 2011). Another example involves women and the crime of robbery. Some scholars highlight how women engage in robbery as solo offenders; how women choose to engage in crime is gendered in that they typically do not engage in overt acts of violence and select other women as their victims (Miller, 1998a). Meanwhile, other cases show women who use their femininity to draw in their victims as part of a larger mixed-gender group (Contreras, 2009). In each of these cases, women use their gender in their favor.

Spotlight on Women and Bank Robbery

Historically, male offenders have dominated the crime of bank robbery. Even in cases where women have been involved in these crimes, they were either coconspirators with a male or were reduced to a minor role. Consider the example of Bonnie Elizabeth Parker (1910–1934) who was romantically involved with Clyde Chestnut Barrow (1909–1934). Barrow and his gang committed over a dozen bank robberies during the Great Depression. Urban legend suggested that Bonnie was an equal participant in these crimes. However, evidence suggests that Bonnie never actually killed a single victim.

While the days of Bonnie and Clyde are long gone and men remain the most likely offender of these crimes, times are changing. Women are becoming more involved in these crimes. In the last decade, the number of bank robberies committed by women has shifted. While there were more females involved in bank robberies in 2003, there were more of these offenses in general. According to the Uniform Crime Reports, women made up 524 of the 9,714 offenders involved in these crimes. This means that women made up 5.5% of all bank robbery offenders in 2003. In 2011, they made up 429 of the offenders for these crimes. However, the overall number of offenders in these cases fell by 37% to 6,088 (Federal Bureau of Investigation [FBI], 2003, 2011).

Perhaps one of the most famous cases of bank robbery involved Patricia Hearst. Hearst was the 19-year-old socialite granddaughter of newspaper publishing mogul William Randolph Hearst. In 1974, Patty Hearst was kidnapped by members of the Symbionese Liberation Army, a domestic terrorist group. The SLA manipulated Hearst to join their criminal actions. During her 18 months under SLA captivity, she participated in three bank robberies and several other criminal activities. Despite her defense that she had been brainwashed by her captors, Hearst was sentenced to 7 years in prison for her part in the robbery. Her sentence was commuted after 2 years by then President Jimmy Carter, and she was pardoned by President Clinton (Cable News Network [CNN], 2001).

A recent example of a female bank robber is Lee Grace Dougherty. In August 2011, Lee Grace, with her brother Ryan and stepbrother Dylan, robbed a local bank in Georgia. While all three had previously been involved with the criminal justice system, Lee Grace drew the attention of the media both for her status as a woman as well as online statements that "I like causing mayhem with my siblings." She was sentenced to 35 years in prison for her involvement in the bank robbery and faces additional time for her subsequent offenses as part of their multistate crime spree (Coffman, 2012; Gast, 2011; MacIntosh, 2011).

Prostitution

Hollywood images of prostitution depict a lifestyle that is rarely found in the real world. Movies such as *Pretty Woman, Leaving Las Vegas,* and *Taxi Driver* paint a picture of the young, beautiful prostitute who is saved from her life on the streets. In reality, there are few Prince Charmings available to rescue these women. The reality that awaits most of these women is one filled with violence, abuse, and addiction—deep scars that are challenging to overcome.

Prostitution involves the act of selling or trading sex for money. Prostitution can take a variety of forms, including escort services, massage parlors, or work in brothels, bars, and truck stops. However, street-level prostitution is perhaps the most visible form of sex work. According to the Uniform Crime Reports, police agencies arrested 36,931 offenders for the crime of prostitution in 2012. Two-thirds of such offenders were female (see FBI, 2011, 2012b). Most of these offenders are workers of the trade and not the traffickers or customers associated with these crimes.

For those women who engage in street-level prostitution, money may not be the only commodity available in exchange for their bodies, because they also trade sex for drugs or other tangibles such as food, clothing, and shelter. In addition, women in this arena experience the high levels of risk for violence and victimization.

The journey into prostitution is not a solitary road. Rather, it involves a variety of individual, contextual, and environmental factors. A history of abuse is one of the most commonly referenced risk factors for prostitution, and research by Dalla (2000) indicates that drug addiction almost always paves the way for work in prostitution. However, poverty also plays a role. In Chapter 5, you learned about the issue of forced prostitution and human trafficking, yet many women choose to enter **street prostitution** and brothel work out of financial need (Karandikar, Gezinski, & Meshelemiah, 2013).

One of the most common pathways for women in prostitution is the experience of early childhood sexual victimization. Although there is no direct link that indicates that the experience of incest is predictive of selling one's body, research indicates that there is a strong correlation between the two (Nokomis Foundation, 2002), and one prostitution recovery program indicates that 87% of their participants experienced abuse throughout their early childhood, often at the hands of a family member. For these women, incest became the way in which they learned about their sexuality as a commodity that could be sold and traded, and some suggest this process of bargaining became a way in which these victims could once again feel powerful about their lives (Mallicoat, 2006). In Chapter 7, you learned about how young girls who have been abused within the home often run away to escape the ongoing violence and victimization. Once on the streets, they are at risk for even more violence. Many of these girls turn to prostitution to support their basic survival needs, such as food and shelter. They also enter prostitution as a way to regain some agency and control of their sexuality, compared to their abusive history where others held the power and control—"because from my childhood, I had been molested. And then as time went on, I was still getting molested, so I got tired. And I said well, if a man is going to take it from me, why not sell myself" (Cobbina & Oselin, 2011). For other girls who enter prostitution during adolescence, the decision to enter prostitution is one that is normalized where prostitution is practiced within the family/community and is viewed as an economic opportunity.

Women in prostitution experience high levels of violence during their careers. On the streets, they witness and experience violence on a daily basis. More than 90% of these women are brutally victimized (Romero-Daza, Weeks, & Singer, 2003). They are robbed, raped, and assaulted by their customers and pimps alike (Raphael & Shapiro, 2004). Violence can also occur at the hands of an intimate partner or pimp (DeHart, Lynch, Belknap, Dass-Brailsford, & Green, 2014). Many do not report these incidents out of fear

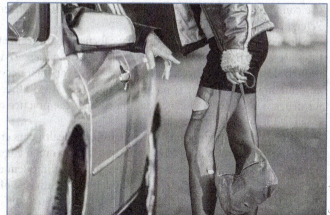

▲ **Photo 8.3** While street prostitution comprises a small proportion of sex work, it is one of the most visible forms. It is also one of the most dangerous forms of sex work. Many women who work the streets risk significant victimization from their clients. Unfortunately, many victims do not report these crimes to the police out of concerns that their cases will not be treated seriously by the justice system.

that they will be arrested for engaging in prostitution, coupled with a belief that the police will do little to respond to these crimes. Indeed, women often return to the streets immediately following their victimization. This temporary intervention is viewed as a delay in work rather than an opportunity to search for an exit strategy. One woman characterized her experience as normal—"society and law enforcement consider a prostitute getting raped or beat as something she deserves. It goes along with your lifestyle. There's nothing that you can do" (Dalla, Xia, & Kennedy, 2003, pp. 1380–1381).

Female sex workers also witness significant acts of violence perpetuated against their peers, an experience that often leads to significant mental health issues. Drug use becomes a way to cope with the violence in their daily lives. As the pressure to make money increases in order to sustain their substance abuse addiction or to provide a roof over their head at night, women may place themselves in increasingly risky situations with their customers (Norton-Hawk, 2004). In an effort to protect against potential harms, women rely on their intuition to avoid potentially violent situations. Many girls indicate that they will not leave a designated area with a client and generally refuse to get into a car with a client. Others carry a weapon, such as a knife. Despite the risks, some women reference the thrill and power they experience when they are able to survive a violent incident (Dalla, Xia, & Kennedy, 2003). Many women are surprised when they reflect on the levels of violence that they experienced on the streets. Some may dissociate themselves from the realities of this journey and believe that the experience was not as traumatic as they originally believed. However, the battle scars from their time on the streets provide the evidence for the trauma they endured, both physically and mentally.

The role of substance abuse is central to the discussion of risk for prostituting women. About 70% of women in prostitution have issues with drug addiction. Some women begin their substance use prior to their entry in prostitution to cope with the pain associated with past or current sexual violence in their lives. They then resort to prostitution to fund their drug habits (Raphael, 2004). For others, entry into substance abuse comes later in an effort to self-medicate against the fear, stress, and low self-esteem resulting from the selling of sex (Nixon, Tutty, Downe, Gorkoff, & Ursel, 2002). As their time on the streets increases, so does their substance abuse (Cobbina & Oselin, 2011). Indeed, the relationship between drug use and prostitution may be a self-perpetuating cycle in which they feed off one another. A sample of women in jail for prostitution had significantly higher rates of drug use compared to women arrested for non-prostitution-related offenses (Yacoubian, Urbach, Larsen, Johnson, & Peters, 2000).

In recent years, media accounts have focused significant attention on the use of crack cocaine by street prostitutes. Research has linked the presence of crack to an increased number of individuals working on the street, which in turn decreases the price that women receive for their services. Addiction to drugs such as crack has created an economy where money is no longer traded for sex. Rather, sexual acts become a commodity to be exchanged for drugs. The levels of violence associated with the practice of selling sex increases in this drug-fueled economy (Maher, 1996).

While drug addiction presents a significant health concern for women in prostitution, additional issues exist for women in terms of long-term physical health. Women engaged in sex work are at risk for issues related to HIV, hepatitis, and other chronic health concerns, including dental, vision, neurological, respiratory, and gynecological problems (Farley & Barkin, 1998). Finally, the death rate of women in prostitution is an astonishingly 40 times higher than the death rate of the overall population (Nokomis Foundation, 2002).

Mental health concerns are also a significant issue for women engaged in the sex trade. Cases of **posttraumatic stress disorder (PTSD)** are directly related to the levels of violence that women experience on the streets, and an estimated two-thirds of prostituted women experience symptoms of PTSD (Schoot & Goswami, 2001). Prostitutes suffering from PTSD may be unable to accurately assess the levels of threat and violence that surround their lives, which in turn places them at increased risk for ongoing physical and sexual victimization (Valera, Sawyer, & Schiraldi, 2000).

The Legalization Debate

The question of whether prostitution should be considered a criminal activity is one of considerable debate. In Nevada, legal prostitution is limited to counties with a population under 400,000, excluding high-traffic areas, such as Reno and Las Vegas, from offering legalized brothels. The laws within Nevada focus almost exclusively on the minimization of risk and reduction of violence for women in prostitution. Since 1986, Nevada has required that prostitutes who work in brothels must submit to weekly exams to assess for any sexually transmitted infections or the presence of HIV. Brothels also implement a variety of regulations to ensure the safety and security of the facility and the women who work there, such as audio monitoring and call buttons in the rooms. Most brothels limit services outside of the brothel environment to control any potentially negative behaviors of clients. Research indicates that women who work in brothel settings feel safe and rarely experience acts of violence while working as prostitutes. Indeed, such safety mechanisms led women to believe that brothel sex work is by far the safest environment in which to engage in prostitution, compared to the violence and danger that street prostitutes regularly experience (Brents & Hausbeck, 2005).

In the Netherlands, the legalization of brothels in 2000 created a new way to govern the sex trade. While the act of prostitution has been legalized since the early 20th century, it was the brothel environment (popularized by the red light district and "window" shopping in the city of Amsterdam and other cities) that was illegal. At the time of brothel legalization, the practice of prostitution in the Netherlands was not an uncommon phenomenon, and estimates suggest that over 6,000 women per day were working in prostitution-related activities (Wagennar, 2006). The effects of the legislation lifted the formal prohibition of the brothel, even though many municipalities tolerated their presence, and agents of social control, such as law enforcement and the courts, largely refrained from prosecuting cases. By creating a system whereby brothels had to be licensed, authorities were able to gain control over the industry by mandating public health and safety screenings for sex workers. As part of the decriminalization of prostitution, the state created the opportunity for brothel owners to have a legal site of business. Labor laws regarding the working conditions for prostitutes were put into effect. In addition, it created a tax base in which revenue could be generated (Pakes, 2005). The goals of decriminalization allowed for the Dutch government to improve the lives of women in prostitution by creating safe working conditions, creating a system of monitoring of the sex trade, and regulating illegal activities that might be associated with the selling of sexuality, such as street crimes associated with prostitution, the exploitation of juveniles, or the trafficking of women into the sex industry (Wagenaar, 2006).

By creating a sustainable economy of prostitution, some proponents suggest not only that the needs of the customer are met but also that these regions create an economic strategy for women, particularly women within challenged economic situations. However, creating a system of legislation is no guarantee that laws will be followed; even with the legalization of prostitution in New South Wales, Australia, the majority of brothels fail to register their businesses and pay little attention to the regulatory rules for operation. In addition, illegal sexual practices have continued to flourish; the Netherlands is identified as a leading destination for pedophiles and child pornographers, many of which operate under the belief that the promotion of legalized prostitution has created opportunities for illegal prostitution in these regions, as well (Raymond, 2004).

Other legislation focuses on the criminalization of the demand for sexual services. In addressing the issue of prostitution in Sweden, legislatures have focused on making the purchasing of sex from women a criminal act. The belief here is that criminalizing the male demand for sex it may significantly decrease the supply of women who engage in these acts. By criminalizing the "johns," Sweden has taken a stand against a practice that the country feels constitutes an act of violence against women (Raymond, 2004). In the passing of these laws, the parliament indicated, "[I]t is not reasonable to punish the person who sells a sexual service. In the majority of cases . . . this person is a weaker partner who is exploited" (Ministry of Labour, Sweden, 1998, p. 4).

In the United States, even in an environment where both the purchaser and seller of sex can be subjected to criminal prosecution, the data indicate that women are significantly more likely to face sanctions for selling sex, compared to men who seek to purchase it (Farley & Kelly, 2000). Although the focus on demand is an important characteristic in the selling of sex, it is not the only variable. Indeed, larger issues such as economics, globalization, poverty, and inequality all contribute to a system where women fall victim to the practices of sexual exploitation.

Farley and Kelly (2000) suggest that even with the legalization of the brothel environment, prostitution remains a significant way in which women are brutalized and harmed. The social stigma of women who engage in the selling of sex does not decrease simply because the act of prostitution becomes legal. Indeed, the restriction of brothels to specific regions only further isolates women from mainstream society and magnifies the stigma they may experience (Farley, 2004). In cases of victimization, women employed in sex work continue to experience significant levels of victim blaming when they are victimized, even if prostitution is decriminalized. The system of public health, which is promoted as a way to keep both the prostitute and her client safe, fails to meet some of the most critical needs of women in this arena, because these efforts toward promoting safety are limited exclusively to physical health, and little to no attention is paid to the mental health needs of women engaged in prostitution (Farley, 2004).

Research indicates that women involved in street prostitution often want to leave the lifestyle, but they express concern over how their multiple needs (including housing, employment, and drug treatment) may limit their abilities to do so. There are few programs that provide adequate levels of services to address the multiple needs of women during this transition. A review of one prostitution recovery program found that affordable safe housing is the greatest immediate need for women in their transition from the streets (Mallicoat, 2011). Homelessness puts women at risk for relapse: "Without reliable housing, it is challenging to escape the cycle of prostituting" (Yahne, Miller, Irvin-Vitela, & Tonigan, 2002, p. 52).

In addition, women must possess necessary skills and have access to support in order to facilitate this process. Women exiting the streets indicate a variety of therapeutic needs, including life skills, addiction recovery programming, and mental health services designed to address the traumas they experienced. An exit strategy needs to acknowledge the barriers to success and continuing struggles that women will experience as a result of these traumas.

Women and Violence

True-crime documentaries and fictionalized television dramas give the perception that the rates of female offending, particularly in cases involving violence, have increased dramatically in recent years. Yet rates of crime for women in these types of cases have actually decreased. This discussion about women and violent crimes investigates three different categories of female offenders. The first topic highlights the role of women in gangs. The second topic looks at general crimes of female violence, including murder. The chapter concludes with a specific type of female homicide with women who kill their children.

Girls and Gangs

While girls have traditionally made up a small proportion of gang members, there was significant media attention on the rise of gang girls throughout the late 20th century. Surveys conducted by law enforcement agencies in the 1990s estimated that between 8% and 11% of gang members were female (Moore & Terrett, 1998). However, not all law enforcement jurisdictions include girls in their counts of gang members, a practice that can skew data about the number of girls involved in gangs (Curry, Ball, & Fox, 1994). Whereas the National Youth Gang Center suggests that these rates have remained consistent and reflect little change in rates of female gang participation (2009), other data tell a different story. Self-report studies during this same time frame reflect a higher percentage of female gang participation compared to law enforcement data and suggest that 38% of the self-identified gang members between the ages of 13 and 15 were female (Esbensen, Deschenes, & Winfree, 1999). Recent self-report data indicate that girls represent between 31% and 45% of gang members (Esbensen & Carson, 2012).

Who are female gang members? Much of the early literature on girls and gangs looked at female gang members as secondary to issues surrounding male gangs. Classic studies by Campbell (1984) and Moore (1991) illustrated that girls entered the gang lifestyle as a result of a brother or boyfriend's affiliation. Girls in the gang were often distinguished from their male counterparts by their sexuality. This sexualization manifested in several ways: (1) as a girlfriend to a male gang member, (2) as one who engages in sex with male gang members, and (3) as one who uses her sexuality in order to avoid detection by rival gang members and law enforcement (Campbell, 1995). Modern research builds on this early work, suggesting that female gangs are not only increasing their membership ranks but also expanding their function and role as an independent entity separate from the male gang. Girls in the gang are no longer the sexual toy of the male gang but have become active participants in crimes of drugs and violence.

The lives of girls in gangs tell a story filled with violence, poverty, racism, disenfranchisement, and limited resources. They come from families who struggle to make ends meet in economically depressed areas. In these communities, opportunities for positive, prosocial activities are significantly limited, and the pressure to join a gang runs rampant. Many of the girls have limited achievements in the classroom, and their educational experience has little to do with books or teachers. Instead, they share stories of disorder, threats, and crime (Molidor, 1996). The majority of their parents never married, and the presence of intimate partner abuse within the home was not uncommon. Many of the girls had a parent or other family members who were involved in the criminal justice system and were either currently incarcerated or had been incarcerated during some part of their lives.

For some girls, membership in a gang is a family affair, with parents, siblings, and extended family members involved in the gang lifestyle. Research by Miller (2000) indicates that 79% of girls who were gang involved had a family member who was a gang member, and 60% of the girls had multiple family members in gangs. For these girls, gang affiliation comes at an early age. During the childhood and preteen years, their gang activities may consist of limited acts of delinquency and drug experimentation. During junior high, girls exhibit several risk factors for delinquency, including risky sexual behavior, school failures, and truancy. By the time these girls become teenagers, they are committed to the gang and criminal activity and participate in a range of delinquent acts, including property crimes, weapons offenses, and violent crimes against persons. The later adolescent years (ages 15–18) represent the most intense years of gang activity (Eghigian & Kirby, 2006).

While the gang is a way of life for some girls, many others find their way to the gang in search of a new family. Many girls involved in gangs have histories of extensive physical and sexual abuse by family members during early childhood. Many of the girls run away from the family residence in an attempt to escape the violence and abuse in their lives. In an attempt to survive on the streets, the gang becomes an attractive option for meeting one's immediate and long-term needs such as shelter, food, and protection. Not only does the gang provide refuge from these abusive home environments but it provides as well a sense of family that was lacking in their families of origin (Joe & Chesney-Lind, 1995). Research by Miller (2000) indicates that it is not so much a specific risk factor that propels girls into the gang but rather the relationship among several life situation factors, such as a neighborhood exposure to gangs, a family involvement in the lifestyle, and the presence of problems in the family, that illustrates the trajectory of girls into the gang lifestyle.

The literature on female gangs indicates that the lifestyle, structure, and characteristics of female gangs and their members are as diverse as male gangs. Some girls hang out with gangs in search of a social life and peer relationships, but they typically do not consider themselves as members of the gang. The structure of the girl gang ranges from being a mixed-gender gang to functioning as an independent unit. For girls involved in mixed-gender gangs, their role ranged from being an affiliate of the male gang unit to even, in some cases, having a "separate but equal" relationship to their male counterparts (Schalet, Hunt, & Joe-Laidler, 2003).

The initiation process for girls varies from being "jumped" in or **walking the line**, whereby the girls were subjected to assault by their fellow gang members, to being "sexed" in or **pulling a train**, an experience that involved having sex with multiple individuals, often the male gang members. However, not all these initiation rites came with a high degree of status within the gang, because those girls who were sexed in general experienced lower levels of respect by fellow gang members (Miller, 2000). Girls who had been "sexed into the gang" were subjected to continued victimization from within the gang. Although not all girls were admitted to the gang in this manner, this image negatively affected all the girls.

> The fact that there was such an option as "sexing in" served to keep girls disempowered, because they always faced the question of how they got in and of whether they were "true" members. In addition, it contributed to a milieu in which young women's sexuality was seen as exploitable. (Miller, 1998a, p. 444)

Recent media attention has targeted the gang girl and [thus created] the perception that violence by these girls is increasing. Yet data indicate that female gang members participate in criminal acts at rates similar to male gang members (Esbensen & Carson, 2012). Research by Fleisher and Krienert (2004) indicated that among girls who described themselves as active members of a gang, almost all (94%) had engaged in a violent crime during the previous 6 months, and two-thirds (67%) had sold drugs during the past 2 months. More than half (55%) had participated in property crimes, such as graffiti or destruction to property, while two-thirds (67%) engaged in economic crimes, such as prostitution, burglary, robbery, or theft, in the previous 6 months. Here, violence is more than just engaging in criminal offenses. Indeed, the participation in a delinquent lifestyle that is associated with gang membership places girls at risk for significant victimization. Girls who are "independent" of a male gang hierarchy tend to experience high levels of violence as a result of selling drugs and their interactions on the streets with other girls. These independent girls are aware of the potential risk they face and take a number of precautionary measures to enhance their safety, such as possessing a weapon, staying off the streets at night, and traveling in groups. While the close relationship with the male gang can often serve as a protective factor, it can also place the girls at risk of rape and sexual assault by their "homeboys" (Hunt & Joe-Laidler, 2001). In addition, girls whose gang membership is connected to a male gang unit tend to experience higher levels of violence on the streets compared to girls who operate in independent cliques. These girls are at a higher risk of victimization due to the levels of violence that they are exposed to from assaults and drive-by shootings that involve the male gang members. Indeed, many of these crimes (and potential risks of victimization) would not be present if they were not involved in the gang lifestyle (Miller, 1998b).

The exit from the gang lifestyle for girls can occur in several ways. For most girls, this exit coincides with the end of adolescence. They may withdraw from the lifestyle, often as a result of pregnancy and the need to care for their young children. For others, their exit is facilitated by an entry into legitimate employment or advanced education. Others will be removed from their gangs as a result of incarceration in a juvenile or adult correctional facility. While some may choose to be "jumped out," most will simply diminish their involvement over time rather than be perceived as betraying or deliberately going against their gang peers (Campbell, 1995). The few women who choose to remain in the gang have several pathways from which to choose. They may continue their gang participation as active members and expand their criminal résumé. Their relationships with male gang members may continue with their choice of marriage partners, which allows them to continue their affiliation in either a direct or indirect role (Eghigian & Kirby, 2006).

Gender and Violent Crime

Despite public perceptions, females make up a small proportion of violent offenders. While violent crime perpetuated by women does occur, it is rare. As you learned earlier in this chapter, men engage in far more acts of violence than females. For example, women's participation in the crime of homicide accounts for less than half of the arrests of men. And as with the rates of male violence, women's participation in these crimes has decreased, with homicide offending rates for females declining from 3.1 offenders per 100,000 in 1980 to 1.6 offenders per 100,000 in 2008 (Cooper & Smith, 2011). Women are more likely to kill someone known to them, compared to a stranger. Research by Kellermann & Mercy (1992) indicates that while 60% of female offenders knew their victims, only 20% of male murders had known victims. Generally speaking, women generally kill their spouses, significant others, or their children (Cooper & Smith, 2011).

Spotlight on Women and Self-Defense

Much of the fascination about women who kill comes from the perception of these offenders either as cold and calculating murderers or cases where women just "snap." But what about those cases of women who kill in self-defense? How do we make sense of these crimes of violence?

Consider the case of Marissa Alexander. During a confrontation with her husband in August 2010, Marissa fired a bullet into the wall to scare her husband. Alexander had a history of abuse with her partner and this incident occurred 9 days after she had given birth to their daughter (Hauser, 2017). She testified that she felt threatened and luckily no one was hurt in the incident. Even though Alexander drew on Florida's Stand Your Ground Law, the jury convicted her of aggravated assault with a deadly weapon, and she was sentenced to 20 years in prison. Her actions triggered a mandatory minimum gun law, which increases the sentence in certain felonies if a gun is brandished or fired. Even lawmakers in the state argued that the intent of the law was not to punish cases like Alexander's but was designed to increase sentences for those who brandished or used a firearm during the commission of a crime such as robbery or assault (Stacy, 2012). Her initial conviction was overturned on appeal for errors by the trial judge in the instructions to the jury, While awaiting a retrial, he accepted a plea deal that allowed her to serve 3 years in prison and 2 years on house arrest. She was released from house arrest in January 2017 and has developed a nonprofit to be an advocate for victims of intimate partner abuse and criminal justice policy reform (Hauser, 2017).

Another case of self-defense that has drawn recent attention involves Sara Kruzan. In 1995, Kruzan was only 16 years old when she was convicted of first-degree murder and sentenced to life without the possibility of parole. She had no juvenile record and had been an honor student as a young child. The victim was her pimp, a 31-year-old man named G. G. Howard, who had begun grooming Sara when she was only 11 years old and had been sexually trafficking her for the past 4 years (Sharma, 2013). Even though her age made it possible for the case to be tried in juvenile court (where the maximum sentence would have resulted in her incarceration until age 25), prosecutors transferred her case to criminal court where she was tried as an adult. In January 2011, new legislation was enacted that allowed for the reconsideration of juvenile cases where life sentences were handed down. Following the new law, then-Governor Schwarzenegger granted clemency to Kruzan and commuted her [life without parole] LWOP sentence to 25 years with the possibility of parole. Additional legislation signed into law by Governor Jerry Brown required parole boards to give special consideration in parole decisions involving juvenile offenders who were tried as adults and who had served at least 15 years of their sentences. After serving 19 years, Kruzan was paroled in part due to these new policies (St. John, 2013).

In both of these cases, public attention played a significant role in raising awareness about these cases. Sara Kruzan was featured in social action campaigns by Abolish Slavery and Human Rights Watch and drew the attention of lawmakers who were seeking changes in how juvenile cases were handled. Kruzan has become the face for thousands of youth who are serving sentences for crimes they committed as juveniles (De Atley, 2013). Similarly, Alexander's case involved a ground of activists and organizations who joined together in a campaign titled Free Marissa Now to which organized grassroot activities such as educational events on domestic violence, social media campaigns, and petitions to state officials on her case. Since her release, the group has continued to advocate for other women who have been incarcerated in cases of domestic and gender-based violence (free marissanow.org).

Much of the fascination about female violent crime stems from how these crimes are portrayed by popular culture. The cable television show *Snapped* (Oxygen network) focuses on true-crime cases of women who kill and their motivations for crime. Movie story lines have included both fictional and "ripped from the headlines" examples of women who stalk, torture, and murder their victims. The 1987 film *Fatal Attraction* tells the story of Alex (portrayed by Glenn Close) who obsesses over her married lover Dan (played by Michael Douglas). Alex engages in all sorts of crimes toward Dan, including pouring acid on his car and killing the family rabbit (Maslin, 1987). The Broadway show (and film adaption) *Chicago* tells the story of Velma Kelly and Roxie Hart who are arrested for the murders of their paramours. The backdrop for this story came from several true-crime cases from the 1920s where women were tried and ultimately acquitted for killing their husbands or lovers. These cases were sensationalized in local newspapers, and these women became celebrities throughout their trials (Perry, 2010). Even popular song lyrics draw attention (and justify) the actions of women who damage the side panel, vandalize its interior, and slash the tires of their cheating boyfriend's car ("Before He Cheats").

Beyond the Hollywood portrayals of violence by women, the public is fascinated by the real-world examples of women who kill. Consider the case of Pamela Smart. Twenty-two years old and married after a quick courtship, she and her husband Gregory Smart had been having significant problems in their marriage and they began to spend time apart. Pamela began spending time outside of her job at Winnacunnet High School with several students. She ultimately began an intimate relationship with one of these youth, William "Billy" Flynn. On May 1, 1990, Smart arrived at her home in Derry, New Hampshire, after the workday to find her husband Gregory dead of a bullet wound to the head. The case immediately aroused the suspicions of the local police. While the crime scene appeared to be staged to look like a robbery gone bad, Gregory Smart had been killed execution style. While Pam had an alibi at the time of the murder, police began to suspect that she was involved in her husband's murder. An anonymous call to the police suggested that Pam had orchestrated the killing. Billy Flynn and two of his friends were arrested for murder. Although the police believed they had the individuals who were responsible for carrying out the murder, they conducted audio surveillance on Pam Smart, where she admitted details of planning the murder of her husband with Flynn (Rideout, 2007). Billy Flynn testified against Smart that she persuaded him to murder her husband so that they could be together (Dinan, 2005). While Flynn was sentenced to 40 years to life, Pamela Smart received a sentence of life without the possibility of parole.

The trial of Pamela Smart gained national attention, and it was the first to be televised on the cable television channel Court TV (Rideout, 2007). By the time the trial began, there were over 400 various articles written about the case in local and national newspapers. By the end of the trial, this number approached 1,200. These articles portrayed Flynn as "hot for teacher" and Smart as seducing her young student (even though Smart was an administrator for the school district and not a teacher). They also described Smart's cold demeanor during the trial, labeling her as the *Ice Princess* (Lyons, 2006). This real-life case became iconized by the movie *To Die For* starring Nicole Kidman and Joaquin Phoenix.

A more contemporary example of the media's fascination with a female murder trial is the case of Casey Anthony, who was tried for the 2008 murder of her 2-year-old daughter Caylee in Orange County, Florida. The police began to suspect Anthony after several discrepancies in her story regarding her daughter's disappearance. Anthony had alleged that Caylee was kidnapped by her nanny (Zenaida Fernandez-Gonzalez), who it was later determined never existed. In addition, Anthony had not reported her daughter missing, which further raised the suspicions of her family and the police. Caylee's decomposed body was found in a wooded area on December 11, 2008 (Casey Anthony, 2014).

Casey Anthony's trial began in June 2011 with significant media attention. In portraying Anthony as responsible for her daughter's death, the state linked [the death to] a search on Casey's computer for chloroform. Remnants of this toxic chemical were found in the trunk of Anthony's car, coupled with the smell of decomposing waste. Anthony was also described as an out of control party animal that did not want to be a mother. However, there was no evidence that directly linked Anthony to the murder of her daughter (Alvarez, 2011). Following her acquittal in July 2011, Anthony's attorneys vilified the press for its role in creating a sensationalized image of Casey to the public that assumed her guilt. However, newspapers were not the only ones to blame for these behaviors. Like Pamela Smart, the trial of Casey Anthony was televised. Twenty years later, however, there are many other sources of information that dominate the public perceptions of crime. These included a live video feed online of the trial, numerous Facebook pages in the names of Casey and her daughter, and even a Twitter account managed by the Ninth Judicial Circuit Court of Florida (Cloud, 2011). This level of intimate accessibility allowed the public to feel as if it were a part of the trial experience and had a personal investment in its outcome. Indeed, the public outcry over Anthony's acquittal was significant. "Because many American murder cases, such as the Casey Anthony trial, are shown on television, they sometimes appear to the public as if they were reality television shows. There is great disappointment, therefore, when the result is a verdict of not guilty" (Dershowitz, 2011, para 8). Not surprisingly, the public's fascination with women who engage in crimes of violence appears to have increased with the times because there are now multiple sources through which one can satisfy their desires for this dramatized portrayal of crime and justice.

These themes were once again displayed in the case of Jodi Arias. Over the course of her four-month trial, every moment of the trial was broadcast on cable television. In addition, there was no shortage of "legal experts" waiting to give their opinion on the events of the day, the evidence presented, or the demeanor of the defendant. Arias was charged and ultimately convicted for the murder of her boyfriend, Travis Alexander. Alexander was found in his shower where he had been stabbed 27 times, his throat had been slit, and he had been shot in the head (Sholchet, 2013). One of the particularly sensationalized parts of the trial involved Arias' own testimony, which lasted 18 days. Under Arizona law, members of the jury are allowed to submit questions to the accused should they choose to take the stand in their own defense. "Some of the questions seemed to serve no other purpose but to mock Arias and illustrate the jurors' annoyance with her claims" (Fagel, 2013). While she was convicted of first-degree murder, the same jury was unable to come to a verdict on whether Arias should be given the death penalty. She is currently serving life in prison without the possibility of parole (Kiefer, 2015).

Spotlight on the Case of Michelle Carter

"You better not be bull sh*ting me and saying you're gonna do this and then purposely get caught."

"Like, are you gonna do it then? Keep being all talk and no action and everyday go throu saying how badly you wanna kill yourself? Or are you gonna try to get better?"

"You're just making it harder on yourself by pushing it off and you say you'll do it but u never do. Its always gonna be that way if u don't take action."

These are just a few of the texts that 17-year-old Michelle Carter sent to her boyfriend Conrad Roy III over a four-week period in 2014. Roy ultimately committed suicide in July 14 by outfitting his truck with tubing connected to his tailpipe so that he could inhale the carbon monoxide (LeBlanc, 2017). Carter was found guilty of involuntary manslaughter and faces up to 20 years in prison. What makes the case particularly interesting to legal scholars is that Carter was not physically present when Roy ultimately took his life. Instead, she was held criminally responsible for encouraging Roy to carry out his suicide. The case hinged both on these text messages, as well as evidence that Carter may have been on the phone with Roy at the time of his death, encouraging him to follow through with the action. Prosecutors contended that Carter was on the phone with Roy and told him to "get back in the truck" when he stepped out of the truck. The call was not recorded and only came to the attention of authorities when Carter told a friend several weeks later via text that she was on the phone with Roy—"his death is my fault, like honestly I could have stopped him. I was on the phone with him and he got out of the car because it was working and he got scared" (Seelye & Bidgood, 2017).

What makes the case particularly interesting is that while Carter's behavior is certainly offensive, is it criminal? Suicide is an act of free will by an individual and typically lacks the legal causation that is required for most offenses. Defense experts also testified that Carter was "involuntarily intoxicated" by her use of antidepressants that were legally prescribed to her (Sanchez & Lance, 2017). Her conviction will likely be appealed and many experts have suggested that her conviction could be overturned because her actions did not directly cause Roy's death. Massachusetts is one of 10 states that does not have any laws that criminalize assisted suicide, though it is possible that the state's legislature may introduce new policy as a result of this case (Suerth, 2017).

Mothers Who Kill Their Children

While the crime of **filicide** is a rare occurrence, it raises significant attention in the media. The case of Andrea Yates is one of the most identifiable cases of filicide in the 21st century. After her husband left for work on June 20, 2001, Yates proceeded to drown each of her five children one at a time in the bathtub of the family home. Her case illustrates several factors that are common to incidents of maternal filicide. Yates had a history of mental health issues, including bipolar disorder, and she had been hospitalized in the past for major depression. She was the primary caretaker for her children and was responsible for homeschooling the older children. She and her husband were devout evangelical Methodists. Yates indicated that she felt inadequate as a mother and wife, believed that her children were spiritually damaged, and stated that she was directed by the voice of Satan to kill her children (Spinelli, 2004).

The case involving the children of Andrea Yates is just one tragic example of a mother engaging in filicide, or the killing of her children. There are several different categories of filicide. **Neonaticide** refers to an act of homicide during the first 24 hours after birth, compared to cases of **infanticide**, which includes acts whereby a parent kills his or her child within the first year of life. Here, the age of the child distinguishes these cases from general acts of filicide, which include the homicide of children older than 1 year of age by their parent. While the practice of filicide does not exclude the murder of a child by its father, mothers make up the majority of offenders in cases of infanticide and neonaticide.

What leads a woman to kill her child? There are several different explanations for this behavior. Research by Resnick (1970) distinguishes five different categories of infanticide. The first category represents cases where the infant was killed for **altruistic** reasons. In these incidents, the mother believes that it is in the best interests of the child to be dead and that the mother is doing a good thing by killing the child. Here, the mother believes (whether real or imagined) that the child is suffering in some way and that the child's pain should end. Based on Resnick's (1970) typology, Yates would be identified as a mother who kills her children out of altruistic reasons. A review of Yates's case indicates two themes common to altruistic filicide. The first theme reflects the pressure that exists in society for women to be good mothers. For Yates, this pressure was influenced by her religious fundamentalism, which placed the importance of the spiritual life of her children under her responsibility. The pressure to be a perfect mother was exacerbated by her history of mental illness. The second theme reflected the pressure of bearing the sole responsibility to care for the children. Here, Yates expressed feeling overwhelmed by the demands of their children's personal, academic, and spiritual needs, in addition to the responsibilities of caring for the family home. She also lacked any support from outside of the family, which further contributed to her feelings of being overburdened (West & Lichtenstein, 2006).

The second category in Resnick's typology refers to the killing of a child by an acutely psychotic woman. These cases are closely linked with explanations of postpartum psychosis where the mother suffers from a severe case of mental illness and may be unaware of her action or be unable to appreciate the wrongfulness of her behaviors. Examples of this type of filicide may involve a woman who hears voices that tell her that she needs to harm her child. The third category represents the killing of an unwanted infant. In many cases, these are cases of neonaticide. Research indicates that there are similar characteristics within the cases of mothers who kill their children within their first day of life. These women tend to be unmarried, under the age of 25, and generally wish to conceal their pregnancy from friends and family. Some women may acknowledge that they are pregnant, but their lack of actions toward preparing for the birth of the child indicate that they may be in denial that they may soon give birth. Others fail to acknowledge that they are pregnant and explain away the symptoms of pregnancy (Miller, 2003). They typically give birth without medical intervention and generally do not receive any form of prenatal care. The majority of these women do not suffer from any form of mental illness, which would help explain the death of their children. Instead, most of the cases of homicide of the infant are simply a result of an unwanted pregnancy. In these instances, the children are typically killed by strangulation, drowning, or suffocation (Meyer & Oberman, 2001). The fourth category involves the "accidental" death of a child following incidents of significant child abuse and maltreatment.

Often, the death of a child occurs after a long period of abuse. The fifth category represents cases where the death of a child is used as an act of ultimate revenge against another. In many cases, these vengeful acts are against the spouse and father of the child (Resnick, 1970).

Mothers who kill their children present a significant challenge to the cultural ideals of femininity and motherhood. Society dictates that mothers should love and care for their children, behave in a loving and nurturing manner, and not cause them harm or place their lives in danger. In many cases, the presence of a psychological disorder makes it easier for society to understand that a mother could hurt her child. Information on postpartum syndromes is used at a variety of different stages of the criminal justice process. Evidence of psychosis may be used to determine whether a defendant is legally competent to participate in the criminal proceedings against her. However, this stage is temporary, because the woman would be placed in a treatment facility until such a time that she is competent to stand trial. Given that postpartum syndromes are generally limited to a short period of time (compared to other forms of psychiatric diagnoses), these court proceedings would be delayed only temporarily.

More often, information about postpartum syndromes is used as evidence to exclude the culpability of the woman during a trial proceeding. In some states, this evidence forms the basis of a verdict of "not guilty by reason of insanity." Here, the courts assess whether the defendant knew that what she was doing at the time of the crime was wrong. "The insanity defense enables female violence to coexist comfortably with traditional notions of femininity. It also promotes empathy toward violent women, whose aberrance becomes a result of external factors rather than conscious choice" (Stangle, 2008, p. 709). In cases where an insanity defense is either not available or is unsuccessful, evidence of postpartum syndromes can be used to argue for the diminished capacity of the offender.

A third option allows for courts to find someone guilty but mentally ill (GBMI). Here, the defendant is found guilty of the crime, but the court may mitigate the criminal sentence to acknowledge the woman's mental health status. For many offenders, this distinction can allow them to serve a portion of their sentence in a treatment hospital or related facility (Proano-Raps & Meyer, 2003). While Andrea Yates was convicted of murder and sentenced to 40 years to life by the state of Texas in 2002, her conviction was later overturned. In her second trial, she was found not guilty by reason of insanity and was committed to a state mental health facility for treatment.

/// SUMMARY

- Women engage in every category of crime, yet their rates of offending are significantly lower than male offending practices.

- Regardless of race, ethnicity, or class, women have similar pathways to addiction: depression, abuse, and social and economic pressures.

- For many women, entry into addiction is rooted in early trauma: Drugs are used for escape, and prostitution and property crimes are then committed for survival.

- The war on drugs has led to increased incarceration rates for both men and women but has had particularly damaging effects for women.

- Women in prostitution face significant mental and physical health issues as a result of their time on the streets. These issues lead to significant challenges as they try to exit prostitution and make a new life off the streets.

- Women are most likely to commit property-based offenses.

- Sexuality can be a component of the gang life for some girls, but it is not necessarily the experience for all girls involved in gangs.

- Although female perpetrated homicide is rare, it is generally sensationalized in the media when it occurs.

- There are several different reasons why mothers may kill their children, but not all involve issues of mental illness.

KEY TERMS

Altruistic 148

Filicide 148

Infanticide 148

Neonaticide 148

Posttraumatic stress
disorder (PTSD) 140

Pulling a train 143

Street prostitution 139

Walking the line 143

DISCUSSION QUESTIONS

1. Why is the media obsessed with the image of the female offender? What implications does this have on understanding the realities of female offending?

2. What does research say about the gender gap in offending?

3. How have drug addiction and the war on drugs become a gendered experience?

4. How are drugs, property crimes, and prostitution connected for many female offenders on the streets?

5. What are the risk factors for prostitution? How do these issues affect a woman's ability to exit the streets?

6. Why are jurisdictions reluctant to legalize or decriminalize prostitution?

7. Why do women engage in property offenses?

8. How do girls use their gender within the gang context?

9. Discuss the types of violent crimes in which women most typically engage.

10. What role does mental illness play in cases of women who kill their children?

WEB RESOURCES

Children of the Night: http://www.childrenofthenight.org

National Gang Center: http://www.nationalgangcenter.gov/

Prostitutes Education Network: http://www.bayswan.org

Prostitution Research and Education: http://www.prostitutionresearch.com

SAMHSA Center for Substance Abuse Treatment: http://www.samhsa.gov/about/csat.aspx

SAMHSA National Center for Trauma-Informed Care: http://www.samhsa.gov/nctic/

The Sentencing Project: http://www.sentencingproject.org

Women and Gender in the Drug War: http://www.drugpolicy.org/communities/women

 Visit **www.sagepub.com/mallicoat3e** to access additional study tools, including eFlashcards, web quizzes, web resources, video resources, and SAGE journal articles.

CHAPTER 9

Processing and Sentencing of Female Offenders

- Processing and sentencing of female offenders
- Treatment of female offenders
- Role of patriarchy, chivalry, and paternalism in processing and sentencing

A s you learned in Chapter 1, the gender gap in crime has remained consistent since 1990. For most crime types, the increase in female arrests reflects not an increase in offending rates of women but rather a shift in policies to arrest and process cases within the criminal justice system that historically had been treated on an informal basis (Rennison, 2009; Steffensmeier & Allan, 1996; Steffensmeier, Zhong, Ackerman, Schwartz, & Agha, 2006). This chapter highlights the different ways in which gender bias occurs in the processing and sentencing of female offenders.

How might we explain the presence of gender bias in the processing of female offenders? Research highlights that women and girls can be treated differently from their male counterparts by agents of social control, such as police, prosecutors, and judges, as a result of their gender. Gender bias can occur in two different ways: (1) Women can receive lenient treatment as a result of their gender, or (2) women may be treated more harshly as a result of their gender. These two competing perspectives are known as the **chivalry** hypothesis and the **evil woman hypothesis**. The chivalry hypothesis suggests that women receive preferential treatment by the justice system. As one of the first scholars on this issue, Otto Pollak (1950) noted that agents of the criminal justice system are reluctant to criminalize women, even though their behaviors may be just as criminal as their male counterparts. However, this leniency can be costly, because it reinforces a system whereby women are denied an equal status with men in society (Belknap, 2007). While most research indicates the presence of chivalrous practices toward women, the potential for sex discrimination against women exists when they are treated more harshly than their male counterparts, even when charged with the same offense. Here, the evil woman hypothesis suggests that women are punished not only for violating the law but also for breaking the socialized norms of gender-role expectations (Nagel & Hagan, 1983).

Research throughout the past 40 years is inconclusive about whether or not girls receive chivalrous treatment. While the majority of studies indicate that girls do receive leniency in the criminal justice system, the presence of chivalry is dependent on several factors. This chapter focuses on five general themes in assessing the effects of chivalry on the processing and treatment of female offenders: (1) the stage of the criminal system, (2) the race and ethnicity of the offender, (3) the effects of the war on drugs for female offenders, (4) the effect of legal and extralegal characteristics, and (5) the effects of sentencing guidelines on judicial decision making. This chapter concludes with a discussion of some of the international sentencing practices of women.

Stage of the Criminal Justice System

Chivalry can occur at different stages of the criminal justice system. Much of the research on whether women benefit from chivalrous treatment looks at only one stage of the criminal justice process. This single snapshot approach makes it difficult to assess the potential effects of chivalrous treatment for each case, region, or time frame. In addition, it can be difficult to determine how the effects of chivalry at one stage of the criminal justice process may impact subsequent decisions as a case moves throughout the system.

Much of our data about crime begins at the arrest stage, since this is generally the first involvement that an offender will have with the criminal justice system. However, the experience of chivalrous treatment can actually begin prior to an arrest. Police officers exercise discretion as part of their everyday duties. As a result, offenders may experience chivalrous treatment as a result of their gender. For example, police use discretion in determining when to engage in stop-and-frisk tactics. Brunson and Miller (2006) noted that African American boys receive greater levels of attention by police officers compared to girls of the same race, yet this may also be dictated by offense type. For example, the girls in this study indicated that their involvement with the police was typically related to incidents of truancy, curfew violations, and other low-level offenses. In contrast, the police generally made contact with the boys over higher criminal offenses, such as drug possession or distribution.

> The police will mess with the males quicker than the females. If it's a group of girls standing across the street and it's a group of dudes standing across the street, [the police] fina [getting ready to] shine they lights on the dudes and they ain't fina mess with the girls. (Brunson & Miller, 2006, p. 539)

Contrary to popular belief, women do not always experience chivalrous treatment. In an early study on gender, chivalry, and arrest practices, Visher (1983) found that it was not just gender that affected whether chivalrous treatment was extended but that variables such as age, race, and behavior also had a strong effect on whether police exercised their discretion in favor of the women. For example, older Caucasian women benefited the most from chivalrous treatment by the police. In comparison, younger women and women of color were significantly more likely to be arrested, even in cases involving similar offenses.

In Chapter 7 you learned about how some of the changes in police practices and school policies have altered how the juvenile justice system has responded to cases of delinquency. We have also seen a ripple effect in the arrests of women as a result of the introduction of mandatory arrest policies in intimate partner abuse cases. Policies such as these have altered how police deal with cases of simple assault, and girls are disproportionately impacted by these changes. Here, the message has been that girls who act outside of traditional normative expectations for behavior are treated more harshly by police (Strom, Warner, Tichavsky, & Zahn, 2010).

Research also indicates that women are more likely to be treated leniently than men by prosecutors who determine the charges that will be filed against an offender and whether charge-reduction strategies will be employed in order to secure a guilty plea. Charge-reduction strategies involve a guilty plea by an offender in exchange for a lesser charge and a reduction in sentence. Some research indicates that women are less likely to have charges filed against them or are more likely to receive charge reductions, compared to their male counterparts (Albonetti, 1986; Saulters-Tubbs, 1993). Research by Spohn, Gruhl, and Welch (1987) found that women of all ethnic groups were more likely, compared to men of all ethnic groups, to benefit from a charge reduction. Given the shift toward determinant sentencing structures and the reduction of judicial discretion, the power of the prosecutor in this practice increases. While research by Wooldredge and Griffin (2005) indicated an increase in the practice of charge reductions under state sentencing guidelines in Ohio, their results indicated that women did not benefit from this practice any more or less than male offenders. While seriousness of crime and criminal history remain the best predictors of receiving a charge reduction, research is inconclusive on the issue of the effect of gender on this process.

At the pretrial stage, the courts are concerned with two primary factors: (1) whether an individual will engage in additional criminal activity if they are not detained prior to trial, and (2) whether they will show up for their court appearances. Most of these decisions are made primarily on an offender's criminal history. Given that women generally have lower criminal histories than men, it is not surprising that women are often treated more leniently during the pretrial stage. Several factors can influence the presence of chivalrous treatment for women at this stage. Offense type affects this process, because female offenders who were charged with property-based offenses were less likely to receive pretrial detention compared to males with similar offenses (Ball & Bostaph, 2009). Generally speaking, females are typically viewed as less dangerous than their male counterparts, making them less likely to be detained during the pretrial process (Leiber, Brubacker, & Fox, 2009). Women are also more likely to have significant ties to the community, such as family and childrearing duties, which make it less likely that they will fail to appear for future court proceedings (Steffensmeier, Kramer, & Streifel, 1993). Offense type also plays a role because women who are charged with drug or property crimes are less likely to be detained prior to trial compared to women who engage in crimes against persons (Freiburger & Hilinski, 2010). This gender bias appears throughout the pretrial process, because women are 30% less likely than men to be detained prior to trial and also receive lower bail amounts than men (and therefore run less risk of being forced to remain in custody because of an inability to make bail) (Pinchevski & Steiner, 2016). However, not all women are treated the same. For example, women who are arrested on higher level crimes and with more serious criminal histories are less likely to be released on their own recognizance and are more likely to be denied bail. Such effects are stronger for women than similarly situated men, proving that judges may punish women (i.e., evil women) who engage in serious crimes more harshly than their male counterparts (Pinchevski & Steiner, 2016). At the same time, women who appear before the court on less serious offenses are often granted greater leniency than their male counterparts (Tillyer, Hartley, & Ward, 2015). The decision to detain someone during the pretrial stage can also have consequences later in the process because women who are detained prior to trial receive longer incarceration sentences compared to those who do not receive pretrial detention (Sacks & Ackerman, 2014).

A related body of work suggests that an offender's needs can also predict whether an individual will be successful. There is limited research on how gender and gender-specific needs impact this process. In a study by Gehring and VanVoohris (2014), issues with substance abuse, mental health, housing instability, a history of abuse and failure to secure employment were also associated with a defendant's failure to appear as well as the likelihood that the offender would engage in additional criminal activity. These findings suggest that using criminal history as the sole predictor of success may not only fail to understand the unique needs of both male and female offenders but could simultaneously set individuals who have high needs but limited criminal histories up for failure. At the same time, there are variables that impact both men and women in similar ways. Research by Zettler and Morris (2015) notes that economic issues can be one of the greatest risks for failure during the pretrial stage. One of the primary causes of failure to appear because of indigence can be transportation issues that prevent offenders from appearing in court or attending pretrial supervision meetings.

Gender also has a significant impact on how cases are disposed of by the courts. In Florida, a felony conviction carries a number of consequences beyond the criminal justice system. Felons lose many of their civil rights as well as professional certifications required for certain occupations, and the restoration of these rights is not an automatic process following the completion of their sentence and requires a lengthy application process. One way of avoiding this process is to avoid a formal conviction and instead be sentenced by the judge to probation. Under state law, the adjudication of the offender is delayed, and if they successfully complete the terms and conditions of their probation, they are not considered a convicted felon (although the case remains a part of their criminal record). Women are more likely to benefit from these withheld adjudications compared to men. This practice continues even in violent offenses, such as assault, and in some cases, women were more likely to benefit from a withheld adjudication for crimes that are dominated by male offenders, such as drug manufacturing (Ryon, 2013).

The appearance of preferential or chivalrous treatment in the early stages of criminal justice processing also affects how women and girls will be treated in later stages. Females who already receive favorable treatment by prosecutors continue to receive such chivalrous treatment as their case progresses. The majority of research indicates that women are more likely to receive chivalrous treatment at sentencing. At this stage of the criminal justice process, women are less likely to be viewed as dangerous (Freiburger & Hilinski, 2010) and are less likely to recidivate (Daly, 1994). Indeed, women are viewed as better candidates for probation supervision compared to male offenders (Freiburger & Hilinski, 2010). Research on the decision to incarcerate reflects that women are less likely to be sent to jail or prison for their crimes, compared to men (Spohn & Beichner, 2000). Offense type also affects the relationship between gender and sentencing, because women are less likely to receive prison sentences for property and drug cases than their male counterparts. In those cases where women are incarcerated for these crimes, their sentences are significantly shorter compared to the sentence length for male property and drug offenders. Here, the disparity in sentencing can be attributed to the levels of discretion exercised by judges in making sentencing decisions (Rodriguez, Curry, & Lee, 2006). Overall, judges are more likely to sentence women to lesser sentences than male offenders (Goulette, Wooldredge, Frank, & Travis, 2015; Ward, Hartley, & Tillyer, 2016). Even in cases where **sentencing guidelines** are used, such as in the federal system, the odds of a substantial assistance departure are significantly greater for women (Ortiz & Spohn, 2014; Spohn & Belenko, 2013). Even in cases where offenders are already involved in the criminal justice system and have received a new charge, women are more likely to receive a substantial assistance departure to either prevent women from having to serve long terms of incarceration or to divert women already under probation supervision from having to go to prison (Ortiz & Spohn, 2014). Although there is a consistent pattern of the preferential treatment in sentencing, not all crime types in all jurisdictions report this experience. While several studies on drug offenders find that women receive preferential treatment by the courts in terms of the decision to incarcerate and the length of the sentence, research by Koeppel (2012) finds that there are no differences in the sentencing practices between male and female property offenders in rural areas.

Race Effects and the Processing of Female Offenders

Historically, African American women have been punished more harshly than White women. This punishment reflected not only a racial bias but also a pattern consistent with their levels of offending, because women of color engaged in higher levels of crimes than White women. In many cases, the types of offenses committed by women of color had more in common with male offenders. Over time, research indicated that the offending patterns of White women shifted such that women, regardless of race or ethnic status, engaged in similar levels of offending.

Significant bodies of research address concerns over the differential processing of male offenders on the basis of race and ethnicity. Here, research consistently agrees that men of color are overrepresented at every stage of the criminal justice system. Given these findings, what effect does discrimination have for female offenders? Several scholars have suggested that chivalry is selective and is more likely to advantage White females over women of color. For example, African American women are less likely to post bail compared to White women (Pinchevsky & Steiner,

2016). This may be an effect of how bail is set by the courts, because minority women receive higher bail amounts than White women (Goulette et al., 2015).

When it comes to sending women to prison, research indicates that the rates of incarceration for White women have increased by 47% between 2000 and 2009; during the same period, incarceration rates for Black women declined 31%. However, women of color still dominate the statistics given their proportion in the population. The rate of incarceration for Black women is 142 per 100,000 (compared to 50 per 100,000 for White women; Mauer, 2013). Not only are women of color more likely to be sent to prison, their incarceration sentences tend to be significantly longer than the sentences given to White women (Goulette, et al., 2015). Given these findings, some researchers have questions on whether discriminatory views about women offenders, and particularly women of color, may negatively influence prosecutorial and judicial decision-making processes (Gilbert, 2001). Even though women of color may be deemed as more "salvageable" than men of color (Spohn & Brennan, 2011), the potential effect of racial bias can be significant considering the significant powers of prosecutors in making charge decisions, offering plea agreements and charge reductions, and making sentence recommendations, as well as on judges who hand down sentences.

You have already learned that gender can impact the decision to hold someone in custody prior to trial. But how does race play into this process? Whereas interactions between gender and race can give the impression that women of color are treated more harshly by the criminal justice system, research findings indicate that the bias may be one of economics rather than race. Katz and Spohn (1995) found that White women are more likely to be released from custody during the pretrial stages, compared to Black women, as a result of the ability to fulfill demands for bail. When defendants cannot make bail, there may be incentives to accept a plea deal that would limit the time spent in custody. Yet this "freedom" comes at a cost, because the label of an *ex-felon* can affect them and limit their opportunities for the rest of their lives. This relationship between race/ethnicity, **legal factors,** and **extralegal factors** can also impact sentencing outcomes. For example, research by Brennan (2006) demonstrated that misdemeanor cases involving female defendants were more likely to be sentenced to incarceration if the offender had a prior criminal history. Here, race serves as an intermediating effect because the Black women in this study had greater criminal histories compared to White and Hispanic women. In addition, women of color were less likely to have strong positive ties to their community. This is a factor that also increased the likelihood of incarceration in these cases.

Research also finds that skin tone can influence the length of a prison sentence for women of color. Black women who are described as "light skinned" received shorter sentences by 12%, compared to offenders that were described as "darker" skinned (Viglione, Hannon, & DeFina, 2011). Similar findings are also demonstrated in research on men of color, whereas darker Black males were more likely to receive harsher punishments by the criminal justice system compared to lighter skinned Black males (Gyimah-Brempong & Price, 2006).

However, not all research demonstrates that girls and women of color suffer from harsher treatment by the courts. Some scholars find evidence that girls and women of color have benefited from chivalrous treatment. Here, scholars suggest that the preferential treatment of African American girls by judges is seen as an attempt to remedy the biased decision making of criminal justice actors during earlier stages of the criminal justice process that may have led to harsher attention (lack of pretrial release and bail options, less likely to receive charge reductions; Leiber et al., 2009). Race can have an effect on the sentencing practices for both adult and juvenile offenders. In one study on sentencing outcomes for juveniles, Guevara, Herz, and Spohn (2008) indicated that race effects did not always mean that girls of color were treated more harshly than White girls. Their results indicate that White females were more likely to receive an out-of-home placement. While many would suggest that an out-of-home placement is a more significant sanction, their research indicates that juvenile court officials may be engaging in "child saving" tactics in an effort to rehabilitate young offenders. In another study involving juvenile court practices, race did not impact the decision to detain youth in detention, because girls of all races and ethnicities were more likely to receive leniency in this decision compared to boys (Maggard, Higgins, & Chappell, 2013).

It is important to note that while research on race, ethnicity, and processing can demonstrate valuable results for women of color in the criminal justice system, these results are significantly limited. Much of the research investigating race and gender effects involves a comparison between White and Black women. It has been only within the last few decades that scholars have extended the discussion to ethnicity and included data on Hispanic/Latina females. Few studies investigate how race can impact the processing for other racial and ethnic groups, such as Asian American, Native Americans, or Pacific Islanders. In addition, while recent implementations of the U.S. Census have utilized the category of "one race or more" to acknowledge that many women of color identify as bi- or multiracial, few studies on the processing of female offenders included this variable in their research. One explanation for this stems from the different sources of data that are used by scholars, such as official data statistics like the Uniform Crime Reports. These sources are limited in how they collect data about race and ethnicity. In many cases, these assessments about race come not from how the offender self-identifies, but from the perceptions of police officers on the streets, court officials, and correctional personnel.

The War on Drugs and Its Effects for Women

The heightened frenzy about the *dangerousness* of drugs has fueled the war on drugs into an epidemic. The war on drugs first appeared as an issue of public policy in 1971, when President Richard Nixon called for a national drug policy in response to the rise of drug-related juvenile violence. Over the next decade, controlled substances, such as cocaine, were illegally smuggled into the United States by drug kingpins and cartels throughout Mexico and South America (National Public Radio, n.d.).

Since the 1980s and the passage of the Anti-Drug Abuse Act, the incarceration rates for both men and women have skyrocketed. Figure 9.1 demonstrates how these new laws impacted the arrest rates for women. Using 1972 data as a baseline, the passage of the first drug bill by President Ronald Reagan led the arrest rates for drug cases to skyrocket (Merolla, 2008). Yet the majority of persons imprisoned on these charges are not the dangerous traffickers who bring drugs into neighborhoods and place families and children at risk. Rather, it is the drug user who is at the greatest risk for arrest and imprisonment. In response to the social fears about crack cocaine in the inner city, lawmakers developed tough-on-crime sentencing structures designed to increase the punishments for crack cocaine. Sentencing disparities between powder and crack created a system whereby drug users were treated the same as mid-level dealers. In 1995, the U.S. Sentencing Commission released a report highlighting the racial effects of the crack and powder cocaine sentencing practices and advised Congress to make changes to the mandatory sentencing practices to reduce the discrepancies. Their suggestions fell on deaf ears among congressional members who did nothing to change these laws. For the next 15 years, cases of crack and powder cocaine perpetuated a 100:1 sentencing ratio, whereby offenders in possession of 5 grams of crack were treated the same as dealers in possession of 500 grams of powder cocaine. In 2010, President Obama signed the Fair Sentencing Act, which reduced the disparity between crack and powder cocaine sentences to a ratio of 18:1. Under this revised law, offenders receive a 5-year mandatory minimum sentence for possessing 28 grams of crack (compared to 5 grams under the old law) and a 10-year sentence for possessing more than 280 grams of crack cocaine.

Prior to the war on drugs and mandatory sentencing structures, most nonviolent drug conviction sentences were handled within community correction divisions. Offenders typically received community service, drug treatment, and probation supervision. The introduction of mandatory minimum sentencing represented a major change in the processing of drug offenders. While these sentencing structures are applied equally to male and female defendants, the extent of women's participation often differs substantially from male involvement in drug-related crimes. With the elimination of judicial discretion, judges were unable to assess the role that women played in these offenses. The result was a shift from community supervision to sentences of incarceration, regardless of the extent of women's participation in criminal drug-related activities (Merolla, 2008).

While the focus by the federal government on drugs shifted criminal justice practices during the mid and late-1980s, it was not until the 1990s that state governments began to alter their policies and practices related to drug

Figure 9.1 • Female Arrests for All Crimes Versus Drug Arrests, 1972–2004

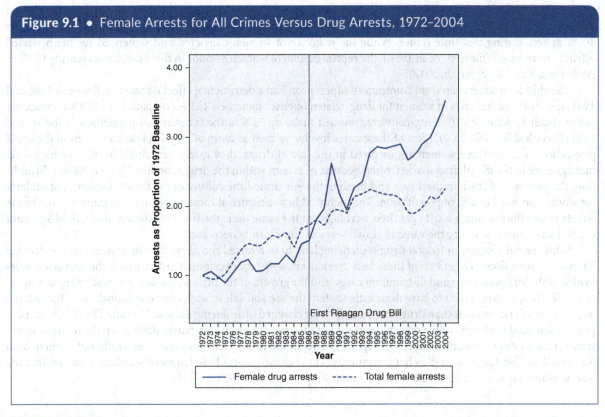

SOURCE: Merolla (2008).

crimes. In Florida, the legislature introduced the Criminal Punishment Code (CPC) in 1994. This new law called for increases not only for drug crimes but for many other crime categories as well. Here, the influence of the war on drugs reflected a shift toward a more punitive and retributive stance by criminal justice agencies. Not only did these changes have a significant effect for women in general but these practices were also particularly detrimental for women of color. In particular, these changes increased the number of racial disparities in sentencing, an ironic consequence given that the focus of the mandatory minimum sentencing practices at the federal level were intended to reduce such disparities by race and ethnicity. For example, prior to the implementation of the CPC in Florida, sentences were 27% higher for Black women and 24% greater for Hispanic/Latina women, compared to those sentences given to White women. By 2003, these disparities had increased to 38% longer sentences for women of color compared to White women.

While much of the attention about the war on drugs has focused on the crack and powder cocaine debate (and the resulting disparities in sentencing between these two substances), these substances no longer reflect the drug of choice trends that currently exist for women. Crack cocaine has been replaced by methamphetamines, to the point where meth has been labeled as the "pink collar crack" (Campbell, 2000). As with the changes that occurred to drug laws about crack and powder cocaine in the 1980s and 90s, recent history has seen changes to the laws on methamphetamine production and use that have not only increased likelihood of incarceration but also increased the sentence length for these crimes as well. As a result, the number of women sentenced for a meth-related drug conviction increased from 10.3% in 1996 to 23.0% in 2006 (Bush-Baskette, 2010). The length of sentences increased 300% as well during this time frame. While the majority of women convicted and sentenced for meth-related offenses were once White (99.5% in 1996), the representation of women of color in these cases is increasing (27% in 2006; Bush-Baskette, & Smith, 2012).

The shift to incarceration from community supervision had a detrimental effect on women. Between 1986 and 1991, the incarceration rates of women for drug-related offenses increased 433%, compared to a 283% increase for males (Bush-Baskette, 2000). Drug-convicted women make up 72% of the incarcerated population at the federal level (Greenfeld & Snell, 2000). Most of these cases involve women as users of illegal substances. Even in the small proportion of cases where women are involved in the sale of drugs, they rarely participate in mid- or high-level management in the illegal drug market, often because of sexism within the drug economy (Maher, 2004a). In addition, the presence of crack in the 1980s and meth in the 90s shifted the culture of the street economy, particularly for women involved in acts of prostitution. The highly addictive nature of these substances led more women to the streets in an effort to find a way to get their next high. At the same time, the flood of women in search of sex work created an economy whereby the value of sexual services significantly decreased.

While recent changes in federal drug sentencing laws have reduced the disparities in sentencing, the damage has already been done. The effects of these laws created a new system of criminal justice where the courts are overloaded with drug possession and distribution cases, and the growth of the prison economy has reached epic proportions. Yet these efforts appear to have done little to stem the use and sale of such controlled substances. Indeed, the overall rates of crimes other than drug-related cases have changed little during the last 40 years. The effects of these policies has produced significant consequences for families and communities, particularly given the increase in the incarceration rates of women. Chapter 10 explores in depth the consequences in the incarceration of women, both for herself and her family, as well as her community. These consequences have led some scholars to suggest that the war on drugs has in effect become a war on women (Chesney-Lind, 1997).

The Effects of Extralegal Factors on Sentencing Women

The assessment of whether women benefit from chivalrous treatment by the criminal justice system is not as simple as comparing the sentences granted to men and women in general. Many factors must be considered, including the severity of the offense, the criminal record of the offender, the levels of injury experienced by the victim, and the culpability, or blameworthiness, of the offender. For example, women generally have a less extensive criminal history than males and are less likely to engage in violent offenses or play a major role in criminal offenses.

In assessing whether women receive chivalrous treatment, it is important to control for these legal and extralegal variables. Research indicates that legal variables do affect the decision-making process for both males and females, albeit in different ways. As you learned earlier in this chapter, the effects of gender vary with each stage of the criminal justice system. For example, offense type and criminal history influence whether a defendant will be detained during the pretrial stages or receive charge reductions and leniency in sentencing. Type of offense also plays a role in whether chivalry will be extended because women who are charged with a drug offense are more likely to be denied bail and less likely to be granted ROR compared to their male counterparts (Pinchevsky & Steiner, 2016).

Not only do legal factors, such as criminal history and offense severity, appear to affect the pretrial decision process for women but extralegal factors, such as the type of attorney, affect as well the likelihood of pretrial release for women. Women who were able to hire a private attorney were 2.5 times more likely to make bail, compared to those women who relied on the services of a public defender. Clearly, the ability to hire (and financially afford) a private attorney is linked to the ability to satisfy the financial demands of bail set by the court. In comparison, women who were represented by a public defender were twice as likely to be detained at the pretrial stage (Ball & Bostaph, 2009). Ties to the community (such as family life) can also serve as an extralegal factor that can mediate sentencing practices. For example, motherhood mitigates the likelihood of a prison sentence, because women with dependent children are less likely to be incarcerated compared to women who do not have children. In these cases, judges appear to consider the social costs of imprisoning mothers and the effects of incarceration on children, particularly in cases of nonviolent or drug offenses (Spohn & Beichner, 2000). Research indicates that variables such as single parenthood and pregnancy have been used by judges to justify a departure from strict sentencing guidelines and offer a reduced sentence (Raeder, 1995). Here, it is not gender specifically that accounts for mitigation but rather concern for the family (as non-"familied" women do not receive similar instances of leniency in sentencing). These departures have been confirmed by the courts in cases such as *U.S. v. Johnson*, 964 F.2d 124 (2d Cir. 1992). Indeed, such departures are not reserved exclusively for women but can also benefit male defendants who are the primary caregiver for minor children (see *U.S. v. Cabell*, 890 F. Supp. 13, 19 [D.D.C. 1995], which granted a departure from the sentencing guidelines for a male offender who was the primary caregiver for the children of his deceased sister).

The Effects of Sentencing Guidelines on Judicial Decision Making

Throughout most of history, judges have had discretion in handing out sentences to offenders. In most cases, judges were free to impose just about any type of sentence, from probation to incarceration. Essentially, the only guidance for decision making came from the judge's own value system and beliefs in justice. This created a process whereby there was no consistency in sentencing, and offenders received dramatically different sentences for the same offenses, whereby the outcome depended on which judge heard their case. While this practice allowed for individualized justice based on the needs of offenders and their potential for rehabilitation, it also left the door open for the potential of bias based on the age, race, ethnicity, and gender of the offender.

During the 1970s, the faith in rehabilitation for corrections began to wane and was replaced with the theory of "just deserts," a retributive philosophy that aimed to increase the punishment of offenders for their crimes against society. In an effort to reform sentencing practices and reduce the levels of discretion within the judiciary, many jurisdictions developed sentencing guidelines to create systems by which offenders would receive similar sentences for similar crimes. At the heart of this campaign was an attempt to regulate sentencing practices and eliminate racial, gender, and class-based discrimination in courts. As part of the Sentencing Reform Act of 1984, the U.S. Sentencing Commission was tasked with crafting sentencing guidelines at the federal level. Since their implementation in November 1987, these guidelines have been criticized for being too rigid and unnecessarily harsh. In many cases, these criticisms reflect a growing concern that judges are now unable to consider the unique circumstances of the crime or characteristics of the offender. Indeed, the only standardized factors that are to be considered under the federal sentencing guidelines are the offense committed, the presence of aggravating or mitigating circumstances, and the criminal history of the offender.

Prior to sentencing reform at the federal level, the majority of female offenders were sentenced to community-based programs, such as probation. Under federal sentencing guidelines, not only are the numbers of incarcerated women expanding, but the length of time that they will spend in custody is increasing well.

Research by Koons-Witt (2006) investigates the effects of gender in sentencing in Minnesota. Minnesota first implemented sentencing guidelines in 1980. As in the case of federal sentencing guidelines, Minnesota founded its guidelines on a retributive philosophy focused on punishment for the offender. The guidelines were designed to be neutral on race, gender, class, and social factors. However, the courts can consider aggravating and mitigating factors, such as the offender's role in the crime, if they make a decision outside of the sentencing guidelines. Koons-Witt investigated the influence of gender at three distinct points in time: prior to the adoption of sentencing guidelines in Minnesota, following their introduction (early implementation 1981–1984), and in 1994, 14 years after the sentencing guidelines were implemented (late implementation). Her research indicated that female offenders were more likely to be older than their male counterparts and have a greater number of dependent children. In contrast, men were faced with more serious crimes, were more likely to be under community supervision at the time of the current offense, and had more significant criminal histories. Prior to the implementation of sentencing guidelines, gender did not appear to have an effect on sentencing guidelines. This finding contradicted the findings of other research, which illustrated that judges did treat female offenders in a chivalrous fashion. The one exception for Koons-Witt's findings was that sentences were reduced for women who had dependent children. Following the early implementation of sentencing guidelines (1981–1984), several legal outcomes increased the potential for incarceration regardless of gender. These legal factors include prior criminal history and pretrial detention. This pattern was repeated during the late implementation time period (1994). However, the influence of extralegal factors reappeared during this time period, whereby women with dependent children were more likely to receive community correctional sentences compared to women who did not have children. In these cases, Koons-Witt suggests that the courts may be using the presence of dependent children as a mitigating factor in their decision to depart from the sentencing guidelines, producing an indirect effect for the preferential treatment of women.

Not all states deal with directive sentencing in the same way. While Minnesota's sentencing guidelines are similar in design to the federal sentencing guidelines, Pennsylvania's sentencing guidelines are not limited to just a retributive focus but also reference tenets of rehabilitation, deterrence, and incapacitation that allow for additional opportunities for judges to exercise their discretion. Pennsylvania first developed its sentencing guidelines in 1982 but suspended the practice and reinstated the practice with new provisions in 1988. Research by Blackwell, Holleran, and Finn (2008) investigated the effects of gender and sentencing during these three time periods (when the sentencing guidelines were in effect [1986–1987 and 1988–1990] and during the suspension [1987–1988]). Their findings demonstrated that Pennsylvania's sentencing guidelines did not reduce the sentencing disparities by sex. However, it is possible that the higher levels of judicial discretion within Pennsylvania's sentencing guidelines may also contribute to this effect.

Like Minnesota and Pennsylvania, Ohio utilizes a guided sentencing structure. Felony crimes are organized into five basic categories. Unlike other state sentencing schemes, Ohio's law allows for increased opportunities for judicial discretion because each category has a wide range of options for sentencing (in terms of sentence length). Unlike other states, which demonstrated increases in the number of offenders sent to prison as well as the sentence length, Ohio documented decreases in both of these categories following its implementation of sentencing guidelines. These decreases were observed for both women and men and in the majority of offense categories (with drug cases as the exception). Racial disparities were also reduced for Black female offenders (Griffin & Wooldredge, 2006).

In contrast to the states that have either implemented or later disbanded sentencing guidelines, South Carolina considered the adoption of sentencing guidelines but ultimately failed to implement a practice. Over the two decades when the state debated whether to adopt such a schema, the state's sentencing commissions collected extensive data from the judicial, corrections, and probation/parole departments on all criminal offenses where the minimum punishment was a $500 fine or greater than 90 days in jail. Research by Koons-Witt, Sevigny, Burrow, and Hester (2012) examines these data to determine how factors such as gender, race, age, and offense type affect sentencing outcomes in a region that did not adopt structured guidelines. Their findings indicate that women benefited from chivalrous treatment by the court, because they were less likely to be incarcerated. When women were sent to prison, they received shorter sentences compared to male offenders. However, this benefit is selective, because it is extended only for White women and not for women of color.

Some critics of gender-neutral sentencing argue that directed sentencing structures such as the federal sentencing guidelines have affected women in a negative fashion. These sentence structures assume that men and women have an equal position in society and, therefore, the unique needs of women do not need to be considered when making sentencing decisions. Whereas the intent behind the creation of sentencing guidelines and mandatory minimums was to standardize sentencing practices so that offenders with similar legal variables received similar sentences, the effect has been an increased length of incarceration sentences for both men and women. Given the inability of judicial officials to consider extralegal factors in making sentencing decisions, these efforts to equalize sentencing practices have significantly affected women.

International Perspectives on the Processing of Female Offenders

While women in the United States have seen significant progress toward equality over the past century, research on gender and criminal justice processing indicate that women still experience gender bias. Here, women either positively benefit from chivalrous treatment or are penalized in part by their gender and receive harsher punishments.

Given these experiences throughout the United States, how do women fare in criminal justice systems in other regions of the world, particularly in countries with significant paternalistic views toward women?

China is one example where the paternalistic treatment of women is integrated within the cultural viewpoint. Women are considered as subordinate members of society. As a result, the legal system may treat women with "kid gloves." This need to protect women can potentially lead to reductions in punishment. As women's participation in criminal activity increases, the legal system is faced with how to respond to these cases. In China, there has been a documented increase in the number of women involved in drug possession and trafficking cases. Research by Liang, Lu, and Taylor (2009) indicates that female drug traffickers received significantly lower punishments than to their male counterparts. In addition, women benefit from chivalrous treatments, even in cases where their offenses and criminal history were similar to male drug traffickers. The most

▲ **Photo 9.1** Amanda Knox reacts after hearing the verdict during her appeal in Perugia on October 3, 2011. The Court of Cassation (Italy's highest court) cleared 24-year-old American Knox and her former boyfriend Raffaele Sollecito of the 2007 murder of British student Meredith Kercher and ordered they be freed after nearly four years in prison. One of the many motives presented by prosecutors argued that Kercher was murdered as part of an orgy gone wrong with Knox and Sollecito. Stories of Knox's sexuality were frequently used in headlines about the case.

© Gene Blevins/LA DailyNews/Corbis

important variable in these cases was the woman's behavior before the court—if the offender was remorseful about her actions and showed respect to the court, she received a more lenient sentence. However, chivalry was extended only to lower-level offenders. In cases where the woman was facing a potential death sentence, the desire for equality between men and women overpowered any influence of patriarchy. The offender's demeanor is an important variable for South Taiwanese women as well. If a female defendant demonstrates a submissive and apologetic demeanor toward the judge, she benefits from leniency in her punishment. To a certain extent, the demeanor of the defendant is just as important as the offense type or the criminal history of the offender (Hsu & Wu, 2011).

Women in South Korea also benefit from chivalry in sentencing. Female offenders are less likely to be sent to prison and received significantly shorter sentences compared to male offenders. In addition, offenders who had a prior criminal history and were detained at the pretrial stage received significantly harsher punishments. This practice echoes many of the findings with women in the American justice system. Drug of choice also has a significant impact on sentence outcomes. While cases involving methamphetamines received harsher punishments compared to marijuana cases (a likely response given stricter legal directives), female offenders were more likely to experience chivalrous treatment in terms of the length of sentence that is handed down, because male offenders received a longer sentence of incarceration than women.

However, chivalry may not be extended to all women. Research on sentencing practices in Australia looks at whether indigenous women receive preferential treatment by the courts. The term *indigenous* refers to a minority group that typifies the early inhabitants of a region. For example, we would identify *Native Americans* as an indigenous group in the United States. In Australia, a person who identifies as indigenous is of either aboriginal or Torres Strait Islander origin. Research by Bond and Jeffries (2012) finds that women of indigenous status do receive preferential treatment by justice officials. In these cases, justice officials appear to consider how unique extralegal variables within these communities (such as the presence of trauma in early childhood and the marginalization of their cultural identity) may have a significant effect on their offending behaviors. These findings suggest that judicial officials weigh the risk that indigenous offenders pose to the community in comparison to the potential consequences that incarcerating indigenous persons for a significant period of time can have for these communities (Bond & Jeffries, 2009, 2012).

Unlike these examples where chivalry can benefit women in certain cases, women in Finland do not benefit from preferential treatment by justice officials. Whereas in many of the jurisdictions where chivalry can have an impact, Finland is much more progressive in policies and practices, and there are greater levels of gender equality between men and women throughout the workplace and home. For example, Finnish family-leave policies are more generous than those in the United States, which has created increased opportunities for mothers to participate in the labor force. Women are also more likely to be active in the political realm in Finland compared to women in the United States. These examples of gender equality have also translated to the criminal justice system, where women and men are considered equal under the law. Gender appears to have no significant effect on sentencing decisions, controlling for legal variables (such as criminal history and crime severity) and social factors (such as employment and family status; Kruttschnitt & Savolainen, 2009).

Conclusion

This chapter reviewed how and when preferential treatment is extended to female offenders. Whether chivalry exists within the criminal justice system is not an easy question to answer, because it is dependent on the stage of the criminal justice system, the intersections of race and ethnicity, legal and extralegal factors, and the implementation of determinate sentencing structures. Even in cases where research suggests that chivalrous treatment serves women through shorter sentences and an increased likelihood to sentence offenders to community-based sanctions over incarceration, not all scholars see this preferential treatment as a positive asset for women. For many, the presence of chivalry is also linked to these gender-role expectations whereby "preferential or punitive treatment is meted out based on the degree to which court actors perceive a female defendant as fitting the stereotype of either a good or bad woman" (Griffin & Wooldredge, 2006, p. 896). Not only does the potential for women to be punished for breaking gender role expectations exist (i.e., the evil woman hypothesis) but there exists as well a double-edged sword in fighting for special treatment models. Gender equality does not necessarily mean "sameness." Rather, this perspective suggests that women possess cultural and biological differences that should be considered in determining the effects of "justice." However, there is a potential danger in treating women differently as a result of these cultural and biological indicators. Given that the law affords reductions in sentencing based on mental capacity and age (juvenile offenders), to extend this treatment toward women can suggest that women "cannot be expected to conform their behavior to the norms of the law . . . thus when women are granted special treatment, they are reduced to the moral status of infants" (Nagel & Johnson, 2004, p. 208).

 ## SUMMARY

- Generally speaking, women are more likely to be released during pretrial stages, receive charge reductions, and receive a jail or probation supervision sentence.

- When women are incarcerated, they typically receive shorter sentences compared to men.

- Research on race and gender is mixed, with some studies indicating that women of color are treated more harshly than Whites, and other researchers finding that women of color are treated in a more lenient fashion.

- Legal factors, such as criminal history and offense type, affect the processing of women.

- Extralegal factors, such as the type of attorney and family status, can affect the likelihood of pretrial release for women.

- Sentencing guidelines have significantly increased the number of women serving time in U.S. prisons.

 ## KEY TERMS

Chivalry 151

Evil woman hypothesis 151

Extralegal factors 155

Legal factors 155

Sentencing guidelines 154

 ## DISCUSSION QUESTIONS

1. Why is it important to study the processing of female offenders at each stage of the criminal justice system, versus just during the final disposition?

2. How do prosecutors and judges use their discretion to give preferential or chivalrous treatment toward women?

3. Which legal and extralegal factors appear to have the greatest impact on the processing of females? Which variables indicate preferential treatment of women in unexpected ways?

4. How do women in foreign countries benefit from chivalrous treatment?

> online resources Visit **www.sagepub.com/mallicoat3e** to access additional study tools, including eFlashcards, web quizzes, web resources, video resources, and SAGE journal articles.

The Supervision of Women
Community Corrections, Rehabilitation, and Reentry

- Gender-responsive treatment and programming for women in the criminal justice system
- Supervision of women in the community
- Reentry challenges for women

This chapter focuses on issues related to the supervision of women within the community corrections setting. This chapter highlights how the differential pathways of female offending affect the unique needs for women and presents a review of the tenets of gender-responsive programming. The chapter then turns to a discussion on how the needs of women can impact their successes and failures on probation. Within this context, this chapter also looks at the role of risk assessment tools and how they are used to make decisions about the supervision of women. The chapter concludes with a discussion on the challenges that female offenders face as they return to their communities following their incarceration.

Gender-Responsive Programming for Women

The needs of women have been significantly neglected by the criminal justice system throughout history. In an effort to remedy the disparities in treatment, several court cases began to challenge the delivery of services for female offenders. Most of these decisions began with the practices in women's prisons; however, their rulings have had implications for women in community correctional settings and programs as well. The case of *Barefield v. Leach* (1974) was particularly important for women because it set the standard through which the courts could measure whether women received a lower standard of treatment compared to men. While *Barefield* was heard in the District Court of New Mexico and could not be applied outside of the state, it was one of the first of its kind to address this issue. Later cases, such as *Glover v. Johnson* (1979) from the District Court of Michigan, held that the state must provide the same opportunities for education, rehabilitation, and vocational training for females as provided for male offenders. Later cases, such as *Cooper v. Morin* (1979) from the Court of Appeals of the State of New York, held that the equal protection clause prevents prison administrators from justifying the disparate treatment of women on the grounds that providing such services for women is inconvenient. Ultimately, the courts have held to a general precedent that "males and females must be treated equally unless there is a substantial reason which requires a distinction be made" (*Canterino v. Wilson*, 1982).

While these cases began to establish a conversation on the accessibility of programming for women, they generally focused on the issue of parity between male and female prisoners. At the time, women constituted only about 5% of the total number of incarcerated offenders. During the 1970s, prison advocates worked toward providing women with the same opportunities for programming and treatment as men. Their efforts were relatively successful in that many gender-based policies were abolished, and new policies were put into place mandating that men and women be treated similarly (Zaitzow & Thomas, 2003). However, feminist criminologists soon discovered that parity and equality for female offenders does not necessarily mean that women benefit from the same treatment as men (Bloom, Owen, & Covington, 2003, 2004). Indeed, research has documented that programs designed for men fail the needs of women (Belknap, 2007).

These findings led to the emergence of a new philosophy of parity for women—**gender-responsive programming**. Gender-responsive or gender-specific programming first emerged in response to the dramatic increase in the number of girls that were appearing before the juvenile court. However, few jurisdictions were prepared to address the needs of this new population. As you learned in Chapter 7, the 1992 reauthorization of the Juvenile Justice and Delinquency Prevention Act mandated that states assess the needs of girls and develop gender-specific options to address the unique needs of female offenders. Following the efforts of the juvenile court, the criminal justice system has engaged in similar conversations regarding the adult female offending population. In an effort to respond to the needs of women and girls, scholars and practitioners were left to determine what it means to be gender responsive in our correctional environments. Research by Bloom et al. (2003, 2004) highlights how six key principles can change the way in which programs and institutions design and manage programs, develop policies, train staff, and supervise offenders. These six principles are (1) gender, (2) environment, (3) relationships, (4) services and supervision, (5) socioeconomic status, and (6) community. Together, these six principles provide guidance for the effective management of female offenders.

The first principle of gender discusses the importance for criminal justice systems and agents to recognize the role that gender plays in the offending of women and the unique treatment needs of women. As you learned earlier in this book, the pathways of women to crime are dramatically different from the pathways of men. Even though they may be incarcerated for similar crimes, their lives related to these offenses are dramatically different. As a result, men and women respond to treatment in different ways and have different issues to face within the context of rehabilitation. To offer the same program to men and women may not adequately address the unique needs for both populations. Given that the majority of programs have been developed about male criminality and are used for male offenders, these programs often fail the unique needs of women.

The second principle of environment focuses on the need for officials to create a place where staff and inmates engage in practices of mutual respect and dignity. Given that many women involved in the criminal justice system come from a background of violence and abuse, it is critical that women feel safe and supported in their journey toward rehabilitation and recovery. Historically, the criminal justice system has emphasized a model of power and control, a model that limits the ability for nurturing, trust, and compassion. Rehabilitative programs for women need to create an environment that is a safe place where women can share the intimate details of their lives (Covington, 1999).

The third principle of relationships refers to developing an understanding of why women commit crimes; the context of their lives prior to, during, and following incarceration; and the relationships that women build while they are incarcerated. In addition, the majority of incarcerated women attempt to sustain their relationships with family members outside the prison walls, particularly with their minor children. Given that the majority of incarcerated women present a low safety risk to the community, women should be placed in settings that are minimally restrictive, offer opportunities for programs and services, and are located within reasonable proximity to their families and minor children. The concept of relationships also involves how program providers interact with and relate to their clients. Group participants need to feel supported by their treatment providers, and the providers need to be able to empower women to make positive choices about their lives (Covington, 1999).

The fourth principle identifies the need for gender-responsive programming to address the traumas that women have experienced throughout the context of their lives. As indicated throughout this text, the cycle to offending for women often begins with the experience of victimization. In addition, these victim experiences continue throughout their lives and often inform their criminal actions. Historically, treatment providers for substance abuse issues, trauma, and mental health issues have dealt with offenders on an individualized basis. Gender-responsive approaches highlight the need for program providers and institutions to address these issues as co-occurring disorders. Here, providers need to be cross-trained in these three issues in order to develop and implement effective programming options for women. In addition, community correctional settings need to acknowledge how these issues translate into challenges and barriers to success in the **reentry** process. This awareness can help support women in their return to the community.

The fifth principle focuses on the socioeconomic status of the majority of women in prison. Most women in prison turn to criminal activity as a survival mechanism. Earlier in this volume, you learned that women in the system lack adequate educational and vocational resources to develop a sustainable life for themselves and their families and struggle with poverty, homelessness, and limited public assistance resources, particularly for drug-convicted offenders. To enhance the possibilities of success following their incarceration, women need to have access to opportunities to break the cycle of abuse and create positive options for their future. Without these skills and opportunities, many women will fall back into the criminal lifestyle out of economic necessity. Given that many women will reunite with their children following their release, these opportunities will help women make a better life not only for themselves but for their children as well.

The sixth principle of community focuses on the need to develop collaborative relationships among providers in order to assist women in their transition toward independent living. Bloom et al. (2003) call for the need to develop wraparound services for women. **Wraparound services** refer to "a holistic and culturally sensitive plan for each woman that draws on a coordinated range of services within her community" (p. 82). Examples of these services include public and mental health systems, addiction recovery, welfare, emergency shelter organizations, and educational and vocational services. Certainly, wraparound services require a high degree of coordination between agencies and program providers. Given the multiple challenges that women face throughout their reentry process, the development of comprehensive services will help support women toward a successful transition. In addition, by having one case manager to address multiple issues, agencies can be more effective in meeting the needs of and supervising women in the community while reducing the levels of bureaucracy and "red tape" in the delivery of resources.

Table 10.1 illustrates how the principles of gender, environment, relationships, services and supervision, socioeconomic status, and community can be utilized when developing gender-responsive policies and programming. These suggestions can assist institutional administrators and program providers in developing policies and procedures that represent the realities of women's lives and reflect ways that rehabilitation efforts can be most effective for women. Within each of these topical considerations, correctional agencies should be reminded that the majority of female offenders are nonviolent in nature, are more likely to be at risk for personal injury versus harmful toward others, and are in need of services.

Table 10.1 • Questions to Ask in Developing a Systemic Approach for Women Offenders

Operational Practices

- Are the specifics of women's behavior and circumstances addressed in written planning, policy, programs, and operational practices? For example, are policies regarding classification, property, programs, and services appropriate to the actual behavior and composition of the female population?

- Does the staff reflect the offender population in terms of gender, race/ethnicity, sexual orientation, language (bilingual), ex-offender, and recovery status? Are female role models and mentors employed to reflect the racial/ethnic and cultural backgrounds of the clients?

- Does staff training prepare workers for the importance of relationships in the lives of women offenders? Does the training provide information on the nature of women's relational context, boundaries and limit setting, communication, and child-related issues? Are staff prepared to relate to women offenders in an empathetic and professional manner?

- Are staff training in appropriate gender communication skills and in recognizing and dealing with the effects of trauma and PTSD?

Services

- Is training on women offenders provided? Is this training available in initial academy or orientation sessions? Is the training provided on an ongoing basis? Is this training mandatory for executive-level staff?

- Does the organization see women's issues as a priority? Are women's issues important enough to warrant an agency-level position to manage women's services?

- Do resource allocation, staffing, training, and budgeting consider the facts of managing women offenders?

Review of Standard Procedures

- Do classifications and other assessments consider gender in classification instruments, assessment tools, and individualized treatment plans? Has the existing classification system been validated on a sample of women? Does the database system allow for separate analysis of female characteristics?

- Is information about women offenders collected, coded, monitored, and analyzed in the agency?

- Are protocols established for reporting and investigating claims of staff misconduct, with protection from retaliation ensured? Are the concepts of privacy and personal safety incorporated in daily operations and architectural design, where applicable?

- How does policy address the issue of cross-gender strip searches and pat downs?

- Does the policy include the concept of zero tolerance for inappropriate language, touching, and other inappropriate behavior and staff sexual misconduct?

Children and Families

- How do existing programs support connections between the female offender and her children and family? How are these connections undermined by current practice? In institutional environments, what provisions are made for visiting and for other opportunities for contact with children and family?

- Are there programs and services that enhance female offenders' parenting skills and their ability to support their children following release? In community supervision settings and community treatment programs, are parenting responsibilities acknowledged through education? Through child care?

Community

- Are criminal justice services delivered in a manner that builds community trust, confidence, and partnerships?

- Do classification systems and housing configurations allow community custody placements? Are transitional programs in place that help women build long-term community support networks?

- Are professionals, providers, and community volunteer positions used to facilitate community connections? Are they used to develop partnerships between correctional agencies and community providers?

SOURCE: Bloom, Owen, & Covington (2003).

The Supervision of Women in the Community

Community-based supervision is the most common form of intervention utilized by the criminal justice system. Within community supervision, the most popular option is **probation**. When offenders are sentenced to probation, they are allowed to remain in the community rather than serve out their sentence in jail or prison. In addition, a sentence to probation allows for offenders to access programs and services that focus on rehabilitation. Offenders on probation must follow specific terms and conditions that allow them to remain in the community. These can include a curfew, participation in therapeutic programs such as anger management counseling and drug treatment, or maintaining a job or enrollment in school. Offenders may also be required to pay fines to the court, restitution to the victim, or to complete community service hours. If an offender fails to follow the directives as ordered by the court and her probation officer, she runs the risk of losing her privilege to remain in the community.

In 2015, 4,650,900 adults were supervised in the community through probation services. According to the Bureau of Justice Statistics, 25% of these probationers were female. This is a slight increase from 2005 where 23% of the probation population were women (Kaeble & Bonczar, 2015). Probation has traditionally been an option offered for many female offenders because it allowed them to remain in the community. This is particularly important given that many women are often the primary caregivers for young children.

The central tenet of probation is about reducing risk to the community. When offenders are sentenced to serve out their sentence under community supervision, how can we be sure that they will be successful? How can we be sure that they are not a danger to themselves or others? In evaluating the risks and needs of women on probation, many agencies use assessment instruments to gauge the risk that an offender presents to the public. At the same time, these tools can help identify what the needs of the offender are, which can help probation officers provide services and supervision for these offenders. However, these *gender-neutral* assessments may not adequately identify the needs of female offenders (Davidson, 2011). In addition, the needs of women are often misrepresented as risks, which can lead to increased punitive punishments by probation officers.

One of the most common assessment tools used in community corrections is the **Level of Service Inventory-Revised (LSI-R)**. While the LSI-R has been validated within the male offender population, research on the LSI-R for female offenders has been mixed. In some cases, the LSI-R fails to identify the gender-specific needs of women. In others, the LSI-R has led to the over-classification of women. Even when the LSI-R is effective in identifying the risks of recidivism, this tool may not be able to assess the context of these risks. Finally, the LSI-R fails to identify some of the most significant needs of women with their abuse histories, health issues, and motherhood issues (Davidson 2011).

Table 10.2 ● Characteristics of Women in Community Corrections		
	Under Community Supervision	**In Jail**
White	62%	36%
African American	27%	44%
Hispanic	10%	15%
Median age	32	31
High school/GED	60%	55%
Single	42%	48%
Unemployed	–	60%
Mother of minor children	72%	70%

▲ **Photo 10.1** Women walk along a corridor at the Los Angeles County women's jail in Lynwood, California, April 26, 2013. The Second Chance Women's Re-entry Court is one of the first in the U.S. to focus on women, and offers a cost-saving alternative to prison for women who plead guilty to nonviolent crimes and volunteer for treatment. Of the 297 women who have been through the court since 2007, 100 have graduated, and only 35 have been returned to state prison.

Given some of these limitations of the LSI-R and other assessment tools, scholars have worked to develop gender-responsive tools to provide a better reflection of the needs of female offenders. The first instrument is shorter in length and is designed to supplement existing assessments that are not gender specific, while the second instrument is designed to replace existing measures and be used as a stand-alone tool in evaluating risk and identifying needs for female offenders. The philosophy behind these new tools is to allow for community correctional agencies to record the high needs that many female offenders may have without increasing their risk levels. (Salisbury, Van Voorhis, Wright, & Bauman, 2009). Another example is the Dynamic Risk Assessment for Offender Reentry (DRAOR), which has been used by Community Probation Services throughout New Zealand and has also been adapted in some U.S. jurisdictions. While this tool was developed for use with male populations, research notes that it can be effective in predicting the risk of recidivism for women (Yesberg, Scanlan, Hanby, Serin, & Polaschek, 2015). These tools allow community correctional agencies to be advocates for female-only and smaller caseloads as well as partner with other agencies and providers in the community to develop wraparound services that will help increase the success levels of women on probation (Van Voorhis, Salisbury, Wright, & Bauman, 2008).

The failure by community-based services to develop and implement gender-responsive programs that meet the needs of offenders is connected to recidivism rates. One example of an effective gender-responsive program for female probationers is the *Moving On* program. The curriculum is designed to help women build tools for resiliency in their personal lives and develop ways to generate support and resources within their communities. Here, the focus of the program is to increase women's self-awareness of their challenges and triggers that might lead to recidivism. Assessments of the *Moving On* program have demonstrated its efficacy, because these women had lower rates of recidivism (in terms of new offenses) compared to those women under traditional probation supervision. While the women from the *Moving On* program were more likely to receive a technical violation of probation, these violations occurred in cases where the women failed to complete the program. These findings conclude that the completion of a gender-responsive program can be an effective tool in reducing the recidivism rates of women on probation (Gehring, Van Voorhis, & Bell, 2010).

Once on probation, gender has an effect on how offenders experience probation, because probation officers view male and female offenders differently, which alters their supervision style. Research by Wyse (2013) indicates that probation officers are more likely to focus on the rules of probation with male probationers. Here, the emphasis was placed on whether the men were employed and desisting from criminal behavior. In these cases, the relationship between the offender and the officer was very formal. In contrast, the relationship between the probation officer and female clients was more intimate and emotional in nature. In many cases, this allowed offenders to develop trust with their probation officers, and offenders seek out their help in finding referrals for treatment and support (Hall, Golder, Conley, & Sawning, 2013). Officers frequently encouraged their clients to find ways to increase their self-esteem. Women were also encouraged to build self-reliance and stay away from romantic relationships in general. Indeed, officers spend far greater time policing these relationships for women, while this is rarely mentioned for male offenders (Wyse, 2013).

Women on Parole

The term **parole** invokes a variety of meanings. On one hand, an offender in prison can be up for parole and have her file reviewed by a board of officials to determine whether she should be released back into the community. At the same time, parole also refers to the supervision of offenders following their release from prison. In 2011, of the 853,900 people who were supervised on parole, 11% of the parole population were women (Maruschak & Parks, 2012). Given that women make up such a small proportion of the offenders placed on parole, it has been challenging to provide appropriate gender-responsive programming and services for this population. While parole supervision was once intended to help offenders successfully transition back to the community, the role of parole officers has shifted. Because of the high caseloads that many parole officers face, the opportunities to provide an individualized case to these offenders are limited. Instead, the majority of their time is spent monitoring offenders, waiting to respond if and when an offender violates the conditions of their release. One woman shares the struggles in meeting these demands, expressing fear and the unknown of her new life and her ability to be successful in her reentry process:

> I start my day running to drop my urine [drug testing]. Then I go see my children, show up for my training program, look for a job, go to a meeting [Alcoholics Anonymous], and show up at my part-time job. I have to take the bus everywhere, sometimes eight buses for 4 hours a day. I don't have the proper outer clothes, I don't have the money to buy lunch along the way, and everyone who works with me keeps me waiting so that I am late to my next appointment. If I fail any one of these things I am revoked. I am so tired that I sometimes fall asleep on my way home from work at 2:00 a.m. and that's dangerous given where I live. And then the next day I have to start over again. I don't mind being busy and working hard . . . that's part of my recovery. But this is a situation that is setting me up to fail. I just can't keep up and I don't know where to start. (Ritchie, 2001, p. 381)

Reentry Issues for Incarcerated Women

The needs of incarcerated women returning to their communities are high. While much of the research on reentry issues has focused on whether offenders will reoffend and return to prison (recidivism), recent scholars have shifted the focus on reentry to discussions on how to successfully transition offenders back into their communities. This process can be quite traumatic, and for women, a number of issues emerge in creating a successful reentry experience.

Consider the basic needs of a woman who has just left prison. She needs housing, clothing, and food. She may be eager to reestablish relationships with friends, family members, and her children. In addition, she has obligations as part of her release—appointments with her parole officer and treatment requirements. In addition, the majority of women find themselves returning to the same communities in which they lived prior to their incarceration, where they face the same problems of poverty, addiction, and dysfunction. Finding safe and affordable housing is challenging, and for many women, the only options place them at risk for relapse and recidivism (Hall et al., 2013). Figure 10.1 highlights the types of short- and long-term housing that women utilize in their exit from prison. Research by the Urban Institute notes that women often sacrifice their safety in exchange for housing: Within the first year of their release, 19% of female ex-offenders in Texas were residing with someone who abused drugs and 22% of women were living with someone who was abusing alcohol (LaVigne, Brooks, & Shollenberger, 2009).

Women are also less likely to have participated in any vocational training programs while behind bars (LaVigne, Brooks, & Shollenberger, 2009). For those few women who were able to receive some therapeutic treatment in prison, most acknowledge that these prison-based intervention programs provided few, if any, legitimate coping skills to deal with the realities of the life stressors that awaited them on their release. Many women also hope to reunite with their children. While a return to motherhood may be a powerful motivation to get their lives back on track, the reality of returning as the authority figure in a family is compromised by a number of factors. These include the separation from her children during incarceration, the loss of her children to other family members or social services, and a lack of confidence to effectively raise her children (Brown & Bloom, 2009). On top of all these struggles, offenders face a new identity on their release from prison—the *ex-offender* status. This identity can place significant challenges for offenders and threaten their ability to be successful on release. Consider the number of employment opportunities that require applicants to disclose whether they have ever been arrested for a crime. In many cases, this automatically excludes the applicant from consideration. For women, the inability to find suitable employment has a significant effect, particularly if she is trying to create a stable home environment to regain custody of her

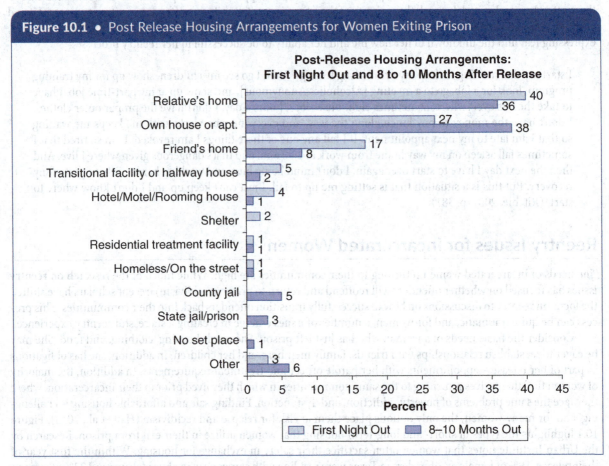

Figure 10.1 ● Post Release Housing Arrangements for Women Exiting Prison

**Post-Release Housing Arrangements:
First Night Out and 8 to 10 Months After Release**

SOURCE: LaVigne, N. G., Brooks, L. E., & Shollenberger, T. L. (2009). *Women on the outside: Understanding the experiences of female prisoners returning to Houston, Texas.* Urban Institute Justice Policy Center. Retrieved at http://www.urban.org/sites/default/files/publication/30401/411902-Women-on-the-Outside-Understanding-the-Experiences-of-Female-Prisoners-Returning-to-Houston-Texas.PDF

children. Many women also reference how their lack of education or training makes it difficult to secure legal and stable employment (Hall et al., 2013). A recent campaign to *ban the box* has many states and companies changing the way they handle ex-convicts' applications for employment. In Minnesota, recent legislation makes it illegal for state employers to ask about an offender's criminal history on a job application. As one of the largest retailers, Target has reformed its hiring policies such that questions about any criminal history are not raised until an applicant has been granted an interview (Strachan, 2013).

In addition to the challenges of returning home from prison, many women continue to battle the demons that led them to criminal activity in the first place. As you learned in Chapter 8, drug addiction is one of the primary reasons why women are involved in criminal activity and ultimately sent to prison. Given the limited availability of treatment options both behind bars and within the community, issues of addiction can lead to recidivism, particularly for women of color (Huebner, DeJong, & Cobbina, 2010). Drug addiction has a multiplying effect in the lives of women—not only can addiction threaten a woman's status on parole, but it impacts as well her ability to maintain stable employment, secure housing, and reunify with her children.

Without community-based resources, many women will return to the addictions and lifestyles in which they engaged prior to their incarceration. In addition, women have limited access to physical and mental health care, often because of a lack of community resources, an inability to pay, or lack of knowledge about where to go to obtain assistance. Sixty-seven percent of women who exit prison have been diagnosed with some sort of chronic health condition, such as asthma, high blood pressure, or an infectious disease. In addition, more than half of the women suffer from mental health issues (LaVigne, Brooks, & Shollenberger, 2009). Given the status of mental and physical health needs of incarcerated women, the management (or lack thereof) of chronic health problems can impede a woman's successful reentry process (Ritchie, 2001). Unfortunately, mental health services within the community overemphasize the use of prescription psychotropic medications. Coupled with the limited availability of therapeutic interventions, these health interventions resemble more of a Band-Aid than a comprehensive stable approach for women (Kitty, 2012). This lack of therapeutic support has a significant impact particularly for women with children because both the women and their children could benefit from these resources (Snyder, 2009). Figure 10.2 highlights the types of services that women say would be the most beneficial in aiding their reentry process. The three most desired resources include job training programs, educational programs, and housing programs. Findings such as this highlight the role of basic sustainability when exiting prison (LaVigne, Brooks, & Shollenberger, 2009).

Reentry can also be challenging depending on the offense that brought women to prison in the first place. You've learned in this chapter about the challenges of reentry for women who continue to struggle with addiction. But what about women who are convicted of one of the most stigmatizing crimes: sexual offenses? What issues do they face? Like other offenders, women convicted of a sexually based offense express concerns about finding housing and a job. In particular, they acknowledged that their offenses come with special terms and conditions of their release such as community notification and residency restrictions. In particular, women were concerned about how this might affect their relationships with their children: Would they be allowed to see them participate in activities such as sports if they were held at their children's school or at a local park? Another concern was the stigma that comes with the all-encompassing label of sex offender, regardless of the nature of their specific offense. Indeed, this label can complicate what is already a difficult transition to the community (Tewksbury, Connor, Cheeseman, & Rivera, 2012).

While women may turn to public assistance to help support their reentry transition, many come to find that these resources are either unavailable or are significantly limited. The **Welfare Reform Act of 1996** imposed not only time limits on the aid that women can receive, but it has also significantly affected the road to success by denying services and resources for women with a criminal record, particularly in cases of women convicted on a felony drug-related charge (Hirsch, 2001). Section 115 of the welfare reform act calls for a lifetime ban on benefits such as Temporary Assistance for Needy Families (TANF) and food stamps to offenders convicted in the state or federal

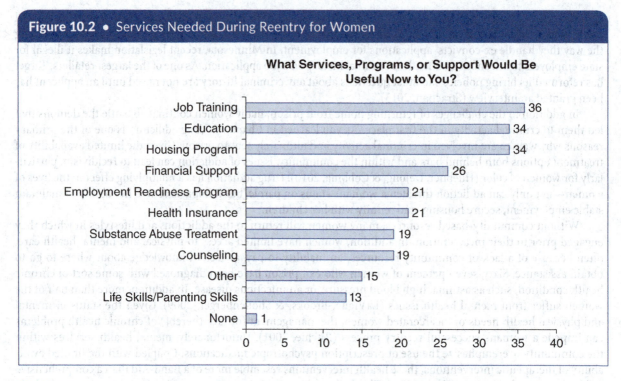

Figure 10.2 • Services Needed During Reentry for Women

What Services, Programs, or Support Would Be Useful Now to You?

Service	Value
Job Training	36
Education	34
Housing Program	34
Financial Support	26
Employment Readiness Program	21
Health Insurance	21
Substance Abuse Treatment	19
Counseling	19
Other	15
Life Skills/Parenting Skills	13
None	1

SOURCE: LaVigne, N. G., Brooks, L. E., & Shollenberger, T. L. (2009). *Women on the outside: Understanding the experiences of female prisoners returning to Houston, Texas.* Urban Institute Justice Policy Center. Retrieved at http://www.urban.org/sites/default/files/publication/30401/411902-Women-on-the-Out-side-Understanding-the-Experiences-of-Female-Prisoners-Returning-to-Houston-Texas.PDF

courts for a felony drug offense. In addition, women convicted of a drug offense are barred from living in public housing developments and, in some areas, a criminal record can limit the availability of Section 8 housing options[1] (Jacobs, 2000). Drug charges are the only offense type subjected to this ban—even convicted murderers can apply for and receive governmental benefits following their release (Sentencing Project, 2006). Indeed, the limits of this ban jeopardize the very efforts toward sustainable and safe housing, education, and drug treatment that are needed in order for women to successfully transition from prison.

How many women are affected by the lifetime bans on assistance? Research by the Sentencing Project indicates that, as of 2011, more than 180,000 women have been affected by the lifetime TANF welfare ban (Sentencing Project, 2015). They also estimate that the denial of benefits places more than 135,000 children at risk for future contact with the criminal justice system because of economic struggles. The ban also disproportionately affects women of color. Since its enactment in 1996, 39 states have rescinded the lifetime ban on resources, either in its entirety or in part. However, 11 states have retained this ban on assistance, placing family reunification efforts between women and their children in jeopardy (Legal Action Center, 2011; Sentencing Project, 2006). In Georgia, a state that has a full ban for both TANF and SNAP benefits for individuals convicted on a drug offense, some legislators have questioned whether such a ban is an effective policy. Georgia State Representative Rich Golick has supported lifting the ban: "You had individuals who were coming out of the system convicted of a violent crime who had the eligibility to apply

---

[1]Section 8 housing provides governmental subsidies for housing in nonpublic housing developments. Here, private landlords are paid the difference between the amount of rent that a tenant can afford, based on his or her available income, and the fair market value of the residence.

Table 10.3 ● State Drug Conviction Policies on Cash Assistance (TANF) and Food Stamps (SNAP)

TANF			SNAP		
Full Ban	**Modified Ban**	**No Ban**	**Full Ban**	**Modified Ban**	**No Ban**
Alaska	Arkansas	Kansas	Alaska	Arkansas	Delaware
Alabama	Arizona	Maine	Alabama	Arizona	Iowa
Delaware	California	Michigan	Georgia	California	Kansas
Georgia	Colorado	New Hampshire	Missouri	Colorado	Maine
Illinois	Connecticut	New Jersey	Mississippi	Connecticut	Michigan
Missouri	Florida	New Mexico	South Carolina	Florida	New Hampshire
Mississippi	Hawaii	New York	Texas	Hawaii	New Jersey
Nebraska	Iowa	Ohio	West Virginia	Iowa	New Mexico
South Carolina	Idaho	Oklahoma	Wyoming	Idaho	New York
South Dakota	Indiana	Pennsylvania		Illinois	Ohio
Texas	Kentucky	Rhode Island		Indiana	Oklahoma
West Virginia	Louisiana	Vermont		Kentucky	Pennsylvania
	Massachusetts	Wyoming		Louisiana	Rhode Island
	Maryland			Massachusetts	South Dakota
	Minnesota			Maryland	Vermont
	Montana			Minnesota	Wyoming
	North Carolina			Montana	
	North Dakota			North Carolina	
	Nevada			North Dakota	
	Oregon			Nevada	
	Tennessee			Oregon	
	Utah			Tennessee	
	Virginia			Utah	
	Washington			Virginia	
	Wisconsin			Wisconsin	
12	**25**	**13**	**9**	**25**	**16**

SOURCE: The Sentencing Project (2015, updated). sentencing project.org/wp-content/uploads/2015/12/A-lifetime-of-punishment.pdf. Reprinted with permission from The Sentencing Project.

for food stamps, whereas someone who went in on a drug charge, including possession, didn't have that ability. You're increasing the changes that they may reoffend because they don't have the ability to make ends meet. Doesn't this go against what we're trying to achieve as they reenter society" (Wiltz, 2016).

Even women without a drug conviction still face significant issues in obtaining public assistance. Federal welfare law prohibits states from providing assistance under programs such as TANF (Temporary Assistance for Needy Families), SSI (Supplementary Security Income), housing assistance, or food stamps in cases where a woman has violated a condition of her probation or parole. In many cases, this violation can be as simple as failing to report for a meeting with a probation officer when she has a sick child. In addition, TANF carries a 5-year lifetime limit for assistance. This lifetime limit applies to all women, not just those under the criminal justice system. In addition, the delay to receive these services ranges from 45 days to several months, a delay that significantly affects the ability of women to put a roof over their children's heads, clothes on their bodies, and food in their bellies (Jacobs, 2000). Ultimately, these reforms are a reflection of budgetary decisions that often result in the slashing of social service and government aid programs, while the budgets for criminal justice agendas, such as incarceration, remain supported by state and governmental officials. These limits affect not only the women who are in the greatest need of services but their children as well, who will suffer physically, mentally, and emotionally from these economic struggles (Danner, 2003).

Despite the social stigma that comes with receiving welfare benefits, women in one study indicated that the receipt of welfare benefits represented progress toward a successful recovery and independence from reliance on friends, family, or a significant other for assistance. A failure to receive benefits could send them into a downward spiral toward homelessness, abusive relationships, and relapse.

> We still need welfare until we are strong enough to get on our feet. Trying to stay clean, trying to be responsible parents and take care of our families. We need welfare right now. If we lose it, we might be back out there selling drugs. We're trying to change our lives. Trying to stop doing wrong things. Some of us need help. Welfare helps us stay in touch with society. Trying to do what's right for us. (Hirsch, 2001, p. 278)

Throughout the reentry process, women also struggle with gaining access to addiction-based services. Without these referrals by probation and parole, most women are denied access to treatment due to the limited availability of services or an inability to pay for such resources on their own. Here, women are actually at risk for recidivism, because their needs continue to be unmet. In addition, many of these programs fail to work within the context of their lives. For example, the majority of inpatient drug treatment programs do not provide the option for women to reside and care for their children. These programs promote sobriety first and rarely create the opportunity for family reunification until women have successfully transitioned from treatment, have obtained a job, and can provide a sustainable environment for themselves. For many women, the desire to reunite with their children is their primary focus, and the inability for women to maintain connection with their children can threaten their path toward sobriety (Jacobs, 2000).

Clearly, women who make the transition from prison or jail back to their communities must achieve stability in their lives. With multiple demands on them (compliance with the terms and conditions of their release; dealing with long-term issues such as addiction, mental health, and physical health concerns; and the need for food, clothing, and shelter), this transition is anything but easy. Here, the influence of a positive mentor can provide significant support for women as they navigate this journey.

> While it is true a woman in reentry has many tangible needs (housing, employment, family reunification, formal education), attention to intangible needs (empowerment, a sense of belonging, someone to talk to) can promote personal growth through positive reinforcement of progress, encouragement and support in the face of defeat and temptation, and a place to feel like a regular person. (Women's Prison Association [WPA], 2008, p. 3)

Several key pieces of legislation have focused on the need for support and mentorship throughout the reentry process and have provided federal funding to support these networks. For example, the Ready4Work initiative (U.S. Department of Labor, 2008), the Prisoner Reentry Initiative (Bush, 2004), and the Second Chance Act (2007) all acknowledged the challenges that ex-offenders face when they exit the prison environment. These initiatives help support community organizations that provide comprehensive services for ex-offenders, including case management, mentoring, and other transitional services (WPA, 2008). Given the struggles that women face as part of their journey back from incarceration, it is clear that these initiatives can provide valuable resources to assist with the reentry process.

Spotlight on Life After Parole

What is it like to experience freedom after spending over 25 years in prison? For women like Brenda Clubine and Glenda Virgil, it's a new life compared to what they experienced prior to entering prison. Both women endured significant abuse by their intimate partner. And both women were incarcerated in the California Institution for Women for killing their abusers.

Brenda Clubine was sentenced to 17 years to life in 1983 for the murder of her husband, Robert Clubine. During their seven-month marriage, she had endured significant beatings and multiple trips to the emergency room. One night, she struck him over the head with an empty wine bottle and he died from blunt force trauma (Hastings, 1993). Glenda Virgil killed her boyfriend with a shotgun when he charged at her with a shovel, threatening to kill her. Similar to Clubine, Virgil was abused physically and sexually throughout their four-year relationship. She was sentenced in 1987 to 15 years to life (CBSLA.com, 2013). Neither woman was allowed to present evidence of their abuse histories during their trials.

Behind the walls of the California prison, Clubine founded a group called Convicted Women Against Abuse where she met women like herself, women like Glenda Virgil. Their stories, as well as the stories of other women like them, were featured in a 2008 documentary called "Sin by Silence." In addition to building a community of abused women behind bars and providing support to each other, the group has been active in trying to change legislation related to abused victims in the criminal courts. During the early 1990s the group was involved in allowing the Battered Women's Syndrome to be used in clemency cases. Their efforts led to the release of several women in the group (Hillard, 2012).

After serving 26 years behind bars, Clubine was released from prison in 2008. Since her release from prison, she has continued her advocacy efforts. In 2012, Governor Brown signed into law new legislation that allowed for victims of domestic violence to petition for new sentencing and parole hearings. During these hearings, inmates are now allowed to present evidence of their abuse and its relationship to their crimes (CISION, 2012). It was under this new law that Glenda Virgil was granted parole after two and a half decades in prison (Ma, 2013). At the time of her release, she had been diagnosed with stage 4 cancer. She passed away in 2017.

Recidivism and Female Offenders

Whether it is probation, prison, or parole, the goal of the corrections is to reduce and prevent recidivism. But does it? Recidivism can be a difficult thing for scholars to measure. What "counts" as recidivism? Is it being arrested or convicted for a new criminal offense? Is it a technical violation of probation or parole? What is the time limit that we use to determine recidivism? One year following release? Five? Ten?

While women are slightly more likely to be successful on parole than to their male counterparts, the failure for women is still high with 47.1% of women returning to prison within one year of release (compared to 59.2% of men returned to prison during the same time period) (Blackburn, Pfeffer, & Harris, 2016). Research by Mears, Cochran, and Bales (2012) indicates that prison can produce a criminogenic effect for women. This means that prison can actually encourage offenders to engage in crime rather than prevent it, at least in terms of particular offenses. While time in prison is more likely to increase property and drug crimes for male offenders, incarceration for women increases their recidivism for property offenses. In addition, prison produces the strongest effect for recidivism, compared to probation. Women who returned to prison during that first year were more likely to have mental health issues that were either untreated or undertreated, a factor that played a significant role in their recidivism (Blackburn, Pfeffer, & Harris, 2016). Women are also more likely to fail on parole due to a technical violation and fail at a faster rate compared to men (Huebner & Pleggenkuhle, 2015). Younger women are also more likely to recidivate (McCoy & Miller, 2013). However, protective factors did serve to inhibit recidivism for women. While romantic and familial relationships increased recidivism risk for male offenders, these relationships (when positive in nature) served to protect women from recidivism (Cobbina, Huebner, & Berg, 2012). These results indicate that the *most punitive* punishment may be the least effective in terms of rehabilitation and that reentry efforts need to consider these factors when providing support.

Building Resiliency for Women

With so much attention on the negative focus of women's lives and their relationships, there has been little discussion within the research about how women involved in the criminal justice system build strength and resiliency in their lives. In Chapter 7, you learned about how factors such as a positive mentor and support networks are important factors for delinquent girls, and the same holds true for incarcerated women. Research by Wright, DeHart, Koons-Witt, and Crittenden (2013) indicates that there are several relationships that can serve as buffers against criminal behavior, including positive family relationships, prosocial peer relationships, supportive significant others, and motherhood. In some cases, family members helped them escape from dangerous situations such as an intimate partner. "Normal" friends may inspire women to want normalcy in their lives. While much has been written about the power of a negative romantic relationship, a healthy relationship can also provide support throughout incarceration and provide a sense of stability on release. Finally, the presence of children may encourage women to turn away from a life of crime and focus on their roles as mothers. While these relationships presented positive opportunities, these women also had negative associations to battle, and it was these bad contexts and relationships that would overpower the positive opportunities in their lives. In the words of one woman,

> It all goes back to trying to please people that you care about. . . . It keeps you focused. If you care about your family and love them, you aren't going to put yourself in a position to have yourself taken away from them. (Wright et al., p. 81)

/// **SUMMARY**

- Probation allows women to receive correctional supervision while remaining in the community.

- On release, many women return to the communities in which they lived prior to their incarceration, where they face issues of addiction and dysfunction in their lives.

- Gender-responsive programming is designed to address the unique needs of female offenders.

KEY TERMS

Barefield v. Leach 165

Canterino v. Wilson 166

Cooper v. Morin 166

Gender-responsive
 programming 166

Glover v. Johnson 165

Level of Service Inventory-Revised
 (LSI-R) 169

Parole 171

Probation 169

Reentry 167

Welfare Reform Act of 1996 173

Wraparound services 167

DISCUSSION QUESTIONS

1. If you were to design a program that reflected gender-responsive principles, what key features would you integrate into your curriculum?

2. What challenges do women face during their reentry process? How does the Welfare Reform Bill limit access to resources for some women following their incarceration?

3. How do traditional risk assessment instruments fail female offenders? What are the implications of these findings?

WEB RESOURCES

Hour Children: http://www.hourchildren.org

Our Place DC: http://www.ourplacedc.org

The Sentencing Project: http://www.sentencingproject.org

Women's Prison Association: http://www.wpaonline.org

 Visit **www.sagepub.com/mallicoat3e** to access additional study tools, including eFlashcards, web quizzes, web resources, video resources, and SAGE journal articles.

CHAPTER 11

Women, Gender, and Incarceration

Chapter Highlights

- Historical trends in the incarceration of women
- Contemporary issues in the incarceration of women

This chapter focuses on patterns and practices in the incarceration of women offenders. Ranging from historical examples of incarceration to modern-day policies, this chapter looks at the treatment and punishment of women in jails and prisons. This chapter also highlights how children become unintended victims in the incarceration of mothers. This chapter concludes with a discussion about the lives of women in prison and their survival strategies as they "do time."

Historical Context of Female Prisons

Prior to the development of the all-female institution, women were housed in a separate unit within the male prison. Generally speaking, the conditions for women in these units were horrendous and were characterized by an excessive use of solitary confinement and significant acts of physical and sexual abuse by both the male inmates and the male guards. Women in these facilities received few, if any, services (Freedman, 1981). At Auburn State Prison in New York, women were housed together in an attic space where they were unmonitored and received their meals from male inmates. In many cases, these men would stay longer than necessary to complete their job duties. To no surprise, there were many prison-related pregnancies that resulted from these interactions. The death of a pregnant woman named Rachel Welch in 1825 as a result of a beating by a male guard led to significant changes in the housing of incarcerated women. In 1839, the first facility for women opened its doors. The Mount Pleasant Prison Annex was located on the grounds of Sing Sing, a male penitentiary located in Ossining, New York. While Mount Pleasant had a female warden at the facility, the oversight of the prison remained in the control of the administrators of Sing Sing, who were male and had little understanding about the nature of female criminality. Despite the intent by administrators to eliminate the abuse of women within the prison setting, the women incarcerated at Mount Pleasant continued to experience high levels of corporal punishment and abuse at the hands of the male guards.

Figure 11.1 • Timeline on the Development of Women's Prisons

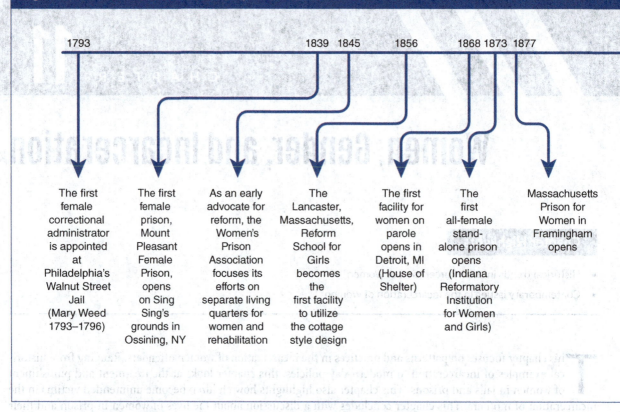

| 1793 | | 1839 | 1845 | 1856 | 1868 | 1873 | 1877 |

The first female correctional administrator is appointed at Philadelphia's Walnut Street Jail (Mary Weed 1793–1796)

The first female prison, Mount Pleasant Female Prison, opens on Sing Sing's grounds in Ossining, NY

As an early advocate for reform, the Women's Prison Association focuses its efforts on separate living quarters for women and rehabilitation

The Lancaster, Massachusetts, Reform School for Girls becomes the first facility to utilize the cottage style design

The first facility for women on parole opens in Detroit, MI (House of Shelter)

The first all-female stand-alone prison opens (Indiana Reformatory Institution for Women and Girls)

Massachusetts Prison for Women in Framingham opens

SOURCES: Freedman, E. B. (1981). *Their Sisters' Keepers: Women's Prison Reform in America 1830–1930*. Ann Arbor: University of Michigan Press; Rafter, N. H. (1985). *Partial Justice: Women, Prisons and Social Control*. New Brunswick, CT: Transaction; Watterson, K. (1996). *Women in Prison: Inside the Concrete Womb*. Boston, MA: Northeastern University Press; Women's Prison Association (n.d., "History & Mission"). Retrieved from http://www.wpaonline.org/about/history

Conditions of squalor and high levels of abuse and neglect prompted moral reformers in England and the United States to work toward improving the conditions of incarcerated women. A key figure in this crusade in the United Kingdom was **Elizabeth Fry** (1780–1845). Her work with the Newgate Prison in London during the early 19th century served as the inspiration for the American women's prison reform movement. Fry argued that women offenders were capable of being reformed and that it was the responsibility of women in the community to assist those who had fallen victim to a lifestyle of crime. Like Fry, many of the reformers in America throughout the 1820s and 1830s came from upper- and middle-class communities with liberal religious backgrounds (Freedman, 1981). The efforts of these reformers led to significant changes in the incarceration of women, including the development of separate institutions for women. (See timeline in Figure 11.1.)

The Indiana Women's Prison (IWP) is identified as the first stand-alone female prison in the United States. It was also the first maximum-security prison for women. At the time of its opening in 1873, IWP housed 16 women (Schadee, 2003). By 1940, 23 states had facilities designed to exclusively house female inmates.

A review of facilities across the United States reveals two different models of institutions for women throughout the 20th century: custodial institutions and reformatories. In **custodial institutions**, women were simply ware-housed, and little programming or treatment was offered to inmates. Women in custodial institutions were typically

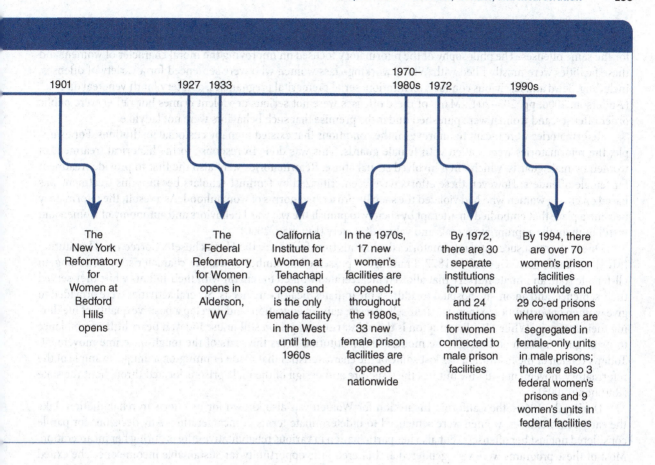

1901	1927	1933	1970–1980s	1972	1990s
The New York Reformatory for Women at Bedford Hills opens	The Federal Reformatory for Women opens in Alderson, WV	California Institute for Women at Tehachapi opens and is the only female facility in the West until the 1960s	In the 1970s, 17 new women's facilities are opened; throughout the 1980s, 33 new female prison facilities are opened nationwide	By 1972, there are 30 separate institutions for women and 24 institutions for women connected to male prison facilities	By 1994, there are over 70 women's prison facilities nationwide and 29 co-ed prisons where women are segregated in female-only units in male prisons; there are also 3 federal women's prisons and 9 women's units in federal facilities

convicted on felony and property-related crimes, with a third of women convicted of violent crimes. The custodial institution was more popular with southern states. In cases where a state had both a reformatory and a custodial institution, the distribution of inmates was made along racial lines—custodial institutions were more likely to house women of color who were determined to have little rehabilitative potential, while reformatories housed primarily White women (Freedman, 1981). Black women were also sent to work on state-owned penal plantations under conditions that mimicked the days of slavery in the South. Women of color generally had committed less serious offenses compared to White women, and yet they were incarcerated for longer periods of time. It was rare to see women of color convicted of moral offenses—since Black women were not held to the same standards of what was considered acceptable behavior for a lady, they were not deemed as in need of the rehabilitative tools that characterized the environments found at the reformatory (Rafter, 1985). Prison conditions for women at the custodial institution were characterized by unsanitary living environments with inadequate sewage and bathing systems, work conditions that were dominated by physical labor and corporal punishment, a lack of medical treatment for offenders, and the use of solitary confinement for women with mental health issues (Kurshan, 2000).

Unlike the custodial institution, which was similar in design and philosophy to most male prisons where inmates were simply housed while they did their time, the **reformatory** offered women opportunities for rehabilitation. This was a new concept in incarceration. Women were sent to the reformatory for an indeterminate period of time. In some cases, this meant that women were incarcerated for longer periods of time than their male counterparts, even for the same offenses. The philosophy of the reformatory focused on improving the moral character of women, and these facilities were mostly filled with White, working-class women who were sentenced for a variety of offenses, including "lewd and lascivious conduct, fornication, serial premarital pregnancies, adultery [and] venereal disease" (Anderson, 2006, pp. 203–204). Many of these offenses were not serious or violent crimes but rather were public order offenses, and women were punished under the premise that such behaviors were not ladylike.

Reformatories were meant to improve on the conditions that existed in many custodial institutions. For example, the reformatories were staffed with female guards. This was done in response to the historical treatment of women by male guards, which often involved sexual abuse. Reformatories were also the first to provide treatment for female offenders. However, these efforts have been criticized by feminist scholars because this treatment was based on curing women who had violated the socially proscribed norms of womanhood. As a result, the reformatory became a place that embodied an attempt by society to punish the wayward behaviors and autonomy of women and instill in them the appropriate morals and values of society (Kurshan, 2000).

One of the most successful reformatories during this time frame was the Massachusetts Correctional Institution (MCI) in Framington. Opened in 1877, Framington possessed a number of unique characteristics, including an all-female staff, an inmate nursery that allowed incarcerated women to remain with their infants while they served their sentence, and an on-site hospital to address the inmates' health care needs. Several activities were provided to give women opportunities to increase their self-esteem, gain an education, and develop a positive quality of life during their sentence. While MCI Framington is the oldest running prison still in use today, it bears little resemblance to its original mission and design; the modern-day institution bears the scars of the tough-on-crime movement. Today's version of the institution has lost some of the characteristics that made Framington a unique example of the reformatory movement and now mimics the structure and design of the male prisons located throughout the state (Rathbone, 2005).

During the 1960s, the California Institution for Women was also known for its efforts in rehabilitation. Like the early reformatories, women were sentenced to indeterminate terms of incarceration. Any decisions for parole considered not just her offense(s) but also her participation in various rehabilitative efforts during her incarceration. Most of these programs were very gendered and offered little opportunity for sustainable income once she exited prison. "Like the ideal mother, each WCS (women's correctional supervisor) also supervised prisoners' training in homemaking, deportment, dress and grooming, and was expected to participate in the moral regulation of prisoners, particularly as this related to their sexuality" (Gartner & Kruttschnitt, 2004, p. 279).

By the mid-1970s, the focus on sentencing had shifted away from rehabilitation and back to punishment as a punitive and retributive ideal. For example, the passage of California's Uniform Determinate Sentencing Act in 1976 meant that group and individualized counseling was no longer mandatory. Indeed, only a few options for rehabilitation were available and were typically run either by community volunteers or by the inmates themselves:

> Work, educational, vocational and volunteer programs were offered as a way for women to empower themselves, boost their self-esteem, and accept personal responsibility for their lives in order to change them. The prisoner was no longer expected to rely on clinical experts to design her route to rehabilitation but had become a rational actor. (Gartner & Kruttschnitt, 2004, pp. 282–283)

Today, most states have at least one facility dedicated to a growing population of female offenders. Unlike male prisons, which allow for different facilities based on the security level of the offender, the smaller incarcerated female population means that women's prisons house offenders of all security levels. In addition, these prison facilities are located in remote areas of the state, far from the cities where most of the women were arrested and where their families reside. The distance between an incarcerated woman and her family plays a significant role in the ways in which she copes with her incarceration and can affect her progress toward rehabilitation and a successful reintegration. In contrast, the sheer number of male facilities increases the probability that these men might reside in a facility closer to their home, which allows for an increased frequency in visitations by family members.

Contemporary Issues for Incarcerated Women

Since the 1980s, the number of women incarcerated in the United States has multiplied at a dramatic rate. As discussed in Chapter 9, sentencing policies, such as mandatory minimum sentences, and the war on drugs have had a dramatic effect on the numbers of women in prison. These structured sentencing formats, whose intent was to reduce the levels of sentencing disparities, have only led to the increases in the numbers of women in custody. At year-end 2015, there were 111,495 women incarcerated in prisons in the United States, a number that makes up 7% of the total incarcerated population. Compared to the previous year, this reflects a reduction of 1.4% fewer women in prison. The majority of this reduction is found in a significant decrease of the number of women in the federal prison system, which saw a 7.5% reduction in its female inmate population. However, several individual states also saw their numbers decrease, including California (largely because of the passage of Proposition 47), Indiana (where inmates with shorter sentences and goodtime credits were transferred to local jail facilities), Florida, and Oklahoma (Carson & Anderson, 2016). Table 11.1 illustrates a profile of women found in the criminal justice system today. Much of the rise in female criminality is the result of minor property crimes, which reflects the economic vulnerability that women experience in society, or cases involving drug-related crimes and the addiction issues facing women.

A review of 2016 census data notes that African Americans are 13.3% of the population, Hispanic/Latinos make up 17.8%, and biracial individuals are 2.6%. However, the demographics of our state and federal prisons note that women of color are significantly overrepresented behind bars. Indeed, research indicates that Black women today are being incarcerated at a greater rate than both White females and Black males (Bush-Baskette, 1998). Figure 11.2 highlights the rates of incarceration of White, Black, and Hispanic women. Women of color have incarceration rates that are up to four times greater than the rates of White women (Carson & Anderson, 2016). While White women are typically incarcerated for property offenses, women of color are more likely to be incarcerated for violent and drug-related offenses (Guerino, Harrison, & Sabol, 2011). Poverty is also an important demographic of incarcerated women, because many women (48%) were unemployed at the time of their arrest, which affects their ability to provide a sustainable environment for themselves and their children. In addition, they tend to come from impoverished

Table 11.1 • Characteristics of Women in Prison	
Race/Ethnicity	
White	33%
African American	48%
Hispanic	15%
Median age	33
High school/GED	56%
Single	47%
Unemployed	62%
Mother of minor children	65%

Figure 11.2 • Rate of Incarceration of Women by Race/Ethnicity

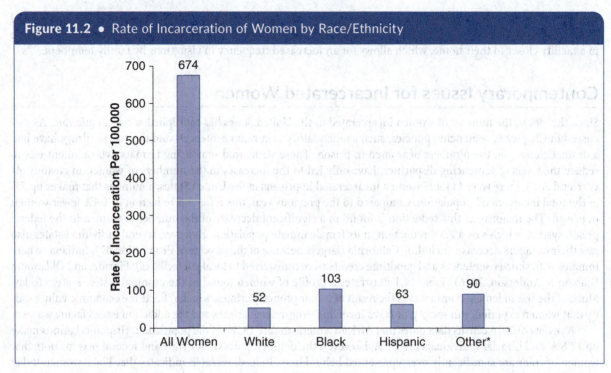

SOURCE: Carson & Anderson (2016).

*Includes American Indians and Alaska Natives; Asians, Native Hawaiians, and other Pacific Islands; and persons of two or more races.

areas, which may help explain why women are typically involved in economically driven crimes, such as property, prostitution, and drug-related offenses. Women also struggle with limited education and a lack of vocational training, which places them at risk for criminal behavior. The majority of women in state prisons across the United States have not completed high school and struggle with learning disabilities and literacy challenges. For example, 29% of women in custody in New York have less than a fifth-grade reading ability. Yet many prison facilities provide limited educational and vocational training, leaving women ill prepared to successfully transition to the community following their release. For example, of the 64% of women who enter prison without a high school diploma, only 16% receive their GED, and only 29% participate in any form of vocational training while they are incarcerated (Women's Prison Association [WPA], 2003, 2009a).

The rise in the female prison population means that many facilities are overcrowded, which creates a strain on basic resources within the facility and impacts the delivery of services of women. Overcrowding also can increase stress and anxiety levels leading to increases in negative mental health issues, such as depression, self-harm, and suicidal ideation. As a result, not only may women be unable to receive the treatment that they need but also staff may be unable to recognize when women are at risk for negative mental health issues. Given the effects that overcrowding can have for female inmates, it is important that prisons be able to provide adequate resources to screen for potential self-harming behaviors and develop necessary therapeutic resources to address these issues (Clements-Nolle, Wolden, & Bargmann-Losche, 2009).

Spotlight on California Prison Realignment and Its Effect on Female Inmates

In 2011, the U.S. Supreme Court ruled that the current state of overcrowding and the resulting conditions of the state's prisons were a violation of the prisoners' Eighth Amendment protection against cruel and unusual punishment. As a result, the California Department of Corrections was required to substantially reduce the state's prison population. To bring the prison population to 137.5% of the institutional design capacity, the state needed to reduce its prison population by 40,000 prisoners (*Brown v. Plata*, 2011).

As part of the efforts to reduce the population in the state prison, correctional officials have shifted many of the correctional supervision of lower level offenders, parolees, and parole violators, to the local governments. In particular, the state legislature has altered how the state punishes felony crimes. Historically, felons were sent to the state prison and only misdemeanor offenders served their time in local jail facilities. The introduction of Assembly Bill 109 reclassified certain felonies (nonviolent, nonserious, and nonsexual offenses) to permit offenders to serve their time in county jails. Additional legislation allows offenders to receive good time credits based on time served as well as participation in specialized programming (Smude, 2012).

As a result of California's realignment plan, the state prison population has seen dramatic changes in 2011 and 2012, both in terms of its overall size and also in terms of the types of offenders that remain housed in these state prison facilities. While some decreases were noted in 2011,[1] the full effects of realignment are apparent with 2012 data. While there have been noted changes in the prison population for both male and female offenders, women have seen proportionally greater reductions. Table 11.2 highlights how the population of California's female population has shifted as a result of realignment. Not only has the number of women in prison decreased by 39% but the types of offenders are [also] more likely to be violent offenders. As a result of realignment practices, nonviolent and drug offenders are now no longer housed in state prison facilities. This represents a dramatic change in practices since the growth of women in prison during the late 20th and early 21st centuries. Table 11.3 highlights the types of sentences that women are now incarcerated on in California's state prisons. Both men (44.0%) and women (55.4%) are most likely to receive a determinate sentence. This means that once they have completed their specific sentence, they are released from custody. Similar to this category are second strikers, who have had one prior serious or violent felony in their criminal history. Their sentences are double the length of the specific offense term and they are released on the earliest possible date without having to appear before the parole board. 21.6% of incarcerated women are considered second strikers. To be considered for parole, third strikers and lifers must appear before the parole board after they have served a specific number of years in custody. Approximately 19% of women in California prisons fall into this category (CDCR, 2013).

Each county has handled its realignment efforts differently. Some have utilized alternative-to-incarceration programs, such as drug treatment or probation. Meanwhile, other counties, such as Los Angeles County, have simply shifted their population from the prison yard to the county jail where, due to limited programming or other opportunities to earn good time credits, women may actually serve longer sentences compared to what they would have spent in state prison (Ryon, 2013).

---

[1]The California Public Safety Realignment program was enacted on October 1, 2011. By end of year 2011, the program had been in effect for only 3 months. 2012 represents the first full year of the program.

Table 11.2 • Profile of Women in California's State Prisons

Offense	2010 (n = 9,759)	2012 (n = 5,992)	Percent Change
Violent Crime	40.9%	62.4%	+21.5
• Murder	14.7%	24.6%	+9.9
• Manslaughter	1.3%	2.0%	+0.7
• Rape	0.1%	0.2%	+0.1
• Robbery	9.9%	14.5%	+4.6
• Aggravated or Simple Assault	9.6%	13.4%	+3.8
Property Crime	33.3%	22.3%	−10.0
• Burglary	11.2%	10.9%	−0.3
• Larceny-Theft	9.9%	4.8%	−5.1
• Motor Vehicle Theft	3.3%	1.7%	−1.6
• Fraud	6.3%	3.0%	−3.3
Drug Offenses	21.1%	10.9%	−10.2

SOURCE: Carson & Golinelli (2013).

Table 11.3 • California's Prison Sentences by Gender (2013)

	Gender				Total	
	Female		Male			
	N	%	N	%	N	%
Total	5,982	100%	128,178	100%	134,160	100%
2nd Strike	1,294	21.6%	33,405	26.1%	34,699	25.9%
3rd Strike	64	1.1%	7,911	6.2%	34,699	25.9%
Determinate Sentence	3,317	55.3%	56,402	44%	59,719	44.5%
Lifer	1,072	17.9%	25,023	19.5%	26,095	19.5%
LWOP	186	3.1%	4,501	3.5%	4,687	3.5%
Death	20	0.3%	714	0.6%	734	0.5%

SOURCE: California Department of Corrections and Rehabilitation (CDCR) (2013). Prison Census Data as of June 30, 2013. Table 10 Prison Census Data, Total Institution Population. Offenders by Sentence Status and Gender. Retrieved at www.cdcr.ca.gov/Reports_Research/Offender_Information_Services_Branch/Annual/Census/CENSUSd1306.pdf

With all the challenges that women face within prison, how do they develop social support networks within the prison walls? Research by Severance (2005) finds that women rely on a variety of experiences to develop these internal support structures. For example, women who are from the same neighborhoods or did time together in jails may bond together. The dormitory style housing environment in prisons can also provide women the opportunity to develop these emotional connections. While being in close proximity can help establish relationships, it can also be challenging for some women to build trust within these environments, particularly given the lack of privacy and the high levels of gossip that exist within these correctional settings (Severance, 2005).

The level of attachment and trust can vary because inmates have different types of relationships within the prison walls. Research by Severance (2005) describes four different categories of relationships that are found within women's prisons: acquaintances, friends, family, and girlfriends. Acquaintances are superficial relationships that involve low levels of trust between inmates. Friends are more meaningful than acquaintances because they involve an increased level of trust. Unlike acquaintances, which are typically temporary relationships, friends have the potential to continue once the women have left prison. While family relationships, or **pseudo-families,** can also provide supportive networks, these relationships are not always positive experiences due to the lack of respect that can occur between family members. Finally, girlfriends can provide emotional and romantic support. What makes this type of relationship unique is that the majority of women in prison do not identify as homosexual.

▲ **Photo 11.1** A woman spends time with a family member during a no-contact visit. A no-contact visit means that the inmate cannot touch or hug her family and friends when they come to visit. For many women, the lack of physical contact with their loved ones can contribute to the stress and loneliness of incarceration.

These relationships are generally not for sexual purposes but rather are for emotional support and companionship. Intimate relationships can also serve to provide economic benefits, particularly in cases where one partner has more resources (i.e., money for canteen supplies) than the other. Here, sex becomes a commodity that can be exchanged. Unlike the "girlfriends" described by Severance (2005), these relationships are often engaged in by offenders with shorter sentences and are purely sexual (Einat & Chen, 2012).

Physical and Mental Health Needs of Incarcerated Women

Women in custody face a variety of physical and mental health issues. In many cases, the criminal justice system is ill equipped to deal with these issues. Incarcerated women are 3.7 times more likely to experience physical or sexual trauma in their lives compared to women in the general population (Grella, Lovinger, & Warda, 2013). Given the high rates of abuse and victimization that these women experience throughout their lives, it is not surprising that the incarcerated female population has a high demand for mental health services. Women in prison have significantly higher rates of mental illness than women in the general population. Official data indicate that 13% of women in federal facilities and 24% of women in state prisons have been diagnosed with a mental disorder (General Accounting Office, 1999).

The pains of imprisonment, including the separation from family and adapting to the prison environment, can exacerbate mental health conditions. In addition, many offenders with life sentences (45%) often experience suicidal ideation on receiving this sentence. The experience of prison can also exacerbate mental health conditions, such as depression, particularly given the life experiences of many female inmates. In addition, women with limited support from family on the outside also experience suicidal ideation (Dye & Aday, 2013).

Unfortunately, the standard course of treatment in many facilities involves prescription psychotropic medications. Often these medications are prescribed in excess and often in lieu of counseling or other therapeutic interventions. For example, one study indicates that 21 of the 22 participants were given the prescription Seroquel,[2] which is used to treat bipolar disorder. Yet only one of the women was actually officially diagnosed with bipolar disorder. Although the manufacturer or Seroquel recommends that people who take this medication should be reassessed at regular intervals, few of the women actually received such treatment while in prison. While some drugs were readily available, the same did not hold true for all psychotropic medications. In some cases, women noted that prison doctors would prescribe new drugs to the women rather than continue to offer prescriptions for drugs that had been effective in the past. "Prison doctors just do whatever they want—the opposite of what you were getting before you went in so that they can show you who's boss. It's just a way for them to show you how much control they have" (Kitty, 2012, p. 171). Not only can the failure to comply with a prescribed medication protocol be grounds for a disciplinary action while in prison but such behaviors can also be used against an offender during a parole hearing.

Some women believe that their mental health status improves during incarceration because they were appropriately medicated, were no longer using illicit substances, and were engaged in therapeutic support programs. However, the majority of women believed that incarceration exacerbated their mental health issues and that a number of variables contributed to this. First, incarceration is a stressful experience and stress can increase feelings of anxiety and insecurity. Second, the majority of resources for mental health were focused on crisis intervention and not therapeutic resources. In particular "lifers" felt that they were often placed at the end of the list and were denied services due to their sentence. Finally, many of the women felt degraded and abused by the staff, which added to their trauma (Harner & Riley, 2013).

Women also face a variety of physical health needs. Women in prison are more likely to be HIV positive compared to women in the community, presenting a unique challenge for the prison health care system. While women in the general U.S. population have an HIV infection rate of 0.3%, the rate of infection for women in state and federal facilities is 3.6%, a tenfold increase. In New York state, this statistic rises to an alarming 18%, a rate 60 times that of the national infection rate. These rates are significantly higher than the rates of HIV-positive incarcerated men. Why is HIV an issue for women in prison? Women who are HIV positive are more likely to have a history of sexual abuse, compared to women who are HIV negative (WPA, 2003). While the rates of HIV-positive women have declined since an all-time high in 1999, the rate of hepatitis C infections has increased dramatically within the incarcerated female population. Estimates indicate that between 20% and 50% of women in jails and prisons are affected by this disease. Hepatitis C is a disease that is transmitted via bodily fluids, such as blood, and can lead to liver damage if not diagnosed or treated. Offending women are at a high risk to contract hepatitis C given their involvement in sex and drug crimes. Few prison facilities routinely test for hepatitis C, and treatment can be expensive due to the high cost of prescriptions (Van Wormer & Bartollas, 2010).

While the physical health needs of women in prison are significant, there are often limited resources for treatment within the prison walls. The medical staff is generally overwhelmed with the high number of inmates that require medical care. In addition, many women expressed concerns about the environment in prison and felt that

---

[2]The manufacturer of Seroquel indicates that "Seroquel is an antipsychotic medication, useful as a mono-drug therapy or as an adjunct to the drugs lithium or divalproex for the treatment of schizophrenia and the acute manic and depressive episodes in bipolar disorder" (Kitty, 2012, p. 168).

it put them at risk for increased health issues in a number of ways, such as the physical conditions of the prison and housing that combine healthy inmates with inmates with chronic and communicable illnesses. Finally, the women expressed a desire for increased health education on issues such as prevention, diet, and exercise (Morgan, 2013).

Spotlight on the Financial Challenges Behind Bars

One of the myths about prison life is that everything is provided for inmates. "Three hots and a cot" is a term thrown about that notes that inmates have food and shelter. There have also been criticisms levied by the public over "free" medical care and education. However, a review of these sorts of programs notes that prison life is anything but free. Medical care is one of the top five greatest expenditures for correctional institutions, costs that are only expected to increase because tough on crime sentencing practices mean that inmates will have increased demands on prison medical systems as they age (The Pew Charitable Trusts and the John D. and Catherine T. MacArthur Foundation, 2014). A recent case of an female inmate who was dying of pancreatic cancer cost the State of California over $100,000 in overtime fees alone for guards to supervise her during the 36 days that she was hospitalized prior to her death (Henry, 2013). As state institutions look for ways to reduce costs, many have adopted health-care payment fees, which can range from $2 to $5. That may not sound like much compared to the $15–$20 that most insurance plans charge for the average individual, but consider the context. Inmate jobs pay very little: The Prison Policy Initiative notes that inmate wages can be as low as $0.13 per hour with the average prison job paying $0.93 per hour. Depending on the state, these wages are taxed at anywhere between 30–50%. One inmate who worked in the prison kitchen netted between $5.25 and $8.75 per week after administrative costs (Bozelko, 2017). Given this context, paying between $2.00 and $5.00 for a medical visit is a significant burden. In addition, women in prison are more likely to utilize prison healthcare services at a higher rate than male inmates (Marshall, Simpson, & Stevens, 2001). Research notes that many women end up negotiating between paying for a health visit and other expenses, such as phone cards or letter writing supplies in order to stay connected to family members. Phone calls can be prohibitively expensive; a 15-minute call can range from $5.15 to $10.00 (Harner, Wyant, & Da Silva, 2017).

The availability of funds in an inmate's commissary account can also be a status symbol behind bars. However, this could also be a difficult relationship to negotiate, both inside and out. Family members could deposit funds for their loved one. However, these funds often took a significant amount of time to be processed. In addition, such contributions were subjected to fees by the institution. In California, deposits to an inmate's commissary account are taxed at 50% to satisfy any restitution orders with an additional 10% administrative fee (CDCR, n.d.). Many inmates expressed feeling guilty for asking their family members to contribute to their accounts, knowing that it was a burden for them to do so. For others, having family members send money (or withhold money) became a symbol of their relationship: Inmates with strong relationships with family members were likely to have deposits made to their accounts while inmates who had deteriorating or poor relationships were less likely to receive such support (Smoyer, 2015).

Given the tenuous financial circumstances that many women find themselves in prior to arriving at prison, the costs of life behind bars can not only exacerbate preexisting physical and mental health conditions but also place additional strain on the relationships that are essential to recovery, rehabilitation, and reentry.

Considering the number of women that come to prison on drug-related charges, or whose criminal activity is related to their drug use, the demand for drug treatment in prison is high. Women are more likely to participate in prison-based drug treatment (Belenko & Houser, 2012), and those who participate have lower rates of recidivism

© Spencer Weiner/Los Angeles Times via Getty Images

▲ **Photo 11.2** The rise of female incarceration has had significant impacts on the lives of their children, who are left to grow up without their mothers. Here, CYA inmate Angela Rodrigiez holds her daughter for the first time during a visit.

over the long term (Grella & Rodriguez, 2011). Many of the drug treatment programs in prison have been based on therapeutic community (TC) models. The TC model is designed to provide individuals with tools to help them live a drug-free lifestyle. However, TC programming may not adequately address some of the gender-specific needs of the female incarcerated population. Research by Messina, Grella, Cartier, and Torres (2010) found that women in the gender-specific drug treatment program were more likely to stay away from drugs for a longer period of time and were more successful on parole compared to those who participated in a TC treatment program. These findings indicate the importance in offering programs designed with the unique needs of women in mind.

While women inmates have a higher need for treatment (in terms of both prevalence and severity of conditions) than male inmates, the prison system is limited in its resources and abilities to address these issues. For example, most facilities are inadequately staffed or lack the diagnostic tools needed to address women's gynecological issues. Women also have higher rates of chronic illnesses than the male population (Anderson, 2006). However, the demands for these services significantly outweigh their availability, and the lack of accessible services ranks high on the list of inmate complaints regarding quality of life issues in prison (WPA, 2003).

Children of Incarcerated Mothers: The Unintended Victims

Children of **incarcerated mothers** (and fathers) deal with a variety of issues that stem from the loss of a parent, including grief, loss, sadness, detachment, and aggressive or at-risk behaviors for delinquency. Additionally, these children are at high risk for ending up in prison themselves as adults. The location of many prisons makes it difficult for many children to retain physical ties with their mother throughout her incarceration. While more than two-thirds of incarcerated mothers have children under the age of 18, only 9% of these women will ever get to be visited by their children while they are incarcerated (Van Wormer & Bartollas, 2010).

A small number of women enter prison already pregnant. Estimates indicate that approximately 6% of women in jail, 4% to 5% of women in state prisons, and 3% of women in federal prison are pregnant when they were arrested for their crimes (Glaze & Maruschak, 2008). While pregnancy is generally a happy time for most expectant mothers, these mothers-to-be face high levels of stress over how their incarceration might affect the lives of their children. One concern centers on the quality of prenatal care that she might experience behind bars. Here, women are concerned about how their physical health before and during their incarceration will impact their unborn child. Most of these women will give birth and return to prison within a few days without their new baby. This separation between mother and child can lead to mental health complications for the mother. In addition, they may be concerned over who will care for their child and fear they will miss out on the physical and emotional connections that mothers traditionally experience with a new baby (Wismont, 2000).

Giving birth while incarcerated can be a traumatizing experience. Consider the following scenario:

> A nurse in the labor room goes to attend to one of her patients who is in active labor and is ready to deliver her baby. The correctional officer removes the women's leg shackles and hand cuffs and immediately replaces them after the baby is born. (Ferszt, 2011, p. 254)

In 2012, 33 states had policies that permitted women to be shackled while they were in labor. Yet even those states that prohibit the practice demonstrate great variability of the law. Some prohibit the use of shackles only during the labor and delivery process. Rhode Island has one of the most comprehensive and liberal laws, in that it prohibits the use of restraints at any time during the second and third trimester, as well as during postpartum (World Law Direct, 2011). These laws state that prisoners needed to be restrained due to safety and security concerns. Several professional organizations, including the American Congress of Obstetricians and Gynecologists and the American Medical Association, have expressed concerns over these policies because they can lead to health risks to both the mother and her baby (Berg, 2011). For example, if a woman is shackled (meaning her legs are either restrained to each other or to the side of the bed), it can be difficult for hospital staff to assist a woman during a

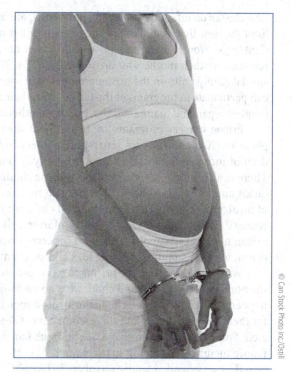

© Can Stock Photo Inc./Ostill

▲ **Photo 11.3** While many states have outlawed the practice of shackling women during childbirth, the use of restraints on pregnant women continues to present a number of health risks for both the mother and the child.

normal childbirth experience and can significantly complicate the delivery during an emergency situation. This has potentially disastrous effects for both the woman and her baby. "If the fetal heart beat slows, and an immediate Caesarian-section is required, the time lost to fumbling with shackle locks could cause brain damage and even death" (WPA, n.d., "Laws Banning," para. 4).

Over the past several years, a number of states have passed new laws that forbid the practice of shackling female inmates during delivery. For example, Florida recently abolished the use of shackling of any pregnant woman during labor and delivery, the first such law in a southern state (Lopez, 2012). California recently passed a law that prohibits the use of shackles (feet), handcuffs (hands), or belly chains during childbirth ("Shackling Pregnant Inmates", 2012). However, some jurisdictions have been slow to respond to new laws in their jurisdiction. While Illinois in 1999 outlawed shackling inmates during labor, the practice continued up until 2012 at places such as the Cook County Jail in Chicago. Eighty women filed a class action suit alleging that they were unnecessarily shackled during birth and recovery and were awarded 4.1 million dollars in damages in May 2012 (Mastony, 2012).

In an effort to both improve the emotional well-being of the mother and encourage attachment and bonding between a mother and her infant, nine states (New York, California, Illinois, Indiana, Ohio, Nebraska, South Dakota, Washington, and West Virginia) have integrated prison nurseries into their facilities, which allow women to remain with their infant children for at least part of their sentence (WPA, 2009b). The oldest prison nursery program is located at Bedford Hills Correctional Facility in New York. Founded in 1901, this program is the largest in the country and allows 29 mothers to reside with their infant children. Women who participate in these prison nursery programs take classes on infant development and participate in support groups with other mothers. Although most programs limit the time that a child can reside with his or her mother (generally 12–18 months), the Washington Correctional Center for Women is unique in that its prison nursery program allows children born to incarcerated women to remain with their mothers for up to 3 years (WPA, 2009b). Other states allow overnight visits with children, either in special family units on the prison grounds or in specialized cells within the facility. At Bedford Hills, older children can participate in programs at the facility with their mothers (Van Wormer & Bartollas, 2010). These programs help families repair and maintain ties between a mother and her child(ren) throughout her incarceration.

Prison nursery programs are not without their critics, because some suggest that prison is an inappropriate place for children. However, separating mothers and their children can also have detrimental effects, because children of incarcerated mothers are more likely to have educational challenges and limited emotional attachments. There is also a cycle of incarceration because children of imprisoned parents have an increased risk toward delinquent and criminal behaviors. Not only do these programs such as the mother-baby nurseries help end the cycle of incarceration for both the mother and child but they also assist in the reduction of recidivism once a woman is released from custody (WPA, 2009b). Unfortunately, many prison administrators are unaware of the benefits that a prison nursery can supply. Additional concerns involve the costs of implementing such a program and a belief that prison was an inappropriate place for children (Campbell & Carlson, 2012).

While the concept of the prison nursery and programming for children of incarcerated mothers helps promote the bond between parent and child, what about those states where these types of programs are not available? What happens to these children? The majority of women in the criminal justice system are the primary custodial parents for their young children, and these women must determine who will care for their children while they are incarcerated. Some may have a husband or children's father to turn to for assistance, though many will seek out extended family members, including grandparents. Seventy-nine percent of children who have an incarcerated parent are raised by an extended family member (WPA, 2003). In cases where an extended family member is unable or unavailable to care for a woman's minor child(ren), social services will place them in foster care. When a woman faces a long term of incarceration, the Adoption and Safe Families Act of 1997 terminates the parental rights in cases where children have been in foster care for 15 months (out of the previous 22 months). Given the increases in strict sentencing practices, the effects of this law mean that the majority of incarcerated women will lose their children if a family member is unable to care for them while the mother serves her sentence (Belknap, 2007).

Given that many of these women will regain custody of their children following the completion of their sentence, it is important that they maintain a connection with their children during this time. This can be a challenging prospect. In many cases, prison facilities are far removed from where these children reside. The cost of traveling to visit a parent can be prohibitive, particularly for families that struggle with the day-to-day economics of raising a child. This means that the majority of women in custody do not receive regular physical visits from their children. While 35% of women correspond with their children via the telephone and 49% communicate via letters, this means that half of the children do not have a relationship with their mother during her incarceration. This can have a detrimental impact on the parent–child relationship. In cases where the women will return to an authoritative parental role following their release from prison, it is important for families to maintain a parent–child bond. Here, extended family members play a crucial role in maintaining the connection between incarcerated women and their children (Stringer & Barnes, 2012).

Given that the majority of women in prison are mothers and that many were the primary caregiver of minor children prior to their incarceration, facilities have begun to implement parenting programs designed to help inmates develop effective parenting skills. Not only can these programs help provide a better relationship between a mother and her child(ren), but it can also help prevent recidivism. As a result of this curriculum, these mothers increased their knowledge about childhood development, altered their attitudes about physical discipline, and developed an understanding about the needs and well-being of their children (Sandifer, 2008).

Spotlight on the Girl Scouts Beyond Bars Program

Funded by the National Institute of Justice, the first Girl Scouts Beyond Bars (GSBB) program was offered at the Maryland Correctional Institution for Women in November 1992 (Girl Scouts [GSA], 2008). As part of the program, mothers meet with their daughters twice a month on prison grounds to work on troop projects, such as math and science projects, as well as creative activities that focus on topics such as self-esteem, relationships, and teen development/pregnancy prevention. By 2008, there were over 37 programs nationwide. Research has shown that the Girl Scouts Behind Bars program has been effective in a number of ways. First, the program facilitates regular contact between mothers and their daughter(s), which allows the mothers to have an active role in childrearing. Spending quality time together also strengthens the mother-child bond even though she is incarcerated (Moses, 1995). Research indicates that the majority (85%) of girls who participated in these programs had a closer bond with their mom following their participation in the program (GSA, 2008). Second, the program benefits the children, because research documents that their behavior at home and educational involvement improve (Block & Potthast, 1998). Additionally, the girls learned a variety of prosocial behaviors, such as respect and leadership, and developed a positive attitude about their personal futures (GSA, 2008).

While there are significant benefits to be gained by participating in the Girl Scouts Beyond Bars program, they do require significant emotional and physical investments by its supporters. Similar to traditional Girl Scouts (GS) programs, GSBB programs are run primarily by volunteers. In traditional GS programs, parents serve as the troop leaders. GSBB programs require a commitment by the community and family members to help organize and lead these programs (Block, 1999). Despite these challenges, the Girl Scouts Beyond Bars represents a program with positive effects for both a mother and her daughter.

/// SUMMARY

- The first prison for women was opened in 1839 in response to the growing concerns of abuse of women in male prison facilities.

- The reformatory prison was designed to rehabilitate women from their immoral ways.

- The custodial institution offered very little in terms of rehabilitative programming for incarcerated women.

- Women of color are overrepresented in women's prisons.

- While in prison, women develop acquaintances, friendships, pseudo-families, and romantic relationships to provide emotional support.

- Women in custody face a variety of unique issues, many of which the prison is ill equipped to deal with.

- Some facilities have prison nursery programs, which allow mothers to remain with their infant children while incarcerated.

- Programs such as Girl Scouts Beyond Bars help provide the parent–child bond while mothers are incarcerated.

KEY TERMS

Custodial institutions 182

Fry, Elizabeth 182

Incarcerated mothers 192

Pseudo-families 189

Reformatory 183

DISCUSSION QUESTIONS

1. If you were to build a women's prison that reflected gender-responsive principles, what key features would you integrate into your facility?

2. Discuss the profile for women who are incarcerated in our prison facilities. In what ways are incarcerated women different from incarcerated men?

3. What challenges do incarcerated women face? How does prison impact the children of these mothers?

WEB RESOURCES

Hour Children: http://www.hourchildren.org

Our Place DC: http://www.ourplacedc.org

The Sentencing Project: http://www.sentencingproject.org

Women's Prison Association: http://www.wpaonline.org

Visit **www.sagepub.com/mallicoat3e** to access additional study tools, including eFlashcards, web quizzes, web resources, video resources, and SAGE journal articles.

Women Professionals and the Criminal Justice System

Police, Corrections, and Offender Services

Chapter Highlights

- The gendered experience of women employed in the criminal justice system
- Challenges for women in victim services, policing, corrections, probation, and parole
- Future directions for females working in the criminal justice system

Throughout history, criminal justice occupations have been dominated by men. Whether the job was that of a police officer or working within the field of corrections, the common perception was that the duties of apprehending and managing dangerous felons was outside the perceptions of what women could—or should—do. Women first began to appear in criminal justice occupations within police organizations in the early 20th century. However, their early presence within the academy was significantly limited, because many believed that policing was a *man's job* and therefore unsuitable as an occupation for women. The duties in these occupations focused on traditional masculine traits, such as aggression, physical skill, and being tough—traits that many argued were lacking for women, making them inherently less capable of doing the job (Appier, 1998).

Society generally assumes that work in the criminal justice system is dominated by events that are dangerous, exciting, and violent. These themes are echoed and reinforced in examples of popular culture, such as television, film, and news outlets, by stories of dangerous offenders and crimes that destroy peaceful communities (Lersch & Bazley, 2012). Certainly criminal justice officials in fields such as policing, corrections, and probation and parole can and do face dangerous situations during their careers. However these extreme examples misrepresent the reality of criminal justice work, which often involves long delays, extensive paperwork, and spending time talking with residents of the community. Unlike the adrenaline rush that is depicted in the media, criminal justice personnel spend significant portions of their time dealing with situations that require empathy, compassion, and nurturing—traits that are stereotypically classified as *feminine* characteristics. For example, the typical duties of a police officer are not limited to the pursuit and capturing of the "bad guys" and more often include responding to victims of a crime and dealing with the welfare of community members. Given the various skills and traits required in criminal justice professions, has the number of women increased in these fields? How does gender contribute to these professions? Are there other differences in how women are hired, do their jobs, and establish careers in criminal justice? This chapter follows these issues through the fields of policing, corrections, and offender services.

Women in Policing

An examination of the history of policing indicates that the work of moral reformers was instrumental in the emergence of policewomen. During the late 19th century, women's advocacy groups were heavily involved in social issues. Examples of their efforts include the creation of a separate court for juvenile offenders as well as crime prevention outreach related to the protection of young women from immoral sexual influences. However, women were not a formal part of the justice system and served as informal advocates and, when employed, as paid social workers.

With the start of the 20th century, women entered the police force as bona fide, sworn officers. However, there is some debate as to who was the first female police officer. One report indicates that the first female police officer may have been **Marie Owens**. She was a Chicago factory inspector who transferred to the police department in 1891 and served 32 years with the city (Mastony, 2010). Other scholars point to **Lola Baldwin**, who was reportedly hired in 1908 by the Portland, Oregon, police department as a supervisor to a group of social workers (Corsianos, 2009). However, it is unclear whether Baldwin served as a sworn officer (Los Angeles Almanac, 2012). But it is **Alice Stebbins Wells**, who was hired by the Los Angeles Police Department (LAPD) in 1910, who is most often cited as the first sworn female police officer in the United States. At the time of her hiring, her job duties revolved around working with female offenders and juvenile cases. Her philosophy as a female police officer reinforced the ideal of feminine traits of policing when she stated, "I don't want to make arrests. I want to keep people from needing to be arrested, especially young people" (Appier, 1998, p. 9). As a result of the national and international attention of her hiring, she traveled the country promoting the benefits of hiring women in municipal policing agencies. As an officer with the LAPD, Wells advocated the protection of children and women, particularly when it came to sexual education. As part of her duties, she inspected dance halls, movie theaters, and locations for public recreation throughout the city. When she came into contact with girls of questionable moral status, she would lecture them on the dangers of premarital sex and advocate for the importance of purity.

Following in the footsteps of Alice Stebbins Wells, many women sought out positions as police officers. The hiring of women by police agencies throughout the early 20th century did not mean that these women were assigned the same duties as male police officers. Rather, these policewomen were essentially social workers armed with a badge. Their duties focused on preventing crime rather than responding to criminal activity. While hundreds of women joined the ranks of local law enforcement agencies between 1910 and 1920, they were a minority within most departments. Female officers were generally limited to working with juvenile and female offenders, and the male officers resented their presence in the

▲ **Photo 12.1** Captain Edyth Totten and the Women Police Reserve, New York City, 1918.

Library of Congress

department. In an effort to distinguish the work of policewomen, many cities created separate branches within their organization. These women's bureaus were tasked with servicing the needs of women and girls in the community. Many of these bureaus were housed outside of the walls of the city police department in an attempt to create a more welcoming environment for citizens in need. Some scholars suggest that by making women's bureaus look more like a home, rather than a bureaucratic institution, women and children would be more comfortable and therefore more likely to seek out the services and advice of policewomen.

The mid-20th century saw significant growth in the numbers of women in policing. In 1922, there were approximately 500 policewomen in the United States—by 1960, more than 5,600 women were employed as officers (Schulz, 1995). Throughout this time, the majority of these policewomen remained limited in their duties, due in large part to a traditional policing (i.e., male) model. Policewomen were not permitted to engage in the same duties as policemen, out of fear that it was too dangerous and that women would not be able to adequately serve in these positions. Most importantly the "all boys club" that existed in most departments simply did not want or welcome women intruding on their territory.

Despite these issues, women occasionally found themselves receiving expanded duties, particularly during times of war. With the decrease in manpower during World War I and II, many women found themselves placed in positions normally reserved for male officers, such as traffic control. In an effort to maintain adequate staffing levels during this period, the number of women hired within police agencies increased. However, the end of these wars saw the return of men to their policing posts and the displacement of women back to their gendered roles and **gendered assignments** within their respective departments (Snow, 2010).

As in many other fields during the 1960s, the civil rights and women's movements had a tremendous effect on the presence of women in policing. Legal challenges paved the way toward gendered equality in policing by opening doors to allow women to serve in more active police capacities, such as patrol. In 1964, **Liz Coffal** and **Betty Blankenship** of the Indianapolis Police Department became the first women in the United States to serve as patrol officers, an assignment that was previously restricted to male officers throughout the country. As policewomen, Coffal and Blankenship were resented by their male colleagues, who believed that the work of a police officer was too dangerous for women. Coffal and Blankenship received little training for their new positions and often had to learn things on their own. They found that dispatch often gave them the mundane and undesirable tasks, such as hospital transports. It soon became clear to Blankenship and Coffal that the likelihood of being requested for any sort of pursuit or arrest cases was slim. In an effort to gain increased experience in their position, they began to respond to calls at their own discretion. Armed with their police radio, they learned to interpret radio codes and began to respond to cases in their vicinity. They successfully navigated calls that most male officers believed they could not handle. As a result of their positive performances in often tense situations, Coffal and Blankenship began to gain some respect from their male colleagues. However, they knew that any accolades could be short lived—one mistake and they ran the risk of being removed from their patrol status, and the traditional philosophy of "police work isn't for women" would be justified. While they eventually returned to some of the "traditional feminine roles" for women in policing, their experiences in patrol set the stage for significant changes for future policewomen (Snow, 2010).

In addition to the differences in their duties, policewomen were historically subjected to different qualification standards for their positions. At the 1922 annual conference of the International Association of the Chiefs of Police, members suggested that policewomen should have completed college or nursing school (Snow, 2010). This standard is particularly ironic, given that male officers were not required to have even a high school diploma in most jurisdictions until the 1950s and 1960s. As a result, the career path of policewomen attracted women of higher educational and intellectual standing.

Not only were policewomen limited by their roles and duties within the department they faced significant barriers as well in terms of the benefits and conditions of their employment. Like in many other fields, policewomen were paid less for their work compared to policemen, even though these women often had higher levels of education than their male colleagues. In addition, the advancement and promotional opportunities for women were significantly limited, because most departments did not allow women to participate in the exam process that would grant them access to promotional opportunities. Generally speaking, the highest position that a policewoman could hold during this time was the commander of the women's bureau. Still, many agencies disagreed with that level of leadership, suggesting that women did not have the necessary skills or abilities to supervise officers or run a division. In some jurisdictions, women were forced to quit their positions when they got married, because many felt that women did not have enough time to care for a home, care for their husband, and fulfill their job duties. As one male officer explained it, "When they marry they have to resign. You see, we might want them for some job or other when they have to be home cooking their husband's dinner. That would not be much use to us, would it?" (Snow, 2010, p. 23).

In 1967, the President's Commission on Law Enforcement and the Administration of Justice advocated expanding the numbers of policewomen and diversifying their duties beyond the traditional female roles to which they were typically assigned. In 1967, the commission wrote, "The value should not be considered as limited to staff functions or police work with juveniles; women should also serve regularly in patrol, vice and investigative functions" (p. 125). Despite these assertions, few departments followed these recommendations, arguing that as members of a uniformed police patrol, officers required significant levels of upper-body strength in order to detain resistant offenders. In addition, many agency administrators argued that the job was simply too dangerous for women.

Until the 1970s, women represented only 1% of all sworn officers in the United States (Appier, 1998). However, new legislation and legal challenges in the 1960s and 1970s led to further changes involving the presence and role of policewomen. While the **Civil Rights Bill of 1964** was generally focused on eliminating racial discrimination, the word *sex* was added to the bill during the eleventh hour by House members, who hoped that this inclusion would raise objections among legislators and prohibit its passing. To the dismay of these dissenters, the bill was signed into law. In 1969, President Richard Nixon signed legislation that prohibited the use of sex as a requirement for hiring—meaning that jobs could not be restricted to men only (or women only). In addition, the Law Enforcement Assistance Administration (LEAA) mandated that agencies with federal funding (and police departments fell under this category) were prohibited from engaging in discriminatory hiring practices based on sex. While sex was now a protected category in terms of employment discrimination, the bill did little on its face to increase the presence of women in sworn policing roles. While the act prohibited discriminatory hiring practices, it had little effect on the types of assignments that were given to women once they joined the police force.

The passage of the Civil Rights Bill began a trend within departments to introduce women into ranks that were previously reserved exclusively for men. While several departments took the initiative to place women into patrol positions, many men in these departments issued strong objections against the practice. Thus, women in these positions often found themselves ostracized, with little support from their colleagues. Eight years later, in 1972, the Civil Rights Act was amended to extend employment protections to state and municipal government agencies, which opened the door to allow women to apply to all law enforcement jurisdictions as sworn officers without restrictions. While these changes increased the number of positions available to women (and to minorities), they also shifted the roles of policing away from the social service orientation that had been historically characteristic for women in policing. Their jobs now included the duties of crime fighting and the maintenance of order and public safety, just like their male counterparts (Schulz, 1995).

Over the past four decades, there have been significant increases in the number of women employed as sworn law enforcement officers. In 1922, there were approximately 500 policewomen in the United States—by 1960, more than 5,600 women were employed as officers, approximately 1.1% of all sworn officers (Rabe-Hemp, 2008; Schulz, 1995). By 1986, approximately 8.8% of municipal officers were female (Rabe-Hemp, 2008), a proportion that almost doubles by 2008 (15.2%). Women are more likely to be employed in larger jurisdictions (22%) and federal agencies (24%) compared to smaller jurisdictions (defined as departments with fewer than 500 officers) where women make up 8% of all sworn personnel (Langton, 2010). Unfortunately, these few women that serve in rural communities are relegated to lower positions within the agency and experience higher degrees of discrimination compared to women in larger metropolitan departments (Rabe-Hemp, 2008).

Why is the representation of women so low in the field of policing? While legal challenges have mandated equal access to employment and promotional opportunities for women in policing, research indicates that the overemphasis on the physical fitness skills component of the hiring process excludes a number of qualified women from employment (Lonsway, Carrington, et al., 2002). Physical fitness tests typical of law enforcement positions have been criticized as a tool to exclude women from policing, despite evidence that it is not the physical abilities of officers that are most desirable. Rather, it is their communication skills that are the best asset for the job. The number of push-ups that a woman can complete compared to a man says little about how well each will complete their duties. Yet standards such as these are used as evidence to suggest that women are inferior to their male colleagues. Women who are able to achieve the male standard of physical fitness are viewed more favorably by male colleagues, compared to women who satisfy only the basic requirements for their gender (Schulze, 2012).

While some agencies have embraced the inclusion of women on the force, women as sworn police officers still experience discrimination and isolation within some agencies. Some male officers still refuse to accept female officers, while others are indifferent to the presence of women on the force. Research indicates that younger male officers and male officers of color are more likely to accept women among the ranks compared to older and/or White officers (Renzetti, Goodstein, & Miller, 2006).

©Thinkstock/Darrin Klimek

▲ **Photo 12.2** Legal changes have increased opportunities in policing for both women and people of color. Today, police officers reflect a greater diversity among the force than in the past. However, women continue to struggle in this male-dominated field.

Despite the continued increase of women in policing, the majority of these women serve within the general ranks because the upper management positions within agencies are still dominated by men. While court rulings in the 1970s opened the possibilities for promotion for policewomen, few women have successfully navigated their way to the top position of police chief. In 2009, there were 212 women serving in the top-ranking position in their departments nationwide (O'Connor, 2012). Most of these women serve in small communities or lead agencies with a specific focus, such as university police divisions or transit authorities (Schulz, 2003). Within metropolitan agencies (more than 100 sworn officers), only 7.3% of the top-level positions and 9.6% of supervisory positions are held by women. Additionally, women of color make up only 4.8% of sworn officers, and minority women are even less likely to appear in upper-level management positions, with only 1.6% of top-level positions and 3.1% of supervisory roles filled by a woman of color. The situation is even bleaker for small and rural agencies, where only 3.4% of the top-level positions are staffed by women (Lonsway, Carrington, et al., 2002). At the federal level it wasn't until 2003 that a woman led a major federal law enforcement agency with the appointment of Karen P. Tandy, who served as the lead administrator for the Drug Enforcement Administration (Schulz, 2004). One explanation for the limited number of women in supervisory positions is that there is low turnover generally in higher ranking positions. Limited turnover means limited opportunities for women and minorities to advance to these positions. In agencies such as the NYPD, there has been an overall reduction in the number of supervisory positions. So even when you have qualified women who score highly on promotion exams, there is a limited number of positions to place qualified candidates (Guajardo, 2016). In some cases, female candidates may be unaware of promotion opportunities (Yu, 2015). Finally, it is plausible that women are choosing not to advance, either due to limited mentoring opportunities or concerns over work-life balance (Harrington & Lonsway, 2004; Schulz, 2004). Indeed, women are more likely to choose to stay in their current positions rather than promote through the ranks due to family issues, compared to men (Rabe-Hemp, 2008). Other studies have noted a lack of mentoring for female officers (Yu, 2015). Such programs would not only assist in the recruitment and retention of female officers but would also create support for officers as they pursue opportunities for career growth and promotion.

Given the historical context of women in policing, it is not surprising that attributes such as compassion, fear, or anything else that is considered *feminine* are historically maligned, particularly by male officers. Given this masculine subculture that exists in policing, how does this affect women who are employed within the agency? What does it mean to be a woman in law enforcement?

Although women in policing have made significant advances over the past century, research is mixed on whether the contemporary situation is improving for women in law enforcement. Female officers today note that the lack of respect by their male colleagues continues to be the greatest barrier for women in law enforcement. A quarter of female officers in federal agencies state that such negativity is pervasive and makes it difficult to manage daily life on the job (Yu, 2015). While legal challenges have required equal access to employment and promotion within law enforcement, research indicates that many women continue to be *passed over* for positions that were ultimately filled by a male officer. In many cases, women felt that they continually had to prove themselves to their male colleagues, regardless of the number of years that they spent within an organization (Rabe-Hemp, 2012).

In many jurisdictions, female officers acknowledge that sexual harassment by their male peers and superior officers is part of the landscape of policing. Studies note that 40% of federal officers have experienced sexual discrimination or sexual harassment in the workplace (Yu, 2015). For example, one female officer was often told by a male superior, "Why don't you go home and be a normal woman barefoot and in the kitchen," and another was "slapped . . . across my ass after he told me that he likes women on their knees in front of him" (Lonsway, Paynich, & Hall, 2013, pp. 191, 193). Many of these cases go unreported (Yu, 2015). Research indicates that women in higher ranking positions are less willing to tolerate sexual harassment and discrimination. While some younger officers dealt with sexual harassment by avoiding and ignoring the behaviors, others confronted their colleagues in an effort to end such behaviors early in their tenure (Haarr & Morash, 2013). Still, many others ignored the behavior because they feared retaliation or believed that nothing would be done (Lonsway et al., 2013).

Despite reports of discrimination and harassment within their agencies, they acknowledge that the culture of policing has become more accepting to women throughout their careers and that such experiences do not deter them from the field (Yu, 2015). However, these ideals of peace were not easily won and required daily support and maintenance by the women. Female officers reduce the stress of sexual harassment by developing strong social bonds with other officers within their departments (Harrison, 2012). While such an approach may not reduce or eliminate the presence of harassment, it can help mediate its effects. Research by Rabe-Hemp (2008) identifies three additional ways in which policewomen gain acceptance within the **masculine culture** of policing: (1) experiences in violent confrontations requiring the use of force, (2) achieving a high rank within the department structure, and (3) distinguishing themselves as different from their male counterparts in terms of their skills and experience. Female police officers acknowledge that acceptance in the male-dominated police culture often comes with significant costs to their personal life and ideals. In many cases, policewomen talk about putting up with disrespect and harassment in order to achieve their goals. For others, they renegotiate their original goals and settle for "second best."

While the historical acceptance of women in policing was less than enthusiastic, there have been a few trends in policing, which have emphasized characteristics that are traditionally feminine. One such example is the emergence of community policing philosophies in the 1990s, which provided a shift in police culture that increased

Spotlight on Pregnancy and Policing

To date, there is limited research on how many policewomen become pregnant or give birth. When we consider the increasing participation of women in policing, coupled with data that there are 43.5 million mothers in the United States, it is not surprising to think that these two populations would join together (U.S Census, 2016). Historically, pregnant officers were either forced to take time off without pay or would leave the police force. In 1983, the *New York Times* published an article on the work-life challenges for women in policing. At the time, women made up only 6% of the sworn officers on the NYPD force. The article highlighted that the department had recently come out with a new maternity uniform to accommodate a growing number of women on the force who were pregnant. What was unique about this shift is that the NYPD was the first major police force in the country to create a maternity uniform for its officers (New York Times, 1983). This was significant progress compared to the challenges that pregnant officers had historically experienced. In 1978, two female officers were victorious in a wrongful termination case against the NYPD. Rather than assess whether these officers were able to return to their regular duties on the force following giving birth, the agency disqualified the women on the basis of their status as mothers. Both officers were reinstated and provided back pay (New York Times, 1978).

The Pregnancy Discrimination Act of 1978 prohibits the denial of employment because of pregnancy. Pregnancy is considered a temporary disability under the law and employers cannot discriminate against someone due to a disability. However, many companies and agencies, including police departments, have struggled with how to manage pregnancy for active duty officers. During the mid-1980s, many agencies implemented drug screening tests for both police recruits and current officers as part of their personnel processes. In 1987, police officials in Washington, DC, confirmed that women who applied for positions with the agency were tested for pregnancy without their consent. When testing candidates for drug use, the lab was also directed to test the female candidates to see if they were pregnant. One woman who applied for the position was informed by the agency that she was pregnant and was told that she "would have to reapply after her pregnancy." While the practice of testing female candidates began in 1985 out of concern that the physical training could be dangerous to the woman or her fetus, the practice was never recorded as an official policy, nor were potential candidates notified that they would be screened for pregnancy (Churchville, 1987). Despite concerns that such policies could open the agency up to legal challenges on the basis of discrimination, the practice continued within DC police until the early-2000's. Today, the Metropolitan Police Department allows for limited duty work assignments throughout the course of pregnancy.

In a study on maternity policies from the top 25 U.S. police departments of female sworn officers, Rabe-Hemp and Humiston (2015) noted that while 82% of the departments they surveyed had written maternity policies, a third of these policies were discretionary, meaning that the implementation of the policy was left up to the administration. In addition, only two-thirds of these policies had been updated in the last 5 years.

In acknowledging the need for policy revision, the Women in Federal Law Enforcement (2011) and the International Association of Chiefs of Police (2010) drafted model policies for agencies, which encourages departments to develop opportunities to retain female officers in meaningful assignments throughout their pregnancies. Examples such as this are evidence of progress toward family-friendly policies in policing. However, there is still work to be done. In 2016, The Justice Department proposed a resolution in a case involving the city of Florence, Kentucky, who was sued by two female officers who were denied a light duty assignment during their pregnancy. Prior to this decision, the department had limited their light duty policy to cases of on-the-job injury. The policy of distinguishing between pregnancy and on-the-job injury for cases of light duty assignments was ruled as discriminatory. Given that many officers today resign from active duty or from policing altogether because of family issues, the implementation of policies on pregnancy, light work duty, and work-life balance is important in ensuring that police agencies have opportunities for pregnant and familied women who wish to continue to serve in the same capacities as they did prior to becoming a parent (Rabe-Hemp, 2011).

the number of women working in the field. The values of **community policing** emphasize relationships, care, and communication between officers and citizens. It allows officers to develop rapport with members of their community and respond to their concerns. Effective community policing strategies have led to improved relationships and respect of officers by residents. Research indicates that policewomen have been particularly successful within models of community policing because of their enhanced problem-solving skills through communication (Lersch & Bazley, 2012). These traditionally female skills serve as an asset to departments that include community-oriented and problem-oriented policing characteristics as part of their mission as well as in dealing with certain offenders such as juveniles and women who have been victimized (Rabe-Hemp, 2009). Even though they may bring a different set of skills to the job, many female officers believe that they do the job just as well as their male counterparts, albeit in different ways. Many female officers argued that their feminine traits served them well on the job. As one officer notes:

> I think they [female officers] are very similar to male officers. They do their job. They just handle it differently. They handle calls differently. Where maybe a male might use strength, I think a female might use strength up here [pointing to her head], you know and strength here [pointing to her mouth]. (Morash & Haarr, 2012, p. 13)

Rather than feel that these female traits made them less competent, some research indicates that female officers believed that their male counterparts appreciated the value of feminine qualities in police work (Morash & Haarr, 2012). For example, women officers may have better relationships with members of their community, have fewer citizen complaints compared to their male counterparts, and are less likely to "jump" to physical interventions (Harrington & Lonsway, 2004; Lonsway, Wood, et al., 2002; Rabe-Hemp, 2009). Feminine traits, such as care and compassion, were also viewed as an asset particularly when dealing with victims, although some female officers resisted the label that they possessed these traits because of their gender (Morash & Haarr, 2012). While feminine traits are viewed as an asset in some realms of policing, some scholars have noted that being perceived as more feminine can also impact mentoring experiences and feelings of job satisfaction. Research by Barratt, Bergman, and Thompson (2014) found that women who exhibited more masculine traits received better mentoring than officers who are viewed as feminine, particularly when they are assigned a male mentor. In addition, officers who are more masculine report higher levels of job satisfaction (Swan, 2016). Such patterns highlight the need for improving both the quality of mixed gender mentoring relationships as well as increasing the number of female mentors.

Gender also impacts how officers approach their job as officers. In addition to the communication and problem-solving skills that many female officers use in their daily experiences, women officers are typically not involved in cases of police brutality and corruption. Research indicates that male officers are more than 8.5 times more likely than female officers to be accused of excessive force (Lonsway, Wood, et al., 2002). Female officers are more likely to be engaged in education and service on topics where victims are disproportionately female. Female officers are more likely to pursue education on issues such as sexual assault, while only one-third of officers reported attending more than 30 hours of such specialized education, compared to two-thirds of female officers. Female officers are also more likely to collaborate with victim advocates (Rich & Seffrin, 2014).

Perhaps the most masculine of all policing environments is the SWAT (Special Weapons and Tactics) team. Few women serve in these environments, and their participation within these ranks is a fairly new phenomenon. Because SWAT is one of the most physically demanding assignments in policing, some have suggested that few women possess the abilities to work within such an intense setting (Snow, 2010). Indeed, there are significant barriers (both perceived and real) that limit the number of women who may seek out and accept these types of positions. First, many female officers view SWAT as the pinnacle of hypermasculinity in policing that would exclude women from its ranks. Second, the nature of SWAT includes physical challenges and abilities that may discourage many women from applying. Here, many of the women acknowledged that they believed they would be accepted by the *team* if they were strong enough. Finally, both male and female officers see that women would be challenged by the male SWAT officers and need to prove that they had the skills necessary to do the job, not unlike the early experiences of women in policing:

> I would see it as a constant, day-to-day battle. Any woman in that type of unit would be forced to "do more and do it better" in order to prove herself to the men in the group. This is how women were first initiated into police work, and that type of probative acceptance continues and may even be more pronounced in units such as SWAT. (Dodge, Valcore, & Klinger, 2010, p. 229)

Despite the significant increases that women have made in the realm of policing, female officers are still viewed differently from their male counterparts. For example, female officers often prefer male officers to another female as backup. This may not reflect a distrust of their fellow female officers but rather serve as a way to distance themselves from a feminine identity and reinforce their validity in a male-dominated arena (Carlan, Nored, & Downey, 2011). At the same time, many women still struggle to separate themselves from the stereotypes of days gone by in many ways, in that they are well suited to dealing with cases involving women, children, and victims in general. These perceptions influence not only beliefs about the abilities of female officers but also ultimately have an impact on the types of work assignments that they receive (Kurtz, Linnemann, & Williams, 2012).

Women in Corrections

Correctional officers are a central component of the criminal justice system. Responsible for the security of the correctional institution and the safety of the inmates housed within its walls, correctional officers are involved with every aspect of the inmate life. Indeed, correctional officers play an important part in the lives of the inmates as a result of their constant interaction. Contrary to other work assignments within the criminal justice field, the position of the correctional officer is integrated into every aspect of the daily life of prisoners. Duties of the correctional officer range from enforcing the rules and regulations of the facility to responding to inmate needs, to diffusing inmate conflicts, and to supervising the daily movement and activities of the inmate (Britton, 2003).

Historically, the workforce of corrections has been largely male and White, regardless of the race or gender of the offender. As discussed earlier, the treatment of female offenders by male guards during the early days of the prison led to significant acts of neglect and abuse of female inmates. These acts of abuse resulted in the hiring of female matrons to supervise the incarcerated female population. However, these early positions differed significantly from the duties of male officers assigned to supervise male inmates, and opportunities for female staff to work outside the population of female-only inmates were rare. For those women who were successful in gaining employment in a male institution, their job duties were significantly limited. In particular, prison policies did not allow female correctional officers to work in direct supervision roles with male offenders. Similar to the realm of policing, the culture within correctional occupations reflected a masculine identity, and administrators believed it was too dangerous to assign a woman to supervise male inmates. In male facilities, female guards were restricted to positions that had little to no inmate contact, such as administrative positions, entry and control booths, and general surveillance (Britton, 2003).

Despite the increased access to employment opportunities for women through the 1970s, many female guards resented these gendered restrictions on their job duties and filed suit with the courts, alleging that the restriction of duties because they were women constituted sex discrimination. While many cases alleged that the restriction of female guards from male units was done to maintain issues of privacy for the offenders, the courts rejected the majority of these arguments. In *Griffin v. Michigan Department of Corrections* (654 F. Supp. 690, 1982), the court held that inmates do not possess any rights to be protected against being viewed in stages of undress or naked by a correctional officer, regardless of gender. In addition, the court held that the positive aspects of offender rehabilitation outweighed any potential risks of assault for female correctional officers; therefore, they should not be barred from working with a male incarcerated population. Other cases such as *Grummett v. Rushen* (779 F.2d 491, 1985) have concluded that the pat-down search of a male inmate (including their groin area) does not violate the Fourth Amendment protection against unreasonable search and seizure. However, the courts have held that the inverse gender relationship can be considered offensive. In *Jordan v. Gardner* (986 F.2d 1137, 1992), the court found that pat-down policies designed to control the introduction of contraband into a facility could be viewed as unconstitutional if conducted by male staff members against female inmates. Here, the court held that a cross sex search could amount to a deliberate indifference with the potential for psychological pain (under the Eighth Amendment) given the high likelihood of a female offender's history of physical and sexual abuse.

As a result of equal employment opportunity legislation, the doors of prison employment have been opened for women to serve as correctional officers. Today, women are increasingly involved in all areas of supervision of both male and female offenders, and all ranks and positions today. Many women choose corrections as a career out of interest in the rehabilitation services, as well as a perception that such a career provides job security (Hurst & Hurst, 1997). According to the 2007 Directory of Adult and Juvenile Correctional Departments, Institutions and Agencies and Probation and Parole Authorities, women made up 37% of correctional officers in state adult facilities and 51% of juvenile correctional officers (American Correctional Association, 2007). Within these facilities, both men and women are assigned to same-sex as well as cross-sex supervision positions. In addition, more women are working as correctional officers in exclusively male facilities, where they constitute 24.5% of the correctional personnel in these institutions (DiMarino, 2009).

Despite significant backlash and criticism against women in corrections, research indicates that the integration of women into the correctional field has significant benefits for prison culture. First, female correctional officers are less likely than male officers to be victimized by inmates. This finding contradicts traditional concerns that women would be at risk for harm if they were responsible for the direct supervision of male offenders (Tewksbury & Collins, 2006). However, women are more likely to fear victimization by inmates (Gordon, Proulx, & Grant, 2013). Second, women officers are more likely than male officers to use communication skills, rather than physical acts of force, to obtain compliance from inmates. Finally, female officers indicate a greater level of satisfaction from their work than male officers (Tewksbury & Collins, 2006).

How does gender affect the perceptions of work in a correctional setting? As with other criminal justice occupations, how do female correctional officers "do" gender in the context of their job duties? Many female correctional officers are hyperaware of their status as women and how gender affects interactions with both fellow staff and inmates. In some cases, female officers utilize skills and techniques that many scholars identify as feminine traits—communication and care for the inmates, mutual respect between inmates and staff, and so on. Female staff members often

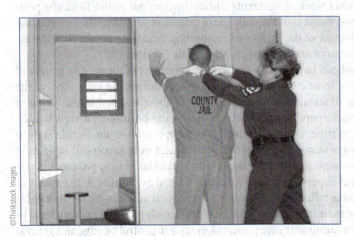

© Thinkstock Images

▲ **Photo 12.3** In the early history of prisons, women were hired to work only with female inmates. In response to equal opportunity policies and lawsuits by women in correctional fields, women today are now assigned to all types of supervision duties within the prison. Here, a female correctional officer engages in a "pat-down" search of an inmate to look for weapons or other contraband items.

become very aware of their physical status as a woman, particularly when working with male offenders, and respond by dressing down, wearing baggier clothing (in facilities where officers are not required to dress in uniform), and donning understated hairstyles and makeup to limit physical displays of gender in the workplace.

Women working in the correctional field are more likely to emphasize the "social worker" aspects of the job, compared to their male counterparts (Stohr, Mays, Lovrich, & Gallegos, 1996). Here, women use their gender to their advantage; by drawing on their communication skills, they are able to defuse potentially dangerous situations before violence ensues. However, it is important to find balance between the feminine traits and masculine traits; too much communication between staff and inmates can be viewed negatively, out of fear that staff will grow too close to an inmate and risk being taken advantage of (Britton, 2003). At the same time, some female correctional officers perceive that they are not promoted because they are viewed as less capable than their male counterparts (Matthews, Monk-Turner, & Sumter, 2010). Research indicates that gender can affect how officers approach their position, regardless of the inmate's sex. For women involved in the supervision of male inmates, their philosophies often differ significantly from that of male officers. For example, Britton (2003) found that, whereas male officers functioned within a paramilitary role and were ready to use force if necessary, women saw their role as mentors and mothers, and they focused on the rehabilitation of the inmates.

Given the increase of the prison population and the opportunities for employment, it is important for facilities to recognize the strengths and weaknesses for women who work in this field and their relationships with the incarcerated population.

However, women still struggle in this masculine, male-dominated environment. Research indicates that female correctional officers are frequent targets of sexual harassment (Chapman, 2009). The **good ol' boy network** remains quite pervasive in many facilities. Many women in leadership positions face significant challenges navigating this culture. For example, as one female officer puts it, "Men will perceive being assertive as a good quality in a guy, [but for women] they will still say, 'oh she's such a bitch.' So you need to couch what you're saying a little differently so as not to offend these poor guys over here" (Greer, 2008, p. 5). However, the perpetration of sexual harassment is not limited to other staff members. Female officers indicate that they experience persistent occurrences of sexual harassment by inmates. However, studies suggest these experiences do not affect female officers' job satisfaction—indeed many accept that incidents of sexual harassment come with the territory of being a woman working in a male-dominated arena (Chapman, 2009).

Given these challenges, are women happy working in the correctional field? Research tells us that women do tend to like their job in corrections more than their male counterparts. This is particularly interesting given that corrections is a male-dominated field, and many women have had to battle for their presence in the correctional setting (Lambert, Paoline, Hogan, & Baker, 2007). There are a number of interacting variables that determine things such as job stress and job satisfaction. For example, female correctional officers report higher levels of job stress than male officers. But what factors influence this stress? Cheeseman and Downey (2012) indicate that women who have low levels of job satisfaction will report higher levels of job-related stress. Even in cases where men and women experience on-the-job stress, the source of this stress varies by gender. While both men and women relate an increased stress level to lower levels of trust in their supervisor, men are more concerned with their abilities of their supervisor to effectively assess their job performance. In comparison, women are more likely to believe that their supervisors place unreasonable expectations on them and treat them poorly in the context of the work environment (Lambert, Hogan, Altheimer, & Wareham, 2010). Women are also more likely to experience increased stress when they have ambiguity within their role (clear rules and expectations, and an understanding about their authority and responsibilities) (Paoline, Lambert, & Hogan, 2015).

While much of the literature on women in corrections focuses on career trajectories and on the job challenges, some scholars also look at how the inmate population can have gendered implications on the work environment. Inmates often have conflicting perceptions about women working in the correctional field. Studies indicate that on their first interactions, male inmates draw on stereotypical assumptions regarding female officers. Yet women in these positions possess the unique opportunity to offer a positive image of women (Cheeseman & Worley, 2006). In addition, many line officers express disdain when they are assigned to work with female offenders. They suggest that girls are much more difficult to work with than the boys and state that the female inmates are more dramatic, manipulative, needy, emotional, and time consuming. Research by Pollock (1986) provides details on why male and female correctional officers believe that working with women is less desirable than supervising men. While both male and female staff members believe that women inmates are more demanding, defiant, and complaining, male officers also express concerns about being accused of inappropriate behaviors against female inmates. Female officers express that they would prefer to work with male inmates because they feel that they are more likely to be respected and appreciated by the male inmates than female inmates. Belief systems such as these have a significant impact on perceptions of working with female offenders and translate into a belief that working with women is an undesirable assignment (Rasche, 2012). Research indicates that among both male and female correctional officers (and regardless of rank), there appears to be a **male inmate preference**, despite the increased risks for violence associated with this population.

Community Corrections: Female Probation and Parole Officers

While there has been a fair amount of research on women in policing and corrections, the same cannot be said for women who work as parole and probation officers. While probation and parole agents are sworn officials like police officers, their work focuses only on convicted offender populations, whereas police officers deal with the general population as well. Given the high demand on probation services as a tool of the correctional system, it is fair to say that probation officers deal with the largest criminal justice population.

The origins of probation date back to the Middle Ages and English criminal law. In the United States, John Augustus became the first volunteer probation officer in 1841. In 1925, the federal government passed the National Probation Act and established the U.S. Federal Probation Service. By 1951, probation departments were established in every state. One of the earliest female probation officers was Catherine F. Brattan, who has been referenced as the first woman probation officer in California in 1910 (Sawyers, 1922). In contrast, parole was first implemented in the United States by Zebulon Brockway in 1876 and was implemented nationwide by 1942 (Peterselia, 2000). Indeed, like some of the early women in policing, many of these early women in probation and parole were charged with supervising juvenile offenders and, later, female offenders. In 1970, most states limited the caseloads of female parole officers to female offenders. Following the passage of the Civil Rights Act, states began to allow for cross sex supervision (Schoonmaker & Brooks, 1975). In 2012, there were 90,300 probation officers and correctional treatment specialists in the United States (Bureau of Labor Statistics [BLS], 2014). However, it is unclear how many of these positions are held by women.

As you learned earlier in this chapter, there has been a significant body of work investigating the cultural environment of women in policing and corrections and the challenges that they face. Could the same be said for women who work in probation and parole? Do they face these same challenges in this male-dominated environment? The answer to this question is yes. Research indicates that women in parole have similar experiences with sexual harassment and marginalization as do women in policing (Ireland & Berg, 2008). Working with highly intense populations also means extensive exposure to acts of violence. Over time, this exposure can desensitize probation officers (Petrillo, 2007).

In addition, women experience high levels of stress as part of their job duties. The presence of stress can be found in four different areas of the job: internal organizational stress, external organizational stress, job and/or task-related stress, and personal stress. Research indicates that male and female probation officers experience different categories of stress. Female probation officers register higher levels of physical stress, whereas male probation officers register high levels of internal organization, job-related, and personal stress. However, each of these types of stress was greater for officers in supervisory positions (and men were more likely to serve in these roles). At the same time, it is possible that women have lower registered levels of stress because they are more likely to be aware of the early warning signs of stress and take action (Wells, Colbert, & Slate, 2006). Despite this, many women acknowledge that these stressful on-the-job experiences often spill over into their lives. Much of the literature on criminal justice occupations (such as policing and corrections) focuses on the masculine nature of these careers and the challenges that women face within these environments. However, literature on parole officers indicates that female officers utilize gendered strategies as part of their management strategies. Like female police officers, communication skills were invaluable in the daily aspects of their job as a parole officer. As one female parole agent expressed,

> We have to have good communication skills; we have to be able to recognize volatile situations; and you have to be able to know how to handle those situations by using your communication skills. I have been involved in situations that could have easily turned volatile, but my manner, my demeanor, my communication skills, and the manner in which I dealt with these individuals has made a very big difference in the way they have responded to me. (Ireland & Berg, 2008, p. 483)

Developing rapport with their clients was also an important skill that contributed to their on-the-job safety. While male officers were more likely to use force in their cases (a reflection of their identity with policing), female agents aligned themselves with a social worker mentality, which allowed for more of a rehabilitative focus (Ireland & Berg, 2008). Particularly in cases where female officers were involved in supervising male offenders, gender became a way to challenge the offender's perceptions and stereotypes about women. However, male offenders would often challenge these female officers, using tricks from intimidation to flirting to regain some power over the situation. At the same time, their interactions with these offenders gave a unique insight as to how victims experience interactions with these offenders, particularly in cases of intimate partner violence and sexual offenses (Petrillo, 2007). In addition, female officers emphasized the role of respect between themselves and their parolees as a way to manage their caseload. "Parolees, if you treat them well and you do your job, even when you have to lock them up, they will respect you and understand that you are just doing your job. If you treat them like a piece of crap, that's what you're going to get back" (Ireland & Berg, 2008, p. 485).

While parole officers appear to engage in cross-sex supervision, probation officers are often assigned caseloads that are specialized, such as around a particular offense (drug crimes, sexual offending), need (mental health treatment), or gender of the offender. Since female probation officers are more likely to be assigned to supervise female offenders, this creates an opportunity to engage in gendered strategies. While these approaches reflect the needs of the offender, it may also be related to how officers do their job. For example, female officers are more likely to engage with their clients on an emotional level and build relationships with their clients. In this way, the probation officer serves as a positive role model for her clients (Wyse, 2013).

Conclusion

At the heart of the research for each of these fields, two major themes emerge: (1) Gender can affect the way in which women who work in these fields satisfy the demands of their positions, and (2) gender affects the experiences that they have within their jobs. These factors are multiplied for women of color, whereby race serves as yet another variable through which discrimination and other challenges can persist. For some of the most masculine positions, such as policing and corrections, women must fight against firmly held beliefs that such jobs are inappropriate for women. While equal employment opportunity legislation has opened the doors for access for women in these traditionally male-dominated fields, women still face an uphill battle because they have been denied opportunities and promotions throughout history. Despite these struggles, women remain an important presence in these fields with significant contributions that need to be encouraged and acknowledged, particularly for future generations of women in these fields.

SUMMARY

- Traditional male occupations, such as policing and corrections, historically excluded employment options for women on the grounds that the work was too dangerous.

- Early policewomen were involved in crime prevention efforts, primarily with juvenile and female populations.

- While equal opportunity legislation may have opened access for women in policing and corrections, institutional cultures and standards continued to create barriers for women in these occupations for entry and advancement.

- Women in police, corrections, and community supervision use different tools and techniques in their daily experiences in their positions, compared to male officers.

- Few women have successfully navigated to the top levels of their fields in law enforcement and corrections.

- As workers in these fields, women are subjected to issues with job satisfaction, stress, and burnout.

- There are more females employed in probation than any other law enforcement or correctional environment.

KEY TERMS

Baldwin, Lola 198

Blankenship, Betty 199

Civil Rights Bill 200

Coffal, Liz 199

Community policing 204

Gendered assignments 199

Good ol' boy network 207

Griffin v. Michigan Department of Corrections 205

Grummett v. Rushen 206

Jordan v. Gardner 206

Male inmate preference 208

Masculine culture 202

Owens, Marie 198

Wells, Alice Stebbins 198

DISCUSSION QUESTIONS

1. Based on the research, how do women do gender within traditional male-dominated criminal justice occupations?

2. What challenges do women who work in criminal justice occupations face that their male counterparts do not?

3. What suggestions can be made to improve the status of women within criminal justice occupations?

WEB RESOURCES

American Correctional Association: http://www.aca.org

Association of Women Executives in Corrections: http://www.awec.us

National Center for Women and Policing: http://www.womenandpolicing.org

 Visit **www.sagepub.com/mallicoat3e** to access additional study tools, including eFlashcards, web quizzes, web resources, video resources, and SAGE journal articles.

Women Professionals and the Criminal Justice System

Courts and Victim Services

Chapter Highlights

- The gendered experience of women employed in the legal field
- Future directions for females working in courts and the law
- The role of victims' advocates in rape-crisis and domestic violence agencies

Women and the Law

Like women in many of the occupations discussed in Chapter 12, women in the legal field have historically been underrepresented. The 1800s saw several notable examples of women in these occupations. In 1869, Belle Mansfield became the first woman admitted to a state bar (Iowa) in the U.S (Morello, 1986; Robinson, 1890). Charlotte E. Ray became the first African American woman admitted to the bar for the District of Columbia in 1872 (Law Library of Congress, n.d.; Robinson, 1890). By 1879, antidiscrimination laws had changed, and Belva Ann Lockwood became the first woman to practice law before the U.S. Supreme Court (Cook, 1997; Law Library of Congress, n.d.; Smith, 1998). However, it was not until 1918 that the first women—Mary B. Grossman of Cleveland, Ohio, and Mary Florence Lathrop of Denver, Colorado, were admitted to the American Bar Association. These appearances by women into the legal profession were rare, and most of these women held positions with low prestige (Drachman, 1998). In the 21st century, the presidency of the American Bar Association has been filled by a woman in six of the past sixteen terms. While times have improved significantly for women in this field, they still endure several challenges based on gender.

Today, women have reached near parity in terms of law school enrollment and faculty positions. Women make up almost half of all students enrolled in law school (49.3% in 2014-2015) with 13.2% of these women identifying as women of color, compared to 10.4% men of color (American Bar Association [ABA], 2017). This equality is also

▲ **Photo 13.1** The number of women in the legal field is increasing. Here, a female lawyer talks with a witness during a trial.

reflected in women's representation on law reviews, where women make up 54% of those in leadership positions and 49% of the editors-in-chief positions. Women also make up a significant presence among law school faculty. According to the American Bar Association (2010), women make up 54.6% of the tenured, tenure-track, or visiting full-time faculty at law schools across the nation. In addition, more women are finding their way into the top administrative positions within these schools. While women are less likely than men to hold the highest office (31.1% of dean positions are staffed by women), they are more likely than men to hold the office of associate or vice dean (60.6%) and assistant dean or director (69.7%).

While women have moved up the ranks within the legal academy, the number of male attorneys far exceeds the number of female attorneys in the United States. According to the American Bar Association (2017), only 36% of practicing attorneys in the United States are female. In addition, many positions are inaccessible for women. Women make up only 2% of the managing partners within the 200 largest law firms in the United States. Within Fortune 500 corporations with in-house counsel, women make up 24.8% of these positions and only a small proportion (13%) of these are staffed by women of color (National Association for Law Placement, 2010; National Association of Women Lawyers, 2009, 2010; ABA, 2017). In addition, women are less likely to make partner than men (Noonan, Corcoran, & Courant, 2008). Women make up 21% of partners at major U.S. law firms. Women of color are even more underrepresented in these roles—only 2.55% of these positions are filled by women of color (NALP, 2015). This contributes to disparities in pay between men and women. However, things are improving significantly. In 2009, female lawyers made 75% of the salaries of men. In 2015, this increased to 90%. This means that male lawyers today make approximately 10% more than their female counterparts, a significant improvement compared to just a few years ago when the disparity equaled 25% (ABA, 2017). However, not all ranks show this level of improvement because the typical female partner in a top-earning firm continues to make 20% less in compensation compared to her male colleagues.

The number of women in the legal field is increasing; over a five-year period between 2012 and 2017, the proportion of female practicing attorneys increased 5% from 31% to 36% and the number of women serving as in-house counsel with Fortune 500 companies increased 6.8%. As more women enter the profession, there will be more women seeking upper level positions. What remains to be seen is whether women within the legal field will face some of the same challenges that you learned about in Chapter 12 with limited turnover in the upper ranks, which creates fewer opportunities for women to move into these higher ranked positions. Currently, women make up almost half of the associates positions in private practice (45%) (ABA, 2017).

Consider the organizational structure of high-profile private firms. Traditionally, the ranks of private law firms were divided into three categories. Associates, or the entry tier, is filled with new lawyers fresh out of law school who are battling for a place within the firm. Associates spend 5 to 7 years with 80-hour work weeks in an effort to demonstrate that they should be selected as a partner. These positions are often probationary and those who are not selected for a partnership are let go. Partnership offers both financial and job security. However, this structure has shifted in recent decades. Nonequity partnerships were introduced into the mix. Lawyers at this rank have demonstrated their success as an associate but have not advanced to an equity partnership, meaning that they do not share in the firm's financial successes. Similar non-partner track positions such as staff attorneys and career associates were also created. It is not surprising that these lower paid positions were more likely to be staffed by women (Sterling, 2016).

Like many of the fields within the criminal justice system, women in the legal profession also face challenges with balancing the needs of their career with the demands of motherhood and family life. Within the corporate model of the legal system, the emphasis on billable hours requires attorneys to work long hours, both during the week and on weekends. In recent decades, the demand for billable hours by firms on their associates has increased significantly. Even with these high demands, billable hours are only part of the daily work that lawyers might engage in. The demands of this type of position often conflict with family responsibilities. For many women, the work-life conflict results in either delaying the start of a family or choosing their career over motherhood entirely. Others choose to leave their legal positions prior to making partner or leave their positions for ones that are less stressful and afford greater flexibility. In many cases, for women who exercise part-time options in an effort to create **work-family balance,** work and family life are often viewed as less ambitious compared to their male (and other female) counterparts.

While firms may offer opportunities for part-time work, research indicates that few women avail themselves of these opportunities for fear that doing so would damage their potential for career advancement. For those women who chose these career trajectories, research indicates that these positions did not necessarily involve compensatory reductions in workload, forcing many to bring their work home with them, work for which they do not receive compensation. In addition, these women often believed that a reduction in time spent in the office could ultimately affect their chances for promotion and earning potential, and it also fostered negative assumptions regarding their work ethic and level of commitment among their colleagues (Bacik & Drew, 2006). One suggestion to remedy the demands created by the billable hours model is to move toward a value billing (where the costs of the legal work are based on the nature and complexity of the case) or fixed fee (costs are quoted up front for the project) billing system. Both of these models create work efficiency and allow for a greater work-life balance (Durrani & Singh, 2011).

As women in private law practice become discouraged regarding their likelihood of achieving partner status, many make the decision to leave their positions. Indeed, men are two to three times more likely to become partners than women and also earn significantly higher salaries (ABA, 2011). While the decisions to get married, have children, and take time away from their jobs, or reduce their employment status to part-time, do not have a significant effect for men or women in their likelihood to leave private practice, these variables are associated with levels of satisfaction surrounding the balance of work and family needs. Here, satisfaction is the key, not their decisions regarding family status (Noonan & Corcoran, 2008, Kay, Alarie, & Adjei, 2013).

The majority of research on women in the legal profession lacks any discussion of how race and ethnicity interact with gender for women of color. What is available indicates that race and ethnicity have significant effects on the gendered nature of legal work. Generally speaking, men were more likely to be assigned high-profile cases, whereas women were assigned cases related to educational and other social issues. In addition, one respondent indicated that although White women and women of other minority groups were more likely to be viewed as "good attorneys," Chicanas were less likely to be viewed as valuable professionals in their field. Here, women of color are put in a position wherein they need to constantly prove themselves to their colleagues. As one female of color commented, "They just didn't appreciate me; (they) didn't think I was capable" (Garcia-Lopez, 2008, p. 598). In addition, Chicana women were more likely than White women to be overburdened with larger, lower profile caseloads. They also felt as though they were the key representatives and spokespersons for their racial-ethnic group. As another observed, "It's like they expect you to answer for the entire Latino population; like you should know everything there is to know about Latinos" (p. 601). Unlike other racial, ethnic, and gender groups, Chicana women attorneys did not define their success by financial achievements. Rather, social justice and helping people in their community play a key function in their concept of success and happiness with their lives and careers (Garcia-Lopez, 2008). In addition, many Latina law associates believe that the **glass ceiling** exists and can limit opportunities for promotion based on their gender and ethnic identity (Foley, Kidder, & Powell, 2002).

Scholars debate whether or not women can achieve equality in the legal profession. Some suggest that as older (and mostly male) partners retire, younger attorneys will be more likely to include a greater representation of women, given the increase in the number of women who attend and graduate from law school (French, 2000). Others argue that this theory neglects the fact that any change in the culture of the law firm will be slow in coming due to the small numbers of women who choose to work within these types of positions and are successful on the partnership track (Reichman & Sterling, 2001).

Spotlight on Women in Politics

In 1894, Colorado was the first state in the nation to elect a woman to a state legislative post. In fact, they elected three—Clara Cressingham, Carrie Clyde Holly, and Frances Klock. All three women were involved in political activity around improving the lives of girls and women. Both Cressingham and Klock supported bills to create homes for delinquent and destitute girls. But it was Holly who was perhaps the most active on women's rights. She was the nation's first woman to sponsor a bill and championed equal rights for men and women. She also worked to raise the age of sexual consent from 16 to 18 (NWHM, n.d.). Today, 1,830 women make up 24.8% of the elected representatives to the state legislatures. Women who are elected at the state level are more likely to be members of the Democratic Party (15%) compared to the Republican Party (9%) (NCSL, 2017).

At the federal level, Jeannette Rankin (MT) was the first woman elected to Congress in the House of Representatives in 1922. Her tenure lasted one day. It wasn't until 1931 when Hattie Caraway was first elected to succeed her husband and was subsequently reelected to a six-year term (Manning, Brudnick, & Shogan, 2015). Today, women comprise 19.6% of the elected officials (105 of the 535 members). Twenty-one women are members of the Senate (21%) and 84 (19.3%) represent their states in the House of Representatives. There are also five female delegates in the House who represent the District of Columbia and U.S. Territories. Like state legislatures, women in Congress are more likely to be Democrats. Women in Congress are also more likely to represent diverse backgrounds, because 38 of the 104 are women of color (CAWP, 2017). In comparison, only 64 of the men in Congress are members of a minority group (Marcos, 2016).

The 2016 election saw three newly elected women to the U.S. Senate. Tammy Duckworth (IL) is a retired U.S. Army Lieutenant Colonel and the first disabled woman to be elected to Congress. She lost both of her legs in combat during the Iraq War in 2004. Catherine Cortez Masto (NV) previously served as the Attorney General of Nevada and is the first Latina to serve in the Senate. Like Cortez-Masto, Kamala Harris (CA) also served as the Attorney General prior to joining the Senate. Harris is the first Indian American to serve in the U.S. Senate. All three women represent the Democratic Party and have been very active since their entry to Washington. Duckworth introduced the Friendly Airports for Mothers Act in June, which calls for medium- and large-sized airports to provide lactation rooms for breastfeeding mothers (S. 1110). In July 2017, Harris (joined by Senators Booker (NJ), Durbin (IL), and Warren (MA)) cosponsored the Dignity for Incarcerated Women Act, which would require federal prisons to provide free tampons and sanitary pads to women. It would ban the shackling of pregnant women or placing them in solitary confinement. The bill would assist in maintaining ties between an incarcerated woman and her family by considering the location of children when determining where she will be housed for her sentence. It would also create policies that would extend the visiting time and eliminate phone charges for women and the families (S. 1524).

There is an extensive amount of research on the legislative actions of women. Much of these findings note that women are traditionally involved in political activity (sponsor and vote) on female-centric legislation.

Examples of these activities include bills that promote women's rights, increased care and resources for families and children, and increased equality for women. Even when female legislators differ in their ideological views (Democratic vs. Republican), both sides agree that they have an obligation to represent women and will often work across party lines to accomplish these goals (Hawkesworth, Casey, Jenkins, & Kleeman, 2001). While many of these issues are often framed as "women's issues," the reality is that legislation on issues such as families, education, and social welfare are gender-neutral issues that impact both men and women. Research has noted that when there are more women serving in leadership roles in the political arena, there is an increase in the number of laws on women's issues. There is also an increase in the gendered content of these laws. However, success of these laws is dependent on their male colleagues offering their support (Wittmer & Bouche, 2013). In addition to their successes on passing laws in favor of women's rights, female participation within the legislature can also help prevent antiwomen legislation (Berkman & O'Connor, 1993). Given the current makeup of legislatures both at the state and federal level, it's clear that women are making a significant impact on the lives of men, women, and children.

Women and the Judiciary

In the judiciary, the representation of women has grown substantially over the last several decades. Although most of the conversations about women in the judiciary focus on the women that have been appointed to the U.S. Supreme Court, we have seen increases in the number of women appointed to the judiciary at all levels in recent times for both the state and federal legal systems. In light of these changes, how is this reflected in the proportion of women who serve in these positions? What is the current status of women in the judiciary?

Most female judges are assigned to courts of general jurisdiction. For example, 92% of women judges in California serve in trial courts (Williams, 2007). Similar trends are noted in the nationwide data, where 84% of women judges serve in courts at the trial level (National Association of Women Lawyers, 2010). While this might seem staggering in terms of the number of women that have been relegated to these lower level positions, we need to think about these data within the context of the number of positions at each level. For example, the majority of all justices (regardless of gender) serve in these general (and other lower level) jurisdiction courts, simply because there are so many opportunities (and high demand) for these positions. In contrast, there are few justices at the appellate and higher levels, which means fewer positions for women in general. However, the proportion of women in these positions is increasing. Nationwide, women represent 34.6% of the judges at the state supreme court level and 34.7% at the intermediate appellate jurisdiction courts. Overall, women occupy 5,596 of the 18,006 positions in state court judicial positions across the United States. Within the federal level, women occupy 60 of the 167 available positions in the Federal Circuit Court of Appeals (35.9%)

Steve Petteway, photographer for the Supreme Court of the United States

▲ **Photo 13.2** The four women of the U.S. Supreme Court. From left to right: Sandra Day O'Connor, Sandra Sotomayor, Ruth Bader Ginsburg, and Elena Kagan.

and 33% in the District Courts (ABA, 2017). So, while the physical number of women in these positions is somewhat small, their effect is significant given the few positions that exist at this level.

What factors affect the appointment of women to the judiciary? Williams (2007) suggests that more women receive a judicial appointment as a result of a nonpartisan election, compared to partisan elections. Liberal states are more likely to have women in judicial positions, compared to conservative states. In addition, the presence of female attorneys in the state also increases the representation of women as judges in the trial courts. At the appellate level, three variables affect the representation of women in these positions: (1) As more seats are generally available on the appellate bench, the representation of women at this level increases; (2) as the number of female attorneys in a state increases, so does the number of women judges at the appellate level; (3) states that use the merit selection process to fill seats have an increased number of women on the bench, compared to those states that rely on a partisan election to fill these positions. In addition, research indicates that women in the judiciary have a greater interest in elevating their career trajectory than male judges (Jensen & Martinek, 2009).

Spotlight on Women and the Supreme Court

The U.S. Supreme Court is an institution unlike any other in the nation. The first Court was established in 1789 with six members: a chief justice and five associate justices. Today, there are a total of nine justices—eight associates plus the chief justice. Over the past 211 years, there have been 112 justices and 17 chief justices. Turnover on the Court is a slow process as members of the Supreme Court are appointed for life (and many serve until their death; Supreme Court, n.d.). The presence of women on the Supreme Court is a new practice. It wasn't until 1981 that the first female justice was appointed to the Court. To date, there have been only four women to serve on the Supreme Court: Sandra Day O'Connor, Ruth Bader Ginsburg, Sonia Sotomayor, and Elena Kagan.

In 1981, President Ronald Reagan appointed Sandra Day O'Connor as the first woman to grace the Supreme Court's bench. At the time of her appointment, there were few women in high-ranking judicial positions at the state and federal level. O'Connor began her tenure on the Court as a conservative voice, and she voted with her conservative colleagues in the overwhelming majority of her decisions ("Nine Justices," 2004). While she was initially appointed as a conservative voice on the Court, she was not always aligned with the political right and became the swing vote alongside more liberal justices in some high-profile cases before the Court. For example, in *Lawrence v. Texas* (2003), she ruled with her liberal colleagues that laws banning sodomy for homosexuals but not for heterosexuals were unconstitutional. She retired from the Court in January 2006.

O'Connor remained the lone woman on the Court until 1993, when Clinton appointed a second woman to the Court—Ruth Bader Ginsburg. During her tenure as a lawyer, she appeared before the Court on six separate occasions in cases involving women's rights. She was first appointed to the federal bench by President Carter in 1981 to serve on the U.S. Court of Appeals. During her tenure on the Court, Ginsburg has presented a balanced view in her decision making—sometimes voting with her liberal colleagues and other times serving as the swing vote for the conservative voice. One of her noted decisions on gender equality involved the case of *United States v. Virginia* (1996), which involved a challenge against the single-sex admission policy of Virginia Military Institute. In writing for the majority opinion, Ginsburg stated that "neither federal nor state government acts compatibly with equal protection when a law or official policy denies to women, simply because they are women, full citizenship stature—equal opportunity to aspire, achieve, participate in and contribute to society based on their individual talents and capacities" (518 U.S. 515, 532).

Recently, Ginsburg has been joined by two additional female justices: Sonia Sotomayor (2009) and Elena Kagan (2010). Their appointments mark a shift in the judiciary of the highest Court in the land. Sotomayor is the first woman of color, a Latina, to serve on the Supreme Court, and the inclusion of Kagan creates a historical first, because this is the first time in history that three women have served simultaneously on the Court.

Sotomayor began her career as a prosecutor and spent time in private practice before she was appointed to the judiciary (federal district court) by President George H. W. Bush in 1991. She was elevated to the Second [U.S. Circuit] Court of Appeals by President Clinton in 1997. Perhaps her most famous decision came in 1995 when she ruled against the administrators of Major League Baseball and subsequently ended the baseball strike ("Sonia Sotomayor," 2012). As the first appointment of President Obama in 2009, she has been involved in several landmark decisions, including health care reform and immigration laws. While a moderate voice early in her career, on the Court she has served as a liberal voice and is often viewed as a champion for the rights of the downtrodden (Savage, 2009).

Few presidents have the opportunity to nominate even one member to the Supreme Court. During his tenure, President Obama has made two appointments. His second appointment came in 2010 with the confirmation of Elena Kagan (Center for American Women and Politics, n.d.). Kagan's career included a variety of positions in private practice, tenure at University of Chicago Law, and even a stint in the White House as a deputy domestic policy advisor under President Clinton. She became a professor at Harvard Law School and was later named its first woman dean. In 2009, President Obama appointed Kagan to serve as the solicitor general. However, this position was short lived because she was nominated and confirmed to the Supreme Court in 2010. While some viewed her lack of experience in the judiciary as a negative, she has positioned herself as one of the more influential leaders on the Court. Indeed, she has participated in two of the recent landmark decisions by the Court involving gay marriage: *Hollingsworth v. Perry* (2013; overturned California's Prop. 8) and *U.S. v. Windsor* (overturned the Defense of Marriage Act). In each of these cases, Kagan sided with the majority opinion in support of gay marriage as a component of fairness and dignity.

With three female justices on the Court, Ginsburg, Sotomayor, and Kagan make history and represent a significant increase of women in the judiciary. While the progress is certainly significant, the long tenure of justices may mean that the addition of more women to the Court will not occur in the near future. However, as new appointees, the voices of Sotomayor and Kagan will certainly shape the decisions of the Court for a significant future.

Does being female affect the way in which judges make decisions? In a study involving hypothetical vignettes, the findings indicated several areas where gender differences existed among judges who participated in the survey. In most of the scenarios, the female judges imposed longer sentences in cases of simple assault and were less likely to award civil damages for these cases. However, when damages were to be awarded, female judges awarded significantly higher monetary levels compared to male judges (Coontz, 2000). When reviewing outcomes in real-life cases, the results are mixed. Research by Steffensmeier and Hebert (1999) finds that women judges tend to be harsher in their sentencing decisions compared to their male counterparts. Controlling for offender characteristics, the presence of a woman on the bench increases both the likelihood of prison time for offenders (10%) and the length of their sentences (+5 months longer). In addition, property offenders and repeat offenders are the ones most likely to bear the brunt of this increased severity when facing a female judge. In contrast, research by McCall (2007) indicates that female judges are generally more liberal in their decision making. Similar research on gender differences in sentencing by Songer, Davis, and Haire (1994) indicates that male and female judges do not differ in judicial decision making in federal cases involving obscenity charges or criminal search and seizure cases, but female judges were significantly more likely to decide in favor of the victim in cases of employment discrimination. At the state supreme court level, research indicates that not only do women tend to vote more liberally in death penalty and obscenity cases but also that the presence of a woman on the court increases the likelihood that the male judges will vote in a liberal fashion (Songer & Crews-Meyer, 2000).

Women and Work in Victim Services

A violation of the criminal law is considered a crime against the state, regardless of the offense or the harm to the victim. Victims have generally played a minor role throughout the criminal justice process and have had limited rights. For example, victims were not entitled to information about the case, nor were they invited to take an active role in the process. The fight for victims' rights began to emerge during the 1970s as a grassroots effort. One of the first victim services programs was the Bay Area Women Against Rape in San Francisco, which was the first rape-crisis center. In 1975, the National Organization for Victim Assistance (NOVA) was created as a resource for victims' rights groups across the United States and provides a voice to the needs of victims of crime (Young & Stein, 2004).

With the increased attention on victims' rights at the national level, the number of agencies began to multiply. While some of these groups were nonprofit community-based organizations, there was also a push for victims' services within local and state government bureaus. The funding source varies from organization to organization. While many of these programs receive state and federal funds, these resources alone are not enough to support the needs of the organization. As a result, many programs seek out grants and private subsidies to sustain their efforts (California Emergency Management Agency [Cal EMA], 2011).

While crime and victimizations cut across race, class, and gender lines (as well as other demographic identities), women are disproportionately represented within certain categories of crime, such as rape, sexual assault, and intimate partner abuse. One of the unique factors of many victim service organizations that focus on these particular types of victims is that the workforce tends to be predominantly female. In addition, many of these workers identify as survivors of these crimes. This feminine dynamic within the workplace brings a unique perspective to these agencies, particularly compared to the majority of occupations affiliated with the criminal justice system that are male dominated. Within the victims' services field, feminine traits, such as compassion, care, and support, are a critical part of the daily work environment. This concept of survivor-as-advocate or survivor-to-survivor model began during the battered women shelter movement whereby individuals who had successfully terminated a violent relationship were available to support those who were currently going through the process (Ferraro, 1981). As the work within intimate partner violence organizations began to become more professionalized, the personal experiences of workers continued to serve as a calling to the work. For others, work within the IPV field was a reflection of their social justice philosophy (Wood, 2017). At the same time, formal education in fields such as victimology, psychology, criminology, social work, and sociology

iStock/monkeybusinessimages

▲ **Photo 13.3** Many women are drawn to work in the field of victims' services. Here, a counselor provides support to a young girl at a domestic violence center.

as well as specialized training on issues such as victim services, law, and the criminal justice system are invaluable for this field (Neff, Patterson, & Johnson, 2012).

However, it is important to consider that victimization is a highly sensitive experience, and the people that work within these fields are often faced with high exposure to emotion within the context of their work. Over time, this can take its toll. The following chapters highlight some of the challenges that **victim advocates** face in the workplace with agencies that provide services for victims of intimate partner violence and sexual assault.

Advocates for Intimate Partner Abuse

The decision to seek out assistance in cases of intimate partner abuse can be difficult for many victims. As you learned in Chapter 4, victims may experience fear and shame as a part of their abuse, believe that nothing can be done to change the situation, or may fail to even identify themselves as a victim. Despite these challenges, the demand for services for victims of these crimes is in high demand. Advocates in these cases may involve a variety of duties, including providing services (or referrals for services), helping victims secure temporary and transitional housing, and providing support in legal cases (Camacho & Alarid, 2008; Slattery & Goodman, 2009).

Within the context of their daily work, advocates are exposed to stories filled with episodes of physical, sexual, and psychological abuse. In addition, advocates deal with clients in emergent and pressure-filled situations. The intensity of these events can take their toll on advocates and lead to **burnout**. Not only may advocates experience emotional exhaustion because of the high levels of on-the-job stress, these experiences can lead advocates to become less connected to their work and their clients. As a result, many may question whether these costs are worth it and whether it makes a difference (Babin, Palazzolo, & Rivera, 2012). It is when an advocate feels that they are ineffective that the risk for burnout is at its highest. To a certain extent, these feelings of efficacy are perpetuated by the cycle of violence. Victims of intimate partner abuse often leave several times before they are able to completely sever their relationship. When a victim returns to her batterer, the advocate may feel that she has failed. Over time, this can have a significant impact on whether the advocate has sympathy for her client, which in turn can limit delivery of services (Kolb, 2011). In an effort to continue to support their clients, advocates will often excuse or justify their clients' actions so as to not take this decision as a personal rejection. One advocate expressed this experience in the following way:

> It takes the heat off (the client) and it makes it easier, especially with abusers, to say that we made them do it, we made them take out the charges. It's frustrating, but that's what an advocate does. (Kolb, 2011, p. 110)

For survivor-advocates, working in support for victims can represent a way of giving back to the support systems that personally helped them. Some advocates would use their individual experiences with victimization to connect with their clients. For others, working with victims provided a unique mirror of their own pathways to healing

> I guess when you kind of get a little sidetracked and you see women and how they struggle with being independent and getting all the assistance they need, it kind of makes me realize how far I've come along and just reminds me to remember where I was at one point and it helps me to understand that I have healed and that I'm in a better place now. And it also motivates me to try to help them so they can one day feel the same way that I do now. That's my goal. (Wood, 2017 p. 321)

The emotional nature of work as a domestic violence advocate can have a significant impact on his or her mental health. Advocates may experience their own psychological strain or secondary trauma stress. **Secondary trauma stress** is similar to post-traumatic stress disorder (PTSD) and is defined as "stress resulting from helping or wanting to help a traumatized or suffering person" (Figley, 1995, p. 7). One of the greatest predictors of secondary trauma stress is whether advocates have a history of their own intimate partner abuse (Slattery & Goodman, 2009). Since many advocates in the field have a personal history of victimization by an intimate partner, this is important to consider because it can create challenges in setting boundaries and lead to emotional triggers that can be harmful for both the worker and their client (Wood, 2017). However, organizational support structures within the workplace can serve as a protective factor against developing secondary trauma stress (Slattery & Goodman, 2009). Examples of these include fostering an environment of peer-to-peer support among the workers as well as developing formal mentor programs for new employees (Babin et al., 2012).

Spotlight on Self-Care for Victim Advocates

The concept of self-care involves activities and practices that help with stress management and the maintenance of our physical and emotional well-being. Self-care can involve a variety of different activities, including exercise, healthy living, mindfulness activities such as meditation, social activities with friends and family, and engagement in spiritual activity. Working with victims of crime can be an intense and emotional experience day in and day out. As a result, individuals who work within these fields often suffer from secondary trauma victimization, compassion fatigue, and burnout. Given these challenges, self-care becomes incredibly important in both the health and well-being of individual workers and volunteers, as well as the structure of the organization.

One area that has garnered attention on self-care for individuals who work with victims of intimate partner violence and sexual assault is art therapy. Art therapy can take a variety of different approaches such as viewing and creating paintings, spoken word poetry, dance, and theater. Even within service-oriented populations, reaching out can be internalized as appearing incompetent in their position (Taylor & Furlonger, 2011). Art therapy can provide nonverbal ways to manage compassion fatigue. It can also create new mediums for expression and communication (Huet & Holttum, 2016). These shared experiences can also create peer connections between colleagues (Ifrach & Miller, 2016). These connections and coping skills can help support each other in their daily work.

One of the greatest challenges for individuals is recognizing the early signs of STS, compassion fatigue, and burnout. Not only is self-care important in terms of employee retention, such traumas could also impact the delivery of services to victims. It is also important for workers to be able to admit when they need help. Organizations need to create safe spaces for employees and volunteers to be able to reach out. Many organizations include discussions of personal well-being into their training programs or create opportunities for practices such as "wellness days" with coordinated activities designed to foster support within the group (Howlett & Collins, 2014).

Rape-Crisis Workers

As one of the first examples of victims' services in the 1970s, rape-crisis organizations began as community-based grassroots agencies. Initially, these organizations were run primarily by a volunteer and female workforce. Many of these women had survived a rape or sexual assault at some point in their lifetime (Mallicoat, Marquez, & Rosenbaum, 2007). In addition to providing support for victims of sexual assault, many of these early centers worked on legislative actions in pursuit of victims' rights in sexual assault cases (Maier, 2011). During the 1980s and 1990s, rape-crisis organizations began to collaborate with other service providers, such as hospitals, police departments, and other community-based services. While much of the collaboration was driven by the budget cuts and the need to develop new ways to share resources, the effect was a professionalization of these agencies and their missions (Mallicoat et al., 2007). In addition, state governments began to take an interest in making sure that crime victims had access to services (Maier, 2011). As a result, contemporary rape-crisis organizations can provide a variety of services, including crisis hotlines (many of which are staffed 24 hours a day), crisis counseling, and legal and medical advocates for victims (Ullman & Townsend, 2007) as well as services for non-English speakers and proactive education on rape and sexual assault (Maier, 2011). While work within these organizations has become a full-time professional occupation, organizations must call on volunteers to help serve the needs of the community (Mallicoat et al., 2007). In addition, today's rape-crisis centers are usually less focused on the political activism that was a core component of the early rape-crisis centers of the 1970s (Maier, 2011).

There is significant variability within the different types of rape-crisis organizations in terms of the types of populations they serve (rural vs. urban and multicultural populations), the types of services that are provided (direct services vs. community outreach), and their connection to other community agencies (Gornick, Burt, & Pitman, 1985). Despite these differences, rape-crisis organizations have a similar philosophy that places victim advocacy as a primary focus (Mallicoat et al., 2007).

Earlier in this chapter, you learned that the majority of the workforce within a rape-crisis center is female and that many of these women are survivors of sexual victimization. Survivors of these crimes may be drawn to work within this field for a variety of reasons. Many volunteers see working in a rape-crisis organization as a way of giving back to a community that assisted them with their own victimization experience or use it to continue to work through their own victim experience (Mallicoat et al., 2007). Rape-crisis workers also believe that it is their purpose to empower their clients by creating opportunities for the victims to be in control of their lives, which is something that was taken away during their assault (Ullman & Townsend, 2008).

Rape-crisis workers also help limit or prevent secondary victimization. As you learned in Chapter 2, secondary victimization occurs when victims of sexual assault have a negative experience with the interventions, and these experiences can cause further trauma to the victim as a result. How does this revictimization occur? The process of a police investigation can further traumatize victims; they are often required to provide the details of their attack multiple times. While the intent of this process is to document the assault in detail, victims can potentially feel that they are blamed for the assault. Other stages of the investigation also carry the risk for potential revictimization, such as the rape exam, which is an extensive process. The rape exam requires specific training of professionals (such as a sexual nurse examiner) in order to ensure that evidence is collected in the correct manner. Errors in this process can not only jeopardize the case but can also cause additional emotional trauma for the victim (Maier, 2008a). As a case moves forward in the criminal justice system, victims may experience additional acts of revictimization. They may receive little information about their case as it moves through the system. They may have to "re-live" the assault when testifying as a witness and, in cases where a plea bargain is offered, be denied the opportunity to confront their accuser in court (Kelleher & McGilloway, 2009). However, the presence of an advocate appears to positively impact these difficult events because victims indicate that they encounter less distress as a result of their interactions with the police and medical professionals. Victims also receive an enhanced standard of care by hospital staff when a crisis counselor is present (Campbell, 2006).

While rape-crisis counselors and advocates provide valuable services for victims and the community, these workers can face a number of barriers in their attempts to deliver services. In Chapter 3, you learned about rape myths and how this can lead to misperceptions in society about the reality of these crimes. Research by Ullman and Townsend (2007) acknowledges that this can make it difficult to provide support for the victim. In addition, budget constrictions can limit the ability of a rape-crisis organization to provide services for the victims. Finally, many victims do not know where to turn for help. It is important that rape-crisis organizations not only conduct outreach to let victims know where they can turn for help but also engage in public education to help dismantle these misperceptions about rape and sexual assault (Kelleher & McGilloway, 2009).

Rape and sexual assault exists in every community. However, the availability of services can vary from organization to organization. Those agencies with the largest budgets (and largest staff and number of volunteers) are able to provide the most resources. Most of these agencies are located in larger urban areas. For victims in rural communities, accessible resources may be limited, and workers in these communities face their own set of unique challenges. Consider that in rural communities, anonymity about people and their lives is rare. Everyone knows everybody (and their business), which can limit privacy and jeopardize confidentiality in these cases. Victims may also be less likely to report these assaults, particularly when cases involve a family member or when victims experience backlash and blame for their victimization (Annan, 2011). Victim blaming practices are also heavily influenced by cultural factors, such as the acceptance of traditional gender roles or conservative religious values, in these rural communities (McGrath, Johnson, & Miller, 2012). Finally, there can be significant challenges in the delivery of services for these victims. Given that rural agencies may draw from a large geographical area, poverty and a lack of available transportation can significantly limit the delivery of support and resources to some communities (McGrath et al., 2012). Despite these challenges, rape-crisis workers in rural communities do see assets to their small stature as they can provide consistent care and attention to their clients as their cases move throughout the system. There is less of a risk that their cases will get handed off to other professionals or get lost within the system. In addition, the tight-knit community allows advocates to develop close relationships with related practitioners, which improves the continuum of care for victims (Annan, 2011).

In Chapter 3, you learned about how women of color have different experiences of sexual assault, which demonstrated in a variety of ways, including prevalence rates, reporting behaviors, disclosure practices, help-seeking behaviors, and responses by the justice system. First, race, ethnicity, and culture have a significant impact on reporting sexual assault. For example, victims in Hindu Indian cultures believe that to be sexually assaulted means that they are no longer "pure," which is a high status symbol within the community. Rather than bring shame to their family, the women have chosen to remain silent and not report these victimizations. Second, the limited availability of resources designed for victims from different races, ethnicities, and cultures can reduce the likelihood that victims will seek out assistance. In addition, many advocates expressed that many victims seemed to accept their victimization, as if this is a normal experience within their community and that it is not necessary to make a big deal about it. Finally, racism can lead to differential treatment of victims of color by the criminal justice system, particularly for cases of interracial victimization. In the words of one advocate,

> If a woman of color is assaulted by a White man there is almost a guarantee of hopelessness—nothing is going to happen. If a White woman is assaulted by a person of color, the whole thing changes. It is going to be on the front page of the news. (Maier, 2008b, p. 311)

Like other occupations within the criminal justice field, rape-crisis workers are faced with issues such as job satisfaction and burnout. While many advocates in this field express high levels of job satisfaction in their work with victims (despite comparatively low salaries), the emotionally taxing nature of the work can lead to high levels of burnout. Earlier in this chapter, you learned about issues of burnout and secondary trauma for domestic violence advocates. Not surprising, rape-crisis counselors deal with many of the same issues in the context of their work environments. Indeed, the physical and emotional toll for advocates can be significantly taxing:

> Having to dedicate energies on such issues has, at times, created a critical event for me, placing me under such stress that I have suffered insomnia and sleep deprivation, urinary nocturnal frequency, migraines, lack of time to attend to exercise, etc.

> The awareness that there are perpetrators who live, work, and "play" among us who are capable of inflicting such atrocities for pleasure, for power and control, and/or for profit if they are engaged in pedophilic/adult pornographic crime scene exploitation created a deep change in men, physically, psychologically, and cognitively. (Coles, Astbury, Dartnall, & Limherwala, 2014, pp. 101–102)

Research notes that age can be a significant predictor in secondary traumatic stress (STS) because younger advocates experience higher levels of STS. Organizational structure can also impact STS. Advocates who have high caseloads or who work in organizations with limited structure and supervision are at a greater risk for secondary trauma stress (Dworkin, Sorell, & Allen, 2016). As a result, it is important that workers balance the demands of work with healthy physical and emotional outlets outside of the workplace (Mallicoat et al., 2007).

Conclusion

Despite the gains of women in traditionally male-dominated criminal justice occupations, they continue to confront a glass ceiling in terms of equal representation, compensation, and opportunity within these fields. In cases such as the legal field, women in these fields become a symbol for all things gender. In other examples such as domestic violence and rape-crisis advocacy work, the organization itself becomes gendered in response to its feminist foundations, and many women are drawn to work within these environments as a result. While equal employment opportunity legislation has opened the doors for access for women in these traditionally male-dominated fields, women still face an uphill battle because they have been denied opportunity and promotion throughout history. In occupations such as attorneys and judges, the proportion of women in these fields has significantly increased in recent decades. While women are represented at both upper and lower levels of the judiciary, their presence may still be as token females. In the case of victims' services agencies, the majority of these organizations are female-centric, creating a unique environment. However, many advocates in these fields suffer from emotional burdens and challenges to gender normative values that can impact their ability to deliver services to victims. Despite these struggles, women remain an important presence in these fields with significant contributions that need to be encouraged and acknowledged, particularly for future generations of women in these fields.

 ## SUMMARY

- Women in the legal field struggle with balancing work demands with family life. These struggles can affect the advancement of women in their field.

- While the number of women in the judiciary has increased, the majority of these positions are at the lower levels.

- Many rape-crisis and intimate partner violence organizations are predominantly staffed by women.

- Many women who serve as victims' advocates have their own personal experience with victimization.

- Victim advocates face issues of burnout and secondary trauma that can affect not only their levels of job satisfaction but also their abilities to offer care to victims and survivors of these crimes.

- Advocates working with victims of color need to consider the cultural issues in these communities when providing services and outreach.

- Rural communities face unique considerations in providing services and support for victims of crime.

KEY TERMS

Burnout 219	Secondary trauma stress 219	Work-family balance 213
Glass ceiling 213	Victim advocates 219	

/// DISCUSSION QUESTIONS

1. Based on the research, how do women do gender within the traditional male-dominated legal occupations?

2. What challenges do women who work in law-related occupations face that their male counterparts do not?

3. What suggestions can be made to improve the status of women within law-related occupations?

4. How can organizations help support women in these occupations to improve job satisfaction and limit burnout?

5. How do the challenges for specialized populations (race/ethnicity, culture, and rural environments) impact the delivery of services for victims?

/// WEB RESOURCES

International Association of Women Judges: http://www.iawj.org

National Association of Women Judges: http://www.nawj.org

National Association of Women Lawyers: http://www.nawl.org

 Visit **www.sagepub.com/mallicoat3e** to access additional study tools, including eFlashcards, web quizzes, web resources, video resources, and SAGE journal articles.

Glossary

Acquaintance rape: the victim knows the perpetrator; it usually accounts for the majority of rape and sexual assault cases.

Adler, Freda: her works were inspired by the emancipation of women that resulted from the effects of the second wave of feminism. Adler suggested that women's rates of violent crime would increase.

Age-of-consent campaign: designed to protect young women from men who preyed on the innocence of girls by raising the age of sexual consent to 16 or 18 in all states by 1920.

Altruistic: one explanation for infanticide where the mother believes that it is in the best interest of her child to be dead and that the mother is doing a good thing by killing her child.

Attachment: the bond that people have with the values of society as a result of their relationships with family, friends, and social institutions.

Baldwin, Lola: hired in 1908 by the Portland, Oregon, police department to provide supervisory assistance to a group of social workers. Her employment sparked debates as to whether she was a sworn officer or a social worker.

Barefield v. Leach (1974): held that states could not justify disparities in the programs for female inmates based on a smaller female incarcerated population and the costs of program delivery.

Battered women's movement: shelters and counseling programs established throughout the United States to help women in need as a result of the feminist movements in the 1960s and 1970s. It led to systemic changes in how the police and courts handled cases of domestic violence.

Belief: a general acceptance of society's rules.

Blankenship, Betty: one of the first women in the United States to serve as a patrol officer; she worked for the Indianapolis Police Department in 1964, and she helped set the stage for significant changes for the future of policewomen.

Bootstrapping: modern-day practice of institutionalizing girls for status offenses.

Burnout: the feeling of being under high levels of emotional and physical duress. This feeling is often categorized into three stages: (1) emotional

exhaustion due to stress, (2) depersonalization, and (3) reduced personal accomplishment.

Campus sexual assault: refers to acts of rape and sexual assault that occur during the collegiate experience. Can involve, but is not limited to, crimes that occur on a college campus

Canterino v. Wilson (1982): males and females must be treated equally unless there is a substantial reason that requires a distinction be made.

Chivalry: instances in which women receive preferential treatment by the justice system.

Civil Rights Bill of 1964: focused on eliminating racial discrimination; however, the word *sex* was added to the bill, prohibiting the use of sex as a requirement for hiring.

Coffal, Liz: one of the first women in the United States to serve as a patrol officer for the Indianapolis Police Department in 1964; she helped set the stage for significant changes for the future of policewomen.

Commitment: the investment that an individual has to the normative values of society.

Community policing: a policing strategy that is based on the idea that the community is extremely important in achieving shared goals; it emphasizes community support from its members, which can help reduce crime and fear.

Cooper v. Morin (1980): held that the equal protection clause prevents prison administrators from justifying the disparate treatment of women on the grounds that providing such services for women is inconvenient.

Core rights of victims: vary by jurisdiction; however, the following core rights have been found in many state constitutions: right to attend, right to compensation, right to be heard, right to be informed, right to protection, right to restitution, right to return of property, right to a speedy trial, and right to enforcement.

Custodial institutions: similar to male institutions, women are warehoused and little programming or treatment is offered to the inmates.

Cyberstalking: incidents of stalking that use electronic forms of technology such as e-mail, text, GPS, and the Internet.

Cycle of victimization and offending: explains how young girls often run away from home in an attempt to escape from an abusive situation, usually ending up as offenders themselves.

Cycle of violence: conceptualized by Lenore Walker in 1979 to help explain how perpetrators of intimate partner abuse maintain control over their victims over time. The cycle is made up of three distinct time frames: tension building, the abusive incident, and the honeymoon period.

Dark figure of crime: crimes that are not reported to the police and therefore not represented in official crime statistics, such as the Uniform Crime Reports and the National Incident-Based Reporting System.

Dating violence: intimate partner abuse in relationships where people are unmarried and may or may not be living together; violence that occurs between two people who are unmarried; teenagers are seen as the most at-risk population.

Debt bondage: a form of forced labor trafficking that requires victims to pay off debt through labor.

Differential association theory: focuses on the influence that one's social relationships may have in encouraging delinquent behavior. This theory also incorporated various characteristics of the social learning theory, suggesting that criminality is a learned behavior.

Discretionary arrest: police officers have the option to arrest or not arrest the offender based on their free choice within the context of their professional judgment.

Drug-facilitated rape: an unwanted sexual act that occurs after a victim voluntarily or involuntarily consumes drugs or alcohol.

Economic abuse: refers to acts of intimate partner abuse that involve control over personal finances (such as denial of money, prohibitions on work).

Emotional abuse: refers to acts of intimate partner abuse that involve tools of emotional or psychological control rather than physical.

Evil woman hypothesis: women are punished not only for violating the law but also for breaking the socialized norms of gender-role expectations.

Extralegal factors: can include the type of attorney (private or public defender), which can significantly affect the likelihood of pretrial release for women.

Fear of victimization: a gendered experience where women experience higher rates of fear of crime compared to males. This idea is based on the distorted portrayal of the criminal justice system by the media.

Femicide: the killing of women based on gender discrimination. The murders often involve sexual torture and body mutilation.

Feminism: a series of social and political movements (also referred to as the *three waves of feminism*) that advocated for women's rights and gender equality.

Feminist criminology: developed as a reaction against traditional criminology, which failed to address women and girls in research. It reflects several of the themes of gender roles and socialization that resulted from the second wave of feminism.

Feminist pathways perspective: provides some of the best understanding of how women find themselves stuck in a cycle that begins with victimization and leads to offending.

Feminist research methods: process of gathering research that involves placing gender at the center of the conversation, giving women a voice, and changing the relationship between the researcher and the subject to one of care and concern versus objectivity.

Filicide: the homicide of children older than one year of age by their parent.

Formal processing: a petition is filed requesting a court hearing, which can initiate the designation of being labeled as a delinquent.

Fry, Elizabeth: a key figure in the crusade to improve the conditions of incarcerated women in the United Kingdom and an inspiration for the American women's prison reform movement.

Gender gap: refers to the differences in male and female offending for different types of offenses.

Gender-responsive programming: creates parity in offender programming and is designed to meet the unique needs of women. Generally involves consideration of six key principles: gender, environment, relationships, services and supervision, socioeconomic status, and community.

Gender-specific programming: must be able to address the wide variety of needs of the delinquent girl. Efforts by Congress have been made to allocate the resources necessary for analyzing, planning, and implementing these services.

Gendered assignments: job duties that were usually assigned to officers based on their gender; female officers were more inclined to receive social service positions rather than patrol and crime-fighting positions.

Gendered justice: also referred to as *injustice*; it is the discrimination of individuals based on their gender. This idea is often seen in the criminal justice system where females' needs and unique experiences go unmet because of the fact that the theories of offending have come from the male perspective.

Genital mutilation: also known as female circumcision and involves the vandalism or removal of female genitalia for the purposes of protecting girls' virginity and eliminating the potential for sexual pleasure.

Glass ceiling: a term used to describe the invisible barriers that limit the ability of women and minorities from achieving high rank opportunities in the workplace.

Glover v. Johnson (1979): held that the state must provide the same opportunities for education, rehabilitation, and vocational training for female offenders as provided for male offenders.

Good ol' boy network: a social network of people who provide access and grant favors to each other. It is usually made up of elite White males, and they tend to exclude other members of their community.

Griffin v. Michigan Department of Corrections (1982): held that inmates do not possess any rights to be protected against being viewed in stages of undress or naked by a correctional officer, regardless of gender.

Grummett v. Rushen (1985): the pat-down search of a male inmate (including the groin area) does not violate one's Fourth Amendment protection against unreasonable search and seizure.

Hagan, John: developed the power control theory; his research focused on the roles within the family unit, especially that of patriarchy.

Harassment: acts that are indicative of stalking behaviors but do not ignite feelings of fear in the victim.

Hirschi, Travis: proposed the social bonds theory; his research focused primarily on delinquency and the reasons why people may not become involved in criminal activity.

Honor-based violence: murders that are executed by a male family member and are a response to a belief that the woman has offended a family's honor and has brought shame to the family.

Human trafficking: the exploitation and forced labor of individuals for the purposes of prostitution, domestic servitude, and other forms of involuntary servitude in agricultural and factory industries.

Incapacitated rape: an unwanted sexual act that occurs after a victim voluntarily consumes drugs or alcohol.

Incarcerated mothers: have a significant effect on children. The geographical location of the prison and length of sentencing determine whether mothers can have ties with their children; in many cases, the children are either cared for by family members or are placed in foster care.

Infanticide: an act in which a parent kills his or her child within the first year.

Intimate partner abuse: abuse that occurs between individuals who currently have, or have previously had, an intimate relationship.

Involvement: one's level of participation in conventional activities (studying, playing sports, or participating in extracurricular activities).

Jail the offender and protect the victim models: prioritization is given to the prosecution of offenders over the needs of the victims; however, these models are widely criticized due to their limitations and inability to deter individuals from participating in the offenses.

Jordan v. Gardner (1992): the pat-down policy designed to control the introduction of contraband into the facility could be viewed as unconstitutional if conducted by male staff members against female inmates.

Just world hypothesis: society has a need to believe that people deserve whatever comes to them; this paradigm is linked to patterns of victim blaming.

Juvenile delinquency: the repeated committing of crimes by young children and adolescents.

Juvenile Justice and Delinquency Prevention (JJDP) Act of 1974: provides funding for state and local governments to help decrease the number of juvenile delinquents and to help provide community and rehabilitative programs to offenders.

Labor trafficking: the recruitment, harboring, transportation, provision, or obtaining of a person for labor or services, through the use of force, fraud, or coercion for the purpose of subjection to involuntary servitude, peonage, debt bondage, or slavery.

Laub, John: codeveloped the life course theory; his research has primarily focused on the following criminological and sociological topics: deviance, the life course, and juvenile delinquency and justice.

Legal factors: have an impact on the decision-making process for both males and females in different ways. They vary from jurisdiction to jurisdiction and they can range from criminal history to offense severity.

Level of Service Inventory-Revised (LSI-R): a risk assessment tool used for correctional populations.

Life course theory: examines how adverse life events impact criminality over time and can provide insight on both female and male offending patterns.

Lifestyle theory: developed to explore the risks of victimization from personal crimes and seeks to relate the patterns of one's everyday activities to the potential for victimization.

Lombroso, Cesare, and William Ferrero: the first criminologists to investigate the nature of the female offender; they worked together to publish *The Female Offender* in 1985.

Male inmate preference: women inmates are perceived as more demanding, defiant, and harder to work with, so male and female officers would much rather work with male inmates.

Mandatory arrest: surfaced during the 1980s and 1990s with the intention to stop domestic violence by deterring offenders. It clarified the roles of police officers when dealing with domestic violence calls and removed the responsibility of arrest from the victim.

Masculine culture: also known as the *male-dominated police culture*; while attempting to gain acceptance into this culture, females are often disrespected and harassed by their male counterparts.

Masked criminality of women: Otto Pollak's theory that suggested that women gain power by deceiving men through sexual playacting, faked sexual responses, and menstruation.

Mendelsohn, Benjamin: distinguished categories of victims based on the responsibility of the victim and the degree to which the victim had the power to make decisions that could alter his or her likelihood of victimization.

Minneapolis Domestic Violence Experiment: helped show the decrease in recidivism rates when an actual arrest was made in misdemeanor domestic violence incidents, in comparison to when a police officer just counseled the aggressor.

National Crime Victimization Survey (NCVS): gathers additional data about crimes to help fill in the gap between reported and unreported crime (also known as the dark figure of crime).

National Incident-Based Reporting System (NIBRS): An incident-based system of crimes reported to the police. The system is administered by the Federal Bureau of Investigation as part of the annual Uniform Crime Reports.

National Intimate Partner and Sexual Violence Survey (NISVS): An annual survey by the Centers for Disease Control and Prevention designed to measure the prevalence of intimate partner violence, sexual violence, and stalking.

National Violence Against Women Survey (NVAWS): A telephone survey of 8,000 men and 8,000 women in the United States (English and Spanish speaking) that was conducted by the Centers for Policy Research to measure the prevalence of violence against women.

Neonaticide: an act of homicide of an infant during the first 24 hours after the birth of the child.

Net widening: refers to the practice whereby programs such as diversion were developed to inhibit the introduction of youth into the juvenile justice system. However, these programs expanded the reach of the juvenile court and increased the number of youth under the general reach of the system, both informally and formally.

No-drop policies: developed in response to a victim's lack of participation in the prosecution of her batterer; these policies have led to the disempowering of victims.

Owens, Marie: a contender for the title of first female police officer; she worked as a Chicago factory inspector, transferred to the police department in 1891, and allegedly served on the force for 32 years.

Parens patriae: originated in the English Chancery Courts; this practice gives the state custody of children in cases where the child has no parents or the parents are deemed unfit care providers.

Parole: (1) a form of post-incarceration supervision of offenders in the community; (2) a method of releasing offenders from prison prior to the conclusion of their sentence.

Pollak, Otto: wrote *The Criminality of Women* in 1961 to further explain his belief that crime data sources failed to reflect the true extent of female crime.

Post-traumatic stress disorder (PTSD): may develop after a person experiences a traumatic life event. PTSD can include flashbacks, avoidance of emotional contexts, and recurrent nightmares and may inhibit normal daily functioning abilities.

Power control theory: looks at the effects of patriarchy within the family unit as a tool of socialization for gender roles.

Probation: a form of community-based supervision that imposes restrictions and regulations on offenders but allows for them to serve their sentence in the community compared to jail or prison.

Pseudo-families: the relationship among individuals who are not related; these relationships are common in the prison system and are often created as a means to provide emotional support to one another during their imprisonment.

Pulling a train: also known as *sexed in*; example of the gang initiation process that requires sexual assault by multiple male members.

Rape: sexual intercourse under force, threat of force, or without the legal consent of the individual. In many jurisdictions, the term *rape* specifically applies in cases of penile-vaginal forced intercourse.

Rape myth acceptance: false beliefs that are seen as justifiable causes for sexual aggression against women.

Reauthorization of the Juvenile Justice and Delinquency Prevention (JJDP) Act (1992): acknowledged the need to provide gender-specific services to address the unique needs of female offenders.

Reentry: the transition from an incarcerated setting to the community; it usually involves meetings with parole officers who provide referrals to receive treatment; unsuccessful reentry often leads to recidivism.

Reformatory: a new concept that saw incarceration as an institution designed with the intent to rehabilitate women from their immoral ways.

Resiliency: also known as *protective factors*; these can enable female victims and female offenders to succeed.

Restraining order: available in every jurisdiction; it is designed to provide the victim with the opportunity to separate from the batterer and prohibit the batterer from contacting the victim.

Risk factors for female delinquency: include a poor family relationship, a history of abuse, poor school performance, negative peer relationships, and issues with substance abuse.

Routine activities theory: created to discuss the risk of victimization in property crimes. It suggests that the likelihood of a criminal act or the likelihood of victimization occurs when an offender, a potential victim, and the absence of a guardian that would deter said offender from making contact with the victim are combined.

Same-sex intimate partner abuse: intimate partner abuse that occurs in a same-sex relationship. Research is significantly limited on this issue, and many victims fear reporting these acts or seeking help because of concerns of being "outed" or concerns about homophobia.

Same-sex sexual assault: often refers to male-on-male assault, because of the limited research on woman-on-woman sexual violence.

Sampson, Robert: codeveloped the *life course theory*; his research has focused on a variety of topics within the fields of criminology and sociology.

Secondary trauma stress (STS): high levels of stress that result from the need and/or desire to help a victim; victim advocates are often affected by this type of stress.

Secondary victimization: the idea that victims become more traumatized after the primary victimization. It can stem from victim blaming or from the process of collecting evidence (physical or testimonial).

Sentencing guidelines: created in conjunction with the Sentencing Reform Act of 1984; the only factors to be considered in imposing a sentence were offense committed, the presence of aggravating or mitigating circumstances, and the criminal history of the offender.

Sexual assault: often used as an umbrella term for all forms of unwanted sexual activity other than rape, sexual assault includes acts such as penetration other than vaginal-penile penetration, penetration by objects, sodomy, forced oral copulation, sexual touching, and other lewd acts.

Simon, Rita: hypothesized that women would make up a greater proportion of property crimes as a result of their "liberation" from traditional gender roles and restrictions.

Social bond theory: focused on four criteria, or bonds, which prevent people from acting on potential criminological impulses or desires. Travis Hirschi identified these bonds as attachment, commitment, involvement, and belief.

Spousal rape: involves emotional coercion or physical force against a spouse to achieve nonconsensual sexual intercourse; it can often lead to domestic violence.

Stalking: a course of conduct directed at a reasonable person that could cause them to feel fearful. It includes acts such as unwanted phone calls or messages, being followed or spied on, and making unannounced visits.

Status offenses: noncriminal behaviors such as running away, immorality, truancy, and indecent conduct that allowed youth to come under the jurisdiction of the juvenile court.

Statutory rape: sexual activity that is unlawful because it is prohibited by stature or code; it generally involves someone who is not of legal age to give consent.

Stranger rape: the perpetrator is unknown to the victim and is usually associated with a lack of safety, such as walking home at night or not locking the doors.

Street prostitution: an illegal form of prostitution that takes place in public places.

Sutherland, Edwin: proposed the differential association theory; his research focused on one's social relationships and their influence on delinquent behavior.

Symbolic assailant: a perpetrator, often of minority ethnicity, who hides in dark shadows awaiting the abduction, rape, or murder of unknown innocents. He or she attacks at random, is unprovoked, and is difficult to apprehend.

Trafficking Victims Protection Act of 2000: designed to punish traffickers, protect victims, and facilitate prevention efforts in the community to fight against human trafficking.

T-visa: visas issued by the United States for victims; the T-visa is issued for human trafficking victims.

Uniform Crime Reports (UCR): An annual collection of reported crime data from police departments. It is compiled by the Federal Bureau of Investigation.

Victim advocates: trained professionals who support victims of a crime. Victim advocates can provide emotional support, knowledge about the legal process and the rights of crime victims, and provide information and resources for services and assistance.

Victim blaming: shifting the blame of rape from the offender to the victim; by doing so, the confrontation of the realities of victimization is avoided.

Violence Against Women Act (VAWA): passed in 1994; this federal law provides funding for training and research on intimate partner abuse as well as sets forth policies for restitution and civil redress. VAWA established the Office on Violence Against Women within the Department of Justice; it provided funding for battered women's shelters and outreach education, funding for domestic violence training for police and court personnel, and the opportunity for victims to sue for civil damages as a result of violent acts perpetuated against them.

von Hentig, Hans: his theory of victimization highlights 13 categories of victims and focuses on how personal factors such as biological, social, and psychological characteristics influence risk factors for victimization.

Walking the line: gang initiation process for girls in which they are subjected to assault by their fellow gang members.

Welfare Reform Act of 1996: Section 115 of this act bans women with a felony drug conviction from collecting welfare benefits and food stamps.

Wells, Alice Stebbins: the first female police officer hired in the United States by the Los Angeles Police Department in 1920; she advocated for the protection of children and women, especially when it came to sexual education.

Work-family balance: a term used to describe the prioritization of family life (marriage, children, and lifestyle) within the demands of the workplace.

Wraparound services: holistic and culturally sensitive plans for each woman that draw on a coordinated range of services within her community, such as public and mental health systems, addiction recovery, welfare, emergency shelter organizations, and educational and vocational services.

References

Abad-Santos, A. (2013, January 3). Everything you need to know about Steubenville High School football "rape crew." *The Wire*. Retrieved from http://www.thewire.com/national/2013/01/steubenville-high-football-rape-crew/60554/

Abe-Kim, J., Takeuchi, D. T., Hong, S., Zane, N., Sue, S., Spencer, M. S., . . . Alegría, M. (2007). Use of mental health-related services among immigrant and U.S.-born Asian Americans: Results from the National Latino and Asian American Study. *American Journal of Public Health, 97*(1), 91.

Abdul, M., Joarder, M., & Miller, P. W. (2014). The experiences of migrants trafficked from Bangladesh. *The ANNALS of the American Academy of Political and Social Science, 653*(1), 141–161.

Acoca, L., & Dedel, K. (1997). *Identifying the needs of young women in the juvenile justice system*. San Francisco, CA: National Council on Crime and Delinquency.

Acoca, L., & Dedel, K. (1998a). *Identifying the needs of young women in the juvenile justice system*. San Francisco, CA: National Council on Crime and Delinquency.

Acoca, L., & Dedel, K. (1998b). *No place to hide: Understanding and meeting the needs of girls in the California juvenile justice system*. San Francisco, CA: National Council on Crime and Delinquency.

Adler, F. (1975). *Sisters in crime: The rise of the new female criminal*. New York: McGraw-Hill.

After court order, Madonna faces accused in stalker case. (1996, January 4.). *New York Times*. Retrieved from http://www.nytimes.com/1996/01/04/us/after-court-order-madonna-faces-accused-in-stalker-case.html

Agnew, R. (1992). Foundation for a general strain theory of crime and delinquency. *Criminology, 30*, 47–88.

Agosin, M. (2006). *Secrets in the sand: The young women of Juarez*. New York: White Pine Press.

Air Force Times. (2012, December 2). Sex assault victims seeking help sooner. Retrieved from http://www.airforcetimes.com/article/20121202/NEWS/212020308/

Akintunde, D. O. (2010). Female genital mutilation: A socio-cultural gang up against womenhood. *Feminist Theology, 18*(2), 192–205.

Alabama Coalition Against Domestic Violence (ACADV). (n.d.). *Dating violence*. Retrieved from http://www.acadv.org/dating.html

Albonetti, C. A. (1986). Criminality, prosecutorial screening, and uncertainty: Toward a theory of discretionary decision making in felony case processing. *Criminology, 24*(4), 623–645.

Alderden, M., & Long, L. (2016). Sexual assault victim participation in police investigations and prosecution. *Violence and Victims, 31*(5), 819–836.

Alexy, E. M., Burgess, A. W., Baker, T., & Smoyak, S. A. (2005). Perceptions of cyberstalking among college students. *Brief Treatment and Crisis Intervention, 5*(3), 279–289.

Alpert, E. (2013, February 18). Murder charges filed after woman burned alive in Papua New Guinea. *Los Angeles Times*. Retrieved from http://articles.latimes.com/2013/feb/18/world/la-fg-wn-woman-burned-alive-papua-new-guinea-20130218

Althaus, D. (2010). Ciudad Juarez women still being tortured by killers. *Houston Chronicle*. Retrieved from http://www.chron.com/news/nation-world/article/Ciudad-Juarez-women-still-being-tortured-by-1703010.php

Alvarez, L. (2011, July 5). Casey Anthony not guilty in slaying of daughter. *New York Times*. Retrieved from http://www.nytimes.com/2011/07/06/us/06casey.html?pagewanted=all&_r=0

American Bar Association (ABA). (2010). *Law school staff by gender and ethnicity*. Retrieved from http://www.americanbar.org/content/dam/aba/migrated/legaled/statistics/charts/facultyinformationbygender.authcheckdam.pdf

American Bar Association (ABA). (2011). A current glance at women in the law, 2011. Retrieved from http://www.americanbar.org/content/dam/aba/marketing/women/current_glance_statistics_2011.authcheckdam.pdf

American Bar Association (ABA). (2017). A current glance at women in the law, 2011. Retrieved from http://www.americanbar.org/content/dam/aba/marketing/women/current_glance_statistics_january2017.authcheckdam.pdf

American Bar Association (ABA). (2012). Goal III Report: An annual report on women's advancement into leadership positions in the American Bar Association. Retrieved from http://www.americanbar.org/content/dam/aba/administrative/women/2012_goa13_women.authcheckdam.pdf

American Bar Association Commission on Domestic Violence. (2008). *Domestic violence Civil Protection Orders (CPOs) by state*. Retrieved from http://www.americanbar.org/content/dam/aba/migrated/domviol/pdfs/CPO_Protections_for_LGBT_Victims_7_08.authcheckdam.pdf

American Correctional Association. (2007). *Directory of adult and juvenile correctional departments, institutions and agencies and probation and parole authorities*. Alexandria, VA: Author.

American Society of Criminology (ASC). (n.d.). History of the American Society of Criminology. Retrieved from http://www.asc41.com

Americans for the Arts. (2000). Arts facts: Arts programs for at-risk youth. Retrieved from http://www.americansforthearts.org/sites/default/files/pdf/get_involved/advocacy/research/2008/youth_at_risk08.pdf

Amnesty International. (1999). *Document—Pakistan: Violence against women in the name of honour*. Retrieved from http://amnesty.org/en/library/asset/ASA33/017/1999/en/53f9cc64-e0f2-11dd-be39-2d4003be4450/asa330171999en.html

Amy Elizabeth Fisher. (2014). The Biography.com website. Retrieved from http://www.biography.com/people/amy-fisher-235415.

Anderson, T. L. (2006). Issues facing women prisoners in the early twenty-first century. In C. Renzetti, L. Goodstein, & S. L. Miller (Eds.), *Rethinking gender, crime and justice* (pp. 200–212). Los Angeles: Roxbury.

Annan, S. L. (2011). "It's not just a job. This is where we live. This is our backyard": The experiences of expert legal and advocate providers with sexually assaulted women in rural areas. *Journal of the American Psychiatric Nurses Association, 17*(2), 139–147.

Anuforo, P. O., Oyedele, L., & Pacquiao, D. F. (2004). Comparative study of meanings, beliefs and practices of female circumcision among three Nigerian tribes in the United States and Nigeria. *Journal of Transcultural Nursing, 15*(2), 103–113.

Appier, J. (1998). *Policing women: The sexual politics of law enforcement and the LAPD*. Philadelphia: Temple University Press.

Arin, C. (2001). Femicide in the name of honor in Turkey. *Violence Against Women, 7*(7), 821–825.

Associated Press. (2012, July 21). Air Force instructor sentenced to 20 years in prison after raping female recruit and sexually assaulting several other women. Retrieved from http://www.dailymail.co.uk/news/article-2177097/Lackland-Air-Force-instructor-Luis-Walker-sentenced-20-years-prison-guilty-rape-sexual-assault.html

Atchison, A. J., & Heide, K. M. (2011). Charles Manson and the family: The application of sociological theories to multiple murder. *International Journal of Offender Therapy and Comparative Criminology 55*(5), 771–798.

Australian Bureau of Statistics (ABS). (2016). Recorded crime—Offenders. Retrieved from http://www.abs.gov.au/ausstats/abs@.nsf/Lookup/by%20Subject/4519.0~2012-13~Main%20Features~Offenders,%20Australia~4

Babin, E. A., Palazzolo, K. E., & Rivera, K. D. (2012). Communication skills, social support and burnout among advocates in a domestic violence agency. *Journal of Applied Communication Research, 40*(2), 147–166.

Bachman, R., Zaykowski, H., Lanier, C., Poteyeva, M., & Kallmyer, R. (2010). Estimating the magnitude of rape and sexual assault against American Indian and Alaska Native (AIAN) women. *Australian & New Zealand Journal of Criminology, 43*(2), 199–222.

Bacik, I., & Drew, E. (2006). Struggling with juggling: Gender and work/life balance in the legal professions. *Women's Studies International Forum, 29*, 136–146.

Baillargeon, J., Binswanger, I. A., Penn, J. V., Williams, B. A., & Murray, O. J. (2009). Psychiatric disorders and repeat incarcerations: The revolving prison door. *American Journal of Psychiatry, 166*, 103–109.

Baker, C. K., Holditch Niolon, P., & Oliphant, H. (2009). A descriptive analysis of transitional housing programs for survivors of intimate partner violence in the United States. *Violence Against Women, 15*(4), 460–481.

Ball, J. D., & Bostaph, L. G. (2009). He versus she: A gender-specific analysis of legal and extralegal effects on pretrial release for felony defendants. *Women and Criminal Justice, 19*(2), 95–119.

Balsam, K. F., Molina, Y., Blayney, J. A., Dillworth, T., Zimmerman, L., & Kaysen, D. (2015). Racial/ethnic differences in identity and mental health outcomes among young sexual minority women. *Cultural Diversity and Ethnic Minority Psychology, 21*(3), 380–390.

Banyard, V. L., Moynihan M. M., & Plante, E. G. (2007). Sexual violence prevention through bystander education: An experimental evaluation. *Journal of Community Psychology, 35*(4), 463–481.

Barata, P. C., & Schneider, F. (2004). Battered women add their voices to the debate about the merits of mandatory arrest. *Women's Studies Quarterly, 32*(3/4), 148–163.

Barefield v. Leach, Civ. Act. No. 10282 (D.N.M. 1974).

Barratt, C. L., Bergman, M. E., & Thompson, R. J. (2014). Women in federal enforcement: The role of gender role orientations and sexual orientation in mentoring. *Sex Roles, 71*(1–2), 21–32.

Barrick, K., Lattimore, P. K., Pitts, W. J., & Zhang, S. X. (2014). When farmworkers and advocates see trafficking but law enforcement does not: Challenges in identifying labor trafficking in North Carolina. *Crime, Law, and Social Change, 61*: 205–214.

Bates, K. A., Bader, C. D., & Mencken, F. C. (2003). Family structure, power-control theory and deviance: Extending power-control theory to include alternate family forms. *Western Criminological Review, 4*(3), 170–190.

Baum, K., Catalano, S., Rand, M., & Rose, K. (2009). Stalking victimization in the United States. U.S. Department of Justice, Bureau of Justice Statistics. Retrieved from http://ojp.usdoj.gov/content/pub/pdf/svus.pdf

BBC. (2013, May 7). Profile: Amanda Berry, Georgina De Jesus and Michelle Knight. Retrieved from http://www.bbc.co.uk/news/world-us-canada-22433057

Beck, A. J., Harrison, P. M., & Guerino, P. (2010). Sexual victimization in juvenile facilities reported by youth, 2008–2009. U.S. Department of Justice, Bureau of Justice Statistics. Retrieved from http://bjs.ojp.usdoj.gov/content/pub/pdf/svjfry09.pdf *NALS of*

Belanger, D. (2014). Labor migration and trafficking among Vietnamese migrants in Asia. *The ANNALS of the American Academy of Political and Social Science 653*(1), 87-106.

Belenko, S., & Houser, K. A. (2012). Gender differences in prison-based drug treatment participation. *International Journal of Offender Therapy and Comparative Criminology, 56*(5), 790–810.

Belknap, J. (2007). *The invisible woman: Gender, crime and justice.* Belmont, CA: Thomson-Wadsworth.

Belknap, J., Dunn, M., & Holsinger, K. (1997). *Moving toward juvenile justice and youth serving systems that address the distinct experience of the adolescent female* (Report to the Governor). Columbus, OH: Office of Criminal Justice Services.

Belknap, J., & Holsinger, K. (1998). An overview of delinquent girls: How theory and practice failed and the need for innovative change. In R. Zaplin (Ed.), *Female crime and delinquency: Critical perspectives and effective interventions* (pp. 31–64). Gaithersburg, MD: Aspen.

Belknap, J., & Holsinger, K. (2006). The gendered nature of risk factors for delinquency, *Feminist Criminology, 1*(1), 48–71.

Bennett, L., Riger, S., Schewe, P., Howard, A., & Wasco, S. (2004). Effectiveness of hotline, advocacy, counseling, and shelter services for victims of domestic violence: A statewide evaluation. *Journal of Interpersonal Violence, 19*(7), 815–829.

Bennett-Smith, M. (2013, February 7). Accused "witch" Kepari Leniata burned alive by mob in Papua New Guinea. *Huffington Post.* Retrieved from http://www.huffingtonpost.com/2013/02/07/kepari-leniata-young-mother-burned-alive-mob-sorcery-papua-new-guinea_n2638431.html

Bennice, J. A., & Resick, P. A. (2003). Marital rape history, research, and practice. *Trauma, Violence, & Abuse, 4*(3), 228–246.

Bent-Goodley, T. B. (2004). Perceptions of domestic violence: A dialogue with African American women. *Health and Social Work, 29*(4), 307–316.

Berg, A. (2011, September 4). Stop shackling pregnant prisoners. *The Daily Beast.* Retrieved from http://www.thedailybeast.com/articles/2011/09/04/stop-shackling-pregnant-prisoners-new-push-to-ban-controversial-practice.html

Berkman, M. B., & O'Connor, R. E. (1993). Do women legislators matter? Female legislators and state abortion policy. *American Politics Quarterly, 21*(1), 102–124.

Bernard, T. J. (1992). *The cycle of juvenile justice.* New York: Oxford University Press.

Bernhard, L. A. (2000). Physical and sexual violence experienced by lesbian and heterosexual women. *Violence Against Women, 6*(1), 68–79.

Beynon, C. M., McVeigh, C., McVeigh, J., Leavey, C., & Bellis, M. A. (2008). The involvement of drugs and alcohol in drug-facilitated sexual assault: A systematic review of the evidence. *Trauma, Violence, & Abuse, 9*(3), 178–188.

Black, M. C., Basile, K. C., Breiding, M. J., Smith, S. G., Walters, M. L., Merrick, M. T., . . . Stevens, M. R. (2011). *The National Intimate Partner and Sexual Violence Survey (NISVS): 2010 summary report.* Atlanta, GA: National Center for Injury Prevention and Control, Centers for Disease Control and Prevention. Retrieved from http://www.cdc.gov/ViolencePrevention/pdf/NISVS_Report2010-a.pdf

Blackburn, A. G., Pfeffer, R. D., & Harris, J. A. (2016). Serious about change: A gendered examination of the impact of offense type on parole success. *Women & Criminal Justice, 26*(5), 340–353.

Blackwell, B. S., Holleran, D., & Finn, M. A. (2008). The impact of the Pennsylvania sentencing guidelines on sex differences in sentencing. *Journal of Contemporary Criminal Justice, 24*(4), 399–418.

Blackwell, D. B. (2012, June 15). Through my eyes: Surviving sexual assault. Retrieved from http://www.usafa.af.mil/shared/media/document/AFD-120619-023.pdf

Block, C. R. (2003). How can practitioners help an abused woman lower her risk of death. *National Institute of Justice (NIJ) Journal, 250,* 4–7. Retrieved from http://www.ncjrs.gov/pdffiles1/jr000250c.pdf

Block, K. J. (1999). Bringing scouting to prison: Programs and challenges. *The Prison Journal, 79*(2), 269–283.

Block, K. J., & Potthast, M. J. (1998). Girl Scouts Beyond Bars: Facilitating parent-child contact in correctional settings. *Child Welfare, 77*(5), 561–579.

Bloom, B., Owen, B., & Covington, S. (2003). *Gender-responsive strategies: Research, practice, and guiding principles for women offenders.* Washington, DC: National Institute of Corrections. U.S. Department of Justice. Retrieved from http://nicic.gov/pubs/2003/018017.pdf

Bloom, B., Owen, B., & Covington, S. (2004). Women offenders and the gendered effects of public policy. *Review of Policy Research, 21*(1), 31–48.

Bloom, B., Owen, B., Deschenes, E. P., & Rosenbaum, J. (2002a). Improving juvenile justice for females: A statewide assessment in California. *Crime and Delinquency, 48*(4), 526–552.

Bloom, B., Owen, B., Deschenes, E. P., & Rosenbaum, J. (2002b). Moving toward justice for female offenders in the new millennium: Modeling gender-specific policies and programs. *Journal of Contemporary Criminal Justice, 18*(1), 37–56.

Blumberg, J. (2007, October 24). A brief history of the Salem witch trials. *The Smithsonian.* Retrieved from http://www.smithsonianmag.com/history/a-brief-history-of-the-salem-witch-trials-175162489/

Boivin, R., & Leclerc, C. (2016). Domestic violence reported to the police: Correlates of victims' reporting behavior and support to legal proceedings. *Violence and Victims, 31*(3), 402–415.

Bond, C., & Jeffries, S. (2009). Does indigeneity matter? Sentencing indigenous offenders in South Australia's higher courts. *Australian & New Zealand Journal of Criminology, 42,* 47–71.

Bond, C. E. W., & Jeffries, S. (2012). Harsher sentences? Indigeneity and prison sentence length in Western Australia's higher courts. *Journal of Sociology, 48*(3), 266–286.

Boone, R. (2017, March 2). School collected evidence before alerting authorities in locker-room sex assault of disabled black teen. *Chicago Tribune.* Retrieved from http://www.chicagotribune.com/news/nationworld/ct-coat-hanger-assault-disabled-black-teen-20170302-story.html

Bornstein, D. R., Fawcett, J., Sullivan, M., Senturia, K. D., & Shiu-Thornton, S. (2006). Understanding the experiences of lesbian, bisexual and trans survivors of domestic violence. *Journal of Homosexuality, 51*(1), 159–181.

Bourduin, C. M., & Ronis, S. T. (2012). Research note: Individual, family, peer and academic characteristics of female serious juvenile offenders. *Youth Violence and Juvenile Justice, 10*(4), 386–400.

Bowles, M. A., DeHart, D., & Webb, J. R. (2012). Family influences on female offenders' substance use: The role of adverse childhood events among incarcerated women. *Journal of Family Violence, 27*, 681–686.

Boyd, C. (2001). The implications and effects of theories of intergenerational transmission of violence for boys who live with domestic violence. *Australian Domestic & Family Violence Clearinghouse Newsletter, 6*, 6–8.

Boykins, A. D., Alvanzo, A. A., Carson, S., Forte, J., Leisey, M., & Plichta, S. B. (2010). Minority women victims of recent sexual violence: Disparities in incident history. *Journal of Women's Health, 19*(3), 453–461.

Boyle, E. H., McMorris, B. J., & Gomez, M. (2002). Local conformity to international norms: The case of female genital cutting. *International Sociology, 17*(1), 5–33.

Bozelko, C. (2017, January 11). Give working prisoners dignity—and decent wages. *National Review*. Retrieved from www.nationalreview.com/article/443747/prison-labor-laws-wages-make-it-close-slavery

Branum, D. (2013, January 8). USAFA reports show increased trust in system, better reporting. *Air Force Print News Today*. Retrieved from http://www.usafa.af.mil/news/story_print.asp?id=123331120

Brennan, P. K. (2006). Sentencing female misdemeanants: An examination of the direct and indirect effects of race/ethnicity. *Justice Quarterly, 23*(1), 60–95.

Brennan, T., Breitenbach, M., Dieterich, W., Salisbury, E. J., & van Voorhis, P. (2012). Women's pathways to serious and habitual crime: A person-centered analysis incorporating gender responsive factors. *Criminal Justice and Behavior, 39*(11), 1481–1508.

Brents, B. G., & Hausbeck, K. (2005). Violence and legalized brothel prostitution in Nevada: Examining safety, risk and prostitution policy. *Journal of Interpersonal Violence, 20*(3), 270–295.

Bright, C. L., Ward, S. K., & Negi, N. J. (2011). "The chain has to be broken": A qualitative investigation of the experiences of young women following juvenile court involvement. *Feminist Criminology, 6*(1), 32–53.

Britton, D. M. (2003). *At work in the iron cage: The prison as a gendered organization*. New York: New York University Press.

Broidy, L., & Agnew, R. (1997). Gender and crime: A general strain theory perspective. *Journal of Research in Crime and Delinquency, 34*, 275–306.

Brown v. Plata, 563 U.S. 493 (2011).

Brown, L. M., Chesney-Lind, M., & Stein, N. (2007). Patriarchy matters: Towards a gendered theory of teen violence and victimization. *Violence Against Women, 13*(12), 1249–1273.

Brown, M., & Bloom, B. (2009). Reentry and renegotiating motherhood: Maternal identity and success on parole. *Crime & Delinquency, 55*(2), 313–336.

Brown, M. J., & Groscup, J. (2009). Perceptions of same-sex domestic violence among crisis center staff. *Journal of Family Violence, 24*, 87–93.

Brumfield, B., & Simpson, D. (2013, October 9). Malala Yousafzai: Accolates, applause and a grim milestone. CNN. Retrieved from http://www.cnn.com/2013/10/09/world/asia/malal-shooting-anniversary/

Brunovskis, A., & Surtees, R. (2012). Coming home: Challenges in family reintegration for trafficked women. *Qualitative Social Work, 12*(4), 454–472.

Brunson, R., & Miller, J. (2006). Gender, race and urban policing: The experience of African American youths. *Gender & Society, 20*, 531–552.

Bryant-Davis, T., Chung, H., & Tillman, S. (2009). From the margins to the center: Ethnic minority women and the mental health effects of sexual assault. *Trauma, Violence, & Abuse, 10*(4), 330–357.

Bui, H. (2007). The limitations of current approaches to domestic violence. In R. Muraskin (Ed.), *It's a crime* (4th ed., pp. 261–276). Upper Saddle River, NJ: Pearson Prentice Hall.

Bui, H., & Morash, M. (2008). Immigration, masculinity and intimate partner violence from the standpoint of domestic violence service providers and Vietnamese-origin women. *Feminist Criminology, 3*(3), 191–215.

Bunch, J., Clay-Warner, J., & Lei, M. (2012, December 6). Demographic characteristics and victimization risk: Testing the mediating effects of routine activities. *Crime & Delinquency*. Advance online publication. Retrieved from http://cad.sagepub.com/content/early/2012/12/05/0011128712466932.full.pdf+html

Bundeskriminalamt (BKA). (2015). *Police crime statistics 2015*. Retrieved from https://www.bka.de/EN/CurrentInformation/PoliceCrimeStatistics/2015/pcs2015.html?nn=39580

Bureau of Justice Statistics (BLS). (2006). *Intimate partner violence*. Office of Justice Programs. Retrieved from http://bjs.ojp.usdoj.gov/content/pub/press/ipvpr.cfm

Bureau of Labor Statistics (BLS). (2009). Median weekly earnings of full-time wage and salary workers by detailed occupation and sex. Retrieved from www.bls.gov/cps/cpsaat39.pdf

Bureau of Labor Statistics (BLS). (2014). *Occupational outlook handbook, 2014–15 Edition*. Probation Officers and Correctional Treatment Specialists. Retrieved from http://www.bls.gov/ooh/community-and-social-service/probation-officers-and-correctional-treatment-specialists.htm

Burgess-Jackson, K. (Ed.). (1999). *A most detestable crime: New philosophical essays on rape*. New York: Oxford University Press.

Burgess-Proctor, A. (2006). Intersections of race, class, gender and crime: Future directions for feminist criminology. *Feminist Criminology, 1*(1), 27–47.

Burgess-Proctor, A. (2012). Backfire: Lessons learned when the criminal justice system fails help-seeking battered women. *Journal of Crime and Justice, 35*(1), 68–92.

Burgess-Proctor, A., Pickett, S. M., Parkhill, M. R., Hamill, T. S., Kirwan, M., & Kozak, A. T. (2016). College women's perception of and inclination to use campus sexual assault resources: Comparing the views of students with and without sexual victimization histories. *Criminal Justice Review, 41*(2), 204–218.

Burke, J. (2012, November 2). Kashmir parents accused of killing daughter in acid attack. *The Guardian.* Retrieved from http://www.theguardian.com/world/2012/nov/02/paresnts-accused-kashmir-acid-attack

Burks, A. C., Cramer, R. J., Henderson, C. E., Stroud, C. H., Crosby, J. W., & Graham, J. (2015). Frequency, nature, and correlates of hate crime victimization experiences in an urban sample of lesbian, gay, and bisexual community members. *Journal of Interpersonal Violence.* DOI: 10.1177/0886260515605298.

Burton, V. S., Cullen, F. T., Evans, D., Alarid, L. F., & Dunaway, G. (1998). Gender, self-control and crime. *Journal of Research in Crime and Delinquency, 35*(2), 123–147.

Bush, G. W. (2004). State of the Union Address. Prisoner Reentry Initiative. Available at https://georgewbush-whitehouse.archives.gov/government/fbci/pri.html

Bush-Baskette, S. (1998). The war on drugs as a war on Black women. In S. L. Miller (Ed.), *Crime control and women* (pp. 113–129). Thousand Oaks, CA: Sage.

Bush-Baskette, S. (1999). The war on drugs: A war against women? In S. Cook & S. Davies (Eds.), *Harsh punishment: International experiences of women's imprisonment* (pp. 211–229). Boston, MA: Northeastern University Press.

Bush-Baskette, S. R. (2000, December). The war on drugs and the incarceration of mothers. *Journal of Drug Issues, 30,* 919–928.

Bush-Baskette, S. R. (2010). *Misguided justice: The war on drugs and the incarceration of Black women.* New York: iUniverse.

Bush-Baskette, S. R., & Smith, V. C. (2012). Is meth the new crack for women in the war on drugs? Factors affecting sentencing outcomes for women and parallels between meth and crack. *Feminist Criminology, 7*(1), 48–69.

Cable News Network (CNN). (2001). Patty Hearst profile. Retrieved from http://www.cnn.com/CNN/Programs/people/shows/hearst/profile.html

Calderon Gamboa, J. (2007, Winter). Seeking integral reparations for the murders and disappearances of women in Ciudad Juárez: A gender and cultural perspective. *Human Rights Brief, 14*(2), 31–35. Retrieved from http://www.wcl.american.edu/hrbrief/14/2calderon.pdf

California Department of Corrections and Rehabilitation (CDCR) (2013). Prison Census Data as of June 30, 2013. Table 10 Prison Census Data, Total Institution Population. Offenders by Sentence Status and Gender. Retrieved from www.cdcr.ca.gov/Reports_Research/Offender_Information_Services_Branch/Annual/Census/CENSUSd1306.pdf

California Department of Corrections and Rehabilitation (CDCR) (n.d.). How to send money to an inmate. Retrieved from www.cdcr.ca.gov/visitors/sending-money-to-inmates.html.

California Emergency Management Agency (Cal EMA). (2011). Victim services programs. Retrieved from http://www.calema.ca.gov/PublicSafetyandVictimServices/Pages/Victim-Services-Programs.aspx

Camacho, C. M., & Alarid, L. F. (2008). The significance of the victim advocate for domestic violence victims in Municipal Court. *Violence and Victims, 23*(3), 288–300.

Campbell, A. (1984). *The girls in the gang.* New Brunswick, NJ: Rutgers University Press.

Campbell, A. (1995). Female participation in gangs. In M.W. Klein, C. L. Maxson, & J. Miller (Eds.), *The modern gang reader* (pp. 70–77). Los Angeles, CA: Roxbury.

Campbell, J., & Carlson. J. R. (2012). Correctional administrators' perceptions of prison nurseries. *Criminal Justice and Behavior, 39*(8), 1063–1074.

Campbell, J. C., Webster, D., Koziol-McLain, J., Block, C. R., Campbell, D., Curry, M. A., . . . Wilt, S. (2003). Assessing risk factors for intimate partner homicide. *National Institute of Justice (NIJ) Journal, 250,* 14–19. Retrieved from http://www.ncjrs.gov/pdffiles1/jr000250e.pdf

Campbell, N. D. (2000). *Using women: Gender, drug policy and social justice.* New York: Routledge.

Campbell, R. (2006). Rape survivors' experiences with the legal and medical systems: Do rape victim advocates make a difference? *Violence Against Women, 12*(1), 30–45.

Campbell, R., Ahrens, C. E., Sefl, T., Wasco, S. M., & Barnes, H. E. (2001). Social reactions to rape victims: Healing and hurtful effects on psychological and physical health outcomes. *Violence and Victims, 16,* 287–302

Canada honor killing trial verdict: Shafia family found guilty. (2012, January 29). *Huffington Post.* Retrieved from http://www.huffingtonpost.com/2012/01/29/canada-honor-killing-shafia-family-guilty_n_1240268.html

Canterino v. Wilson, 546 F. Supp. 174 (W.D. Ky. 1982).

Caputo, G. A., & King, A. (2011). Shoplifting: Work, agency and gender. *Feminist Criminology, 6*(3), 159–177.

Carbone-Lopez, K., Gatewood Owens, J., & Miller, J. (2012). Women's "storylines" of methamphetamine initiation in the Midwest. *Journal of Drug Issues, 42*(3), 226–246.

Carey, K. B., Durney, S. E., Shepardson, R. L., & Carey, M. P. (2015). Incapacitated and forcible rape of college women: Prevalence across the first year. *Journal of Adolescent Health, 56:* 678–680.

Carlan, P. E., Nored, L. S., & Downey, R. A. (2011). Officer preferences for male backup: The influence of gender and police partnering. *Journal of Police and Criminal Psychology, 26*(1), 4–10.

Carr, N. T., Hudson, K., Hanks, R. S., & Hunt, A. N. (2008). Gender effects along the juvenile justice system: Evidence of a gendered organization. *Feminist Criminology, 3*(1), 25–43.

Carson, E. A., & Anderson, E. (2016). Prisoners in 2015. U.S. Department of Justice, Office of Justice Programs, Bureau of Justice Statistics. Retrieved from https://www.bjs.gov/content/pub/pdf/p15.pdf

Carson, E. A., & Golinelli, D. (2013). Prisoners in 2012—Advance counts. U.S. Department of Justice, Bureau of Justice Statistics. Retrieved from http://www.bjs.gov/content/pub/pdf/p12ac.pdf

Casey Anthony. (2014). The Biography.com website. Retrieved from http://www.biography.com/people/casey-anthony-20660183.

Cass, A., & Mallicoat, S. L. (2014). College student perceptions of victim action: Will targets of stalking report to police? *American Journal of Criminal Justice*. doi: 10.1007/s12103-014-9252-8

Catalano, S. (2007). *Intimate partner violence in the United States*. Bureau of Justice Statistics. Washington, DC: U.S. Department of Justice. Retrieved from http://bjs.ojp.usdoj.gov/content/pub/pdf/IPAus.pdf

Catalano, S. (2012). *Intimate partner violence in the United States*. Bureau of Justice Statistics, Office of Justice Programs. Retrieved from http://bjs.ojp.usdoj.gov/content/intimate/ipv.cfm

Catterall, J. S., Dumais, S. A., & Hampden-Thompson, G. (2012). The arts and achievement in at-risk youth: Findings from four longitudinal studies. National Endowment for the Arts. Retrieved from http://arts.gov/sites/default/files/Arts-At-Risk-Youth.pdf

CBSLA.com. (2013, July 3). Woman recently released from prison for killing abusive boyfriend speaks out. Retrieved from http://losangeles.cbslocal.com/2013/07/03/women-recently-released-from-prison-for-killing-abusive-boyfriend-speaks-out/

CBS News. (2009, February 11). Air Force rape scandal grows. Retrieved from http://www.cbsnews.com/2100-201_162-543490.html

Center for American Women and Politics. (n.d.). Women on the U.S. Supreme Court. Retrieved from http://www.cawp.rutgers.edu/fast_facts/levels_of_office/USSupremeCourt.php

Center for American Women and Politics. (2017). Women in the U.S. Congress 2017. Retrieved from http://www.cawp.rutgers.edu/women-us-congress-2017.

Centers for Disease Control and Prevention (CDC). (1992–2004). Youth risk behavior surveillance—United States 1991–2004. CDC surveillance summaries. Department of Health and Human Services. Retrieved from http://www.cdc.gov/

Centers for Disease Control and Prevention (CDC). (2003). *Costs of intimate partner violence against women in the United States: 2003*. Atlanta, GA: National Centers for Injury Prevention and Control.

Centers for Disease Control and Prevention (CDC). (n.d.). Intimate partner violence. Retrieved from http://www.cdc.gov/ViolencePrevention/intimatepartnerviolence/definitions.html

Centers for Disease Control and Prevention (CDC). 1991-2015 High School Youth Risk Behavior Survey Data. Retrieved from http://nccd.cdc.gov/youthonline/

Cerulli, C., Kothari, C., Dichter, M., Marcus, S., Kim, T. K. Wiley, J., & Rhodes, K. V. (2015). Help-seeking patterns among women experiencing intimate partner violence: Do they forgo the criminal justice system if their adjudication wishers are not met? *Violence and Victims, 30*(1), 16–31.

Chamberlain, L. (2007, March 28). 2 cities and 4 bridges where commerce flows. *New York Times*, p. 28.

Chancer, L. (2016). Introduction to special 10th anniversary issue of feminist criminology: Is criminology still male dominated? *Feminist Criminology, 11*(4), 307–310.

Chapman, S. B. (2009). *Inmate-perpetrated harassment: Exploring the gender-specific experience of female correctional officers*. (Doctoral dissertation). City University of New York, New York. Retrieved from ProQuest Dissertations and Theses database, http://media.proquest.com/media/pq/classic/doc/1679173831/fmt/ai/rep/NPDF?_s=uODFIQqrVIzWJxoNj7uj9lddn8I%3D

Chasmar, J. (2013, June 10). Teacher publically tortured, beheaded for witchcraft in Papua New Guinea. *Washington Times*. Retrieved from http://www.washingtontimes.com/news/2013/jun/10/teacher-publicly-tortured-beheaded-witchcraft-papu/

Cheeseman, K. A., & Downey, R. A. (2012). Talking 'bout my generation: The effect on "generation" on correctional employee perceptions of work stress and job satisfaction. *The Prison Journal, 92*(1), 24–44.

Cheeseman, K. A., & Worley, R. M. (2006). A "captive" audience: Legal responses and remedies to the sexual abuse of female inmates. *Criminal Law Bulletin–Boston, 42*(4), 439.

Chesler, P. (2010). Worldwide trends in honor killings. *Middle East Quarterly, 17*(2), 3–11.

Chesney-Lind, M. (1973). Judicial enforcement of the female sex role. *Issues in Criminology, 8*, 51–70.

Chesney-Lind, M. (1997). *The female offender: Girls, women and crime*. Thousand Oaks, CA: Sage.

Chesney-Lind, M. (2006). Patriarchy, crime and justice: Feminist criminology in an era of backlash. *Feminist Criminology, 1*(1), 6–26.

Chesney-Lind, M., & Chagnon, N. (2016). Criminology, gender, and race: A case study of privilege in the academy. *Feminist Criminology, 11*(4), 311–333.

Chesney-Lind, M., & Shelden, R. G. (2004). *Girls, delinquency and juvenile justice*. Belmont, CA: West/Wadsworth.

Chika, I. S. (2011). Legalization of marital rape in Nigeria: A gross violation of women's health and reproductive rights. *Journal of Social Welfare & Family Law, 33*(1), 39–46.

Chiricos, T., Padgett, K., & Gertz, M. (2000). Fear, TV news and the reality of crime. *Criminology, 38*(3), 755–786.

Cho, H. (2012a). Intimate partner violence among Asian Americans: Risk factor differences across ethnic subgroups. *Journal of Family Violence, 27*(3), 215–224.

Cho, H. (2012b). Use of mental health services among Asian and Latino victims of intimate partner violence. *Violence Against Women, 18*(4), 404–419.

Cho, S-Y, Dreher, A., & Neumayer, E. (2011). *The spread of anti-trafficking policies—Evidence from a new index*. Cege Discussion Paper Series No. 119, Georg-August-University of Goettingen, Germany.

Churchville, V. (1987, November 5). Applicants for D.C. Police secretly tested for pregnancy: Officials reassess policy after complaint D.C. Police reassess pregnancy test policy. *The Washington Post*, p. A1.

Ciong, Z. B., & Huang, J. (2011). Predicting Hmong male and female youth's delinquent behavior: An exploratory study. *Hmong Studies Journal, 12,* 1–34. Retrieved from http://www.hmong-studies.org/XiongandHuangHSJ12.pdf

CISION. (2012, October 5). Assaulted, betrayed and jailed but ultimately triumphant, Brenda Clubine fights for abused women. Retrieved from http://www.prnewswire.com/news-releases/assaulted-betrayed-and-jailed-but-ultimately-triumphant-brenda-clubine-fights-for-abused-women-172869521.html

Clear, T., & Frost, N. (2007). Informing public policy. *Criminology & Public Policy, 6*(4), 633–640.

Clements-Nolle, K., Wolden, M., & Bargmann-Losche, J. (2009). Childhood trauma and risk for past and future suicide attempts among women in prison. *Women's Health Issues, 19,* 185–192.

Cloud, J. (2011, June 16). How the Casey Anthony murder case became the social media trial of the century. *Time Magazine*. Retrieved from http://content.time.com/time/nation/article/0,8599,2077969,00.html

Cobbina, J. E., Huebner, B. M., & Berg, M. T. (2012). Men, women and postrelease offending: An examination of the nature of the link between relational ties and recidivism. *Crime & Delinquency, 58*(3), 331–361.

Cobbina, J. E., & Oselin, S. S. (2011). It's not only for the money: An analysis of adolescent versus adult entry into street prostitution. *Sociological Inquiry, 81*(3), 310–332.

Coffman, K. (2012, April 30). Dougherty gang sentenced in Colorado for police shootout. *Reuters*. Retrieved from http://news.yahoo.com/dougherty-gang-sentenced-colorado-police-shootout-230049502.html

Cohen, A. K. (1955). *Delinquent boys*. Glencoe, IL: Free Press.

Cohen, L. E., & Felson, M. (1979). Social change and crime rate trends: A routine activity approach. *American Sociological Review*, 588–608.

Coles, J., Astbury, J., Dartnall, E., & Limjerwala, S. (2014). A qualitative exploration of research trauma and researchers' responses to investigating sexual violence. *Violence Against Women, 20*(1), 95–117.

Connor, T. (2013, October 16). Ariel Castro victim reparations bill gets initial approval. *NBC News*. Retrieved from http://usnews.nbcnews.com/_news/2013/10/16/20988996-ariel-castro-victim-reparations-bill-gets-initial-approval?lite

Contreras, R. (2009). "Damn, yo—Who's that girl?" An ethnographic analysis of masculinity in drug robberies. *Journal of Contemporary Ethnography, 38*(4), 465–492.

Cook, C. L., & Fox, K. A. (2012). Testing the relative importance of contemporaneous offenses: The impacts of fear of sexual assault versus fear of physical harm among men and women. *Journal of Criminal Justice 40*(2), 142–151.

Cook, F. A. (1997). *Belva Ann Lockwood: For peace, justice, and president*. Stanford, CA: Women's Legal History Biography Project, Robert Crown Law Library, Stanford Law School. Retrieved from http://wlh-static.law.stanford.edu/papers/LockwoodB-Cook97.pdf

Cook, J. A., & Fonow, M. M. (1986). Knowledge and women's interests: Issues of epistemology and methodology in feminist sociological research. *Sociological Inquiry, 56,* 2–29.

Coontz, P. (2000). Gender and judicial decisions: Do female judges decide cases differently than male judges? *Gender Issues, 18*(4), 59–73.

Cooper, A., & Smith, E. L. (2011). Homicide trends in the United States. Annual rates for 2009 and 2010. U.S. Department of Justice. Retrieved from http://bjs.ojp.usdoj.gov/content/pub/pdf/htus8008.pdf

Cooper, H. (2017, March 15). Reports of sexual assault increase at two military academies. *The New York Times*. Retrieved from https://www.nytimes.com/2017/03/15/us/politics/sexual-assault-military-west-point-annapolis.html?_r=0

Cooper v. Morin, 49 N.Y.2d 69 (1979).

Copp, J. E., Giordano, P. C., Longmore, M. A., & Manning, W. D. (2015). Stay or leave decision making in nonviolent and violent dating relationships. *Violence and Victims, 30*(4), 581–599.

Cops, D., & Pleysier, S. (2011). "Doing Gender" in fear of crime: The impact of gender identity on reported levels of fear of crime in adolescents and young adults. *British Journal of Criminology, 51*(1), 58–74.

Corman, H., Dave, D. M., & Reichman, N. E. (2014). Effects of welfare reform on women's crime. *International Review of Law and Economics, 40,* 1–14.

Corsianos, M. (2009). *Policing and gendered justice: Examining the possibilities*. Toronto, Canada: UTP Higher Education.

Covington, S. (1999). *Helping women recover: A program for treating substance abuse*. San Francisco, CA: Jossey-Bass.

Cox, L., & Speziale, B. (2009). Survivors of stalking: Their voices and lived experiences. *Affilia: Journal of Women and Social Work, 24*(1), 5–18.

Crandall, M., Senturia, K., Sullivan, M., & Shiu-Thornton, S. (2005). No way out: Russian-speaking women's experiences with domestic violence. *Journal of Interpersonal Violence, 20*(8), 941–958.

Crime in the United States 2010 (CIUS). (2010). Forcible rape. Uniform Crime Reports. U.S. Department of Justice, Federal Bureau of Investigation. Retrieved from http://www.fbi.gov/about-us/cjis/ucr/crime-in-the-u.s/2010/crime-in-the-u.s.-2010/violent-crime/rapemain

Crime in the United States 2012 (CIUS). (2012). About crime in the U.S. Uniform Crime Reports. U.S. Department of Justice, Federal Bureau of Investigation. Retrieved from http://www.fbi.gov/about-us/cjis/ucr/crime-in-the-u.s/2012/crime-in-the-u.s.-2012

Crime in the United States 2015 (CIUS). (2015). 10-year UCR arrest trends. Retrieved from https://ucr.fbi.gov/crime-in-the-u.s/2015/crime-in-the-u.s.-2015

Crosnoe, R., Erickson, K. G., & Dornbusch, S. M. (2002). Protective functions of family relationships and school factors on the deviant behavior of adolescent boys and girls. *Youth and Society, 33*(4), 515–544.

Curry, G. D., Ball, R. A., & Fox, R. J. (1994). *Gang crime and law enforcement recordkeeping. Research in brief.* Washington, DC: U.S. Department of Justice, Office of Justice Programs, National Institute of Justice. Retrieved from http://www.ncjrs.gov/txtfiles/gcrime.txt

Dahl, J. (2012, May 16). Fla. woman Marissa Alexander gets 20 years for "warning shot": Did she stand her ground? CBS News. Retrieved from http://www.cbsnews.com/news/fla-woman-marissa-alexander-gets-20-years-for-warning-shot-did-she-stand-her-ground/

Daigle, L. E., Cullen, F. T., & Wright, J. P. (2007). Gender differences in the predictors of juvenile delinquency: Assessing the generality-specificity debate. *Youth Violence and Juvenile Justice, 5*(3), 254–286.

Dalla, R. L. (2000). Exposing the "pretty woman" myth: A qualitative examination of the lives of female streetwalking prostitutes. *Journal of Sex Research, 37*(4), 344–353.

Dalla, R. L., Xia, Y., & Kennedy, H. (2003). "You just give them what they want and pray they don't kill you": Street-level workers' reports of victimization, personal resources and coping strategies. *Violence Against Women, 9*(11), 1367–1394.

Daly, K. (1994). *Gender, crime, and punishment.* New Haven, CT: Yale University Press.

Daly, K., & Chesney-Lind, M. (1988). Feminism and criminology. *Justice Quarterly, 5*(4), 497–538.

Danner, M. J. E. (2003). Three strikes and it's women who are out: The hidden consequences for women of criminal justice policy reforms. In R. Muraskin (Ed.), *It's a crime: Women and justice* (2nd ed., Chapter 44). Upper Saddle River, NJ: Prentice-Hall.

Davidson, J. T. (2011). Managing risk in the community: How gender matters. In R. Sheehan, G. McIvor, & C. Trotter (Eds.), *Working with women offenders in the community.* New York: Willan.

Davies, K., Block, C. R., & Campbell, J. (2007). Seeking help from the police: Battered women's decisions and experiences. *Criminal Justice Studies, 20*(1), 15–41.

Davis, C. P. (2007). At risk girls and delinquency: Career pathways. *Crime and Delinquency, 53*(3), 408–435.

Davis, K. E., Coker, A. L., & Sanderson, M. (2002). Physical and mental health effects of being stalked for men and women. *Violence and Victims, 17*(4), 429–443.

Day, J. C., Zahn, M. A., & Tichavsky, L. R. (2015). What works for whom? The effects of gender responsive programming on girls and boys in secure detention. *Journal of Research in Crime and Delinquency, 52*(1), 93–129.

De Atley, R. (2013, October 28). Sara Kruzan: If sentenced today, hers would be a different story. *The Press-Enterprise.* Retrieved from http://www.pe.com/local-news/local-news-headlines/20131028-kruzan-if-sentenced-today-hers-would-be-a-different-story.ece

De Groof, S. (2008). And my mama said. . . . The (relative) parental influence on fear of crime among adolescent boys and girls. *Youth & Society, 39*(3), 267–293.

DeHart, D., Lynch, S., Belknap, J., Dass-Brailsford, P., & Green, B. (2014). Life history models of female offending: The roles of serious mental illness and trauma in women's pathways to jail. *Psychology of Women Quarterly, 38*(1), 138–151.

DeHart, D., & Moran, M. (2015). Poly-victimization among girls in the justice system: Trajectories of risk and association to juvenile offending. *Violence Against Women, 21*(3), 291–312.

DeJong, C., Burgess-Proctor, A., & Elis, L. (2008). Police officer perceptions of intimate partner violence: An analysis of observational data. *Violence and Victims, 23*, 683–696.

DeLisi, M., Beaver, K. M., Vaughn, M. G., Trulson, C. R., Kisloski, A. E., Drury, A. J., & Wright, J. P. (2010). Personality, gender and self-control theory revisited: Results from a sample of institutionalized juvenile delinquents. *Applied Psychology in Criminal Justice, 6*(1), 31–46.

Deluca, M. (2013, August 1). Ariel Castro victim Michelle Knight: "Your hell is just beginning." Retrieved from http://usnews.nbcnews.com/_news/2013/08/01/19813977-ariel-castro-victim-michelle-knight-your-hell-is-just-beginning?lite

Demuth, S., & Steffensmeier, D. (2004). The impact of gender and race-ethnicity in the pretrial release process. *Social Problems, 51*(2), 222–242.

Dennis, M. L., Scott, C. K., Funk, R., & Foss, M. A. (2005). The duration and correlates of addiction and treatment careers. *Journal of Substance Abuse Treatment, 28*(2), S51–S62.

Department of Defense (2017). DOD annual report on sexual harassment and violence at the military service academies, academic program year 2015–2016. Retrieved from http://www.sapr.mil/public/docs/reports/MSA/APY_15-16/APY_15-16_MSA_InfoPaper.pdf

Dershowitz, A. (2011, July 7). Casey Anthony: The system worked. *Wall Street Journal.* Retrieved from http://online.wsj.com/news/articles/SB10001424052702303544604576429783247016492

De Vaus, D., & Wise, S. (1996, Autumn). Parent's concern for the safety of their children. *Family Matters, 43*, 34–38.

Diep, F. (2013, June 10). Mississippi will test teen mom babies for statutory rape evidence. *Popular Science.* Retrieved from http://www.popsci.com/science/article/2013-06/new-mississippi-teen-moms-babies-statutory-rape

Dietz, N. A., & Martin, P. Y. (2007). Women who are stalked: Questioning the fear standard. *Violence Against Women, 13*(7), 750–776.

DiMarino, F. (2009). Women as corrections professionals. *Corrections.com.* Retrieved from http://www.corrections.com/articles/21703-women-as-corrections-professionals

Dimond, J. P., Fiesler, C., & Bruckman, A. S. (2011). Domestic violence and information communication technologies. *Interacting With Computers, 23*, 413–421.

Dinan, E. (2005, February 27). Where the Smart boys are 14 years later. *Portsmouth Herald.* Retrieved from http://www.hampton.lib.nh.us/hampton/biog/pamsmart/20050227PH.htm

Dissell, R. (2012, September 2). Rape charges against high school players divide football town of Steubenville, Ohio. Cleveland.com. Retrieved from http://www.cleveland.com/metro/index.ssf/2012/09/rape_charges_divide_football_t.html

Dobash, R., & Dobash, R. E. (1992). *Women, violence and social change.* New York: Routledge.

Dodderidge, J. (1632). *The lawes resolutions of women's rights: Or, the law's provision for women.* London, UK: John More, Rare Book and Special Collections Division, Library of Congress.

Dodge, M. Valcore, L., & Klinger, D. A. (2010). Maintaining separate spheres in policing: Women on SWAT teams. *Women & Criminal Justice, 20*(3), 218–238.

Donovan, P. (1996). Can statutory rape laws be effective in preventing adolescent pregnancy? *Family Planning Perspectives, 29*(1). Retrieved from http://www.guttmacher.org/pubs/journals/2903097.html

Dooley, S., Scott, T., Ng, C., & Effron, L. (2016, July 8). Jaycee Dugard on reclaiming her life after being held captive for 18 years: "I have lived a lot of lifetimes." ABC News. Retrieved from http://abcnews.go.com/US/jaycee-dugard-reclaiming-life-held-captive-18-years/story?id=40280031

Dowler, K. (2003). Media consumption and public attitudes toward crime and justice: The relationship between fear of crime, punitive attitudes, and perceived police effectiveness. *Journal of Criminal Justice and Popular Culture, 10*(2), 109–126.

Downey, M. (2007, October 28). Genarlow Wilson is free . . . But other victims of Georgia's sweeping sex offender laws are not. *Atlanta Journal-Constitution*, B1.

Drabble, L., Trocki, K. F., Hughes, T. L., Korcha, R. A., & Lown, A. E. (2013). Sexual orientation differences in the relationship between victimization and hazardous drinking among women in the National Alcohol Survey. *Psychology of Addictive Behaviors, 27*(3), 639–648.

Drachman, V. G. (1998). *Sisters in law: Women lawyers in modern American history.* Cambridge, MA: Harvard University Press.

Dugan, L, Nagin, D., & Rosenfeld, R. (2003). Exposure reduction or retaliation: Domestic violence resources on intimate-partner homicide. *Law & Society Review, 37*(1), 169–198.

Durrani, S., & Singh, P. (2011). Women, private practice and billable hours: Time for a total rewards strategy? *Compensation & Benefits Review, 43*(5), 300–305.

Dworkin, E. R., Sorell, N. R., & Allen, N. E. (2016). Individual- and setting-level correlates of secondary traumatic stress in rape crisis center staff. *Journal of Interpersonal Violence*

Dye, M. H., & Aday, R. H. (2013). "I just wanted to die": Preprison and current suicide ideation among women serving life sentences. *Criminal Justice and Behavior, 40*(8), 832–849.

Egelko, B. (March 16, 2016). Court rejects suit by kidnap survivor Jaycee Duggard. SF Gate. Retrieved from http://www.sfgate.com/crime/article/Court-rejects-suit-by-kidnap-survivor-Jaycee-6892232.php

Eghigian, M., & Kirby, K. (2006). Girls in gangs: On the rise in America. *Corrections Today, 68*(2), 48–50.

Eigenberg, H., & Garland, R. (2008). Victim blaming. In L. J. Moriarty (Ed.), *Controversies in victimology* (pp. 21–36). Newark, NJ: Elsevier Press.

Einat, T., & Chen. G. (2012). What's love got to do with it? Sex in a female maximum security prison. *The Prison Journal, 92*(4), 484–505.

England, L. (2008, March 17). Rumsfeld knew. *Stern Magazine.* Retrieved from http://www.stern.de/politik/ausland/lynndie-england-rumsfeld-knew-614356.html?nv=ct_cb

Esbensen, F. A., & Carson, D. C. (2012). Who are the gangsters? An examination of the age, race/ethnicity, sex and immigration status of self-reported gang members in a seven-city study of American youth. *Journal of Contemporary Criminal Justice, 28*(4), 465–481.

Esbensen, F. A., Deschenes, E. P., & Winfree, L. T., Jr. (1999). Differences between gang girls and gang boys: Results from a multisite survey. *Youth and Society, 31*(1), 27–53.

Esfandiari, G. (2006). Afghanistan: Rights watchdog alarmed at continuing "honor killings." Women's United Nations Report Network. Retrieved from http://www.wunrn.com/news/2006/09_25_06/100106_afghanistan_violence.htm

Estrada, F., & Nilsson A. (2012). Does it cost more to be a female offender? A life-course study of childhood circumstances, crime, drug abuse, and living conditions. *Feminist Criminology, 7*(3), 196–219.

Ewoldt, C. A., Monson, C. M., & Langhinrichsen-Rohling, J. (2000). Attributions about rape in a continuum of dissolving marital relationships. *Journal of Interpersonal Violence, 15*(11), 1175–1183.

Ezell, M., & Levy, M. (2003). An evaluation of an arts program for incarcerated juvenile offenders. *Journal of Correctional Education, 54*(3), 108–114.

Fagel, M. (2013, March 8). Jury questions to Jodi Arias illustrate their frustration with her story. *Huffington Post.* Retrieved from http://www.huffingtonpost.com/mari-fagel/jodi-arias-jury-questions_b_2825167.html

Farid, M. (2014, January 13). On the shelves: "I am Malala": Her first hand story. *The Jakarta Post.* Retrieved from http://www.thejakartapost.com/news/2014/01/13/on-shelves-i-am-malala-her-first-hand-story.html-0

Farley, M. (2004). "Bad for the body, bad for the heart": Prostitution harms women even if legalized or decriminalized. *Violence Against Women, 10*(10), 1087–1125.

Farley, M., & Barkin, H. (1998). Prostitution, violence and post-traumatic stress disorder. *Women and Health, 27*(3), 37–49.

Farley, M., & Kelly, V. (2000). Prostitution: A critical review of the medical and social sciences literature. *Women and Criminal Justice, 11*(4), 29–64.

Farrell, A., McDevitt, J., & Fahy, S. (2010). Where are all the victims? Understanding the determinants of official identification of human trafficking incidents. *Criminology & Public Policy, 9*, 201–233.

Farrell, A., Owens, C., & McDevitt, J. (2014). New laws but few cases: Understanding the challenges to the investigation and prosecution of human trafficking cases. *Crime, Law and Social Change, 61*: 139–168.

Fattah, E. A., & Sacco, V. F. (1989). *Crime and victimization of the elderly.* New York: Springer-Verlag.

Federal Bureau of Investigation (FBI). (2003). Bank crime statistics 2003. Retrieved from http://www.fbi.gov/stats-services/publications/bank-crime-statistics-2003/bank-crime-statistics-bcs-2003

Federal Bureau of Investigation (FBI). (2011). *Crime in the U.S. 2010: Uniform Crime Reports.* Retrieved from http://www.fbi.gov/about-us/cjis/ucr/crime-in-the-u.s/2010/crime-in-the-u.s.-2010

Federal Bureau of Investigation (FBI). (2012a, January 6). Attorney General Eric Holder announces revisions to the Uniform Crime Report's definition of rape: Date reported on rape will better reflect state criminal codes, victim experiences [Press release]. U.S. Department of Justice, Uniform Crime Reports. Retrieved from http://www.fbi.gov/news/pressrel/press-releases/attorney-general-eric-holder-announces-revisions-to-the-uniform-crime-reports-definition-of-rape

Federal Bureau of Investigation (FBI). (2012b). Crime in the United States, 2012. Retrieved from http://www.fbi.gov/about-us/cjis/ucr/crime-in-the-u.s/2012/crime-in-the-u.s.-2012/cius_home

Federal Bureau of Investigation (FBI). (2012c). UCR program changes definition of rape: Includes all victims and omits requirement of physical force. Criminal Justice Information Service, U. S. Department of Justice. Retrieved from http://www.fbi.gov/about-us/cjis/cjis-link/march-2012/ucr-program-changes-definition-of-rape

Feld, B. C. (2009). Violent girls or relabeled status offenders? An alternative interpretation of the data. *Crime and Delinquency, 55*(2), 241–265.

Felix, Q. (2005). Human rights in Pakistan: Violence and misery for children and women. *Asia News.* Retrieved from http://www.asianews.it/news-en/Human-rights-in-Pakistan:-violence-and-misery-for-children-and-women-2554.html

Fellner, J. (2010). Sexually abused: The nightmare of juveniles in confinement. *Huffington Post.* Retrieved from http://www.huffingtonpost.com/jamie-fellner/sexually-abused-the-night_b_444240.html

Ferraro, K. J. (1981). *Battered women and the shelter movement* (Doctoral dissertation). Arizona State University, Tempe.

Ferro, C., Cermele, J., & Saltzman, A. (2008). Current perceptions of marital rape: Some good and not-so-good news. *Journal of Interpersonal Violence, 23*(6), 764–779

Ferszt, G. G. (2011). Who will speak for me? Advocating for pregnant women in prison. *Policy, Politics & Nursing Practice, 12*(4), 254–256.

Figley, C. R. (1995). Compassion fatigue: Toward a new understanding of the costs of caring. In B. H. Stamm (Ed.), *Secondary traumatic stress: Self-care issues for clinicians, researchers and educators* (2nd ed., pp. 3–28). Lutherville, MD: Sidran.

Fisher, B. S., Cullen, F. T., & Turner, M. G. (2000). The sexual victimization of college women. Series: Research report. *NCJ.* Retrieved from https://www.ncjrs.gov/txtfiles1/nij/182369.txt

Fisher, B. S., Daigle, L. E., & Cullen, F. T. (2010). What distinguishes single from recurrent sexual victims? The role of lifestyle-routine activities and first-incident characteristics. *Justice Quarterly, 27*(1), 102–129.

Fisher, B. S., Daigle, L. E., Cullen, F. T., & Turner, M. G. (2003). Reporting sexual victimization to the police and others: Results from a national-level study of college women. *Criminal Justice and Behavior, 30*(1), 6–38.

Fisher, B. S., & May, D. (2009). College students' crime-related fears on campus: Are far-provoking cues gendered? *Journal of Contemporary Criminal Justice, 25*(3), 300–321.

Fisher, B. S., & Sloan, J. J. (2003). Unraveling the fear of sexual victimization among college women: Is the "shadow of sexual assault" hypothesis supported? *Justice Quarterly, 20,* 633–659.

Fleisher, M. S., & Krienert, J. L. (2004). Life-course events, social networks, and the emergence of violence among female gang members. *Journal of Community Psychology, 32*(5), 607–622.

Fleury-Steiner, R., Bybee, D., Sullivan, C. M., Belknap, J., & Melton, H. C. (2006). Contextual factors impacting battered women's intentions to reuse the criminal legal system. *Journal of Community Psychology, 34*(3), 327–342.

Foley, S., Kidder, D. L., & Powell, G. N. (2002). The perceived glass ceiling and justice perceptions: An investigation of Hispanic law associates. *Journal of Management, 28*(4), 471–496.

Ford, M. (2017, May 12). Jeff Sessions reinvigorates the drug war. *The Atlantic.* Retrieved from https://www.theatlantic.com/politics/archive/2017/05/sessions-sentencing-memo/526029/

Foundation for Women's Health, Research and Development (FORWARD). (2012). *Female genital mutilation.* Retrieved from http://www.forwarduk.org.uk/key-issues/fgm

Fox News. (2014, January 7). One of two teens convicted in Steubenville rape case released. Retrieved from http://www.foxnews.com/us/2014/01/07/one-two-teens-convicted-in-steubenville-rape-case-released/

Franiuk, R., Seefelt, J. L., Cepress, S. L., & Vandello, J. A. (2008). Prevalence and effects of rape myths in the media: The Kobe Bryant case. *Violence Against Women, 14,* 287–309.

Freedman, E. B. (1981). *Their sisters' keepers: Women prison reform in America, 1830–1930.* Ann Arbor: University of Michigan Press.

Freeman, H. (2013, June 18). Nigella Lawson: From domestic goddess to the face of domestic violence. *The Guardian.* Retrieved from http://www.theguardian.com/commentisfree/2013/jun/18/nigella-lawson-domestic-goddess-violence

Freiburger, T. L., & Burke, A. S. (2011). Status offenders in the juvenile court: The effects of gender, race and ethnicity on the adjudication decision. *Youth Violence and Juvenile Justice, 9*(4), 352–365.

Freiburger, T. L., & Hilinski, C. M. (2010). The impact of race, gender and age on the pretrial decision. *Criminal Justice Review, 35*(3), 318–334.

French, S. (2000). Of problems, pitfalls and possibilities: A comprehensive look at female attorneys and law firm partnership. *Women's Rights Law Reporter, 21*(3), 189–216.

Frost, N. A., & Clear, T. R. (2007). Doctoral education in criminology and criminal justice. *Journal of Criminal Justice Education, 18,* 35–52.

Frost, N. A., & Phillips, N. D. (2011). Talking heads: Crime reporting on cable news. *Justice Quarterly, 28*(1), 87–112.

Fus, T. (2006, March). Criminalizing marital rape: A comparison of judicial and legislative approaches. *Vanderbilt Journal of Transnational Law, 39*(2), 481–517.

Gaarder, E., & Belknap, J. (2002). Tenuous borders: Girls transferred to adult court. *Criminology, 40*(3), 481–518.

Garcia, C. A., & Lane, J. (2010). Looking in the rearview mirror: What incarcerated women think girls need from the system. *Feminist Criminology, 5*(3), 227–243.

Garcia, C. A., & Lane, J. (2012). Dealing with the fall-out: Identifying and addressing the role that relationship strain plays in the lives of girls in the juvenile justice system. *Journal of Criminal Justice, 40,* 259–267.

Garcia-Lopez, G. (2008). Nunca te toman en cuenta [They never take you into account]: The challenges of inclusion and strategies for success of Chicana attorneys. *Gender and Society, 22*(5), 590–612.

Gartner, R., & Kruttschnitt, C. (2004). A brief history of doing time: The California Institution for Women in the 1960's and the 1990's. *Law and Society Review, 38*(2), 267–304.

Gast, P. (2011, August 10). Siblings wanted in bank robbery, shootout arrested after chase. CNN. Retrieved from http://www .cnn.com/2011/CRIME/08/11/georgia.three.siblings.manhunt. archives/index.html?iref=allsearch

Gavazzi, S. M., Yarcheck, C. M., & Lim, J.-Y. (2005). Ethnicity, gender, and global risk indicators in the lives of status offenders coming to the attention of the juvenile court. *International Journal of Offender Therapy and Comparative Criminology, 49*(6), 696–710.

Gehring, K., & Van Voorhis, P. (2014). Needs and pretrial failure: Additional risk factors for female and male pretrial defendants. *Criminal Justice and Behavior, 41*(8), 943–970.

Gehring, K., Van Voorhis, P., & Bell, V. (2010). "What Works" for female probationers? An evaluation of the *Moving On* program. *Women, Girls and Criminal Justice, 11*(1), 6–10.

General Accounting Office (GAO). (1999). *Women in prison: Issues and challenges confronting U.S. correctional systems.* Washington, DC: U.S. Department of Justice.

Gerbner, G., & Gross, L. (1980, Summer). The "Mainstreaming" of America: Violence profile no. 11. *Journal of Communication,* 10–29.

Giaris, H. (2014, September 8). Don't watch the Ray Rice video. Don't ask why Janay Palmer married him. Ask why anyone would blame a victim. *The Guardian.* Retrieved from https://www .theguardian.com/commentisfree/2014/sep/08/ray-rice-domestic-violence-video-janay-palmer-victim-blaming

Gidycz, C. A., Orchowski, L. M., King, C. R., & Rich, C. L. (2008). Sexual victimization and health-risk behaviors: A prospective analysis of college women. *Journal of Interpersonal Violence, 23*(6), 744–763.

Gilbert, E. (2001). Women, race and criminal justice processing. In C. Renzetti & L. Goodstein (Eds.), *Women, crime and criminal justice: Original feminist readings.* Los Angeles, CA: Roxbury.

Gilfus, M. E. (1992). From victims to survivors to offenders: Women's routes of entry and immersion into street crime. *Women and Criminal Justice, 4*(1), 63–89.

Gillum, T. L. (2008). Community response and needs of African American female survivors of domestic violence. *Journal of Interpersonal Violence, 23*(1), 39–57.

Gillum, T. L. (2009). Improving services to African American survivors of IPV: From the voices of recipients of culturally specific services. *Violence Against Women, 15*(1), 57–80.

Girard, A. L., & Senn, C. Y. (2008). The role of the new "date rape drugs" in attributions about date rape. *Journal of Interpersonal Violence, 23*(1), 3–20.

Girl Scouts of America (GSA). (2008). *Third-year evaluation of Girl Scouts Beyond Bars final report.* Retrieved from http://www .girlscouts.org/research.pdf/gsbb_report.pdf

Girls Incorporated. (1996). *Prevention and parity: Girls in juvenile justice.* Indianapolis, IN: Girls Incorporated National Resource Center & Office of Juvenile Justice and Delinquency Prevention.

Girshick, L. B. (2002). No sugar, no spice: Reflections on research on woman-to-woman sexual violence. *Violence Against Women, 8*(12), 1500–1520.

Glaze, L., & Maruschak, L. (2008). *Parents in prison and their minor children.* Washington, DC: U.S. Department of Justice.

Glover v. Johnson, 478 F. Supp. 1075 (1979).

Glueck, S., & Glueck, E. (1934). *Five hundred delinquent women.* New York: Alfred A. Knopf.

Goddard, C., & Bedi, G. (2010). Intimate partner violence and child abuse: A child-centered perspective. *Child Abuse Review, 19,* 5–20.

Gordon, J. A., Proulx, B., & Grant, P. H. (2013). Trepidation among the "keepers": Gendered perceptions of fear and risk of victimization among corrections officers. *American Journal of Criminal Justice, 38,* 245–265.

Gormley, P. (2007). The historical role and views towards victims and the evolution of prosecution policies in domestic violence. In R. Muraskin (Ed.), *It's a crime* (4th ed., Ch. 13). Upper Saddle River, NJ: Pearson Prentice Hall.

Gornick, J., Burt, M. J., & Pitman, P. J. (1985). Structures and activities of rape crisis centers in the early 1980s. *Crime and Delinquency, 31,* 247–268.

Gottfredson, M., & Hirschi, T. (1990). *A general theory of crime.* Palo Alto, CA: Stanford University Press.

Goulette, N., Wooldredge, J., Frank, J., & Travis III, L. (2015). From initial appearance to sentencing: Do female defendants experience disparate treatment? *Journal of Criminal Justice, 43*: 406–417.

Gover, A. R., Brank, E. M., & MacDonald, J. M. (2007). A specialized domestic violence court in South Carolina: An example of procedural justice for victims and defendants. *Violence Against Women, 13*(6), 603–626.

Gover, A. R., Welton-Mitchell, C., Belknap, J., & Deprince, A. P. (2013). When abuse happens again. Women's reasons for not reporting new incidents of intimate partner abuse to law enforcement. *Women & Criminal Justice, 23*, 99–120.

Gracia, E., & Tomas, J. M. (2014). Correlates of victim-blaming attitudes regarding partner violence against Spanish general population. *Violence Against Women, 20*(1), 26–41.

Greenfeld, L. A. (1997). *Sex offenses and offenders: An analysis of data on rape and sexual assault*. Washington, DC: U.S. Department of Justice, Office of Justice Programs.

Greenfeld, L. A., & Snell, T. L. (2000). *Women offenders*. Washington, DC: Bureau of Justice Statistics. Retrieved from http://bjs.ojp .usdoj.gov/content/pub/pdf/wo.pdf

Greer, K. (2008). When women hold the keys: Gender, leadership and correctional policy. Management and Training Institute. Retrieved from http://nicic.org/Library/023347

Grella, C. E., Lovinger, K., & Warda, U. S. (2013). Relationships among trauma exposure, familiar characteristics, and PTSD: A case-control study of women in prison and in the general population. *Women & Criminal Justice, 23*(1), 63–79.

Grella, C. E., & Rodriguez, L. (2011). Motivation for treatment among women offenders in prison-based treatment and longitudinal outcomes among those who participate in community aftercare. *Journal of Psychoactive Drugs, 43*(1), 58–67.

Griffin v. Michigan Department of Corrections, 654 F. Supp. 690 (1982).

Griffin, T., & Wooldredge, J. (2006). Sex-based disparities in felony dispositions before versus after sentencing reform in Ohio. *Criminology, 44*(4), 893–923.

Grossman, S. F., & Lundy, M. (2011). Characteristics of women who do and do not receive onsite shelter services from domestic violence programs. *Violence Against Women, 17*(8), 1024–1045.

Grossman, S. F., Lundy, M., George, C. C., & Crabtree-Nelson, S. (2010). Shelter and service receipt for victims of domestic violence in Illinois. *Journal of Interpersonal Violence, 25*(11), 2077–2093.

Grothoff, G. E., Kempf-Leonard, K., & Mullins, C. (2014). Gender and juvenile drug abuse: A general strain theory perspective. *Women & Criminal Justice, 24*: 22–43.

Grubb, A., & Turner, E. (2012). Attribution of blame in rape cases: A review of the impact of rape myth acceptance, gender role conformity and substance use on victim blaming. *Aggression and Violent Behvior, 17*(5), 443–452.

Grummett v. Rushen, 779 F.2d 491 (1985).

Guajardo, S. A. (2016). Women in policing: A longitudinal assessment of female officers in supervisory positions in the New York City Police Department. *Women & Criminal Justice, 26*(1), 20–36.

Guerino, P., Harrison, P. M., & Sabol, W. J. (2011). Prisoners in 2010. U.S. Department of Justice, Bureau of Justice Statistics. Retrieved from http://www.bjs.gov/content/pub/pdf/p10.pdf

Guevara, L., Herz, D., & Spohn, C. (2008). Race, gender and legal counsel: Differential outcomes in two juvenile courts. *Youth Violence and Juvenile Justice, 6*(1), 83–104.

Gyimah-Brempong, K., & Price, G. N. (2006). Crime and punishment: And skin hue too? *American Economic Association, 96*(2), 246–250.

Haarr, R. N., & Morash, M. (2013). The effect of rank on police women coping with discrimination and harassment. *Police Quarterly, 16*(4), 395–419.

Hagan, J. (1989). *Structural criminology*. New Brunswick, NJ: Rutgers University Press.

Hall, M., Golder, S., Conley, C. L., & Sawning, S. (2013). Designing programming and interventions for women in the criminal justice system. *American Journal of Criminal Justice, 38*, 27–50.

Hannan, L. (2014, January 10). Marissa Alexander can remain free on bond, but judge clearly upset with home-detention supervisor. *The Florida Times Union*. Retrieved from http://jacksonville.com/breaking-news/2014-01-10/story/marissa-alexander-can-remain-free-bond-judge-clearly-upset-home

Hardesty, J. L., Oswald, R. F., Khaw, L., & Fonseca, C. (2011). Lesbian/bisexual mothers and intimate partner violence: Help seeking in the context of social and legal vulnerability. *Violence Against Women, 17*(1), 28–46.

Harlow, P. (2013, March 17). Guilty verdict in Steubenville rape trial. CNN Transcripts. Retrieved from http://transcripts.cnn.com/TRANSCRIPTS/1303/17/rs.01.html

Harner, H. M., & Riley, S. (2013). The impact of incarceration on women's mental health: Responses from women in a maximum-security prison. *Qualitative Health Research, 23*(1), 26–42.

Harner, H. M., Wyant, B. R., & DaSilva, D. (2017). "Prison ain't free like everyone thinks": Financial stressors faced by incarcerated women. *Qualitative Health Research, 27*(5), 688–699.

Harrington, P., & Lonsway, K. A. (2004). Current barriers and future promise for women in policing. In B. R. Price & N. J. Sokoloff (Eds.), *The criminal justice system and women: Offenders, prisoners, victims and workers* (3rd ed., pp. 495–510). Boston, MA: McGraw Hill.

Harris, K. M., & Edlund, M. J. (2005). Self-medication of mental health problems: New evidence from a national survey. *Health Services Research, 40*(1), 117–134.

Harrison, J. (2012). Women in law enforcement: Subverting sexual harassment with social bonds. *Women & Criminal Justice, 22*(3), 226–238. doi: 10.1080/08974454.2012.687964

Harrison, P. M., & Beck, A. J. (2006). Prison and jail inmates at midyear 2005 [BJS Bulletin]. http://bjs.ojp.usdoj.gov/content/pub/pdf/pjim05.pdf

Hart, T. C., & Rennison, C. M. (2003). *Special report: National Crime Victimization Survey: Reporting crime to the police*. Bureau of Justice Statistics. Retrieved from http://bjs.ojp.usdoj.gov/index.cfm?ty=pbdetail&iid=1142

Hassouneh, D., & Glass, N. (2008). The influence of gender-role stereotyping on female same sex intimate partner violence. *Violence Against Women, 14*(3), 310–325.

Hastings, D. (1993, October 10). National spokeswoman for battered women: Is she telling the truth? California: Brenda Clubine's description of the events that precipitated killing of her husband doesn't match her murder trial testimony. Gov. Pete Wilson denied her bid for clemency, saying she has "repeatedly lied." *Los Angeles Times.* Retrieved from http://articles.latimes.com/1993-10-10/local/me-44254_1_brenda-clubine-sue-osthoff-murder-trial-testimony

Hauser, C. (2017, February 7). Florida woman whose "Stand Your Ground" defense was rejected is released. *New York Times.* Retrieved from https://www.nytimes.com/2017/02/07/us/marissa-alexander-released-stand-your-ground.html

Hawkesworth, M., Casey, K. J., Jenkins, K., & Kleeman, K. E. (2001). Legislating by and for women: A comparison of the 103rd and 104th Congresses. Center for American Women and Politics. Retrieved from www.capwip.org/readingroom/women_103_104.pdf

Haynes, D. F. (2004). Used, abused, arrested and deported: Extending immigration benefits to protect the victims of trafficking and to secure the prosecution of traffickers. *Human Rights Quarterly, 26*(2), 221–272.

Heidensohn, F. M. (1985). *Women and crime: The life of the female offender.* New York: New York University Press.

Heimer, K. (1996). Gender, interaction and delinquency: Testing a theory of differential social control. *Social Psychology Quarterly, 59,* 339–361.

Hennessey, M., Ford, J. D., Mahoney, K., Ko, S. J., & Siegfried, C. B. (2004). Trauma among girls in the juvenile justice system. National Child Traumatic Stress Network Juvenile Justice Working Group. Retrieved from http://www.nctsn.org/nctsn_assets/pdfs/edu_materials/trauma_among_girls_in_jjsys.pdf

Henry, L. (2013, September 17). A death needlessly sad, exorbitantly expensive. Retrieved from http://www.bakersfield.com/columnists/lois-henry-a-death-needlessly-sad-exorbitantly-expensive/article_2614a651-2f64-5c3d-b264-8f5238b4ca35.html

Hensley, J. (2017, March 3). Does Brandon Marshall become an exception to Ravens' domestic violence stance? *ESPN.* Retrieved from http://www.espn.com/blog/nflnation/post/_/id/232290/does-brandon-marshall-become-an-exception-to-ravens-domestic-violence-stance

Hersh, S. M. (2004, May 10). Torture at Abu Ghraib. *The New Yorker.* Retrieved from http://www.newyorker.com/archive/2004/05/10/040510fa_fact?currentPage=all

Hessy-Biber, S. N. (2004). *Feminist perspectives on social research.* New York: Oxford University Press.

Higdon, M. (2008). Queer teens and legislative bullies: The cruel and invidious discrimination behind heterosexist statutory rape laws. *UC Davis Law Review, 42,* 195.

Hillard, G. (2012, October 5). Domestic abuse victims get chance at freedom. *NPR.* Retrieved from http://www.prnewswire.com/news-releases/assaulted-betrayed-and-jailed-but-ultimately-triumphant-brenda-clubine-fights-for-abused-women-172869521.html

Hindelang, M. J., Gottfredson, M. R., & Garofalo, J. (1978). *Victims of personal crime: An empirical foundation for a theory of personal victimization.* Cambridge, MA: Ballinger.

Hines, D. A., Armstrong, J. L., Reed, K. P., & Cameron, A. Y. (2012). Gender differences in sexual assault victimization among college students. *Violence & Victims, 27*(6), 922–940.

Hirsch, A. E. (2001). Bringing back shame: Women, welfare reform and criminal justice. In P. J. Schram & B. Koons-Witt (Eds.), *Gendered (in)justice: Theory and practice in feminist criminology* (pp. 270–286). Long Grove, IL: Waveland Press.

Hirschel, D. (2008). *Domestic violence cases: What research shows about arrest and dual arrest rates.* National Institute of Justice. Retrieved from http://www.nij.gov/nij/publications/dv-dual-arrest-222679/dv-dual-arrest.pdf

Hirschel, D., Buzawa, E., Pattavina, A., Faggiani, D., & Reuland, M. (2007). *Explaining the prevalence, context and consequences of dual arrest in intimate partner cases.* U.S. Department of Justice. Retrieved from https://www.ncjrs.gov/pdffiles1/nij/grants/218355.pdf

Hirschi, T. (1969). *Causes of delinquency.* Berkeley: University of California Press.

Hockenberry, S., & Puzzanchera, C. (2017). *Juvenile Court Statistics 2014.* Pittsburgh: National Center for Juvenile Justice. Retrieved from http://www.ncjj.org/pdf/jcsreports/jcs2014.pdf.

Hollingsworth v. Perry, 133 S.Ct. 2652 (2013).

Holsinger, K., & Holsinger, A. M. (2005). Differential pathways to violence and self-injurious behavior: African American and White girls in the juvenile justice system. *Journal of Research in Crime & Delinquency, 42*(2), 211–242.

Howlett, S. L., & Collins, A. (2014). Vicarious traumatization: Risk and resilience among crisis support volunteers in a community organization. *South African Journal of Psychology, 44*(2), 180–190.

Hsu, H., & Wu, B. (2011). Female defendants and criminal courts in Taiwan: An observation study. *Asian Criminology, 6,* 1–14.

Huebner, A. J., & Betts, S. C. (2002). Exploring the utility of social control theory for youth development: Issues of attachment, involvement, and gender. *Youth & Society, 34*(2), 123–145.

Huebner, B. M., DeJong, C., & Cobbina, J. (2010). Women coming home: Long-term patterns of recidivism. *Justice Quarterly, 27*(2), 225–254.

Huebner, B. M., & Pleggenkuhle, B. (2015). Residential location, household composition, and recidivism: An analysis by gender. *Justice Quarterly, 32*(5), 818–844.

Huet, V., & Holttum, S. (2016). Art therapists with experience of mental distress: Implications for art therapy training and practice. *International Journal of Art Therapy, 21*(3), 95–103.

Huffington Post. (2013, November 25). Steubenville grand jury investigation: Four more school employees indicted. Retrieved from http://www.huffingtonpost.com/2013/11/25/steubenville-grand-jury-investigation_n_4337646.html?utm_hp_ref=steubenville-rape

Human Rights Campaign. (2014). A guide to state-level advocacy following enactment of the Matthew Shepard and James Byrd, Jr. Hate Crimes Prevention Act. Retrieved from http://hrc-assets.s3-website-us-east-1.amazonaws.com/files/assets/resources/HRC-Hate-Crimes-Guide-2014.pdf

Human Rights Watch. (2006). Custody and control: Conditions of confinement in New York's juvenile prisons for girls. Retrieved from http://www.hrw.org/sites/default/files/reports/us0906web-wcover.pdf

Human Rights Watch (2017a). Demogratic Republic of Congo. Retrieved from https://www.hrw.org/africa/democratic-republic-congo

Human Rights Watch (2017b). DR Congo: Ensure justice for killings in the Kasais. Retrieved from https://www.hrw.org/news/2017/02/24/dr-congo-ensure-justice-killings-kasais

Hunt, G., & Joe-Laidler, K. (2001). Situations of violence in the lives of girl gang members. *Health Care for Women International, 22,* 363–384.

Hurst, T. E., & Hurst, M. M. (1997). Gender differences in mediation of severe occupational stress among correctional officers. *American Journal of Criminal Justice, 22*(1), 121–137.

Ifrach, E, R., & Miller, A. (2016). Social action art therapy as an intervention for compassion fatigue. *The Arts in Psychotherapy, 50:* 34–39.

Inciardi, J. A., Lockwood, D., & Pottiger, A. E. (1993). *Women and crack-cocaine.* Toronto, Canada: Maxwell Macmillian.

Ingram, E. M. (2007). A comparison of help seeking between Latino and non-Latino victims of intimate partner violence. *Violence Against Women, 13*(2), 159–171.

Inter-American Commission on Human Rights. (2003). The situation of the rights of women in Ciudad Juárez, Mexico: The right to be free from violence and discrimination. Retrieved from http://www.cidh.org/annualrep/2002eng/chap.vi.juarez.htm

International Association of Chiefs of Police. (2010). Pregnancy & policing: A new policy makes them more compatible. Retrieved from http://www.aele.org/los2010kruger-pregnancy.pdf

International Labour Organization. (2005). *A global alliance against forced labour.* Geneva, Switzerland: United Nations.

Ireland, C., & Berg, B. (2008). Women in parole: Respect and rapport. *International Journal of Offender Therapy and Comparative Criminology, 52*(4), 474–491.

Irwin, J. (2008). (Dis)counted stories: Domestic violence and lesbians. *Qualitative Social Work, 7*(2), 199–215.

Jablonski, R. (January 8, 2015). Steubenville rape convict Trent Mays released from juvenile detention. Retrieved from http://www.cleveland.com/metro/index.ssf/2015/01/steubenville_rape_convict_tren.html

Jacobs, A. (2000). *Give 'em a fighting chance: The challenges for women offenders trying to succeed in the community.* Retrieved from http://www.wpaonline.org/pdf/WPA_FightingChance.pdf

James, D. J., & Glaze, L. E. (2006). *Bureau of Justice Statistics Special Report: Mental Health Problems of Prison and Jail Inmates* (NCJ No. 213600). Washington, DC: U.S. Department of Justice, Office of Justice Programs.

James, S. E., Herman, J. L., Rankin, S., Keisling, M., Mottet, L., & Anafi, M. (2016). *The Report of the 2015 U.S. Transgender Survey.* Washington, DC: National Center for Transgender Equality. Retrieved from http://www.transequality.org/sites/default/files/docs/usts/USTS%20Full%20Report%20-%20FINAL%201.6.17.pdf

Javdani, S., & Allen, N.E. (2016). An ecological model for intervention for juvenile justice-involved girls: Development and preliminary prospective evaluation. *Feminist Criminology, 11*(2), 135–162.

Jefferies, M. (2013, June 19). Nigella Lawson photos: Charles Saatchi reveals why he accepted police caution but makes no public apology. *The Mirror.* Retrieved from http://www.mirror.co.uk/news/uk-news/nigella-lawson-photos-charles-saatchi-1960358

Jensen, J. M., & Martinek, W. L. (2009). The effects of race and gender on the judicial ambitions of state trial court judges. *Political Research Quarterly, 62*(2), 379–392.

Jo, Y., & Bouffard, L. (2014). Stability of self-control and gender. *Journal of Criminal Justice, 42*(4), 356–365.

Joe, K., & Chesney-Lind, M. (1995). Just every mother's angel: An analysis of gender and ethnic variation in youth gang membership. *Gender and Society, 9*(4), 408–430.

Johnson, H. (2004). Drugs and crime: A study of incarcerated female offenders. *Australian Institute of Criminology, 63.* Retrieved from http://www.aic.gov.au/documents/E/B/8/%7BEB8A400C-E611-42BF-9B9F-B58E7C5A0694%7DRPP63.pdf

Johnson, I. M. (2007). Victims' perceptions of police response to domestic violence incidents. *Journal of Criminal Justice, 35,* 498–510.

Johnson, J. E., Esposito-Smythers, C., Miranda, R., Rizzo, C. J., Justus, A. N., & Clum, G. (2011). Gender, social support and depression in criminal justice-involved adolescents. *International Journal of Offender Therapy and Comparative Criminology, 55*(7), 1096–1109.

Johnson, K., Scott, J., Rughita, B., Kisielewski, M., Asher, J., Ong, R., & Lawry, L. (2010). Association of sexual violence and human rights violations with physical and mental health in territories of the Eastern Democratic Republic of the Congo. *Journal of the American Medical Aossociation. 304*(5), 553–562.

Jones-Brown, D. (2007). Forever the symbolic assailant: The more things change, the more they stay the same. *Criminology & Public Policy, 6*(1), 103–121.

Jordan v. Gardner, 986 F.2d 1137 (1992).

Just Detention International (JDI). (2009). Incarcerated youth at extreme risk of sexual abuse. Retrieved from http://www.justdetention.org/en/factsheets/jdifactsheetyouth.pdf

Justice Research and Statistics Association (JRSA). (n.d.). Background and status of incident-based reporting and NIBRS. Retrieved from http://www.jrsa.org/ibrrc/background-status/nibrs_states.shtml

Kaeble, D., & Bonczar, T. P. (2016). Probation and Parole in the United States. U.S. Department of Justice, Office of Justice Programs, Bureau of Justice Statistics. Retrieved from https://www.bjs.gov/content/pub/pdf/ppus15.pdf

Karakurt, G., & Silver, K. E. (2013). Emotional abuse in intimate relationships: The role of gender and age. *Violence and Victims, 28*(5), 804–821.

Karandikar, S., Gezinski, L. B., & Meshelemiah, J. C. A. (2013). A qualitative examination of women involved in prostitution in Mumbai, India: The role of family and acquaintances. *International Social Work, 56*(4), 496–515.

Kardam, N. (2005). The dynamics of honor killings in Turkey: Prospects for action. United Nations Development Programme. Retrieved from http://www.unfpa.org/public/publications/pid/383

Katz, J., & Moore, J. (2013). Bystander education training for campus sexual assault prevention: An initial meta-analysis. *Violence and Victims, 28*(6), 1054–1067.

Katz, C. M., & Spohn, C. (1995). The effect of race and gender and bail outcomes: A test of an interactive model. *American Journal of Criminal Justice, 19*, 161–184.

Kaukinen, C. (2004). Status compatibility, physical violence, and emotional abuse in intimate relationships. *Journal of Marriage and Family, 66*(2), 452–471.

Kaukinen, C., & DeMaris, A. (2009). Sexual assault and current mental health: The role of help-seeking and police response. *Violence Against Women, 15*(11), 1331–1357.

Kay, F. M., Alarie, S., & Adjei, J. (2013). Leaving private practice: How organizational context, time, pressures, and structural inflexibilities share departures from private law practice. *Indiana Journal of Global Legal Studies, 20*: 1223–1260.

KBOI News Staff (2016, September 1). Charges dropped against one teen in alleged Dietrich sexual assault case. Retrieved from http://kboi2.com/news/local/charges-dropped-against-teen-in-alleged-dietrich-sexual-assault-case

Kelleher, C., & McGilloway, S. (2009). "Nobody ever chooses this . . .": A qualitative study of service providers working in the sexual violence sector—Key issues and challenges. *Health and Social Care in the Community, 17*(3), 295–303.

Kellermann, A. L., & Mercy, J. A. (1992). Men, women, and murder: Gender specific differences in rates of fatal violence and victimization. *The Journal of Trauma, 33*(1), 1–5.

Kernsmith, P. (2005). Exerting power or striking back: A gendered comparison of motivations for domestic violence perpetration. *Violence and Victims, 20*, 173–185.

Kiefer, M. (2015, April 13). Jodi Arias sentence: Natural life, no chance of release. Retrieved from www.azcentral.com/story/news/local/mesa/2015/04/13/jodi-arias-faces0life-sentence-to-day-murder-travis-alexander/25608085/

Kilpatrick, D. G., Resnick, H. S., Ruggiero, K. J., Conoscenti, L. M., & McCauley, J. (2007). *Drug-facilitated, incapacitated, and forcible rape: A national study.* Charleston, SC: Medical University of South Carolina, National Crime Victims Research & Treatment Center.

Kim, B., Gerber, J., Henderson, C., & Kim, Y. (2012). Applicability of general power-control theory to prosocial and antisocial risk taking behaviors among women in South Korea. *The Prison Journal, 92*(1), 125–150.

Kim B., Hawkins P. M. (2013). Who's getting cited: Representation of women and non-white scholars in major American criminology and criminal justice journals between 1986-2005. *International Journal of Criminology and Sociology, 2*, 306–321.

Kim, B., & Merlo, A. (2012). In her own voice: Presentations on women, crime and criminal justice at American Society of Criminology meetings from 1999-2008. *Women and Criminal Justice, 22*(1), 66–88.

Kirkwood, M. K., & Cecil, D. K. (2001). Marital rape: A student assessment of rape laws and the marital exemption. *Violence Against Women, 7*(11), 1234–1253.

Kitty, J. M. (2012). "It's like they don't want you to get better": Psy control of women in the carceral context. *Feminism & Psychology, 22*(2), 162–182.

Klein, A. R. (2004). *The criminal justice response to domestic violence.* Belmont, CA: Wadsworth Thomson Learning.

Knoll, C., & Sickmund, M. (2010). *Delinquency cases in juvenile court, 2007.* Office of Justice Programs. Office of Juvenile Justice and Delinquency Prevention. Retrieved from http://www.ncjrs.gov/pdffiles1/ojjdp/230168.pdf

Knoll, C., & Sickmund, M. (2012). *Delinquency cases in juvenile court, 2009.* Office of Juvenile Justice and Delinquency Prevention. Retrieved from http://www.ojjdp.gov/pubs/239081.pdf

Koeppel, M. D. H. (2012, November 28). Gender sentencing of rural property offenders in Iowa. *Criminal Justice Policy Review.* Advance online publication. doi:10.1177/0887403412465308

Kohsin Wang, S., & Rowley, E. (2007). *Rape: How women, the community and the health sector respond.* Geneva, Switzerland: World Health Organization/Sexual Violence Research Initiative

Kolb, K. H. (2011). Sympathy work: Identity and emotion management among victim-advocates and counselors. *Qualitative Sociology, 34*, 101–119.

Konradi, A. (2016). Can justice be served on campus? An examination of due process and victim protection policies in the campus adjudication of sexual assault in Maryland. *Humanity & Society,* 1-32. DOI: 10.1177/0160597616651657.

Koons-Witt, B. (2006). Decision to incarcerate before and after the introduction of sentencing guidelines. *Criminology, 40*(2), 297–328.

Koons-Witt, B. A., Sevigny, E. L., Burrow, J. D., & Hester, R. (2012). Gender and sentencing outcomes in South Carolina: Examining the interactions with race, age, and offense type. *Criminal Justice Police Review, 10*, 1–26.

Koren, M. (2016, June 17). Why the Stanford judge gave Brock Turner six months. *The Atlantic.* Retrieved from https://www.theatlantic.com/news/archive/2016/06/stanford-rape-case-judge/487415/

Kraaij, V., Arensman, E., Garnefski, N., & Kremers, I. (2007). The role of cognitive coping in female victims of stalking. *Journal of Interpersonal Violence, 22*(12), 1603–1612.

Krouse, P. (2013, July 26). Ariel Castro agrees to plea deal: Life in prison, no parole, plus 1,000 years. Retrieved from http://www.cleveland.com/metro/index.ssf/2013/07/ariel_castro_agrees_to_plea_de.html

Kruttschnitt, C., & Savolianen, J. (2009). Ages of chivalry, places of paternalism: Gender and criminal sentencing in Finland. *European Journal of Criminology, 6*(3), 225–247.

Kuriakose, D. (2013, October 9). Malala Yousafzai: From blogger to Nobel Peace Prize nominee—Timeline. *The Guardian*. Retrieved from http://www.theguardian.com/world/interactive/2013/oct/09/malala-yousafzai-timeline

Kurshan, N. (2000). *Women and imprisonment in the United States: History and current reality*. Retrieved from http://www.prison-activist.org/archive/women/women-and-imprisonment.html

Kurtz, D. L., Linnemann, T., & Williams, L. S. (2012). Reinventing the matron: The continued importance of gendered images and division of labor in modern policing. *Women & Criminal Justice, 22*(3), 239–263.

Kyckelhahn, T., Beck, A. J., & Cohen, T. H. (2009). Characteristics of suspected human trafficking incidents. Retrieved from http://www.ojp.usdoj.gov/bjs/abstract/cshti08.htm

La Ganga, M. L. (2017, February 24). Idaho judge rules attack on high school football player was "not a rape' or racist." *The Guardian*. Retrieved from https://www.theguardian.com/us-news/2017/feb/24/idaho-football-player-rape-case-coat-hanger-light-sentence

LaGrange, T. C., & Silverman, R. A. (1999). Low self-control and opportunity: Testing the general theory of crime as an explanation of gender differences in delinquency. *Criminology, 37*(1), 41–72.

Lambert, E. G., Hogan, N. L., Altheimer, I., & Wareham, J. (2010). The effects of different aspects of supervision among female and male correctional staff: A preliminary study. *Criminal Justice Review, 35*, 492–513. doi: 10.1177/0734016810372068

Lambert, E. G., Paoline, E. A. Hogan, N. L., & Baker, D. N. (2007). Gender similarities and differences in correctional staff work attitudes and perceptions of the work environment. *Western Criminology Review, 8*(1), 16–31.

Lambert, E. G., Smith, B., & Geistman, J. (2013). Do men and women differ in the perceptions of stalking: An exploratory study among college students. *Violence and Victims, 28*(2), 195–209.

Lane, J., Gover, A. R., & Dahod, S. (2009). Fear of violent crime among men and women on campus: The impact of perceived risk and fear of sexual assault. *Violence and Victims, 24*(2), 172–192.

Langenderfer-Magruder, L., Walls, N. E., Kattari, S. K., Whitfield, D. L., & Ramos, D. (2016). Sexual victimization and subsequent police reporting by gender identity among lesbian, gay, bisexual, transgendered, and queer adults. *Violence and Victims, 31*(2), 320–331.

Langhinrichsen-Rohling, J., & Monson, C. M. (1998). Marital rape: Is the crime taken seriously without co-occurring physical abuse? *Journal of Family Violence, 13*(4), 433–443.

Langton, L. (2010). Crime data brief: Women in law enforcement. Bureau of Justice Statistics. Retrieved from http://bjs.ojp.usdoj.gov/content/pub/pdf/wle8708.pdf

LaVigne, N. G., Brooks, L. E., & Shollenberger, T. L. (2009). Women on the outside: Understanding the experiences of female prisoners returning to Houston, Texas. Urban Institute Justice Policy Center. Retrieved from http://www.urban.org/sites/default/files/publication/30401/411902-Women-on-the-Outside-Understanding-the-Experiences-of-Female-Prisoners-Returning-to-Houston-Texas.PDF

Law Library of Congress (n.d.). Women lawyers and state bar admission. The Library of Congress. Retrieved from http://memory.loc.gov/ammem/awhhtml/awlaw3/women_lawyers.html

Lawrence v. Texas, 539 U.S. 558 (2003).

Learner, S. (2012). Scarred for life. *Nursing Standard, 26*(18), 20–21.

LeBlanc, P. (2017, June 16). The text messages that led up to teen's suicide. CNN. Retrieved from www.cnn.com/2017/06/08/us/text-message-suicide-michelle-carter-conrad-roy/index.html

Lee, J., Pomeroy, E. C., Yoo, S. K., & Rheinboldt, K. T. (2005). Attitudes toward rape: A comparison between Asian and Caucasian college students. *Violence Against Women, 11*(2), 177–196.

Lee, M. Y., & Law, P. F. M. (2001). Perception of sexual violence against women in Asian American communities. *Journal of Ethnic and Cultural Diversity in Social Work, 10*(2), 3–25.

Lee, R. K. (1998). Romantic and electronic stalking in a college context. *William and Mary Journal of Women and the Law, 4*, 373–466.

Legal Action Center. (2011). State TANF options drug felon ban. Retrieved from http://www.lac.org/doc_library/lac/publications/HIRE_Network_State_TANF_Options_Drug_Felony_Ban.pdf

Leiber, M., Brubaker, S., & Fox, K. (2009). A closer look at the individual and joint effects of gender and race in juvenile justice decision making. *Feminist Criminology, 4*, 333–358.

Leonard, E. B. (1982). *Women, crime, and society.* New York: Longman.

Lerner, M. J. (1980). *The belief in a just world: A fundamental delusion.* New York: Plenum Press.

Lersch, K. M., & Bazley, T. (2012). A paler shade of blue? Women and the police subculture. In R. Muraskin (Ed.), *Women and justice: It's a crime* (5th ed., pp. 514–526). Upper Saddle River, NJ: Prentice-Hall.

Leung, R. (2009, February 11). Abuse of Iraqi POWs by GIs probed. *60 Minutes*. CBS News. Retrieved from http://www.cbsnews.com/stories/2004/04/27/60ii/main614063.shtml

Liang, B., Lu, H., & Taylor, M. (2009). Female drug abusers, narcotic offenders and legal punishment in China. *Journal of Criminal Justice, 37*, 133–141.

Like-Haislip, T. Z., & Miofsky, K. (2011). Race, ethnicity, gender and violent victimization. *Race and Justice, 1*(3), 254–276.

Lindgren, J., Stanglin, D., & Alcindor, Y. (2013, August 7). Ariel Castro's house of horror demolished in Cleveland. *USA Today*. Retrieved from http://www.usatoday.com/story/news/nation/2013/08/07/ariel-castro-cleveland-house-abduction/2626855/

Lipari, R. N., Cook, P. J., Rock, L., & Matos, K. (2008). 2006 gender relations survey of active duty members (DMDC Report No. 2007–022). Arlington, VA: Defense Manpower Data Center.

Lipsky, S., Caetano, R., Field, C. A., & Larkin, G. L. (2006). The role of intimate partner violence, race and ethnicity in help-seeking behaviors. *Ethnicity and Health, 11*(1), 81–100.

Littleton, H., Breitkopf, C. R., & Berenson, A. (2008). Beyond the campus unacknowledged rape among low-income women. *Violence Against Women, 14*(3), 269–286.

Logan, T. K., Evans, L., Stevenson, E., & Jordan, C. E. (2005). Barriers to services for rural and urban survivors of rape. *Journal of Interpersonal Violence, 20*(5), 591–616.

Lombroso, C. (2006). *Criminal man* (M. Gibson & N. Hahn Rafter, Trans.). Durham, NC: Duke University Press.

Lombroso, C., & Ferrero, W. (1895). *The female offender.* New York: Barnes.

Long, L., & Ullman, S. E. (2013). The impact of multiple traumatic victimization on disclosure and coping mechanisms for Black women. *Feminist Criminology, 8*(4), 295–319.

Lonsway, K. A., & Fitzgerald, L. F. (1994). Rape myths in review. *Psychology of Women Quarterly, 18*(2), 133–164.

Lonsway, K. A., Paynich, R., & Hall, J. N. (2013). Sexual harassment in law enforcement: Incidence, impact, and perception. *Police Quarterly, 16*(2), 177–210.

Lonsway, K., Carrington, S., Aguirre, P., Wood, M., Moore, M., Harrington, P., . . . Spillar, K. (2002). *Equality denied: The status of women in policing: 2001.* The National Center for Women and Policing. Retrieved from http://www.womenandpo licing.org/PDF/2002_Status_Report.pdf

Lonsway, K., Wood, M., Fickling, M., De Leon, A., Moore, M., Harrington, P., . . . Spillar, K. (2002). Men, women and police excessive force: A tale of two genders: A content analysis of civil liability cases, sustained allegations and citizen complaints. The National Center for Women and Policing. Retrieved from http://www.womenandpolicing.org/PDF/2002_Excessive_Force.pdf

Lopez, A. (2012). Scott signs "historic" anti-shackling bill for incarcerated pregnant women. *Florida Independent.* Retrieved from http://floridaindependent.com/74661/rick-scott-anti-shackling-bill

Lopez, A. J. (2007). Expert: Victims' path rockier than celebrities'. *Rocky Mountain News.* Retrieved from http://therocky.com/news/2007/mar/15/expert-victims-path-rockier-than-celebrities/

Los Angeles Almanac. (2012). LAPD had the nation's first police woman. Retrieved from http://www.laalmanac.com/crime/cr73b.htm

Lowe, N. C., May, D. C., & Elrod, P. (2008). Theoretical predictors of delinquency among public school students in a mid-southern state: The roles of context and gender. *Youth Violence and Juvenile Justice, 6*(4), 343–362.

Lyons, C. (2006, April 20). "Media circus" atmosphere aggravated case. Retrieved from http://www.hampton.lib.nh.us/hampton/biog/pamsmart/equinox2006_4.htm

Ma, F. (2013, June 24). Domestic abse victim Glenda Virgil is freed. *SFGate.* Retrieved from http://www.sfgate.com/opinion/open-forum/article/Domestic-abuse-victim-Glenda-Virgil-is-freed-4619772.php

MacIntosh, J. (2011, August 9). "Rack" and ruin: Stripper goes on "crime spree" with brothers. *New York Post.* Retrieved from http://www.nypost.com/p/news/national/vixen_faces_rack_ruin_q5hnBQ1AlZJrIImUY4CHCP

Maggard. S. R., Higgins, J. L., & Chappell, A. T. (2013). Pre-dispositional juvenile detention: An analysis of race, gender and intersectionality. *Journal of Crime and Justice, 36*(1), 67–86.

Maguire, B. (1988). Image vs. reality: An analysis of prime-time television crime and police programs. *Journal of Crime and Justice, 11*(1), 165–188.

Maher, L. (1996). Hidden in the light: Occupational norms among crack-using street level sex workers. *Journal of Drug Issues, 26,* 143–173.

Maher, L. (2004a). A reserve army: Women and the drug market. In B. Price & N. Sokoloff (Eds.), *The criminal justice system and women: Offenders, prisoners, victims and workers* (3rd ed., pp. 127–146). New York, NY: McGraw-Hill.

Maher L. (2004b). "Hooked on heroin: Drugs and drifters in a globalized world." *Addiction, 99,* 929–930.

Mahoney, J. (2013, May 9). Death penalty possible for alleged Cleveland kidnapper, prosecutor says. *The Globe and Mail.* Retrieved from http://web.archive.org/web/20130509221120/http://www .theglobeandmail.com/news/world/kidnap-suspect-ariel-castro-due-in-cleveland-court/article11810618/?cmpid=rss1

Mahoney, J. L., Cairns, B. D., & Farmer, T. W. (2003). Promoting interpersonal competence and educational success through extracurricular activity participation. *Journal of Educational Psychology, 95*(2), 409–418.

Maier, S. L. (2008a). "I have heard terrible stories . . ": Rape victim advocates' perceptions of the revictimization of rape victims by the police and medical system. *Violence Against Women, 14*(7), 786–808.

Maier, S. L. (2008b). Rape victim advocates' perception of the influence of race and ethnicity on victims' responses to rape. *Journal of Ethnicity and Criminal Justice, 6*(4), 295–326.

Maier, S. L. (2011). "We belong to them": The costs of funding for rape crisis centers. *Violence Against Women, 17*(11), 1383–1408.

Mallicoat, S. L. (2006, August). *Mary Magdalene project: Kester program evaluation.* Paper presented at the Program Committee of the Mary Magdalene Project, Van Nuys, CA.

Mallicoat, S. L. (2007). Gendered justice: Attributional differences between males and females in the juvenile courts. *Feminist Criminology, 2*(1), 4–30.

Mallicoat, S. L. (2011). Lives in transition: A needs assessment of women exiting from prostitution. In R. Muraskin (Ed.), *It's a crime: Women and justice* (4th ed., pp. 241–255). Upper Saddle River, NJ: Prentice-Hall.

Mallicoat, S. L., Marquez, S. A., & Rosenbaum, J. L. (2007). Guiding philosophies for rape crisis centers. In R. Muraskin (Ed.), *It's a crime: Women and criminal justice* (4th ed., pp. 217–225). Upper Saddle River, NJ: Prentice-Hall.

Mandal, S. (2014). The impossibility of marital rape: Contestations around marriage, sex, violence and the law in contemporary India. *Australia Feminist Studies, 29*(81), 255–272.

Mann, M., Menih, H., & Smith, C. (2014). There is 'hope for you yet': The female drug offender in sentencing discourse. *Australian & New Zealand Journal of Criminology, 47*(3), 355–373.

Manning, J. E., Brudnick, I. A., & Shogan, C. J. (2015). Women in Congress: Historical overview, tables, and discussion. Congressional Research Service. Retrieved from https://fas.org/sgp/crs/misc/R43244.pdf

Marcos, C. (2016, November 17). 115th Congress will be the most racially diverse in history. *The Hill*. Retrieved from thehill.com/homenews/house/306480-115th-congress-will-be0the-most-racially-diverse-in-history

Marcotte, A. (2014, September 11). Ray Rice defenders have found their argument: He's a victim too. *Slate*. Retrieved from http://www.slate.com/blogs/xx_factor/2014/09/11/ray_rice_and_janay_rice_do_not_share_the_blame_at_al.html

Marks, P. (1993, November 16). Buttafuoco is sentenced to 6 months for rape. *The New York Times*. http://www.nytimes.com/1993/11/16/nyregion/buttafuoco-is-sentenced-to-6-months-for-rape.html

Marshall, T., Simpson S., & Stevens, A. (2001). Use of health services by prison inmates: Comparisons with the community. *Journal of Epidemiology and Community Health, 55*(5), 364–365.

Martin, E. K., Taft, C. T., & Resick, P. A. (2007). A review of marital rape. *Aggression and Violent Behavior, 12*(3), 329–347.

Martin, L. (1991). *A report on the glass ceiling commission*. Washington, DC: U.S. Department of Labor.

Maruschak, L., & Parks, E. R. (2012). Probation and parole in the United States, 2011. U.S. Department of Justice, Bureau of Justice Statistics. Retrieved from http://www.bjs.gov/content/pub/pdf/ppus11.pdf

Mary Katherine Schmitz. (2014). The Biography.com website. Retrieved from http://www.biography.com/people/mary-kay-letourneau-9542379.

Maslin, J. (1987, September 17). Fatal attraction [Review]. Retrieved from http://www.nytimes.com/movie/review?res=9B0DE-3DE163CF93BA2575AC0A961948260

Mastony, C. (2010). Was Chicago home to the country's 1st female cop? Researcher uncovers the story of Sgt. Marie Owens. *Chicago Tribune*. Retrieved from http://articles.chicagotribune.com/2010-09-01/news/ct-met-first-police-woman-20100901_1_female-officer-police-officer-female-cop

Mastony, C. (2012, May 23). $4.1 million settlement set for pregnant inmates who said they were shackled before giving birth. *Chicago Tribune*. Retrieved from http://articles.chicagotribune.com/2012-05-23/news/ct-met-shackled-pregnant-women-20120523_1_pregnant-women-pregnant-inmates-shackles-and-belly-chains

Matsueda, R. (1992). Reflected appraisals, parental labeling and delinquency: Specifying a symbolic interactionist theory. *American Journal of Sociology, 97*(6), 1577.

Matthews, C., Monk-Turner, E., & Sumter, M. (2010). Promotional opportunities: How women in corrections perceive their chances for advancement at work. *Gender Issues, 27*, 53–66.

Mauer, M. (2013). The changing racial dynamics of women's incarceration. The Sentencing Project. Retrieved from http://www.sentencingproject.org/doc/advocacy/Changing%20Racial%20Dynamics%20Webinar%20Slides.pdf

Mayell, H. (2002, February 12). Thousands of women killed for family honor. *National Geographic News, 12*.

McAtee, J (2017, March 15). Charges against LA Rams DE Ethan Westbrooks dropped in domestic violence case. SBNation. Retrieved at http://www.turfshowtimes.com/2017/3/15/14937898/la-rams-de-ethan-westbrooks-charges-dropped-domestic-violence-case

McCall, M. (2007). Structuring gender's impact: Judicial voting across criminal justice cases. *American Politics Research, 36*(2), 264–296.

McCann, A. (2014, August 28). The NFL's uneven history of punishing domestic violence. FiveThirtyEight. Retrieved from https://fivethirtyeight.com/features/nfl-domestic-violence-policy-suspensions/

McCartan, L. M., & Gunnison, E. (2010). Individual and relationship factors that differentiate female offenders with and without a sexual abuse history. *Journal of Interpersonal Violence, 25*(8), 1449–1469.

McCoy, L. A., & Miller, H. A. (2013). Comparing gender across risk and recidivism in nonviolent offenders. *Women & Criminal Justice, 23*(2), 143–162.

McGrath, S. A., Johnson, M., & Miller, M. H. (2012). The social ecological challenges of rural victim advocacy: An exploratory study. *Journal of Community Psychology, 40*(5), 588–606.

McKnight, L. R., & Loper, A. B. (2002). The effect of risk and resilience factors on the prediction of delinquency in adolescent girls. *School Psychology International, 23*(2), 186–198.

Mears, D. P., Cochran, J. C., & Bales, W. D. (2012). Gender differences in the effects of prison on recidivism. *Journal of Criminal Justice, 40*, 370–378.

Melton, H. C. (2007). Predicting the occurrence of stalking in relationships characterized by domestic violence. *Journal of Interpersonal Violence, 22*(1), 3–25.

Mendelsohn, B. (1956). A new branch of bio-psychological science: La Victimology. *Revue Internationale de Criminologie et de Police Technique 10*, 782–789.

Merolla, D. (2008). The war on drugs and the gender gap in arrests: A critical perspective. *Critical Sociology, 34*(2), 355–270.

Merton, R. K. (1938). Social structure and anomie. *American Sociological Review, 3*(5), 672–682.

Messina, N., Grella, C. E., Cartier, J., & Torres, S. (2010). A randomized experimental study of gender-responsive substance abuse treatment for women in prison. *Journal of Substance Abuse Treatment, 39*, 97–107.

Meyer, C. L., & Oberman, M. (2001). *Mothers who kill their children: Understanding the acts of moms from Susan Smith to the "Prom mom."* New York: University Press.

Millar, G., Stermac, L., & Addison, M. (2002). Immediate and delayed treatment seeking among adult sexual assault victims. *Women & Health, 35*(1), 53–64.

Miller, J. (1994). Race, gender and juvenile justice: An examination of disposition decision-making for delinquent girls. In M. Schwartz & D. Milovanivoc (Eds.), *Race, gender and class in criminology: The intersection* (pp. 219–246). New York: Garland.

Miller, J. (1998a). Gender and victimization risk among young women in gangs. *Journal of Research in Crime and Delinquency, 35,* 429–453.

Miller, J. (1998b). Up it up: Gender and the accomplishment of street robbery. *Criminology, 36*(1), 37–66.

Miller, J. (2000). *One of the guys: Girls, gangs and gender.* Oxford, UK: Oxford University Press.

Miller, L. J. (2003). Denial of pregnancy. In M. G. Spinelli (Ed.), *Infanticide: Psychosocial and legal perspectives on mothers who kill* (pp. 81–104). Washington, DC: American Psychiatric.

Miller, M. E. (2016, June 6). "A steep price to pay for 20 minutes of action": Dad defends Stanford sex offender. *Washington Post.* Retrieved from https://www.washingtonpost.com/news/morning-mix/wp/2016/06/06/a-steep-price-to-pay-for-20-minutes-of-action-dad-defends-stanford-sex-offender/?utm_term=.448ccd755a77

Miller, S. (2005). *Victims as offenders: The paradox of women's violence in relationships.* New Brunswick, NJ: Rutgers University Press.

Miller, S., Loeber, R., & Hipwell, A. (2009). Peer deviance, parenting and disruptive behavior among young girls. *Journal of Abnormal Child Psychology, 37*(2), 139–152.

Miller, S. L., & Meloy, M. L. (2006). Women's use of force: Voices of women arrested for domestic violence. *Violence Against Women, 12*(1), 89–115.

Miller, S. L., & Peterson, E. S. L. (2007). The impact of law enforcement policies on victims of intimate partner violence. In R. Muraskin (Ed.), *It's a crime* (4th ed., Chapt. 14). Upper Saddle River, NJ: Pearson Prentice Hall.

Ministry of Labour in cooperation with the Ministry of Justice and the Ministry of Health and Social Affairs, Government of Sweden. (1998). *Fact sheet.* Stockholm, Sweden: Secretariat for Information and Communication, Ministry of Labour.

Mintz, Z. (2013, June 10). Witch hunts in Papua New Guinea on the rise, killings connected to economic growth and jealousy. *International Business Times.* Retrieved from http://www.ibtimes.com/witch-hunts-papua-new-guinea-rise-killings-connected-economic-growth-jealousy-1298363

Moe, A. M. (2007). Silenced voices and structured survival: Battered women's help seeking. *Violence Against Women, 13*(7), 676–699.

Moe, A. M. (2009). Battered women, children, and the end of abusive relationships. *Afilia: Journal of Women and Social Work, 24*(3), 244–256.

Moffitt, T. E., Caspi, A., Rutter, M., & Silva, P. A. (2001). *Sex differences in antisocial behavior: Conduct disorder, delinquency and violence in the Dunedin Longitudinal Study.* New York: Cambridge University Press.

Molidor, C. E. (1996). Female gang members: A profile of aggression and victimization. *Social Work, 41*(3), 251–257.

Moon, B., & Morash, M. (2017). Gender and general strain theory: A comparison of strains, mediating, and moderating effects explaining three types of delinquency. *Youth & Society, 49*(4), 484–504.

Moore, J. W. (1991). *Going down to the barrio: Homeboys and homegirls in change.* Philadelphia: Temple University Press.

Moore, J., & Terrett, C. P. (1998). *Highlights of the 1996 National Youth Gang Survey. Fact sheet.* Washington, DC: U.S. Department of Justice, Office of Justice Programs, Office of Juvenile Justice and Delinquency Prevention.

Morash, M., & Haarr, R. N. (2012). Doing, redoing and undoing gender: Variation in gender identities of women working as police officers. *Feminist Criminology, 7*(1), 3–23.

Morash, M., Stevens, T., & Yingling, J. (2014). Focus on the family: Juvenile court responses to girls and their caretakers. *Feminist Criminology, 9*(4), 298–322.

Morello, K. (1986). *The invisible bar: The woman lawyer in America 1638 to the present.* New York: Random House.

Morgan, K. D. (2013). Issues in female inmate health: Results from a southeastern state. *Women & Criminal Justice, 23,* 121–142.

Moses, M. (1995). Girl Scouts Beyond Bars—A synergistic solution for children of incarcerated parents. *Corrections Today, 57*(7), 124–127.

Munge, B. A., Pomerantz, A. M., Pettibone, J. C., & Falconer, J. W. (2007). The influence of length of marriage and fidelity status on perception of marital rape. *Journal of Interpersonal Violence, 22*(10), 1332–1339.

Mungin, L., & Alsup, D. (2013, September 4). Cleveland kidnapper Ariel Castro dead: Commits suicide in prison. CNN Justice. Retrieved from http://www.cnn.com/2013/09/04/justice/ariel-castro-cleveland-kidnapper-death/

Murtha, T. (2013, March 19). From Big Dan's to Steubenville: A generation later, media coverage of rape still awful. RH Reality Check. Retrieved from http://rhrealitycheck.org/article/2013/03/19/from-big-dans-to-steubenville-a-generation-later-media-coverage-of-rape-still-awful/

Mustaine, E. E., & Tewksbury, R. (2002). Sexual assault of college women: A feminist interpretation of a routine activities analysis. *Criminal Justice Review, 27*(1), 89–123.

Myers, R. K., Nelson, D. B., & Forke, C. M. (2016). Occurrence of stalking behaviors among female and male undergraduate students. *Journal of College Student Development, 57*(2), 213–218.

Nagel, I., & Hagan, J. (1983). Gender and crime: Offense patterns and criminal court sanctions. In N. Morris and M. Tonry (Eds.), *Crime and justice* (Vol. 4, pp. 91–144). Chicago, IL: University of Chicago Press.

Nagel, I. H., & Johnson, B. L. (2004). The role of gender in a structured sentencing system: Equal treatment, policy choices and the sentencing of female offenders. In P. Schram & B. Koons-Witt (Eds.), *Gendered (in)justice: Theory and practice in feminist criminology.* Long Grove, IL: Waveland Press.

Nanivazo, M. (2012, May 24). Sexual violence in the Democratic Republic of the Congo. United Nations University. Retrieved from https://unu.edu/publications/articles/sexual-violence-in-the-democratic-republic-of-the-congo.html

Nash, S. T. (2006). Through Black eyes: African American women's constructions of their experiences with intimate male partner violence. *Violence Against Women, 11*(11), 1420–1440.

National Asian Women's Health Organization. (2002). *Silent epidemic: A survey of violence among young Asian American women.* Retrieved from http://www.nawho.org/pubs/NAWHO SilentEpidemic.pdf

National Association for Law Placement. (2010). *Law firm diversity among associates erodes in 2010.* National Association for Law Placement. Retrieved from http://www.nalp.org/uploads/PressReleases/10NALPWomenMinoritiesPressRel.pdf

National Association for Law Placement (NALP). (2015). *Women, black/African-American associates lose ground at major U.S. law firms.* Retrieved from www.nalp.org/lawfirmdiversity_nov2015

National Association of Women Lawyers and The NAWL Foundation. (2009). *Report of the Fourth Annual National Survey on Retention and Promotion of Women in Law Firms.* Retrieved from http://nawl.timberlakepublishing.com/files/2009%20Survey% 20Report%20FINAL.pdf

National Association of Women Lawyers and The NAWL Foundation. (2010). *Report of the Fifth Annual National Survey on Retention and Promotion of Women in Law Firms.* Retrieved from http://nawl.timberlakepublishing.com/files/NAWL%202010%20Final(1).pdf

National Coalition Against Domestic Violence. (n.d.). Mission statement and purpose. Retrieved from www.ncadv.org

National Coalition Against Domestic Violence. (2006). Comparison of VAWA 1994, VAWA 2000 and VAWA 2005 Reauthorization Bill. Retrieved from http://www.ncadv.org/files/VAWA_94_00_05.pdf

National Conference of State Legislatures. (2017). Women in state legislatures for 2017. Retrieved from www.ncsl.org/legislators-staff/legislators/womens-legislative-network/women-in-state-legislatures-for-2017.aspx

National Drug Intelligence Center. (n.d.). Drug-facilitated sexual assault fast facts. Retrieved from http://www.justice.gov/archive/ndic/pubs8/8872/index.htm#Top

National Incident Based Reporting System (NIBRS). (2015). Summary of NIBRS 2015. Retrieved from https://ucr.fbi.gov/nibrs/2015/resource-pages/nibrs-2015_summary_final-1.pdf

National Incident Based Reporting System. (2016a). Summary of NIBRS, 2015. Retrieved from https://ucr.fbi.gov/nibrs/2015/resource-pages/nibrs-2015_summary_final-1.pdf

National Incident Based Reporting System. (2016b). Arrestees, Sex by Arrest Offense Category, 2015. Retrieved from https://ucr.fbi.gov/nibrs/2015/tables/data-tables

National Public Radio. (n.d.). Timeline: America's war on drugs. Retrieved from http://www.npr.org/templates/story/story.php?storyId=9252490

National Women's History Museum (NWHM). (n.d). Women wielding power: Pioneer female state legislators. Retrieved from https://www.nwhm.org/org/online-exhibits/legislators/Colorado.hmtl

National Youth Gang Center. (2009). *National Youth Gang Survey analysis.* Retrieved from http://www.nationalgangcenter.gov/Survey-Analysis

Navarro, J. N., & Jasinski, J. L. (2013). Why girls? Using routine activities theory to predict cyberbullying experiences between girls and boys. *Women & Criminal Justice, 23*, 286–303.

Neff, J. L., Patterson, M. M., & Johnson, S. (2012). Meeting the training needs of those who meet the needs of victims: Assessing service providers. *Violence and Victims, 27*(4), 609–632.

New York Times. (1978, February 22). 2 officers win case on issue of pregnancy. Pg. B3.

New York Times. (1983, February 21). Women balance police work at home. Pg. C18.

Newton, M. (2003). Ciudad Juarez: The serial killers playground. Retrieved from http://www.trutv.com/library/crime/serial_killers/predators/ciudad_juarez/11.html

Ng, C. (2013, March 17). Steubenville, Ohio, football players convicted in rape trial. ABC News. Retrieved from http://abcnews.go.com/US/steubenville-football-players-guilty-ohio-rape-trial/story?id=18748493

Nguyen, H. V., Kaysen, D., Dillworth, T. M., Brajcich, M., & Larimer, M. E. (2010). Incapacitated rape and alcohol use in White and Asian American college women. *Violence Against Women, 16*(8), 919–933.

Nine justices, ten years: A statistical retrospective. (2004). *Harvard Law Review, 118*(1), 521. Retrieved from http://web.archive.org/web/20060327053526/http://www.harvardlawreview.org/issues/118/Nov04/Nine_Justices_Ten_YearsFTX.pdf

Nixon, K., Tutty, L., Downe, P., Gorkoff, K., & Ursel, J. (2002).The everyday occurrence: Violence in the lives of girls exploited through prostitution. *Violence Against Women, 8*(9), 1016–1043.

Nokomis Foundation. (2002). We can do better: Helping prostituted women and girls in Grand Rapids make healthy choices: A prostitution round table report to the community. Retrieved from http://www.nokomisfoundation.org/documents/WeCan DoBetter.pdf

Noonan, M. C., & Corcoran, M. E. (2008). The mommy track and partnership: Temporary delay or dead end? *Annals of the American Academy of Political and Social Science, 596,* 130–150.

Noonan, M. C., Corcoran, M. E., & Courant, P. N. (2008). Is the partnership gap closing for women? Cohort differences in the sex gap in partnership chances. *Social Science Research, 37,* 156–179.

Norton-Hawk, M. (2004). A comparison of pimp and non-pimp controlled women. *Violence Against Women, 10*(2), 189–194.

NY Daily News. (2013, December 20). Congress passed defense bill with provision to crack down on sexual assault in the military. Retrieved from http://www.nydailynews.com/news/politics/sen-gillibrand-military-sexual-assault-bill-passes-article-1.1553722

O'Connor, M. L. (2012). Early policing in the United States: "Help wanted—Women need not apply!" In R. Muraskin (Ed.),

Women and justice: It's a crime (5th ed., pp. 487–499). Upper Saddle River, NJ: Prentice-Hall.

Odem, M. E. (1995). Delinquent daughters: Protecting and policing adolescent female sexuality in the United States: 1885–1920. Chapel Hill: University of North Carolina Press.

O'Donnell, P., Richards, M., Pearce, S., & Romero, E. (2012). Gender differences in monitoring and deviant peers as predictors of delinquent behavior among low-income urban African American youth. *Journal of Early Adolescence, 32*(3), 431–459.

Office for National Statistics. (2014). *Crime in England and Wales, year ending December 2013.* Retrieved from http://www.ons.gov.uk/ons/dcp171778_360216.pdf

Office of Civil Rights, Department of Education. (2011, April 4). Dear Colleague letter. Retrieved from https://www2.ed.gov/about/offices/list/ocr/letters/colleague-201104.pdf

Office on Violence Against Women (OVW). (n.d.). Home. U.S. Department of Justice. Retrieved from http://www.ovw.usdoj.gov

Office on Violence Against Women. (n.d.). VAWA 2013 summary: Changes to OVW-administered grant programs. Retrieved from http://www.ncdsv.org/images/OVW_VAWA+2013+summary+changes+to+OVW-administered+Grant+Programs.pdf

O'Keefe, E. (2013, December 19). Congress approves reforms to address sexual assault, rape in military. *Washington Post.* Retrieved from http://www.washingtonpost.com/politics/congress-poised-to-approve-reforms-to-address-sexual-assault-rape-in-military/2013/12/19/bbd34afa-68c9-11e3-a0b9-249bbb34602c_story.html

Oppel, R. A. (2013, March 17). Ohio teenagers guilty in rape that social media brought to light. *The New York Times.* Retrieved from http://www.nytimes.com/2013/03/18/us/teenagers-found-guilty-in-rape-in-steubenville-ohio.html?pagewanted=all&_r=0

Ortiz, N. R., & Spohn, C. (2014). Mitigating the effect of a criminal record at sentencing: Local life circumstances and substantial assistance departures among recidivists in federal court. *Criminal Justice Policy Review, 25*(1), 3–28.

Otis, M. D. (2007). Perceptions of victimization risk and fear of crime among lesbians and gay men. *Journal of Interpersonal Violence, 22*(2), 198–217.

Owen, B., & Bloom B. (1998). *Modeling gender-specific services in juvenile justice: Final report to the office of criminal justice planning.* Sacramento, CA: OCJP.

OXFAM. (n.d.). Protecting the accused: Sorcery in PNG. Retrieved from http://www.oxfam.org.nz/what-we-do/where-we-work/papua-new-guinea/gender-justice/confronting-sorcery

OXFAM. (2010, October 15). Sorcery beliefs and practices in Gumine: A source of conflict and insecurity. Retrieved from http://www.oxfam.org.nz/sites/default/files/reports/Sorcery_report_FINAL.pdf

Oxman-Martinez, J., & Hanley, J. (2003, February 20). Human smuggling and trafficking: Achieving the goals of the UN protocols? *Cross Border Perspectives: Human Trafficking, 20.*

Ozbay, O., & Ozcan Y. Z. (2008). A test of Hirschi's social bonding theory: A comparison of male and female delinquency. *Internal Journal of Offender Therapy and Comparative Criminology, 52*(2), 134–157.

Pakes, F. (2005). Penalization and retreat: The changing face of Dutch criminal justice. *Criminal Justice, 5*(2), 145–161.

Palmer, B. (2001). Women in the American judiciary: Their influence and impact. *Women and Politics, 23*(3), 91–101.

Panchanadeswaran, S., & Koverola, C. (2005). Voices of battered women in India. *Violence Against Women, 11*(6), 736–758.

Paoline, E. A., Lambert, E. G., & Hogan, N. L. (2015). Job stress and job satisfaction among jail staff: Exploring gendered effects. *Women & Criminal Justice, 25*(5), 339–359.

Parsons, J., & Bergin, T. (2010). The impact of criminal justice involvement on victims' mental health. *Journal of Traumatic Stress, 23*(2), 182–188. doi:10.1002/jts.20505

Patel, S., & Gadit, A. M. (2008). Karo-kari: A form of honour killing in Pakistan. *Transcultural Psychiatry, 45*(4), 683–694.

Pathe, M., & Mullen, P. E. (1997). The impact of stalkers on their victims. *British Journal of Psychiatry, 170,* 12–17.

Patterson, D., & Campbell, R. (2010). Why rape survivors participate in the criminal justice system. *Journal of Community Psychology, 38*(2), 191–205.

Pelissero, T. (2014, August 28). NFL toughens its stance on domestic violence. USA Today. Retrieved from https://www.usatoday.com/story/sports/nfl/2014/08/28/nfl-toughens-its-stance-on-domestic-violence/14746187/

Perona, A. R., Bottoms, B. L., & Sorenson, E. (2006). Research-based guidelines for child forensic interviews. *Journal of Aggression, Maltreatment & Trauma, 12*(3/4), 81–130.

Perry, D. (2010). *The Girls of Murder City: Fame, lust, and the beautiful killers that inspired Chicago.* New York: Penguin Group/Viking Press.

Peterman, A., Palermo, T., & Bredenkamp, C. (2011). Estimates and determinants of sexual violence in the democratic Republic of the Congo. *American Journal of Public Health*

Perselia, J. (2000). Parole and prisoner reentry in the United States. Perspectives. American Probation and Parole Association. Retrieved from http://www.appa-net.org/eweb/resources/pppsw_2013/history.htm

Peterson, F. (2012, July 21). Luis Walker, Lackland boot camp instructor, convicted of rape and sexual assault. *Global Post.* Retrieved from http://www.globalpost.com/dispatch/news/regions/americas/united-states/120721/luis-walker-rape-sex-assault-lackland-texas-sexual-air-force-military-boot

Petrillo, M. (2007). Power struggle: Gender issues for female probation officers in the supervision of high risk offenders. *Probation Journal: The Journal of Community and Criminal Justice, 54*(4), 394–406.

The Pew Charitable Trusts and the John D. and Catherine T. MacArthur Foundation. (2014). State prison health care spending: An examination. Retreved from http://www.pewtrusts

.org/~/media/assets/2014/07/stateprisonhealthcarespendingreport.pdf

Phillips, D. (2017, March 6). Marines shared illicit images of female peers. *The New York Times*. Retrieved from https://www.nytimes.com/2017/03/06/us/inquiry-opens-into-how-30000-marines-shared-illicit-images-of-female-peers.html

Pilon, M. (2017, January 31). Inside the NFL's domestic violence punishment problem. *B/R Mag*. Retrieved from http://mag.bleacherreport.com/nfl-domestic-violence-policy-suspensions/

Pinchevsky, G. M., & Steiner, B. (2016). Sex-based disparities in pretrial release decisions and outcomes. *Crime and Delinquency, 62*(3), 308–340.

Piquero, N. L., Gover, A. R., MacDonald, J. M., & Piquero, A. R. (2005). The influence of delinquent peers on delinquency: Does gender matter? *Youth & Society, 36*(3), 251–275.

Planty, M., Langton, L., Krebs, C., Berzofsky, M., & Smiley-McDonald, H. (2013). Female victims of sexual violence, 1994–2010. U.S. Department of Justice, Bureau of Justice Statistics. Retrieved from http://www.bjs.gov/content/pub/pdf/fvsv9410.pdf

Platt, A. M. (1969). *The child savers*. IL: University of Chicago Press.

Pollak, O. (1950). *Criminality of women*. Baltimore, MD: University of Pennsylvania Press.

Pollak, O. (1961). *The criminality of women*. New York: A. S. Barnes.

Pollak, S. (2013, February 7). Woman burned alive for witchcraft in Papua New Guinea. *Time*. Retrieved from http://newsfeed.time.com/2013/02/07/Woman-burned-alive-for-witchcraft-in-Papua-New-Guinea

Pollock, J. M. (1986). *Sex and supervision: Guarding male and female inmates*. New York: Greenwood Press.

Postmus, J. L., Plummer, S., & Stylianou, A. M. (2016). Measuring economic abuse in the lives of survivors: Revising the scale of economic abuse. *Violence Against Women, 22*(6), 692–703.

Potter, G., & Kappeler, V. (2006). *Constructing crime: Perspectives on making news and social problems* (2nd ed.). Long Grove, IL: Waveland Press.

Potter, H. (2015). *Intersectionality and criminality: Disrupting and revolutionizing studies of crime*. New York: Routledge.

Potter, H. (2006). An argument for Black feminist criminology. *Feminist Criminology, 1*(2), 106–124.

Potter, H. (2007a). Battered Black women's use of religious services and spirituality for assistance in leaving abusive relationships. *Violence Against Women, 13*(3), 262–284.

Potter, H. (2007b). *Battle cries: Understanding and confronting intimate partner abuse against African-American women*. New York: New York University Press.

President's Commission on Law Enforcement and the Administration of Justice. (1967). *The challenge of crime in a free society*. Washington DC: U.S. Government Printing Office.

Proano-Raps, T. C., & Meyer, C. L. (2003). Postpartum syndrome and the legal system. In R. Muraskin (Ed.), *It's a crime: Women and justice* (3rd ed., pp. 53–76). Upper Saddle River, NJ: Prentice-Hall.

Pryor, D. W., & Hughes, M. R. (2013). Fear of rape among college women: A social psychological analysis. *Violence and Victims, 28*(3), 443–465.

Quinn, B. (2013, March 19). Taliban victim Malala Yousafzai starts school in UK. *The Guardian*. Retrieved from http://www.theguardian.com/world/2013/mar/20/taliban-victim-malala-yousafzai-school

Rabe-Hemp, C. (2011). Exploring administrators' perceptions of light-duty assignment. *Police Quarterly, 14*(2), 124–141.

Rabe-Hemp, C. (2012). The career trajectories of female police executives. In R. Muraskin (Ed.), *Women and justice: It's a crime* (5th ed., pp. 527–543). Upper Saddle River, NJ: Prentice-Hall.

Rabe-Hemp, C., & Humiston, G. S. (2015). A survey of maternity policies and pregnancy accommodations in American police deparments. *Police Practice and Research, 16*(3), 239–253.

Rabe-Hemp, C. E. (2008). Survival in an "all boys club": Policewomen and their fight for acceptance. *Policing: An International Journal of Police Strategies and Management, 31*(2), 251–270.

Rabe-Hemp, C. E. (2009). POLICEwomen or PoliceWOMEN? Doing gender and police work. *Feminist Criminology, 4*(2), 114–129.

Raeder, M. S. (1995). The forgotten offender: The effect of the sentencing guidelines and mandatory minimums on women and their children. *Federal Sentencing Reporter, 8*, 157.

Rafferty, Y. (2007). Children for sale: Child trafficking in Southeast Asia. *Child Abuse Review, 16*(6), 401–422.

Rafter, N. H. (1985). *Partial justice: Women in state prisons 1800–1935*. Boston: New England University Press.

Raphael, J. (2000). *Saving Bernice: Battered women, welfare and poverty*. Boston: Northeastern University Press.

Raphael, J. (2004). *Listening to Olivia: Violence, poverty and prostitution*. Boston: Northeastern University Press.

Raphael, J., & Shapiro, D. L. (2004). Violence in indoor and outdoor venues. *Violence Against Women, 10*(2), 126–139.

Raphael, K. G. (2005). Childhood abuse and pain in adulthood: More than a modest relationship? *The Clinical Journal of Pain, 21*(5), 371–373.

Rasche, C. E. (2012). The dislike of female offenders among correctional officers: A need for specialized training. In R. Muraskin (Ed.), *Women and justice: It's a crime* (5th ed., pp. 544–562). Upper Saddle River, NJ: Prentice-Hall.

Rathbone, C. (2005). *A world apart: Women, prison and life behind bars*. New York: Random House.

Raymond, J. G. (2004). Prostitution on demand: Legalizing the buyers as sexual consumers. *Violence Against Women, 10*(10), 1156–1186.

Reichman, N. J., & Sterling, J. S. (2001). Recasting the brass ring: Deconstructing and reconstructing workplace opportunities for women lawyers. *Capital University Law Review, 29*, 923–977.

Reinharz, S. (1992). *Feminist methods in social research*. New York: Oxford University Press.

Rennison, C. M. (2009). A new look at the gender gap in offending. *Women and Criminal Justice, 19*, 171–190.

Renzetti, C. M., Goodstein, L., & Miller, S. E. (2006). *Rethinking gender, crime, and justice: Feminist readings*. New York: Oxford University Press.

Resnick, H., Acierno, R., Holmes, M., Dammeyer, M., & Kilpatrick, D. (2000). Emergency evaluation and intervention with female victims of rape and other violence. *Journal of Clinical Psychology, 56*(10), 1317–1333.

Resnick, P. J. (1970). Murder of the newborn: A psychiatric review of neonaticide. *American Journal of Psychiatry, 126,* 1414–1420.

Revolutionary Worker. (2002). The disappearing women of Juarez. Retrieved from http://revcom.us/a/v24/1161-1170/1166/juarez .htm

Reyns, B. W., Burek, M. W., Henson, B., & Fisher, B. S. (2013). The unintended consequences of digital technology: Exploring the relationship between sexting and cybervictimization. *Journal of Crime and Justice, 36*(1), 1–17.

Reyns, B. W., & Englebrecht, C. M. (2012). The fear factor: Exploring predictors of fear among stalking victims throughout the stalking encounter. *Crime & Delinquency, 59*(5), 788–808.

Rice, S. K., Terry, K. J., Miller, H. V., & Ackerman, A. R. (2007). Research trajectories of female scholars in criminology and criminal justice. *Journal of Criminal Justice Education, 18*(3), 360–384.

Rich, K., & Seffrin, P. (2014). Birds of a feather or fish out of water? Policewomen taking rape reports. *Feminist Criminology, 9*(2), 137–159.

Rickert, V. I., Wiemann, C. M., & Vaughan, R. D. (2005). Disclosure of date/acquaintance rape: Who reports and when. *Journal of Pediatric and Adolescent Gynecology, 18*(1), 17–24.

Rideout, M. (2007). May 1, 1990: The shocking death that started a sensation in N.H. Keene Equinox. Retrieved from http://www .hampton.lib.nh.us/hampton/biog/pamsmart/equinox2006_ 1.htm

Ritchie, B. E. (2001). Challenges incarcerated women face as they return to their communities: Findings from life history interviews. *Crime and Delinquency, 47*(3), 368–389.

Robinson, L. (1890). Woman lawyers in the United States. *The Green Bag, 2,* 10.

Robison, S. M. (1966). A critical review of the Uniform Crime Reports. *Michigan Law Review, 64*(6), 1031–1054.

Rodriguez, S. F., Curry, T. R., & Lee, G. (2006). Gender differences in criminal sentencing: Do effects vary across violent, property and drug offenses. *Social Science Quarterly, 87*(2), 318–339.

Roe-Sepowitz, D. E. (2012). Juvenile entry into prostitution: The role of emotional abuse. *Violence Against Women, 18*(5), 562–579.

Romero-Daza, N., Weeks, M., & Singer, M. (2003). "Nobody gives a damn if I live or die": Violence, drugs, and street-level prostitution in inner city Hartford, Connecticut. *Medical Anthropology, 22,* 233–259.

Rosenbaum, A. (2009). Batterer intervention programs: A report from the field. *Violence and Victims, 24*(6), 757–770.

Rosenbaum, J. L. (1989). Family dysfunction and female delinquency. *Crime and Delinquency, 35,* 31–44.

Rosenbaum, J. L., & Spivack, S. (2013). *Implementing a gender based arts program for juvenile offenders.* Waltham, MA: Elsevier.

Ross, E. (2013, May 10). Air Force sex scandal heats up. Retrieved from http://www.koaa.com/news/air-force-sex-scandal-heats-up/

Rumney, P. N. S. 1999. When rape isn't rape: Court of appeal sentencing practice in cases of marital and relationship rape. *Oxford Journal of Legal Studies, 19*(2), 243–270.

Ryder, J. A., & Brisgone, R. E. (2013). Cracked perspectives: Reflections of women and girls in the aftermath of the crack cocaine era. *Feminist Criminology, 8*(1), 40–62.

Ryon, S. B. (2013). Gender as social threat: A study of offender sex, situational factors, gender dynamics and social control. *Journal of Criminal Justice, 41,* 426–437.

S. v. Modise (2007). South Africa: North West High Court, Mafikeng. ZANWHC 73. As cited in Mandal, S. (2014). The impossibility of marital rape: Contestations around marriage, sex, violence and the law in contemporary India. *Australia Feminist Studies, 29*(81), 255–272.

Sabina, C., Cuevas, C. A., & Schally, J. L. (2012). Help-seeking in a national sample of victimized Latino women: The influence of victimization types. *Journal of Interpersonal Violence, 27*(1), 40–61.

Sacks, M., & Ackerman, A. (2014). Bail and sentencing: Does pretrial detention lead to harsher punishment? *Criminal Justice Policy Review, 25*(1), 59–77.

Salisbury, E. J., Van Voorhis, P., Wright, E., M., & Bauman, A. (2009). Changing probation experiences for female offenders based on women's needs and risk assessment project findings. *Women, Girls and Criminal Justice, 10*(6), 83–84, 92–95.

Salonga, R. (2016, August 11). Jaycee Dugard TV interview: On her daughters, "Room" and the $20 million settlement. *The Mercury News.* Retrieved from http://www.mercurynews.com/2016/ 07/08/jaycee-dugard-tv-interview-on-her-daughters-room- and-the-20-million-settlement/

SAMHSA. (2009). Substance abuse treatment: Addressing the specific needs of women. A treatment improvement protocol TIP 51. Center for Substance Abuse Treatment. Retrieved from http://mentalhealth.samhsa.gov/cmhs/CommunitySupport/ women_violence/default.asphttp://bjs.ojp.usdoj.gov/index .cfm?ty=tp&tid=35

Sampson, R. (2003). Acquaintance rape of college students. *Public Health Resources, 92.*

Sampson, R., & Laub, J. (1993). *Crime in the making: Pathways and turning points through life.* Cambridge, MA: Harvard University Press.

Sanchez, R., & Lance, N. (2017, June 17). Judge finds Michelle Carter guilty of manslaughter in texting suicide case. CNN. Retrieved from www.cnn.com/2017/06/16/michelle-carter-texting-case/ index.html

Sandifer, J. L. (2008). Evaluating the efficacy of a parenting program for incarcerated mothers. *The Prison Journal, 88*(3), 423–445.

Saulters-Tubbs, C. (1993). Prosecutorial and judicial treatment of female offenders. *Federal Probation,* 37–42.

Savage, D. G. (2009). Sotomayor takes her seat. *American Bar Association Journals, 95*(10), 24–25.

Sawyers, E. T. (1922). History of Santa Clara County, California. Retrieved from http://www.mariposaresearch.net/santaclara- research/SCBIOS/cfbrattan.html

Schadee, J. (2003). Passport to healthy families. *Corrections Today, 65*(3), 64.

Schalet, A., Hunt, G., & Joe-Laidler, K. (2003). Respectability and autonomy: The articulation and meaning of sexuality among girls in the gang. *Journal of Contemporary Ethnography, 32*(1), 108–143.

Schemo, D. J. (2003, August 29). Rate of rape at academy is put at 12% in survey. Retrieved from http://www.nytimes.com/2003/08/29/national/29ACAD.html?th

Schoonmaker, M. H., & Brooks, J.S. (1975). Women in probation and parole, 1974. *Crime & Delinquency, 21*(2), 109–115.

Schoot, E., & Goswami, S. (2001). *Prostitution: A violent reality of homelessness. Chicago:* Chicago Coalition for the Homeless.

Schulz, D. M. (1995). From social worker to crime fighter: Women in United States municipal policing. Westport, CT: Praeger.

Schulz, D. M. (2003). Women police chiefs: A statistical profile. *Police Quarterly, 6*(3), 330–345.

Schulz, D. M. (2004). Invisible no more: A social history of women in U.S. policing. In B. R. Price & N. J. Sokologg (Eds.), *The criminal justice system and women* (pp. 483–494). New York: McGraw-Hill.

Schulze, C. (2012). The policies of United States police departments: Equal access, equal treatment. In R. Muraskin (Ed.), *Women and justice: It's a crime* (5th ed., pp. 500–513). Upper Saddle River, NJ: Prentice-Hall.

Schwartz, M. D., & DeKeseredy, W. S. (2008). Interpersonal violence against women: The role of men. *Journal of Contemporary Criminal Justice, 24*(2), 178–185.

Schwartz, M. D., DeKeseredy, W. S., Tait, D., & Alvi, S. (2001). Male peer support and a feminist routing activities theory: Understanding sexual assault on the college campus. *Justice Quarterly, 18*(3), 623–649.

Scott-Ham, M., & Burton, F. C. (2005). Toxicological findings in cases of alleged drug-facilitated sexual assault in the United Kingdom over a 3-year period. *Journal of Clinical Forensic Medicine, 12*(4), 175.

The Second Chance Act (H.R. 1593). Available at https://www.congress.gov/bill/110th-congress/house-bill/1593/text

Sedlak, A. J., McPherson, K. S., & Basena, M. (2013). Nature and risk of victimization: Findings from the survey of youth in residential placement [Bulletin]. Office of Juvenile Justice and Delinquency Prevention. Retrieved from http://www.ojjdp.gov/pubs/240703.pdf

Seelye, K. Q., & Bidgood, J. (2017). Guilty verdit for young woman who urged friend to kill himself. *New York Times.* Retrieved from https://www.nytimes/2017/06/16/us/suicide-texting-trial-michelle -carter-conrad-roy.html

Seghetti, L. M., & Bjelopera, J. P. (2012). The Violence Against Women Act: Overview, legislation and federal funding. Congressional Research Service. Retrieved from http://www.fas.org/sgp/crs/misc/R42499.pdf

Sellers, C., & Bromley, M. (1996). Violent behavior in college student dating relationships. *Journal of Contemporary Criminal Justice, 12*(1), 1–27.

Sengstock, M. C. (1976). *Culpable victims in Mendelsohn's typology.* Retrieved from https://www.ncjrs.gov/App/publications/Abstract.aspx?id=48998

Sentencing Project. (2006). *Life sentences: Denying welfare benefits to women convicted of drug offenses.* Retrieved from http://www.sentencingproject.org/doc/publications/women_smy_lifesentences.pdf

Severance, T. A. (2005). "You know who you can go to": Cooperation and exchange between incarcerated women. *The Prison Journal, 85*(3), 343–367.

Shackling pregnant inmates banned under California law, but many states allow the practice. (2012, October 11). *Huffington Post.* Retrieved from http://www.huffingtonpost.com/2012/10/11/pregnant-women-shackles-giving-birth-two-thirds-33-states_n_1958319.html

Shannon-Lewy, C., & Dull, V. T. (2005). The response of Christian clergy to domestic violence: Help or hindrance? *Aggression and Violent Behavior, 10*(6), 647–659.

Sharma, A. (2013, October 31). Sara Kruzan released from prison 18 years after killing pimp as teen. Retrieved from http://www.kpbs.org/news/2013/oct/31/sara-kruzan-killed-pimp-teen-goes-free/

Sharp, S. F., Peck, B. M., & Hartsfield, J. (2012). Childhood adversity and substance use of women prisoners: A general strain theory approach. *Journal of Criminal Justice, 40*, 202–211.

Sharpe, G. (2009). The trouble with girls today: Professional perspectives on young women's offending. *Youth Justice, 9*(3), 254–269.

Sheeran, T. J. (2013, July 17). Ariel Castro pleads not guilty to 977 counts in Ohio kidnapping indictment. *Huffington Post.* Retrieved from http://www.huffingtonpost.com/2013/07/17/ariel-castro-arraignment-charges_n_3609793.html

Shekarkhar, Z., & Gibson, C. L. (2011). Gender, self-control and offending behaviors among Latino youth. *Journal of Contemporary Criminal Justice, 27*(1), 63–80.

Shelden, R. G. (1981). Sex discrimination in the juvenile justice system: Memphis, Tennessee, 1900–1917. In M. Q. Warren (Ed.), *Comparing male and female offenders* (pp. 52–72). Beverly Hills, CA: Sage.

Shenoy, D. P., Neranartkomol, R., Ashok, M., Chiang, A., Lam, A. G., & Trieu, S. L. (2010). Breaking down the silence: A study examining patterns of sexual assault and subsequent disclosure among ethnic groups of Asian American college women. *Californian Journal of Health Promotion, 7*(2), 78–91.

Shepherd, S. M., Luebbers, S., & Dolan, M. (2013, April–June). Identifying gender differences in an Australian youth offender population. *Sage Open, 3*, 1–12.

Sherman, L. W., & Berk, R. A. (1984). The Minneapolis Domestic Violence Experiment. *Police Foundation Reports.* Retrieved from http://www.policefoundation.org/pdf/minneapolisdve.pdf

Sholchet, C. (2013, May). Jodi Arias guilty of first degree murder: Death penalty possible. CNN. Retrieved from http://www.cnn.com/2013/05/08/justice/arizona-jodi-arias-verdict/

Shorey, R. C., Cornelius, T. L., & Strauss, C. (2015). Stalking in college student dating relationships: A descriptive investigation. *Journal of Family Violence, 30*: 935–942.

Shufelt, J. L., & Cocozza, J. J. (2006). Youth with mental health disorders in the juvenile justice system: Results from a multi-state prevalence study. National Center for Mental Health and Juvenile Justice. Retrieved from http://www.ncmhjj.com/pdfs/publications/PrevalenceRPB.pdf

Sigurvinsdottir, R., & Ullman S. E. (2015). The role of sexual orientation in the victimization and recovery of sexual assault survivors. *Violence and Victims, 3*(4), 636–648.

Silva, S. A., Pires, A. P., Guerreiro, C., & Cardoso, A. (2012). Balancing motherhood and drug addiction: The transition to parenthood of addicted mothers. *Journal of Health Psychology, 18*(3), 359–367.

Silverman, J. G., Raj, A., Mucci, L. A., & Hathaway, J. E. (2001). Dating violence against adolescent girls and associated substance use, unhealthy weight control, sexual risk behavior, pregnancy and suicidality. *Journal of American Medical Association, 285*(5), 572–579.

Silverman, J. R., & Caldwell, R. M. (2008). Peer relationships and violence among female juvenile offenders: An exploration of differences among four racial/ethnic populations. *Criminal Justice and Behavior, 35*(3), 333–343.

Simkhada, P. (2008). Life histories and survival strategies amongst sexually trafficked girls in Nepal. *Children and Society, 22,* 235–248.

Simmons, W. P. (2006, Spring). Remedies for the women of Ciudad Juárez through the Inter-American Court of Human Rights. *Northwestern Journal of International Human Rights, 4*(3). Retrieved from http://www.law.northwestern.edu/journals/jihr/v4/n3/2/Simmons. pdf

Simon, R. (1975). *Women and crime.* Lexington, MA: D. C. Heath.

Skolnick, J. (1966). Justice without trial. New York: Wiley.

Slattery, S. M., & Goodman, L. A. (2009). Secondary traumatic stress among domestic violence advocates: Workplace risk and protective factors. *Violence Against Women, 15*(11), 1358–1379.

Smith, E. L., & Farole, D. J., Jr. (2009). *Profile of intimate partner violence cases in large urban counties.* Bureau of Justice Statistics, U.S. Department of Justice. Retrieved from http://bjs.ojp.usdoj.gov/content/pub/pdf/pipvcluc.pdf

Smith, J. C. (1998). *Rebels in law: Voices in history of Black women lawyers* (KF299.A35 R43 1998). Ann Arbor: University of Michigan.

Smith-Spark, L., & Nyberg, P. (2013, July 31). Nigella Lawson and Charles Saatchi take step toward divorce. CNN. Retrieved at http://www.cnn.com/2013/07/31/world/europe/nigella-lawson-saatchi-divorce/

Smoyer, A. B. (2015). Feedling relationships: Foodways and social networks in a women's prison. *Affilia: Journal of Women and Social Work, 30*(1), 26–39.

Smude, L. (2012). Realignment: A new frontier for California criminal justice. In C. Gardiner & S. Mallicoat (Eds.), *California's criminal justice system* (pp. 153–168). Durham, NC: Carolina Academic Press.

Snedker, K. A. (2012). Explaining the gender gap in fear of crime: Assessments of risk and vulnerability among New York City residents. *Feminist Criminology, 7*(2), 75–111.

Snell, C., Sorenson, J., Rodriguez, J. J., & Kuanliang, A. (2009). Gender differences in research productivity among criminal justice and criminology scholars. *Journal of Criminal Justice, 37*(3), 288–295.

Snow, R. L. (2010). *Policewomen who made history: Breaking through the ranks.* Lanham, MD: Rowman and Littlefield.

Snyder, H. N., & Sickmund, M. (2006). *Juvenile offenders and victims: 2006 national report.* National Center for Juvenile Justice. Office of Juvenile Justice and Delinquency Prevention. Retrieved from http://www.ojjdp.gov/ojstatbb/nr2006/

Snyder, J. A., Fisher, B. S., Scherer, H. L, & Daigle, L. E. (2012). Unsafe in the camouflage tower: Sexual victimization and perceptions of military academy leadership. *Journal of Interpersonal Violence, 27*(16), 3171–3194.

Snyder, Z. K. (2009). Keeping families together: The importance of maintaining mother-child contact for incarcerated women. *Women & Criminal Justice, 19,* 37–59.

Sokoloff, N. J. (2004). Domestic violence at the crossroads: Violence against poor women and women of color. *Women Studies Quarterly, 32*(3/4), 139–147.

Songer, D. R., & Crews-Meyer, K. A. (2000). Does judge gender matter? Decision making in state supreme courts. *Social Science Quarterly, 8*(3), 750–762.

Songer, D. R., Davis, S., & Haire, S. (1994). A reappraisal of diversification in the federal courts: Gender effects in the court of appeals. *Journal of Politics, 56*(2), 425–439.

Sonia Sotomayor. (2012). *The New York Times.* Retrieved from http://topics.nytimes.com/top/reference/timestopics/people/s/sonia_sotomayor/index.html?8qa

Spears, J. W., & Spohn, C. C. (1996). The genuine victim and prosecutors' charging decisions in sexual assault cases. *American Journal of Criminal Justice, 20,* 183–205.

Spencer, G. C. (2004/2005). Her body is a battlefield: The applicability of the Alien Tort Statute to corporate human rights abuses in Juarez, Mexico. *Gonzaga Law Review, 40,* 503.

Spinelli, M. G. (2004). Maternal infanticide associated with mental illness: Prevention and the promise of saved lives. *American Journal of Psychiatry, 161,* 1548–1557.

Spitzberg, B. H. (2016). Acknowledgment of unwanted pursuit, threats, assault, and stalking in a college population. *Psychology of Violence* Advance online publication. http:// dx.doi.org/10.1037/a0040205

Spitzberg, B. H., & Cupach, W. R. (2003). What mad pursuit? Obsessive relational intrusion and stalking related phenomena. *Aggression and Violent Behavior, 8,* 345–375.

Spohn, C., & Beichner, D. (2000). Is preferential treatment of female offenders a thing of the past? A multisite study of gender, race, and imprisonment. *Criminal Justice Policy Review, 11*(2), 149–184.

Spohn, C., & Belenko, S. (2013). Do the drugs do the time? The effect of drug abuse on sentences imposed on drug offenders in three U.S. District Courts. *Criminal Justice and Behavior, 40*(6), 646–670.

Spohn, C., & Brennan, P. K. (2011). The joint effects of offender race/ethnicity and gender on substantial assistance departures in federal courts. *Race and Justice 1*(1), 49–78.

Spohn, C., Gruhl, J., & Welch, S. (1987). The impact of the ethnicity and gender of defendants on the decision to reject or dismiss felony charges. *Criminology, 25*(1), 175–192

Sports Illustrated (2017, February 17). Former NFL RB Trent Richardson arrested on domestic violence charge. Retrieved from https://www.si.com/nfl/2017/02/17/trent-richardson-arrested-domestic-violence-charge-alabama

Srinivas, T., & DePrince, A. P. (2015). Links between the police response and women's psychological outcomes following intimate partner violence. *Violence and Victims, 30*(1), 32–48.

St. John, P. (2013, October 26). Jerry Brown Oks freedom for woman imprisoned at 16 for killing pimp. *Los Angeles Times*. Retrieved from http://articles.latimes.com/2013/oct/26/local/la-me-ff-kruzan-20131027

Stacy, M. (2012, May 19). Marissa Alexander gets 20 years for firing warning shot. *Huffington Post*. Retrieved from http://www.huffingtonpost.com/2012/05/19/marissa-alexander-gets-20_n_1530035.html

Stalens, L. J., & Finn, M. A. (2000). Gender differences in officers' perceptions and decisions about domestic violence cases. *Women and Criminal Justice, 11*(3), 1–24.

Stangle, H. L. (2008). Murderous Madonna: Femininity, violence, and the myth of postpartum mental disorder in cases of maternal infanticide and filicide. *William and Mary Law Review, 50*, 699–734.

Starzynski, L. L., Ullman, S. E., Townsend, S. M., Long, L. M., & Long, S. M. (2007). What factors predict women's disclosure of sexual assault to mental health professionals? *Journal of Community Psychology, 35*(5), 619–638.

Stattin, H., & Magnusson, D. (1990). *Pubertal maturation in female development* (Vol. 2). Hillsdale, NJ: Erlbaum.

Steer, J. (2013, May 6). Cleveland police: Missing teens Amanda Berry and Gina DeJesus found alive, appear to be OK. Retrieved from http://www.newsnet5.com/news/local-news/cleveland-metro/cleveland-police-dispatch-missing-teens-amanda-berry-and-gina-dejesus-found-alive

Steffensmeier, D., & Allan, E. (1996). Gender and crime: Toward a gendered theory of female offending. *American Review of Sociology, 22*, 459–487.

Steffensmeier, D., & Hebert, C. (1999). Women and men policymakers: Does the judge's gender affect the sentencing of criminal defendants? *Social Forces, 77*(3), 1163–1196.

Steffensmeier, D., Kramer, J., & Streifel, C. (1993). Gender and imprisonment decisions. *Criminology, 31*, 411–446.

Steffensmeier, D., Schwartz, J., Zhong, H., & Ackerman, J. (2005). An assessment of recent trends in girls' violence using diverse longitudinal sources: Is the gender gap closing? *Criminology, 43*, 355–405.

Steffensmeier, D., Zhong, H., Ackerman, J., Schwartz, J., & Agha, S. (2006). Gender gap trends for violent crimes, 1980 to 2003: A UCR-NCVS comparison. *Feminist Criminology, 1*(1), 72–98.

Stephens, E., & Melton, H. (2016). The impact of children on intimate partner abuse victims' service-seeking. *Women & Criminal Justice.* DOI: 10.1080/08974454.2016.1247773

Sterling, J. S., & Reichman, N. (2016). Overlooked and undervalued: Women in private law practice. *Annual Review of Law and Social Science, 12*: 373–393.

Stevenson, T., & Love, C. (1999). *Her story of domestic violence: A timeline of the battered women's movement.* Safework: California's Domestic Violence Resource. Retrieved from http://www.mincava.umn.edu/documents/herstory/herstory.html

Stewart, C. C., Langan, D., & Hannem, S. (2013). Victim experiences and perspectives on police responses to verbal violence in domestic settings. *Feminist Criminology, 8*(4), 269–294.

Stohr, M. K., Mays, G. L., Lovrich, N. P., & Gallegos, A. M. (1996). *Partial perceptions: Gender, job enrichment and job satisfaction among correctional officers in women's jails.* Paper presented at the Annual Meeting of the Academy of Criminal Justice Sciences, Las Vegas, Nevada.

Stotzer, R. L. (2014). Law enforcement and criminal justice personnel interactions with transgender people in the United States: A literature review. *Aggression and Violent Behavior, 19*(3), 263–277.

Strachan, M. (2013, October 29). Target to drop criminal background questions in job applications. *Huffington Post*. Retrieved from http://www.huffingtonpost.com/2013/10/29/target-criminal-history-questions_n_4175407.html

Stringer, E. C., & Barnes, S. L. (2012). Mothering while imprisoned: The effects of family and child dynamics on mothering attitudes. *Family Relations, 61*, 313–326.

Strom, K. J., Warner, T. D., Tichavsky, L., & Zahn, M. A. (2010, September 8). Policing juveniles: Domestic violence arrest policies, gender and police response to child-parent violence. *Crime & Delinquency*. Advance online publication. Retrieved from http://www.sagepub.com/journals/Journal200959

Suerth, J. (2017, June 16). Afer guilty verdit in texting suicide case, what's next for Michelle Carter? CNN. Retrieved from www.cnn.com/2017/06/16/us/michelle-carter-whats-next/index.html.

Sullivan, M., Senturia, K., Negash, T., Shiu-Thornton, S., & Giday, B. (2005). For us it's like living in the dark: Ethiopian women's experiences with domestic violence. *Journal of Interpersonal Violence, 20*(8), 922–940.

Supreme Court. (n.d.). The Supreme Court of the United States—History. Retrieved from http://www.judiciary.senate.gov/nominations/SupremeCourt/SupremeCourtHistory.cfm

Surette, R. (2003). The media, the public, and criminal justice policy. *Journal of the Institute of Justice & International Studies, 2*, 39–52.

Sutherland, E., & Cressey, D. (1974). *Criminology* (9th ed.). Philadelphia: H. B. Lippincott.

Sutton, J. R. (1988). *Stubborn children: Controlling delinquency in the United States, 1640–1981.* Berkeley: University of California Press.

Svensson, R. (2003). Gender differences in adolescent drug use. *Youth and Society, 34*, 300–329.

Svensson, R. (2004). Shame as a consequence of the parent-child relationship: A study of gender differences in juvenile delinquency. *European Journal of Criminology, 1*(4), 477–504.

Swan, A. A. (2016). Masculine, feminine, or androgynous: The influence of gender identity on job satisfaction among female police officers. *Women & Criminal Justice, 26*(1), 1–19.

Tamborra, T. L. (2012). Poor, urban, battered women who are stalked: How can we include their experiences. *Feminist Criminology, 7*(2), 112–129.

Tasca, M., Zatz, M., & Rodriguez, N. (2012). Girls' experiences with violence: An analysis of violence against and by at-risk girls. *Violence Against Women, 18*(6), 672–680.

Taylor, S. C., & Norma, C. (2012). The "symbolic protest" behind women's reporting of sexual assault crime to the police. *Feminist Criminology, 7*(1), 24–47.

Taylor, W., & Furlonger, B. (2011). A review of vicarious traumatization and supervision among Australian telephone and online counsellors. *Australian Journal of Guidance and Counselling, 21*: 225–235.

Testa, R. J., Sciacca, L. M., Wang, F., Hendricks, M. L., Goldblum, P., Bradford, J., & Bongar, B. (2012). Effect of violence on transgender people. *Professional Psychology: Research and Practice, 43*(5), 452–459.

Tewksbury, R., & Collins, S. C. (2006). Aggression levels among correctional officers. *The Prison Journal, 86*(3), 327–343.

Tewksbury, R., Connor, D. P., Chesseman, K., & Rivera, B. L. (2012). Female sex offenders' anticipations for reentry: Do they really know what they're in for? *Journal of Crime and Justice, 35*(3), 451–463.

The Florida Senate. (2011). Examine Florida's "Romeo and Juliet" law (Issue brief 2012–2014). Retrieved from http://www.flsenate.gov/PublishedContent/Session/2012InterimReports/2012-214cj.pdf

Thompson, D. (2017, June 22). Parole deined for Manson follower Krenwinkle in California. ABC News. Retrieved from http://abcnews.go.com/US/wireStory/manson-follower-longest-serving-female-inmate-seeks-parole-48211374

Thompson, M., & Petrovic, M. (2009). Gendered transitions: Within-person changes in employment, family and illicit drug use. *Journal of Research in Crime and Delinquency, 46*(3), 377–408.

Tiby, E. (2001). Victimization and fear among lesbians and gay men in Stockholm. *International Review of Victimiology, 8*: 217–243

Tille, J. E., & Rose, J. C. (2007). Emotional and behavioral problems of 13-to-18 year-old incarcerated female first-time offenders and recidivists. *Youth Violence and Juvenile Justice, 5*(4), 426–435.

Tillman, S., Bryant-Davis, T., Smith, K., & Marks, A. (2010). Shattering silence: Exploring barriers to disclosure for African American sexual assault survivors. *Trauma, Violence, & Abuse, 11*(2), 59–70.

Tillyer, R., Hartley, R. D., & Ward, J. T. (2015). Differential treatment of female defnendants: Does criminal history moderate the effects of gender on sentence length in Federal narcotics cases? *Criminal Justice and Behavior, 42*(7), 703–721.

Tjaden, P. G., & Thoennes, N. (2006). *Extent, nature, and consequences of rape victimization: Findings from the National Violence Against Women Survey.* Washington, DC: U.S. Department of Justice, Office of Justice Programs, National Institute of Justice.

Tonsing, J., & Barn, R. (2016). Intimate partner violence in South Asian communities: Exploring the notion of "shame" to promote understandings of migrant women's experiences. *International Social Work.* DOI: 10.1177/0020872816655868

Topping, A., & Quinn, B. (2013, June 18). Nigella Lawson assault: Charles Saatchi accepts police caution. *The Guardian.* Retrieved from http://www.theguardian.com/uk/2013/jun/18/saatchi-lawson-police-caution-assault?guni=Article:in%20body%201ink

Torre, I. (2013, October 9). Pakistan's educational challenges. CNN. Retrieved from http://www.cnn.com/2013/10/09/world/asia/infographic-pakistan-education/index.html?iid=article_sidebar

Truman, J. L. (2011). *Criminal victimization, 2010.* Washington, DC: Bureau of Justice Statistics.

Truman, J. L., & Morgan, R. E. (2016). Criminal Victimization, 2015. U.S. Department of Justice, Bureau of Justice Statistics. Retrieved from https://www.bjs.gov/content/pub/pdf/cv15.pdf

Turrell, S. C., & Cornell-Swanson, L. (2005). Not all alike: Within group differences in seeking help for same-sex relationship abuses. *Journal of Gay & Lesbian Social Services, 18*(1), 77–88.

Turvill, W. (2013, November 1). Saatchi decides not to sue Nigella and reveal the "truth" over their break-up as he "wants to get on with his life." *Daily Mail.* Retrieved from http://www.dailymail.co.uk/news/article-2483393/Charles-Saatchi-wont-sue-Nigella-Lawson-divorce-truth.html

Ullman, S. E., & Townsend, S. M. (2007). Barriers to working with sexual assault providers. *Violence Against Women, 13*(4), 412–443.

Ullman, S. E., & Townsend, S. M. (2008). What is an empowerment approach to working with sexual assault survivors? *Journal of Community Psychology, 36*(3), 299–312.

United Nations. (2000). *Protocol to prevent, suppress and punish trafficking in persons, especially women and children.* Geneva, Switzerland: Author.

United Nations. (2008). UN-backed container exhibit spotlights plight of sex trafficking victims. UN News Centre. Retrieved from http://www.un.org/apps/news/story.asp?NewsID=25524&Cr=trafficking&Cr1

United Nations. (2010). Impunity for domestic violence, "honor killings" cannot continue. UN News Centre. Retrieved from http://www.un.org/apps/news/story.asp?NewsID=33971&Cr=violence+against+women&Cr1

United Nations Office on Drugs and Crime (UNODC). (2016). Global Report on Trafficking in Persons 2016 Retrieved from http://www.unodc.org/documents/data-and-analysis/glo-tip/2016_Global_Report_on_Trafficking_in_Persons.pdf

United Nations Office on Drugs and Crime (UNODC) (2017). United Nations Survey of Crime Trends and Operations of Criminal Justice Systems (2016 UN-CTS). Retrieved from https://www.unodc.org/unodc/en/data-and-analysis/statistics/crime/cts-data-collection.html

United Nations Office of the Special Representative of the Secretary General for Sexual Violence in Conflict. (2015). Democratic Republic of the Congo. Retrieved from http://www.un.org/sex-ualviolenceinconflict/countries/democratic-republic-of-the-congo/

United States v. Virginia, 518 U.S. 515, 532 (1996).

UN News Centre. (2013, May 31). UN human rights office regrets Papua New Guinea's decision to resume death penalty. Retrieved from http://www.un.org/apps/news/story.asp?NewsID=45049&Cr=death+penalty&Cr1=&Kw1=sorcery&Kw2=&Kw3=#.UtR6byjiOI4

UN: "Sorcery" murders must end. (2013, April 13). *New Zealand Herald*. Retrieved from http://www.nzherald.co.nz/world/news/article.cfm?c_id=2&objectid=10877300

U.S. Bureau of the Census. (2000). Profiles of general demographic characteristics. Retrieved from http://www2.census.gov/cen-sus_2000/datasets/demographic_profile/0_United_States/2kh00.pdf

U.S. Census. (2013). Quick facts, Stubenville, OH. Retrieved from http://quickfacts.census.gov/qfd/states/39/3974608.html

U.S. Census (2016). Facts for Features, Mother's Day. Retrieved from https://www.census.gov.newsroom/facts-for-features/2016/cb-16-ff09.html

U.S. Department of Defense. (2010). *DoD fiscal year (FY) 2009 annual report on sexual assaults in the military services*. Washington, DC: Office of the Secretary of Defense, Sexual Assault Prevention and Response Office. Retrieved from http://www.sapr.mil/media/pdf/reports/fy09_annual_report.pdf

U.S. Department of Health and Human Services. (2011). *National human trafficking resource center fact sheet*. U.S. Department of Health and Human Services. Retrieved from http://www.hhs.gov/

U.S. Department of Justice, Office of Justice Programs. (1998). *New directions from the field: Victims' rights and services for the 21st century*. Washington, DC: U.S. Government Printing Office.

U.S. Department of Justice. (2003). *Criminal victimization, 2003*. Washington, DC: Author.

U.S. Department of Labor (2008). Ready4Work: Final Research Project. Retrieved from https://wdr.doleta.gov/research/FullText_Documents/Ready4Work%20Final%20Research%20Report.pdf

U.S. Department of State. (2008). *Trafficking in Persons Report 2008*. U.S. Department of State. Retrieved from http://www.state.gov

U.S. Department of State. (2009). *Trafficking in Persons Report 2009*. U.S. Department of State. Retrieved from http://www.state.gov

U.S. Department of State. (2011). *Trafficking in Persons Report 2011*. U.S. Department of State. Retrieved from http://www.state.gov/j/tip/rls/tiprpt/2010/index.htm

U.S. Department of State. (2012). *Trafficking in Persons Report 2012*. U.S. Department of State. Retrieved from http://www.state.gov

U.S. Department of State. (2013). *Trafficking in Persons Report 2013*. U.S. Department of State. Retrieved from http://www.state.gov/documents/organization/210737.pdf

U.S. v. Cabell, 890 F. Supp. 13, 19 [D.D.C. 1995].

U.S. v. Johnson, 964 F.2d 124 (2d Cir. 1992).

U.S. v. Windsor, 133 S.Ct. 2675 (2013).

Valera, R. J., Sawyer, R. G., & Schiraldi, G. R. (2000). Violence and post-traumatic stress disorder in a sample of inner city street prostitutes. *American Journal of Health Studies, 16*(3), 149–155.

van der Put, C. E., Dekovic, M., Hoeve, M., Stams, G., van der Laan, P. H., & Langewouters, F. (2014). Risk assessment of girls: Are there any sex differences in risk factors for re-offending and in risk profiles. *Crime and Delinquency, 60*(7), 1033–1056.

Van Outtsel, J., Ponnet, K., & Walrave, M. (2016). Cyber dating abuse victimization among secondary school students from a life-style-routine activities theory perspective. *Journal of Interpersonal Violence*. DOI: 10.1177/08862605166293990

Vanassche, S., Sodermans, A. K., Matthijs, K., & Swicegood, G. (2014). The effects of family type, family relationships and parental role models on delinquency and alcohol use among Flemish adolescents. *Journal of Child and Family Studies, 23*(1), 128–143.

Van Voorhis, P., Salisbury, E., Wright, E., & Bauman, A. (2008). *Achieving accurate pictures of risk and identifying gender respon-sive needs: Two new assessments for women offenders*. Washington, DC: United States Department of Justice, National Institute of Corrections.

Van Wormer, K. S., & Bartollas, C. (2010). *Women and the criminal justice system*. Boston: Allyn and Bacon.

Ventura Miller, H., Miller, J. M., & Barnes, J. C. (2016). Reentry programming for opioid and opiate involved female offenders: Findings from a mixed methods evaluation. *Journal of Criminal Justice,* 129–136.

VictimLaw (n.d.). About victims' rights. Retrieved from https://www.victimlaw.org/victimlaw/pages/victimsRight.jsp

Viglione, J., Hannon, L., & DeFina, R. (2011). The impact of light skin on prison time for Black female offenders. *The Social Science Journal, 48*, 250–258.

Villagran, L. (n.d.). The victims' movement in Mexico. Retrieved from https://www.wilsoncenter.org/sites/default/files/05_victims_movement_villagran.pdf

Visher, C. A. (1983). Gender, police arrest decisions, and notions of chivalry. *Criminology, 21*, 5–28.

von Hentig, H. (1948). *The criminal and his victim: Studies in the sociobiology of crime*. Cambridge, MA: Yale University Press.

Wagenaar, H. (2006). Democracy and prostitution: Deliberating the legalization of brothels in the Netherlands. *Administration and Society, 38*(2), 198–235.

Walker, L. E. (1979). *The battered woman*. New York: Harper and Row.

Walsh, D. (2012, October 9). Taliban gun down girl who spoke up for rights. *New York Times*. Retrieved from http://www.nytimes

.com/2012/10/10/world/asia/teen-school-activist-malala-yousafzai-survives-hit-by-pakistani-taliban.html? pagewanted+all&_r=0

Walters, M. L., Chen, J., & Breiding, M. J. (2013). The National Intimate Partner and Sexual Violence Survey (NISVS): 2010 Findings on victimization by sexual orientation. Atlanta, GA: National Center for Injury Prevention and Control, Centers for Disease Control and Prevention.

Wang, M. C., Horne, S. G., Levitt, H. M., & Klesges, L. M. (2009). Christian women in IPV relationships: An exploratory study of religious factors. *Journal of Psychology and Christianity, 28*(3), 224–235.

Wang, Y. (2011). Voices from the margin: A case study of a rural lesbian's experience with woman-to-woman sexual violence. *Journal of Lesbian Studies, 15*(2), 166–175.

Ward, J. T., Hartley, R. D., & Tillyer, R. (2016). Unpacking gender and racial/ethnic biases in the federal sentencing of drug offenders: A causal mediation approach. *Journal of Criminal Justice, 46*: 196–206.

Warr, M. (1984). Fear of victimization: Why are women and the elderly more afraid. *Social Science Quarterly, 65*(3), 681–702.

Warr, M. (1985). Fear of rape among urban women. *Social Problems*, 238–250.

Warshaw, R. (1994). *I never called it rape.* New York: Harper Perennial.

Washington, P. A. (2001). Disclosure patterns of Black female sexual assault survivors. *Violence Against Women, 7*(11), 1254–1283.

Watterson, K. (1996). *Women in prison: Inside the concrete womb.* Boston: Northeastern University Press.

Webster v. Reproductive Health Services, 492 U.S. 490 (1989).

Weerman, F. M., & Hoeve, M. (2012). Peers and delinquency: Are sex differences in delinquency explained by peer factors. *European Journal of Criminology, 9*(3), 228–244.

Wells, T., Colbert, S., & Slate, R. N. (2006). Gender matters: Differences in state probation officer stress. *Journal of Contemporary Criminal Justice, 22*(1), 63–79.

Welsh-Huggins, A. (2013a, March 17). Teen in Steubenville rape case: "I could not remember anything." *Huffington Post.* Retrieved from http://www.huffingtonpost.com/2013/03/16/steubenville-rape-case-teen-cant-recall-assault_n_2893398.html?utm_hp_ref=steubenville-rape

Welsh-Huggins, A. (2013b, May 2). Steubenville Rape: Teen girls guilty of threatening rape victim on Twitter. *Huffington Post.* Retrieved from http://www.huffingtonpost.com/2013/05/02/steubenville-rape-teen-girls-guilty-threats-twitter_n_3204301.html

Wesely, J. K. (2006). Considering the context of women's violence: Gender, lived experiences, and cumulative victimization. *Feminist Criminology, 1*(4), 303–328.

West, C. M. (2004). Black women and intimate partner violence: New directions for research. *Journal of Interpersonal Violence, 19*(12), 1487–1493.

West, D. A., & Lichtenstein, B. (2006). Andrea Yates and the criminalization of the filicidal maternal body. *Feminist Criminology, 1*(3), 173–187.

Westervelt, S. D., & Cook, K. J. (2007). Feminist research methods in theory and action: Learning from death row exonerees. In S. Miller (Ed.), *Criminal justice research and practice: Diverse voices from the field* (pp. 21–37). Boston: University Press of New England.

Westmarland, N. (2001). The quantitative/qualitative debate and feminist research: A subjective view of objectivity. *Forum: Qualitative Social Research, 2*(1). Retrieved from http://www.qualitative-research.net/index.php/fqs/article/view/974/2125

Weymouth, M. (2014, September 9). Wait, people are still victim blaming Janay Rice? *Philadelphia Magazine.* Retrieved from http://www.phillymag.com/news/2014/09/09/people-still-victim-blaming-janay-rice/

Whaley, R. B., Hayes-Smith, J., & Hayes-Smith, R. (2010). Gendered pathways: Gender, mediating factors and the gap in boys' and girls' substance use. *Crime and Delinquency, 59*(5), 651–669.

Whaley, R. B., Hayes, R., & Smith, J. M. (2014). Differential reactions to school bonds, peers, and victimization in the case of adolescent substance use: The moderating effect of sex. *Crime & Delinquency, 62*(10), 1263–1285.

Whitaker, M. (2014, April 2). Marisa Alexander in court, seeking "stand your ground" immunity. MSNBC. Retrieved from http://www.msnbc.com/politicsnation/florida-mom-seeks-stand-your-ground

Widom, C. S. (1989). The cycle of violence. *Science, 244,* 160–166.

Wies, J. R. (2008). Professionalizing human services: A case of domestic violence shelter advocates. *Human Communication, 67*(2), 221–233.

Williams, M. (2007). Women's representation on state trial and appellate courts. *Social Science Quarterly, 88*(5), 1192–1204.

Wiltz, T. (2016, August 9). More states lift welfare restrictions for drug felons. Stateline. The PEW Charitable Trusts. Retrieved from http://www.pewtrusts.org/en/research-and-analysis/blogs.stateline/2016/08/09/more-states-life-welfare-restrictions-for-drug-felons

Wismont, J. M. (2000). The lived pregnancy experience of women in prison. *Journal of Midwifery and Women's Health, 45*(4), 292–300.

Wittmer, D. E., & Bouche, V. (2013). The limits of gendered leadership: Policy implications of female leadership on "women's issues". *Politics & Gender, 9*, 245–275.

Women in Federal Law Enforcement. (2011). Pregnancy guidelines for federal law enforcement. Retrieved from http://www.wifle.org/pregnancyguidelines.pdf

Women's Health. (2004). *UMHS Women's Health Program.* Retrieved from http://www.med.umich.edu/whp/newsletters/summer04/p03-dating.html

Women's Prison Association (WPA). (2003). *WPA focus on women and justice: A portrait of women in prison.* Retrieved from http://www.wpaonline.org/pdf/Focus_December 2003.pdf

Women's Prison Association (WPA). (2008). *Mentoring women in reentry.* Retrieved from http://www.wpaon line.org

Women's Prison Association (WPA). (2009a). *Quick facts: Women and criminal justice 2009.* Retrieved from http://www.wpaonline.org

Women's Prison Association (WPA). (2009b). Mothers, infants and imprisonment: A national look at prison nurseries and community-based alternatives. Retrieved from http://www.wpaoline.com

Women's Prison Association. (WPA). (n.d.). History & mission. Retrieved from http://www.wpaonline.org/about/history

Women's Prison Association (WPA). (n.d.). Laws banning shackling during childbirth gaining momentum nationwide. Retrieved from http://66.29.139.159/pdf/Shackling%20Brief_final.pdf

Wood, L. (2017). "I look across from me and I see me": Survivors as advocates in intimate partner violence agencies. *Violence Against Women, 23*(3), 309–329.

Wooditch, A. (2011). The efficacy of the *Trafficking in Persons Report*: A review of the evidence. *Criminal Justice Policy Review, 22*(4), 471–493.

Woodlock, D. (2017). The abuse of technology in domestic violence and stalking. *Violence Against Women, 23*(5), 584–602.

Wooldredge, J., & Griffin, T. (2005). Displaced discretion under Ohio sentencing guidelines. *Journal of Criminal Justice, 33,* 301–316.

World Health Organization. (2012). *Sexual and reproductive health.* Retrieved from http://www.who.int/reproductivehealth/about_us/en/index.html.

World Law Direct. (2011). Shackling laws. Retrieved from http://www.worldlawdirect.com/forum/law-wiki/43470-shackling-laws.html

Wright, E. M., DeHart, D. D., Koons-Witt, B. A., & Crittenden, C. A. (2013). "Buffers" against crime? Exploring the roles and limitations of positive relationships among women in prison. *Punishment & Society, 15*(1), 71–95.

Wyse, J. J. B. (2013). Rehabilitating criminal selves: Gendered strategies in community corrections. *Gender & Society, 27*(2), 231–255.

Yacoubian, G. S., Urbach, B. J., Larsen, K. L., Johnson, R. J., & Peters, R. J. (2000). A comparison of drug use between prostitutes and other female arrestees. *Journal of Alcohol and Drug Education, 46*(2), 12–26.

Yahne, C. E., Miller, W. R., Irvin-Vitela, L., & Tonigan, J. S. (2002). Magdalena Pilot Project: Motivational outreach to substance abusing women street sex workers. *Journal of Substance Abuse Treatment, 23*(1), 49–53.

Yavuz, N., & Welch, E. W. (2010). Addressing fear of crime in public space: Gender differences in reaction to safety measures in train transit. *Urban Studies, 47*(12), 2491–2515.

Yesberg, J. A., Scanlan, J. M., Hanby, L, J., Serin, R. C., & Polaschek, D. L. L. (2015). Predicting women's recidivism: Validating a dynamic community-based 'gender-neutral' tool. *Probation Journal, 62*(1), 33–48.

Yeum, E. B. B. (2010). Eleventh annual review of gender and sexuality law: Criminal law chapter: Rape, sexual assault and evidentiary matters. *Georgetown Journal of Gender & the Law, 11,* 191–869.

Yirga, W. S., Kassa, N. A., Gebremichael, M. W., & Aro, A. R. (2012). Female genital mutilation: Prevalence, perceptions, and effect on women's health in Kersa district of Ethiopia. *International Journal of Women's Health, 4*(1), 45–54.

Yoshihama, M., Ramakrishnon, A., Hammock, A. C., & Khaliq, M. (2012). Intimate partner violence prevention program in an Asian immigrant community: Integrating theories, data and community. *Violence Against Women, 18*(7), 763–783.

Young, M., & Stein, J. (2004). The history of the crime victims' movement in the United States: A component of the Office for Victims of Crime Oral History Project. Washington DC: U.S. Department of Justice. Retrieved from https://www.ncjrs.gov/ovc_archives/ncvrw/2005/pdf/historyofcrime.pdf

Yu, H. (2015). An examiniation of women in federal law enforcement: An exploratory analysis of the challenges they face in the work environment. *Feminist Criminology, 10*(3), 259–278.

Zaitzow, B. H., & Thomas, J. (2003). *Women in prison: Gender and social control.* Boulder, CO: Lynne Rienner.

Zaykowski, H., & Gunter, W. D. (2013). Gender differences in victimization risk: Exploring the role of deviant lifestyles. *Violence and Victims, 28*(2), 341–356.

Zettler, H. R., & Morris, R. G. (2015). An exploratory assessment of race and gender specific predictors of failure to appear in court among defendants released via a pretrial services agency. *Criminal Justice Review, 40*(4), 417–430.

Index

AAPI (Asian American and Pacific Islander population), rape reporting by, 52
Abolish Slavery (ngo), 145
Abuse:
    female delinquency and, 123
    See also entries for specific types of abuse
Abused Women's Active Response Emergency (AWARE), 72
Academy, women and, 3–4
Academy of Criminal Justice Sciences, 4
Ackerman, A. R., 117
Acoca, L., 124
Acquaintance rape, 27, 40–41
Addison, M., 40
Adler, Freda, 106–107
Adoption and Safe Families Act of 1975, 194
African American women, rape and sexual assault of, 51–52
Age-of-consent campaign, 114–115
Agnew, Robert, 105–106
AIAN (American Indian and Alaska Native population), rape rates in, 51
Air Force Academy, 43
Alexander, Marissa, 145
Alexander, Travis, 147
Allan, E., 132–133
Alvi, S., 31
American Bar Association, 211–212
American Congress of Obstetricians and Gynecologists, 193
American Indian and Alaska Native population (AIAN), rape rates in, 51
American Medical Association, 193
American Society of Criminology (ASC), 4
Amnesty International, 93–94
Anthony, Casey, 146–147
Anti-Drug Abuse Act, 156
Arias, Jody, 147
Arts programming for at-risk youth, 126
ASC (American Society of Criminology), 4
Asian American and Pacific Islander population (AAPI), rape reporting by, 52
Assault. *See* Rape and sexual assault
Atkins, Susan, 102–103
Attachment, in social bond theory, 103–104

Auburn State Prison (NY), 181
Augustus, John, 208
Austin, Rodney, 63
Australia, female offender processing in, 162
Australian Bureau of Statistics (ABS), 15
AWARE (Abused Women's Active Response Emergency), 72

Bader, C. D., 107
Baldwin, Lola, 198
Bales, W. D., 178
Baltimore Ravens football team, 25
Bank robberies, 138
Banks, Tyra, 75
Ban the box campaign, 173
Bardo, Robert, 80
Barefield v. Leach (1952), 165
Barratt, C. L., 204
Barrow, Clyde Chestnut, 138
Bates, K. A., 107
Battered Women's Syndrome, 177
Battering:
    battered women's movement, 59–60
    immigrant partners, 69
    intervention programming for, 74
    mandatory arrest policies effect on, 73
Bay Area Women Against Rape (San Francisco, CA), 218
Bedford Hills Correctional Facility (NY), 193
Belief, in social bond theory, 103–104
Belknap, Joanne, 4, 99, 108–109, 111, 125
Bergman, M. E., 204
Berry, Amanda, 30
Black feminist criminology, 3
Black feminist theory, 111
Blackwell, B. S., 160
Blaming victims, 24–26
Blankenship, Betty, 199
Bloom, B. E., 166–167
Bond, C., 162
Boykins, A. D., 51
Brattan, Catherine F., 208

Breitenbach, M., 110
Brennan, P. K., 155
Brennan, T., 110
Brockway, Zebulon, 208
Broidy, L., 105
Brown, Jerry, 145, 177
Brunson, R., 152
Bryant, Kobe, 25
Bui, H., 69
Bullock, Sandra, 75
Bundeskriminalamt (BKA, Federal Criminal Police Office of Germany), 15
Bureau of Justice Statistics, 137, 169
Burgess-Proctor, Amanda, 2, 111
Burrow, J. D., 160
Bush, George H. W., 217

Caldwell, R. M., 105
California Department of Corrections, 187
California Institution for Women, 103, 177, 184
California's Uniform Determinate Sentencing Act of 1954, 184
California Youth Authority, 105, 110
Campbell, A., 143
Campus rape and sexual assault, 47–49
Canales, Ernesto, 24
Caraway, Hattie, 214
Carter, Jimmy, 138, 216
Carter, Michelle, 147
Cartier, J., 192
Case studies:
    arts programming for at-risk youth, 126
    bank robberies, women involved in, 138
    California prison realignment, 187
    Carter, Michelle, 147
    financial challenges behind bars, 191
    gender and kidnapping, 30–31
    Girl Scouts Beyond Bars program, 195
    girl's voices, 126–127
    intimate partner abuse and NFL, 63
    intimate partner abuse in India, 70
    life after parole, 177
    Manson women, 102–103
    men and masculinity, 108
    pregnancy and policing, 203
    rape culture, 40–41
    rape in military, 43–45
    self-care for victim advocates, 220
    self-defense, women and, 145
    sexual abuse of girls in confinement, 121
    stalking on college campuses, 77
    statutory rape, 48–49
    victim's rights in Mexico, 23–24
    witch burnings in Papua New Guinea, 90
    women in politics, 214–215
    Yousafzai, Malala, 95–97

Castro, Ariel, 30
Centers for Disease Control, 14
Charge-reduction strategies, 153
Cheeseman, K. A., 207
Chesler, P., 94
Chesney-Lind, Meda, 109, 111
Chicago (play and film), 146
Chicago Women's Health Risk Study, 22
Children:
    female delinquency in, 123
    incarcerated mothers and, 192–194
    intimate partner abuse impact on, 65
    killing of, 148–149
    leaving abusive relationships and, 71–72
    sexual assault of, 36
Child-saving movement of Progressive Era, 114
China, female offender processing in, 161
Chivalry hypothesis, 151, 154, 161–162
Cho, S.-Y., 87
Civil Rights Act of 1942, 200, 208
Civil Rights Act of 1950, 200
Clinton, Bill, 138, 216–217
Clubine, Brenda, 177
Clubine, Robert, 177
CNN-TV, 41
Cochran, J. C., 178
Code of Hammurabi (ancient Babylonia), 35
Coffal, Liz, 199
Cohen, A. K., 105
Cohen, L. E., 31
College campuses, stalking on, 77
Columbia University, 48
Columbine shootings, 108
Commitment, in social bond theory, 103–104
Community-based corrections, 169–171
Community policing, 202–204
Community Probation Services (New Zealand), 169
Connell, Raewyn, 108
Controlled Substances Act of 1948, 42
Convicted Women Against Abuse, 177
Cooper v. Morin (1957), 166
Copp, J. E., 65
Core rights of victims, 22
Corrections, 165–178
    community-based, 169–171
    gender-responsive programming in, 165–168
    parole, 171
    recidivism, 177–178
    reentry issues, 171–177
    women as professionals in, 205–208
    See also Criminal justice system; Incarceration of women
Court TV, 146
CPC (Criminal Punishment Code, FL), 156
Cressingham, Clara, 214
Crime Survey for England and Wales (CSEW), 16

Crime Victim's Rights Act of 1984, 22
Criminality of Women, The (Pollak), 102
Criminal justice system:
  intimate partner abuse, 72–74
  victimization theories and, 21–26
  work in, 6
  See also Female offenders, processing and sentencing of
Criminal justice system, women as professionals in:
  corrections, 205–208
  judiciary, 215–218
  law and, 211–215
  overview, 197–209
  police, 198–205
  probation and parole officers, 208–209
  victim services, 218–223
Criminal Man, The (Lombroso), 100
Criminal Punishment Code (CPC, FL), 156
Criminology. *See* Female offenders, crimes and; Female offending;
    Women and crime, introduction to
Criminology (journal), 4
Critical race feminist theory, 111
Crittenden, C. A., 178
CSEW (Crime Survey for England and Wales), 16
Culture:
  domestic violence accepted in, 69–70, 75
  leaving abusive relationships and, 71–72
  masculine, in policing, 202
Custodial institutions, 182–183
Cyberstalking and, 78–79
Cycle of victimization and offending, 31–32

Daigle, L. E., 105
Daly, K., 109
Dark figure of crime, 13, 133
Dating violence, 65–67
Davis, S., 217
Debt bondage, 86
Dedel, K., 124
DeHart, D. D., 178
DeJesus, Georgina, 30
DeKeseredy, Walter S., 31
DeLisi, M., 105
Dick, Kirby, 44
Dieterich, W., 110
Dietz, N. A., 80
Differential association theory, 105
Dignity for Incarcerated Women Act, 214
Directory of Adult and Juvenile Correctional Departments,
    Institutions and Agencies and Probation and Parole
    Authorities, 206
Domestic violence, cultural acceptance of, 69–70
Dougherty, Lee Grace, 138
Downey, R. A., 207
DRAOR (Dynamic Risk Assessment for Offender Reentry), 169
Dreher, A., 87

Drug abuse:
  crimes related to, 134–136
  rape and sexual assault facilitated by, 41–45
  sentencing offenders and, 156–158
  See also Substance abuse
Drug Enforcement Administration, 201
Drug-Induced Rape Prevention and Punishment Act of 1974, 42
Dual-arrest situations, 73
Duckworth, Tammy, 214
Dugard, Jaycee, 30–31
Dynamic Risk Assessment for Offender Reentry (DRAOR), 169

Economic abuse, 62–63
Elliott, Exekiel, 63
Elrod, P., 105
Emotional abuse, 62
English Chancery Courts, 113
Estrada, R., 107
Ethnicity. *See* Race and ethnicity
European Union (EU), human trafficking policies of, 87–88
Evil woman hypothesis, 151
Excessive force, by police, 204
Ex-offenders, women as, 5
Extralegal factors, sentencing and, 155, 158–159

Fair Sentencing Act of 1990, 156
Families, female delinquency and, 122–123
Farley, M., 140
Fatal Attraction (film), 145
Federal Bureau of Investigation (FBI), Uniform Crime Reports
    published by, 7
Federal Crime Victims Act, 60
Feld, B. C., 121
Felson, M., 31
Female genital mutilation, 91–92
Female Offender, The (Lombroso and Ferrero), 100
Female offenders, crimes and, 131–150
  drugs and, 134–136
  filicide, 148–149
  overview, 131–134
  property crime, 137–138
  prostitution, 138–142
  violence, women and, 142–147
Female offenders, processing and sentencing of, 151–163
  criminal justice system stage, 152–154
  extralegal factors and, 158–159
  international perspectives on, 161–162
  overview, 151–152
  race and, 154–156
  sentencing guidelines and, 159–161
  war on drugs and, 156–158
Female offending, 99–111
  cycle of victimization and, 31–32
  feminist criminology, 109–111
  historical theories of, 100–103

modern theories of, 106–108
overview, 99–100
traditional theories of, 103–106
victimization intersection with, 6
Femicide, 23, 24, 83, 94
Feminism:
    research methodology in, 17–18
    women and crime influenced by, 2–4
Feminist criminology, 3, 109–111
Feminist pathways perspective on victimization, 32–33
Ferrero, William, 100–101
Filicide (killing one's children), 148–149
Financial challenges in incarceration, 191
Finland, female offender processing in, 162
Finn, M. A., 160
Five Hundred Delinquent Women (Glueck and Glueck), 101
Fleisher, M. S., 144
Flynn, William, 146
Food Stamp programs (SNAP), 173–176
Forke, C. M., 77
Formal processing of juvenile cases, by gender, 117–118
Foster, Jodi, 75
Free Marissa Now campaign, 145
Friendly Airports for Mothers Act, 214
Fry, Elizabeth, 182

Gang membership, girls in, 142–144
Garafalo, R., 31
Garcia, I., 106
Garrido, Nancy, 30–31
Garrido, Phillip, 30–31
GBMI (guilty but mentally ill) verdict, 149
Gehring, K., 153
Gender bias. *See* Female offenders, processing and sentencing of
Gendered assignments, in policing, 199
Gendered equality efforts of 1938s, 199–201
Gendered justice, 1
Gender gap research, 5
Gender-neutral sentencing, 160–161
Gender-responsive programming, 165–168
Gender-specific programming, 125–129
Genital mutilation of females, 91–92
Gibson, C. L., 105
Gilfus, M. E., 111
Gillibrand, Kirsten, 45
Ginsburg, Ruth Bader, 215–217
Giordano, P. C., 65
Girl Scouts Beyond Bars (GSBB) program, 195
Glass ceiling, in law firms, 213
Glover v. Johnson (1957), 165
Glueck, Eleanor, 101–102
Glueck, Sheldon, 101–102
Golick, Rich, 174
Goodell, Roger, 63
"Good ol' boy network," in corrections facilities, 207
Gottfredson, Michael R., 31, 104–105

Great Depression, 138
Grella, C. E., 192
Griffin, T., 153
Griffin v. Michigan Department of Corrections (1970), 205–206
Grossman, Mary B., 211
Gruhl, J., 153
Grummett v. Rushen (1973), 206
GSBB (Girl Scouts Beyond Bars) program, 195
Guevara, L., 155
Guilty but mentally ill (GBMI) verdict, 149

Hagan, John, 107
Hageman, Ra'Shede, 63
Haire, S., 217
Harassment:
    behaviors, 75
    cyberstalking, 79
    defined, 75n5
    honor-based violence and, 95
    right to protection from, 22
    sexual. *See* Sexual harassment
Harlow, Poppy, 41
Harris, Eric, 108
Harris, Kamala, 214
Harvard Law School, 217
Hate crime victimization, 27
HBV (honor-based violence), 92–97
Hearst, Patricia, 138
Hearst, William Randolph, 138
Hebert, C., 217
Heidensohn, Frances, 109
Heimer, Karen, 4
Hegemonic masculinity, 108
Hentig, Hans von, 29
Herz, D., 155
Hester, R., 160
High School Youth Risk Behavior Survey (Centers for Disease Control), 65
Hinckley, John, Jr., 75
Hindelang, M. J., 31
Hipwell, A., 123
Hirschi, Travis, 103–105
Hispanic/Latina women, rape and sexual assault of, 52–53
Holleran, D., 160
Hollingsworth v. Perry (1993), 217
Holly, Carrie Clyde, 214
Holsinger, Kristi, 109, 111, 125
Honor-based violence (HBV), 92–97
Hoskins, Robert Dewey, 75
Howard, G. G., 145
HTRS (Human Trafficking Reporting System, US Department of Justice), 85n
Human Rights Watch (ngo), 145
Human trafficking, 84–90
Human Trafficking Reporting System (HTRS, U.S. Department of Justice), 85n
Humiston, G. S., 203

IACHR (Inter-American Commission on Human Rights), 24
I am Malala (Yousafzai), 97
Immigrants, intimate partner abuse of, 69–70
Incapacitated rape and sexual assault, 41–45
Incarceration of women, 181–195
    children of incarcerated mothers, 192–194
    contemporary issues, 185–189
    historical context of prisons, 181–185
    physical and mental health needs of women in, 189–192
    See also Corrections
Index crimes, 9
India, intimate partner abuse in, 70
Indianapolis Police Department, 199
Indiana Women's Prison (IWP), 182
Inter-American Commission on Human Rights (IACHR), 24
International Association of the Chiefs of Police, 199, 203
International perspectives processing and sentencing, 161–162
International victimization issues, 83–97
    female genital mutilation, 91–92
    honor-based violence, 92–97
    human trafficking, 84–90
    rape as war crime, 91
Intimate partner abuse, 59–81
    barriers to leaving abusive relationships, 71–72
    children of, 65
    cyberstalking and, 78–79
    dating violence, 65
    identifying, 60–63
    immigrant victims of, 69–70
    incarceration of victims of, 177
    LGBTQ and, 66–68
    police, corrections, and victims of, 72–75
    race and ethnicity effects on, 68–69
    stalking and, 75–78
    stalking laws, 80
    victim assistance services for, 219–223
    violence cycle, 64
Invisible No More Campaign, 45
Invisible War, The (Dick and Ziering), 44
Involvement, in social bond theory, 103–104
Italian Supreme Court, 161
IWP (Indiana Women's Prison), 182

Jails. *See* Corrections; Incarceration of women
Jail the offender and protect the victim models,
    for human trafficking, 88–90
Jeanne Clery Disclosure of Campus Security Policy and
    Campus Crime Statistics Act of 1977 and 1991, 77
Jeffries, S., 162
Jessica's Law, 37
Jilani, Hina, 93
JJDP (Juvenile Justice and Delinquency Prevention) Act of 1952, 121
Johnson, H., 137
Jordan v. Gardner (1970), 206
Judiciary, women as professionals in, 215–218
Justice Quarterly, 4

Justicia para Nuestras Hijas (Justice for our Daughters,
    Mexican organization), 24
Just world hypothesis, 25
Juvenile delinquency, 113–130
    drug-related, 156
    nature and extent of, 115–121
    risk factors for, 122–125
    sexual double standard for, 113–115
    status offenses, 121
    unique needs of, 125–129
    "violent" girls, 122–121
Juvenile Justice and Delinquency Prevention (JJDP) Act of 1952, 121

Kagan, Elena, 215–217
Katz, J., 155
Kellermann, A. L., 144
Kelly, V., 140
Kercher, Meredith, 161
Kidnapping, gender and, 30–31
Kilpatrick, D. G., 42
Klay, Ariana, 45
Klebold, Dylan, 108
Klock, Frances, 214
Knight, Michelle, 30
Knox, Amanda, 161
Koons-Witt, B. A., 159–160, 178
Krenwinkel, Patricia, 102–103
Krienert, J. L., 144
Kruttschnitt, Candace, 4
Kruzan, Sara, 145

LaBianca, Leno, 102
LaBianca, Rosemary, 102
Labor trafficking, 86
Lane, J., 106
Language barriers, 70
Lathrop, Mary Florence, 211
Laub, John H., 107–108
Law, women as professionals in, 211–215
Law Enforcement Assistance Administration (LEAA), 200
Lawrence v. Texas (1983), 216
LEAA (Law Enforcement Assistance Administration), 200
Legal factors, sentencing and, 155
Leniata, Kepari, 90
Letterman, David, 75
Level of Service Inventory-Revised (LSI-R) assessment tool, 169
LGBTQ:
    intimate partner abuse of, 66–68
    rape and sexual assault of, 49–51
Liang, B., 161
Life course theory, 107–108
Lifestyle theory of victimization, 31
Lockwood, Belva Ann, 211
Loeber, R., 123
Lohan, Lindsay, 75
Lombroso, Cesare, 100–101

Longmore, M. A., 65
Los Angeles Police Department, 198
Lowe, N. C., 105
LSI-R (Level of Service Inventory-Revised) assessment tool, 169
Lu, H., 161

Madonna, 75
Major League Baseball, 217
Male inmate preference, 208
Maleness, 108
Mandatory arrest policies, 73
Manning, W. D., 65
Mansfield, Belle, 211
Manson, Charles, 102–103
Manson women, 102–103
Marital-rape exception, 37
Marshall, Brandon, 63
Martin, P. Y., 80
Maryland Correctional Institution for Women, 195
Masculine culture of policing, 202
Masculinity, 108
Masked criminality of women (Pollak), 102
Massachusetts Correctional Institution (MCI), 184
Masto, Catherine Cotez, 214
May, David, 105
Mays, Trent, 41
McCall, M., 217
McCaskill, Claire, 45
MCI (Massachusetts Correctional Institution), 184
MDVE (Minneapolis Domestic Violence Experiment)., 60
Mears, D. P., 178
Megan's Law, 37
Men and masculinity, 108
Mencken, F. C., 107
Mendelsohn, Benjamin, 28
Mendelsohn's theory of victimization, 28–31
Mental health:
    addiction and, 135
    acquaintance rape victims and, 40
    children of intimate partner abuse and, 65
    delinquent girls and, 125–127
    domestic violence advocates and, 219
    filicide and, 148–149
    incarceration and, 183, 189–192
    post incarceration, 173, 176, 178
    prison overcrowding and, 187
    sex workers and, 140–142
    stalking victim and, 77–78
    wraparound services and, 167
    See also Post-traumatic stress disorder (PTSD)
Mercy, J. A., 144
Merton, R. K., 105
Messerschmidt, James, 108
Messina, N., 192
Mexico, victim's rights in, 23–24

Military, rape in, 43–45
Military Justice Improvement Act of 1993, 45
Millar, G., 40
Miller, J., 143, 152
Miller, S., 123
Minneapolis Domestic Violence Experiment (MDVE)., 60
Model Penal Code (1933), 36
Moore, J. W., 143
Morash, Merry, 69
Morris, R. G., 153
Mount Pleasant Prison Annex (NY), 181
Moving On program, 169
Myers, R. K., 77

National Alcohol survey, 49
National Center for Injury Prevention and Control, 14
National Center for Transgendered Equality, 50
National Crime Victimization Survey (NCVS), 13–14, 22, 37, 53, 60, 133, 137
National Football League (NFL), intimate partner abuse and, 63
National Incident-Based Reporting System (NIBRS), 11–13
National Institute of Justice, 4, 195
National Intimate Partner and Sexual Violence Survey (NISVS), 14–16, 50
National Organization for Victim Assistance (NOVA), 218
National Prison Rape Elimination Commissions, 121
National Probation Act, 208
National Survey of Youth in Custody, 121
National Violence Against Women Survey (NVAWS), 14, 53, 60, 68, 80, 107
National Youth Gang Center, 142
Naval Academy, 44
NCVS (National Crime Victimization Survey), 13–14, 22, 37, 53, 60, 133, 137
Nelson, D. B., 77
Net widening practices, 114–115
Neumayer, E., 87
Newgate Prison (UK), 182
New York House of Refuge, 114
New York Times, 203
NFL (National Football League), intimate partner abuse and, 63
NIBRS (National Incident-Based Reporting System), 11–13
Nilsson, A., 107
Ninth Judicial Circuit Court of Florida, 146
NISVS (National Intimate Partner and Sexual Violence Survey), 14–16, 50
Nixon, Richard, 156, 200
Nobel Peace Prize, 97
Nogami-Campbell, Michi, 63
NOVA (National Organization for Victim Assistance), 218
NVAWS (National Violence Against Women Survey), 14, 53, 60, 68, 80

Obama, Barack, 156, 217
O'Connor, Sandra Day, 215–216
Offenders. *See* Female offenders *entries*

Offending. *See* Female offending
Office on Violence Against Women (OVW), 60
Overcrowding in prisons, 187. *See also* Incarceration of women
OVW (Office on Violence Against Women), 60
Owens, Marie, 198
Ozbay, O., 104
Ozcan, Y. Z., 104

Panetta, Leon, 45
Papua New Guinea, witch burnings in, 90
Parens patriae doctrine, 113–114
Parker, Bonnie Elizabeth, 138
Parole. *See* Corrections
Patriarchy, 108
Peers, female delinquency and, 123–124
Persky, Aaron, 41
Personal Responsibility and Work Opportunity Reconciliation Act
    (PRWORA), 49
Peterson, Ruth, 4
Petrovic, M., 107–108
"Pink collar" crack, 137, 157
Piquero, Nicole, 4
Police. *See* Criminal justice system
Politics, women in, 214–215
Pollak, Otto, 102, 151
Pollock, J. M., 208
Post-traumatic stress disorder (PTSD):
    rape and sexual assault resulting in, 54
    secondary trauma stress and, 219–220, 223
    sex workers' experience of, 140
Potter, G., 68
Potter, H., 111
Power control theory, 107
Pregnancy and policing, 203
Pregnancy Discrimination Act of 1956, 203
President's Commission on Law Enforcement and the Administration
    of Justice, 200
Prisoner Reentry Initiative, 177
Prison Policy Initiative, 191
Prisons. *See* Corrections; Incarceration of women
Probation, 169
Processing and sentencing of offenders. *See* Female offenders, processing
    and sentencing of
Property crime, 137–138
Prostitution:
    crack cocaine addiction and, 158
    criminal offense of, 138–142
    legalization debate, 141–142
Protocol to Prevent, Suppress and Punish Trafficking in Persons,
    especially Women and Children (United Nations), 87
PRWORA (Personal Responsibility and Work Opportunity
    Reconciliation Act), 49
Pseudo-families, in prisons, 189
PTSD. *See* Post-traumatic stress disorder (PTSD)
Pulling a train, in gangs, 143

Queer criminology. *See* LGBTQ

Rabe-Hemp, C. E., 202–203
Race and ethnicity:
    differential association theory of crime and, 105
    glass ceiling in law firms and, 213
    intimate partner abuse and, 68–69
    processing and sentencing offenders affected by, 154–156
    rape and sexual assault and, 15, 51–53, 220
    See also Incarceration of women
RAINN (Rape, Abuse and Incest National Network), 38
Rankin, Jeannette, 214
Rape, Abuse and Incest National Network (RAINN), 38
Rape and sexual assault, 35–57
    acquaintance, 27
    acquaintance *v.* stranger, 40–41
    campus, 47–49
    drug facilitated/incapacitated, 41–45
    girls in confinement experience of, 121
    historical perspectives on, 35–37
    LGBTQ, 49–51
    myths about, 38–39
    prevalence of, 38
    race, ethnicity and, 15
    racial differences in, 51–53
    sexual victimization defined, 37–38
    spousal, 46–47
    victims' roles in, 53–55
    war crimes as, 91
Rape myth acceptance, 26
Ray, Charlotte E., 211
Ready4Work initiative, 177
Reagan, Ronald, 75, 156, 216
Reauthorization of the Juvenile Justice and Delinquency Prevention
    (JJDP) Act of 1970, 121
Recidivism. *See* Corrections
Reentry. *See* Corrections
Reformatories, 182–184
Rehabilitation. *See* Corrections
Rennison, C. M., 133
Resiliency:
    corrections programs for building, 178
    delinquency *v.,* 124, 129
Resnick, P. J., 148
Restraining orders, 68, 70
Revictimization, in rape cases, 219
Rice, Janay, 25–26, 63
Rice, Ray, 25–26, 63
Richmond, Ma'lik, 41
Rickert, V. I., 40
Robberies, women involved in, 138
Rodriguez, Nancy, 4, 121
Routine activities theory of victimization, 31–32
Roy, Conrad, III, 147
"Rule of thumb," 59

Salisbury, E. J., 110
Same-sex intimate partner abuse, 66
Same-sex sexual assault, 36
Sampson, Robert J., 107–108
SAPR (Sexual Assault Prevention and Response) team, 44, 98
Schaeffer, Rebecca, 80
Schools, 124
Schwartz, J., 117
Schwartz, M. D., 31
Schwarzenegger, Arnold, 145
Secondary trauma stress, 219–220, 223
Secondary victimization, 26
Second Chance Act of 1987, 177
Second Chance Women's Re-entry Court (CA), 169
Self-care for victim advocates, 220
Self-control, in social bond theory, 105
Self-defense, women and, 145
Sentencing:
    guidelines, 154, 159–161
    See also Female offenders, processing and sentencing of
Sentencing Project, 174
Sentencing Reform Act of 1972, 159
SES (socioeconomic status) of offenders, 167
Sessions, Jefferson, 136
Severance, T., 189
Sevigny, E. L., 160
Sexual assault. *See* Rape and sexual assault
Sexual Assault Prevention and Response (SAPR) team, 44
Sexual double standard for juvenile delinquency of girls, 113–115
Sexual harassment:
    campus sexual assault and, 47
    labor trafficking and, 86
    military and, 43–44
    school and, 124
    women in corrections and, 208
    women in policing and, 18, 202, 207
Sexually transmitted infections (STI), 115
Shafia, Mohammad, 94
Share Art Program (MI), 126
Shekarkhar, Z., 105
Shoplifting, 137
Silverman, J. R., 105
Simon, Rita, 106–107
Sin by Silence (documentary), 177
Smart, Gregory, 146
Smart, Pamela, 146
Snapped (TV show), 145
Social bond theory, 103–104
Socioeconomic status (SES) of offenders, 167
Sollecito, Raffaele, 161
Songer, D. R., 217
Sorcery Act of 1949 (Papua New Guinea), 90
Sotomayor, Sandra, 215–217
South Korea, female offender processing in, 162

Special Weapons and Tactics (SWAT), in policing, 204–205
Spohn, C., 153, 155
Spousal rape and sexual assault, 46–47
SSI (Supplementary Security Income), 173–176
Stalking:
    cyberstalking, 78–79
    intimate partner abuse and, 75–78
    laws on, 80
Stand Your Ground Law, 145
Stanford University, 41
Status offenses, 121
Statutory rape, 48–49
Steffensmeier, D., 117, 132–133, 217
Stermac, L., 40
STI (sexually transmitted infections), 115
Strain theory, 102, 105–106
Stranger rape, 40–41
Street prostitution, 139
Substance abuse:
    crimes related to, 134–136
    female delinquency and, 124–125
Sulkowicz, Emma, 48
Sundance Movie Festival, 44
Supervision of women offenders. *See* Corrections
Supplemental Victimization Survey (SVS), 75–76
Supplementary Security Income (SSI), 173–176
Survey of Youth in Residential Placement, 121
Sutherland, Edwin, 105
SVS (Supplemental Victimization Survey), 75–76
SWAT (Special Weapons and Tactics), in policing, 204–205
Symbionese Liberation Army, 138

Tait, D., 31
Taliban, 95–97
Tandy, Karen P., 201
TANF (Temporary Assistance for Needy Families), 173–176
Tasca, M., 121
Tate, Sharon, 102–103
Taylor, M., 161
Tehrik-e-Minhaj ul Quran, 93
Temporary Assistance for Needy Families (TANF), 173–176
Theoretical Criminology, 4
Therapeutic community (TC) models, 192
Thoennes, N., 53
Thompson, D., 107–108
Thompson. R. J., 204
Thrasher, F. M., 22
Tjaden, P. G., 53
Torres, S., 192
Totten, Edyth, 198
Townsend, Stephanie M., 219
Trafficking in Persons (TIP) Report, 87
Trafficking Victims Protection Act (TVPA, US), 86, 87
Turner, Brock, 41

T-visa, 87
TVPA (Trafficking Victims Protection Act, US), 86, 87

UCR (Uniform Crime Reports). *See* Uniform Crime Reports (UCR)
Ullman, Sarah E., 219
Uniform Crime Reports (UCR):
    bank robberies in, 138
    crime information from, 7–11
    female offenders in, 131–134
    juvenile offenders in, 115–116
    property crime in, 137
    prostitution in, 139
    rape in, 37
Uniform Military Code of Justice, 45
United Nations:
    honor killings estimated by, 94
    Protocol to Prevent, Suppress and Punish Trafficking in Persons, especially Women and Children, 87
    Survey of Crime Trends and Operations of Criminal Justice Systems (UN-CTS), 16
United States v. Virginia (1974), 216
University of Chicago, 217
Urban Institute, 171
U.S. Department of Education, 47
U.S. Department of Justice, 38, 85n, 203
U.S. Federal Probation Service, 208
U.S. Sentencing Commission, 156, 159
U.S. Supreme Court, 211, 216–217
U.S. v. Johnson (1970), 159
U.S. v. Windsor, 217

Van Houten, Leslie, 102–103
VanVoorhis, P., 110, 153
Vaughan, R. D., 40
VAWA (Violence Against Women Act), 50, 60–61, 69
Vertical prosecution units, 49
Victimization, 21–87
    criminal justice system and, 21–26
    fear of, 26–28
    feminist pathways perspective, 32–33
    Mendelsohn's theories of, 28–31
    offending intersection with, 6
    routine activities theory of, 31–32
Victim services, 218–223. *See also* Rape and sexual assault
Violence:
    cultural acceptance of domestic, 69–70
    cycle of, 64
    dating, 65
    honor-based (HBV), 92–97
    women as victims of, 5
    women initiating, 142–147
Violence Against Women Act (VAWA), 50, 60–61, 69
Violence Against Women survey, 38
"Violent" girls, 122–121
Virgil, Glenda, 177

Virginia Military Institute, 216
Visher, Christy A., 152

Walker, Luis, 45
Walking the line, in gangs, 143
War crimes, rape as, 91
War on drugs, sentencing offenders and, 156–158
Washington, P. A., 52
Welch, Rachel, 181
Welch, S., 153
Welfare Reform Act of 1974, 173
Wells, Alice Stebbins, 198
Wesely, J. K., 109
Westbrooks, Ethan, 63
West Point Military Academy, 44
White House Task Force to Protect Students from Sexual Assault, 47
WHO (World Health Organization), 92
Widom, C. S., 123
Wiemann, C. M., 40
Williams, M., 216
Wilson, Pete, 49
Witch burnings, in Papua New Guinea, 90
Women and crime, data sources on:
    Crime Survey for England and Wales (CSEW), 16
    National Crime Victimization Survey (NCVS), 13–14
    National Incident-Based Reporting System (NIBRS), 11–13
    National Intimate Partner and Sexual Violence Survey (NISVS), 14–16
    National Violence Against Women Survey (NVAWS), 14
    Uniform Crime Reports (UCR), 7–11
Women and crime, introduction to, 1–21
    criminal justice system work, 6
    data sources on
    feminism influence on, 2–4
    feminist methodology for research on, 17–18
    victimization and offending intersection in, 6
    violence victims as, 5
Women in Federal Law Enforcement, 203
Women Police Reserve (NY), 198
Wooldredge, J., 153
Work-family balance, 213
World Health Organization (WHO), 92
Wraparound services, 167
Wright, E. M., 178
Wyse, J. J. B., 169

Yahya, Tooba, 94
Yates, Andrea, 148–149
Yousafzai, Malala, 95–97
YouthARTS development project, 126
Youth Risk Behavior Survey, 122

Zatz, M., 121
Zettler, H. R., 153
Zhong, H., 117
Ziering, Amy, 44

About the Author

Stacy L. Mallicoat is a Professor of Criminal Justice and Chair of the Division of Politics, Administration and Justice at California State University, Fullerton. She earned her BA in Legal Studies and Sociology from Pacific Lutheran University and her PhD from the University of Colorado Boulder in Sociology. She is the author of several books, including *Crime and Criminal Justice: Concepts and Controversies; Women, Gender, and Crime: Core Concepts;* and *Criminal Justice Policy.* Her work also appears in a number of peer-reviewed journals and edited volumes. She is an active member of the American Society of Criminology, the ASC's Division on Women and Crime, and the Academy of Criminal Justice Sciences.